FREED TO LEAD

FREED TO LEAD

HOW YOUR IDENTITY IN CHRIST
CAN TRANSFORM ANY LEADERSHIP ROLE

ROD WOODS

MONARCH
BOOKS

Oxford, UK, and Grand Rapids, USA

Published by Monarch Books
an imprint of
Lion Hudson plc
Wilkinson House, Jordan Hill Road,
Oxford OX2 8DR, England
Email: monarch@lionhudson.com
www.lionhudson.com/monarch

ISBN 978 0 85721 704 2
e-ISBN 978 0 85721 705 9

First edition 2016

Acknowledgments
Scripture quotations taken from The Holy Bible, English Standard Version®
(ESV®) copyright © 2001 by Crossway, a publishing ministry of Good News
Publishers. All rights reserved.

A catalogue record for this book is available from the British Library

Printed and bound in the UK, December 2015, LH36

CONTENTS

Part VI: Overcoming Leadership Pitfalls

ACKNOWLEDGMENTS

I am dedicating this book to my two grandsons, Micah and Judah. I am confident that they will both become influential leaders as they grow. My prayer is that this book might help them to be the leaders God has designed them to be, even when I may no longer be around for them.

Sadly, my mother passed away as I was writing this book so she was never able to see how deeply her example of self-giving and perseverance has influenced everything in my life. I learned more from her than I can possibly express.

In one sense, true honesty would demand that my wife, Karen, be credited as a co-writer of this book. Without her it could never have been written because without her I am not sure I would have survived to write it! She has helped me become the leader I am. She is God's greatest blessing in my life.

I also want to thank all my friends (and perhaps my "enemies") that have been part of the three churches I have served during my career as a minister. You have taught me how to lead. It was in the crucible of City Temple that many of these ideas took form. I want to thank especially all those at City Temple who endured the many earlier versions of the Freed to Lead conference I developed out of which this book has emerged.

I want to thank my good friend, Steve Goss, who gave me the opportunity to develop and pilot these ideas in the broader setting of Freedom in Christ Ministries International and who has joined with me in delivering our Freed to Lead conference. Steve's insights and encouragements have improved the book immeasurably.

Finally, I want to honor my friends Alan and Jenny Rogers. Before his untimely death in July 2010, Alan was like a father to me. Not only was he a great leader, but he also taught me how to become a better leader myself. Jenny remains a dear friend, and an inspiration for how we might develop leaders more effectively. Together, Alan and Jenny encouraged and strengthened Karen and me through some very difficult years, giving us the courage and stamina to continue leading in the midst of adversity.

PREFACE

Great Christian leaders will change the world for Jesus Christ.

You can become a great Christian leader – not necessarily in terms of Western or worldly views of "great", but in terms of God's view of "great". In God's view of "great", your life matters and you have a lasting impact because of your leadership, no matter how "small" you might perceive it to be.

You are not a failure. I deeply desire that you persevere in your leadership as a Christian, because I know that many people give up leading because it gets tough and painful, which makes them think that they are failures – even when they are making a real difference. You may already be a great Christian leader without realizing it.

My passion is to see great Christian leaders rise up all across the world.

This book has grown out of over thirty years' experience of leadership in both church and marketplace contexts. During these years I have learned from many good leaders, both in person and through their books. In many ways impossible to mention, this book has grown from their seeds planted in my life. As Solomon said, "There is nothing new under the sun," and "Of making many books there is no end" (Ecclesiastes 1:9 and 12:12, respectively).

There are many great books on leadership. As I have read many of these books I have noticed three common problems. First, some books come from places of overwhelming success and extraordinary dynamism that simply are not available to most leaders today. These books seem to suggest that if we follow their actions or replicate their strategies then we would have the same level of success wherever we are. Sadly, that is not the case. These books show a naïvety about the "real world" of many leaders. Most leaders simply do not have the resources, context or "luck" that the few superstars have had.

Second, other books suggest that if we would only change ourselves as leaders to become Jack Welch, Jeff Bezos, Larry Page, Steve Jobs, or – dare I say – Jesus Christ, then we would become great leaders and have the same success that they have – apart from Jesus who, after all, was crucified. These books seek to persuade us to make fundamental changes to our personality and activities, assuming that if we simply share the personality traits of some of the greats and do what they do then we would become as successful as they are.

Both these problems have the effect of disempowering most people in leadership. For some, reading these books leads to a depression about themselves and their circumstances which creates a sense of hopelessness. This may lead them to settle for less than God's best for them and their leadership role. For others, reading these books launches them into a never-ending cycle of read "this" book – try to apply it – fail miserably or succeed only partially – abandon the effort – read another book. This often leads to weary leaders and even wearier followers.

The third problem is that most books on leadership, even books written by Christians, seem to minimize or homogenize their Christian content so that it becomes little more than an accessory, a respectful nod to Jesus and the Bible so that the writers can proceed to write whatever they want. The assumption is that since we have done our obligatory obeisance to Jesus then whatever secular principles of leadership we might develop or apply have suddenly become Christianized. Another form of this problem is where the writers acknowledge their faith in Jesus then endorse whatever non-Christian principles that seem to bring about success – no matter what judgment the Bible might have concerning these practices. Similarly, writers might suggest that Christians need to develop a good Christian character (privately) but learn solid worldly leadership practices to apply publicly.

The effect of this third problem is to create the impression that our Christian faith has nothing to offer the public world of leadership, unless it is mere "church" leadership. I have spoken with many Christian leaders in the marketplace, some highly successful in business, who privately despaired that they could not link their faith in Jesus with their business effectiveness. In many of these conversations, it has only taken a few minutes to show these leaders how their faith in Jesus Christ might make them more effective as a leader in the public marketplace without dumbing down their faith and without sacrificing business success.

I hope to avoid these problems by presenting a vision of Christian leadership that is accessible to every Christian, no matter where God has called you to lead. This vision of Christian leadership begins with who you are and where you are right now. It does not begin with learning a bunch of new strategies and techniques. It does not begin by making fundamental changes to your personality. It begins with who you are right now in Jesus Christ.

Most importantly, I hope to avoid all three problems in this book by presenting a vision of our faith in Jesus Christ that might make Christian leaders the most effective leaders in every area of society, without having to proselytize (although I do believe in evangelism) and without having to Christianize society (an impossible task for us) before we experience leadership fruitfulness. As Christians, we must have the conviction that authentically *Christian* leadership will benefit all people and all societies at all times. Perhaps if people in the world saw more genuinely Christian leadership in the marketplace then they would hunger to learn more about the Jesus who has made us such good leaders.

When I originally conceived this book, I had entertained the notion of using a more academic approach in order to make solid arguments about the points I would raise and to consider the counterarguments that others would raise. I wanted to present a comprehensive survey of the literature on leadership and how what I would present fits within that survey. However, I quickly began to realize that most *leaders* would not read such a book! So, I am making no pretense to originality or scholarship, and I realize it would be impossible to credit everyone who has shaped and formed my thinking on the issue of leadership over the past three decades.

My goal is to make this work as readable and as accessible as possible, so that readers might interact with the material and learn more easily. So I have chosen to minimize the use of long quotations and footnotes. I will not take into account all the material that may support my claims – although the literature is considerable – nor will I consider all the various arguments in support of what I write. I do not make any claim to have made a systematic review of all the relevant literature on leadership. I will not review all the possible counterarguments one could make against what I say.

In this preface, I do want to acknowledge the massive debt I have to two writers who have influenced my thinking deeply and whose influence throughout the pages of this book is impossible to attribute properly. The first is Edwin Freidman in his seminal work *A Failure of Nerve*. God brought this book into my life in the dark days of 2007 and it created a new framework by which I might understand not only what was happening in my life and leadership at the time but also what had often happened throughout the previous twenty-five years. His insights regarding the nature and effects of anxiety in our world and on our leadership have helped me immeasurably. One can see his influence most fully in sections three and four of the book.

The second person to acknowledge is Neil T. Anderson, especially his book *Victory over the Darkness*. The Freedom in Christ Ministries International that developed from *Victory over the Darkness* and *The Bondage Breaker* has blessed and encouraged Christians globally for over twenty-five years. The ministry is now much stronger than ever. God used *Victory over the Darkness* to change my life by opening my mind to what the Bible really says about me as a disciple of Jesus Christ, someone who has been saved by grace through faith (see

Ephesians 2:8). As you will see, the implications of his work have a radical impact on our understanding of leadership. I see this work as so foundational to leadership that I would encourage all Christians to read these two books and to participate in the *Freedom in Christ Discipleship Course* and to undertake *The Steps to Freedom in Christ*. Without mastering the biblical concepts about our identity in Christ and fully applying them to our lives it will be difficult for us to become the leaders God has designed us to be.

One final note about my approach in the book is important here: the use of stories and illustrations. Every story or illustration that I use – unless otherwise noted – is true and based on an actual event. However, I have freely altered the details of each story, hopefully to make them largely unrecognizable. In telling my own story and giving examples from my own experience, I will try to change them less but still I will change some of the details. I am making these changes in order to preserve anonymity and privacy as necessary.

In the case of my own story (particularly in chapter two), I am telling it from my own perspective and experience, freely acknowledging that I am not attempting to record alternate viewpoints. Over the years I have discovered that behind any "successful" leader is a group of people who perceive their experience of that person's leadership negatively. I am no exception to this. So I will seek to preserve some of the details, but I will also redact freely. I will center much of the story on myself and my perceptions, rather than pretending to give some unbiased account. Instead of talking about individual people, I will generalize freely. Persons who lived through some of these events alongside me should not try to read themselves or any other person into the narrative. Any similarities are purely coincidental – unless of course you really like what you perceive I have said about you. In that case, it was entirely intentional.

INTRODUCTION

What is leadership? What makes a good leader?

As Steve Goss and I have discussed these questions with people from cultures around the world during our Freed to Lead courses, we have learned two things. First, people generally struggle to define leadership. Very few groups have ever given a concise definition of leadership when asked to deliberate on it. The best they can do is give some ideas about it. Occasionally, groups will come up with some reductionistic definition – such as John Maxwell's "leadership in influence" – but very quickly admit that it is insufficient.

The second thing we have learned is that people generally find it much easier to answer the question about what makes a good leader than to give a definition of leadership. Surprisingly, their answers are remarkably similar across the various cultures of the world – especially when one adjusts the answers a bit in light of that culture's understanding of the answers. For example, "humility" is a common answer about what makes a good leader, but different cultures will express the concept of "humility" in different ways. Also surprisingly, few of the answers about what makes a good leader have much to do with leadership *activities*. Most answers revolve around the personality of leaders, what personality traits people would like to see in their leaders.

As we have discussed these questions with Christians, we have found that very few Christians will answer these questions explicitly in terms of the Bible, let alone have a clear vision for what the Bible says about leadership, other than perhaps a few vague references to "servant leadership" and the personality traits of Jesus. Often, we perceive that Christians experience a strange disconnect between what they believe a Christian leader *should* be and what it takes to be an effective leader in the world. Many Christians have capitulated to the secularizing tendency in society and relinquished the work of defining and maintaining "good" leadership to the business schools and marketplaces of the world. When they discover that a successful (read "wealthy" and "prosperous") businessperson is actually a Christian, they alternate between a sense of surprise and a sense of deep mistrust, assuming that the leader must have compromised their Christianity in order to succeed.

Most of us have presupposed that leadership is leadership, whether it is a Christian, atheist, Muslim or Jedi knight doing the leading. Most of us have presupposed that a person did not have to be a person of some religious persuasion in order to lead well. Of course, to an extent this is true. When John Maxwell states that "leadership is influence", he is stating something true for all leadership in all times and in all places. Without influence there is no leadership, whether in a Christian or secularist society. History is filled with people who were not Christians yet who led well. We would not dispute this.

On the other hand, if the Bible is true, if Jesus really is Lord, and if God is sovereign, then certainly there must be something qualitatively different about leadership that is authentically Christian – that is, leadership that is shaped by the Bible as God's Word in full surrender to the Lordship of Jesus Christ flowing from the redemptive realities of the cross and the empty tomb. Surely authentically Christian leadership would enhance leadership generally, making it more transformational, more beneficial, and more fruitful. Surely being a truly *Christian* leader would amplify our leadership so that we are enabled to go beyond our normal limitations as leaders and experience something transcendent in our leadership – at the risk of sounding a bit mystical.

Recently I custom-ordered a new guitar from one of the finest luthiers in the world (and my friend) – George Lowden. I discovered a dizzying array of choices regarding the types of wood to be used for the top, back, and sides of guitars. The woods I chose are some of the best used in making guitars globally today. When I was discussing these choices with George, he said that most of the woods available (and certainly *all* of the woods he and his team of luthiers would use in his shop) could make very good-sounding guitars. Several of these woods would make a guitar sound among the best 15–20 percent of guitars available. However, he suggested that the woods I chose would make the guitar sound even better, well into the top 5–10 percent of guitars available. So I chose the better woods because I wanted to achieve the best results possible – especially because I bought the new guitar not just for myself but also as a legacy to leave to my grandson.

We can surely achieve effective leadership using the resources commonly available today. We would agree that there are many productive leaders who are not Christians and many Christians who are productive leaders without allowing their Christian faith to influence their leadership. However, just as a craftsman using a great wood might take a guitar into the top 10 percent of guitars in the world, so also leading in an authentically Christian way might take our leadership beyond the normal limits of leadership and into a richer, God-ordained dimension of leadership effectiveness. Certainly it should enable us to lead in a way that leaves a positive legacy for the coming generations.

SOME OF OUR OBJECTIVES

The overarching aim of *Freed to Lead* is to enable Christians to lead confidently from a vision of Christian leadership based in our identity in Christ. We might call this "identity-based" leadership. Identity-based leadership makes us less driven and reduces the risk of burnout. It enables us to survive personal attacks and use conflict positively. It will help us overcome other barriers to effective leadership.

Leading from our identity centered and grounded in Christ, we become far less vulnerable to threats to our status. We cease to have anything to hide (because we can afford to be vulnerable). And we are much less likely to be blown off course by strong-willed people wanting to push their own agendas. As we learn to lead from our freedom and identity in Christ we can become authentic and real in our leadership.

We are not talking about some idealistic vision of leadership. Identity-based leadership is grounded in the gritty reality of trying to lead in the world today. It is also grounded in a realistic assessment of our strengths and weaknesses, foibles and failures, realizing that we are often our own worst enemies when it comes to leadership.

We do not apologize that we are seeking to present an unashamedly *Christian* and *biblical* vision for leadership. Without a faith that leads us to surrender our lives to Jesus Christ, we cannot fully embrace this vision of leadership. Nor should we be able to do so. That said, non-Christians might learn from this approach to leadership as well.

A second aim is to help people learn how to lead in light of the reality of the spiritual world and the battle for our minds. No secular leadership book takes the reality of the spiritual world seriously – although a few may talk about "spirituality" in a generic sense. However, as Christians we know that there are spiritual realities that surround us – angels, demons, God's kingdom, to name but a few – which influence what happens in our world far more than we realize. Failure to consider and account for these realities has led to many leadership failures and caused many problems for leaders. Properly dealing with these realities has often brought fruitfulness in leadership.

Perhaps a couple examples would suffice at this point. Over the years I have counseled many couples who would get into an argument almost every Sunday morning before coming to church. This argument would arise suddenly and sometimes ruin the whole day. Every time I would suggest that perhaps something demonic would want to prevent them from having a good worship experience. I would suggest that when an argument starts to brew they should immediately stop and pray, explicitly commanding anything demonic to leave their presence. Every couple who has followed this advice has seen an almost complete end to the Sunday morning arguments – and many other arguments as well. They were affected by a spiritual reality of which they were unaware.

I heard another church leader tell a story about how his small city had a serious drugs issue. Many pastors had burned out of the ministry in that city. As he sought God in prayer, God gave him a strategy about praying with his elders at several points throughout the city and making a symbolic act. Although it seemed silly to him at the time, he and his elders followed through on the strategy. Within a few weeks the two top drug dealers in the city were converted and there was a major shift in the effectiveness of his leadership.

The reality of the spiritual world is often played out as a battle for our minds. Paul tells us to "take every thought captive to obey Christ" (2 Corinthians 10:5) and to set our minds "on the things of the Spirit" (Romans 8:5). We are in a battle for our minds.

Even non-Christians recognize this battle for our minds. A number of years ago I took a professional training course for life coaching. I noticed quite a number of similarities between life coaching and what the Bible calls "discipleship". One important issue coaches needed to identify was what we called "gremlins". Gremlins are thoughts in our minds that prevent us from doing what we know we need to do. As a Christian, I recognized these "gremlins". But unlike many people on the course, I understood that they were not random thoughts but spiritual forces of evil intent on sabotaging our ability to function well.

A third aim is to help people resolve common personal and spiritual issues regarding leadership. There are common internal issues all leaders face, such as forgiving those followers who wound us and dealing with selfish ambition. These issues are not so much the result of the reality of the spiritual world but the result of our wrestling with our flesh, that sinful aspect of our humanity that constantly draws us away from God.

A final aim to mention is to help people learn to lead in almost any context using almost any healthy leadership style or technique as we renew our minds with truth. We do not believe there is one correct leadership style or one technique that will work at any time in any place. Effective leaders use a number of different tools to lead. We all develop our own style of leadership which may work well in our context.

At the same time, we believe there are many factors that people today have failed to consider which make the real difference concerning leadership success. Too often we blame our failure of leadership on the failure to adopt the right style of leadership or the right leadership technique instead of on our failure to deal with these oft ignored factors. In this book we will address some of these factors.

WHAT NOT TO EXPECT

We also want to let you know what we are *not* going to do. We would hate for you to have false expectations. One book cannot possibly tell you everything about leadership.

We will not provide you with everything you need to know about leading effectively in every context. We hope that we will raise almost as many questions as we answer, questions that will lead you to search out answers for yourself where God has placed you. So many factors determine your leadership fruitfulness that it is impossible to consider them all. However, we will address many of the common factors we have discovered that actually undermine your leadership ability.

We will not cover some very important leadership issues, such as vision and management, that many other authors have covered constructively in countless books and blogs. We encourage you to find three or four of these that speak clearly to you and your context and learn from them. From our experience, we have found that embracing the concepts in *Freed to Lead* will help you integrate the wisdom of these other authors more powerfully in your own leadership.

We will not advocate particular styles of leadership or approaches to leadership, other than giving the vision for leadership that is genuinely Christian. We will discuss the variety of styles briefly in part two. However, we will leave it up to your discernment to decide which styles of leadership work best for you and your context.

Finally, we will not deal with all the issues regarding self-care for leaders and spiritual disciplines for leaders. We will consider some overlooked strategies for self-care and some overlooked spiritual disciplines, but we will leave it to people to research these more fully for themselves. This area is very important for leaders, however, as many recent secular books on leadership attest.

AN OVERVIEW OF THE BOOK

We have arranged *Freed to Lead* in six parts. Part one presents leadership as an adventure and discusses why the adventure is so challenging. Leadership is more difficult and complex than ever before – otherwise there would not be millions of books published about leadership! As leaders, we need to be aware of several significant issues that make the leadership adventure difficult. Any of these issues might challenge the flourishing of our leadership. I will also share some of my personal journey in leadership. Over the years we have found this helpful to encourage people who are in difficult leadership situations. We often need to break through our idealistic distortions about what leading will be like and come into a more balanced understanding of the challenges we face.

In part two, we will present our vision for authentically Christian leadership. We will explain our definition of leadership. We will also present the twofold dynamic of leading we call "being" and "doing".

Part three will review the contexts of leadership. Leadership does not occur in isolation, yet we often assume that our success or failure is down to our own efforts as leaders. What we discover is that this is a delusion. The contexts of leadership affect our fruitfulness more than we want to admit.

Part four will deal with one of the most neglected issues that undermines leadership more often than we realize: anxiety. We will see that anxiety is more than a little nervousness and apprehension. We will examine the social dynamic of anxiety. We will discover that it has a debilitating effect on us as leaders, on our followers, and on our contexts of leadership.

Increasing our effectiveness as a leader will be the focus of part five. In this section, we will consider two important areas that add to our leadership strength: communication and trust. Integrating these areas into our leadership will increase our influence as leaders. They will also increase our joy in leading.

The final part will consider a number of common pitfalls we face as leaders. Avoiding these pitfalls is essential if we are to have the impact as leaders God desires. We will review three types of pitfalls: personal pitfalls, system pitfalls, and leadership delusions.

We will close the book with a chapter that presents a number of factors that enable our leadership to become transformative – both for us and for the people we lead. These factors will be well known to most Christians, but it is surprising how often we fail to incorporate them into our leadership.

We have also included an appendix called "Steps to Freedom for Leaders". This appendix presents a tool to help leaders encounter God and resolve a number of common personal and spiritual issues regarding leadership. This prayer process is something leaders might work through on their own, although it would be most powerful working through this prayer process together with another leader. "Iron sharpens iron, and one [leader] sharpens another" (Proverbs 27:17).

To get the maximum benefit out of this book, we would encourage you to work through *Victory over the Darkness* and *The Bondage*

Breaker by Neil Anderson, or *The Freedom in Christ Discipleship Course* by Neil Anderson and Steve Goss. We would also encourage you to work through the *Steps to Freedom in Christ* for all Christians.

THE BIBLE AND LEADERSHIP

In this book, the Bible is our foundation for understanding leadership. The Bible shows us God's will for how to live, which includes how we lead. In the Bible, we believe that Jesus showed us real leadership. We seek to ground everything we say in the Bible as God's Word. At the same time, we see three common errors made by many in the church today, errors we seek to avoid when it comes to the Bible.

First, many people try to reduce the Bible to a set of principles. They may even seek to reduce Jesus to a set of principles. We can read books talking about the principles that Jesus would apply if he were the CEO of our company. Or we might read about the top ten leadership principles from the Bible, or the life of Nehemiah, or the life of David. In one sense, this is understandable. After all, the Bible is a huge collection of many books and it is difficult to consider everything the Bible might say about leadership. So it is easier to break that down into a neat set of principles or values. However, Jesus and the Bible are more than a set of principles, and learning what the Bible and Jesus have to say about leadership involves an ongoing relationship with God through Jesus in the power of the Holy Spirit that enables us not only to read the Bible but also to live out what it says every day, including in our work as leaders.

The second error is that many people may idealize the leadership of Jesus, or idealize what the Bible says, to the point that it has no relevance in the world today. People might say, "After all, Jesus was the Son of God. Of course, he would be a great leader. But as a mere mortal I could not possibly lead in the way that Jesus led." Regarding the Bible, we may assume that the Bible sets an impossibly high standard, especially for life in the public realm. In this view, Jesus and the Bible might be good for private morality, but they could have little to say to the public world. Yet, we believe the Bible is more relevant than ever before. Certainly the Bible has anticipated the world in which we live.

Finally, some people just ignore the Bible. They assume that since the Bible was written in another time and culture it could not have anything reasonable to say to our present leadership situation. They also ignore the leadership of Jesus. They assume that Jesus did not live in the "real" world of profit and loss, of business and workplace. Instead, they pursue worldly methods and styles of leadership. Although they might seek to live as a Christian at home, they think that living as a Christian in the world of business would lead to failure, ridicule, and loss. However, we believe that Christian leadership – the leadership presented by the Bible and in the life of Jesus – is the leadership really needed by the *public* world today, and not just by the family and the church.

KEY PASSAGES FOR THIS BOOK

Three passages from the Bible run through our understanding of effective Christian leadership: 2 Timothy 1:6–7; John 10:10–13; and Luke 22:24–27.

> **For this reason I remind you to fan into flame the gift of God, which is in you through the laying on of my hands, for God gave us a spirit not of cowardice or timidity stemming from anxiety but of power and love and self-control. (2 Timothy 1:6–7, author's translation)**

Paul challenged Timothy to lead with boldness, out of power and love. Paul reminds us that leadership involves resisting a cowardice or timidity that comes from anxiety (a better way to translate what is often translated as "fear"). He encourages us to fan into flame our unique gifts and lead with self-control, as God has empowered us. This passage is perhaps the theme passage of the book.

> The thief comes only to steal and kill and destroy. I
> came that they may have life and have it abundantly. I
> am the good shepherd. The good shepherd lays down
> his life for the sheep. He who is a hired hand and not a
> shepherd, who does not own the sheep, sees the wolf
> coming and leaves the sheep and flees, and the wolf
> snatches them and scatters them. He flees because he
> is a hired hand and cares nothing for the sheep. (John
> 10:10–13)

In John 10, Jesus contrasts the leadership of the good shepherd with the leadership of the hired hand. The good shepherd is fully committed to the sheep. The hired hand abandons the sheep at the first sign of trouble. So many leaders today abandon their posts when things become difficult. They are merely hired hands. True leadership will come in order to bring abundant life. Obviously, Jesus is the good shepherd and the only one who can really bring life. But leaders created in his image will also become life-bringers to their contexts.

> A dispute also arose among them, as to which of them
> was to be regarded as the greatest. And he said to
> them, "The kings of the Gentiles exercise lordship
> over them, and those in authority over them are
> called benefactors. But not so with you. Rather, let the
> greatest among you become as the youngest, and the
> leader as one who serves. For who is the greater, one
> who reclines at table or one who serves? Is it not the
> one who reclines at table? But I am among you as one
> who serves." (Luke 22:24–27)

In Luke 22, Jesus reminds us that leaders are not called to be the overlord or the boss but are called to serve. "Servant leadership" has become a popular and well-established perspective on leadership, even among secular leadership theorists. We would certainly affirm the concept of leading by serving. We believe the best way a leader can serve is by leading well as a healthy leader.

At the same time, we see great power in the final line of the passage: "I am *among you* as one who serves" (italics added). Truly compelling leaders are those who lead from the midst of us, who are one of us. They do not sit "on high", handing down the latest dictates and benefices. They do not keep themselves separate and afar, as some almost mythical figure. Leaders who make real and lasting change are those who are among us as ones who serve. We will come to see how important this often neglected aspect of this passage is for leadership, especially Christian leadership.

These passages and many others permeate our understanding of Christian leadership. Throughout the book, we will not seek to prooftext everything with a cursory quote from the Bible. Instead, we hope everyone will see how to integrate the truth of the Bible into every facet of our leadership as we renew our minds with the truth of God's Word.

Lead on!

PART I
THE ADVENTURE OF LEADERSHIP

Men make history and not the other way around. In periods where there is no leadership, society stands still. Progress occurs when courageous, skillful leaders seize the opportunity to change things for the better.

Harry S. Truman

Anyone can hold the helm when the sea is calm.

Publilius Syrus

Tough times never last but tough people do.

Robert Schuller

Great leaders don't need to act tough. Their confidence and humility serve to underscore their toughness.

Simon Sinek

Leadership is an adventure. It takes us places we never dreamed of going. It stretches and challenges us to the limits of our endurance. This adventure enables us to shape the course of history in powerful ways. Whether the adventure seems great or insignificant at the time, we can never fully anticipate what leadership might accomplish in the world. Seemingly small steps of leaders, like walking across a bridge in a small Alabama town (as did Dr. Martin Luther King, Jr.), may resound across the face of the earth, changing the course of nations.

The leadership adventure engages seemingly ordinary people in seemingly ordinary roles – mother, father, supervisor, entrepreneur, boss, pastor – in processes and activities that transform lives and shape our societies. We, as leaders, may think of ourselves as small and insignificant – we may not even think of ourselves as "leaders" at all – but God uses us in ways often beyond our perception.

No adventure worth having is easy. Adventures worthy of the name test our stamina and courage. We may often want to quit, but something compels us forward. We often do not choose the adventure of leadership for ourselves, but people or circumstances – or God – seem to choose us instead.

Whatever else it is, the adventure of leadership is often tough, and requires us to be tough as well. The word "tough" has a variety of meanings. When something is very difficult and demanding, tiring and exhausting, we say that it is "tough". When we have something that is durable and resilient, something that will last, we also say it is "tough". So when it comes to leadership and leaders, what does it mean to say that "leadership is tough"? What does it mean to say that "leaders are tough"?

Regardless of who you are reading this book, I know that you are tougher than you might think you are. I have had the privilege of working with leaders around the world. I have learned of their compassion, determination, love, commitment, creativity, calling, vision, and hopes. I have also learned that they are always tougher than they think. Many of the people I have met did not even think of themselves as leaders, but they were fully engaged in the leadership adventure.

1

THE TOUGH ADVENTURE

If you are going through hell, keep going.

Winston Churchill

Character cannot be developed in ease and quiet. Only through experience of trial and suffering can the soul be strengthened, ambition inspired, and success achieved.

Helen Keller

These are the hard times in which a genius would wish to live. Great necessities call forth great leaders.

Abigail Adams

An accidental encounter with a leader almost twenty years ago has become one of the most profound experiences of my life regarding leadership. While traveling through the state of Pennsylvania, we noticed that we would be passing close by the battlefield of Gettysburg, now a national park in the United States. We had some time to spare so we thought it would be fun to stop and see this famous historic site. Little did I know, it was there I would encounter one of the greatest leaders in US history: Abraham Lincoln.

The Battle of Gettysburg was fought on July 1–3, 1863, during the American Civil War. It was one of the bloodiest battles of the Civil War, claiming somewhere around 50,000 casualties. Many historians believe that it was the turning point of the entire Civil War. It does not cover a very large area, and it is extraordinary to think of the sacrifices made on those days.

Admittedly, it was a chance encounter with President Lincoln and, no, I did not meet him personally. But as I was walking around the battlefield, I encountered the place from which Lincoln gave the famous "Gettysburg Address". Lincoln visited the battle site the following November and gave the speech on November 19, 1863, at the dedication of the Soldiers National Cemetery. A short speech, it had been preserved on a plaque on the ground, so I thought it might be interesting to read it out loud. These are the words of the address:

> Four score and seven years ago our fathers brought
> forth on this continent, a new nation, conceived in
> Liberty, and dedicated to the proposition that all men
> are created equal.
>
> Now we are engaged in a great civil war, testing
> whether that nation, or any nation so conceived and
> so dedicated, can long endure. We are met on a great
> battle-field of that war. We have come to dedicate a
> portion of that field, as a final resting place for those
> who here gave their lives that that nation might live. It
> is altogether fitting and proper that we should do this.
>
> But, in a larger sense, we can not dedicate – we
> can not consecrate – we can not hallow – this ground.
> The brave men, living and dead, who struggled here,
> have consecrated it, far above our poor power to add or
> detract. The world will little note, nor long remember
> what we say here, but it can never forget what they did
> here. It is for us the living, rather, to be dedicated here
> to the unfinished work which they who fought here
> have thus far so nobly advanced. It is rather for us to
> be here dedicated to the great task remaining before
> us – that from these honored dead we take increased
> devotion to that cause for which they gave the last

full measure of devotion – that we here highly resolve
that these dead shall not have died in vain – that this
nation, under God, shall have a new birth of freedom –
and that government of the people, by the people, for
the people, shall not perish from the earth.

I did not read the words very loudly nor did I read them dramatically. When I began reading there was no one standing around me. However, before I had finished reading the words on the ground, a small group of people had spontaneously gathered around me. They listened respectfully and patiently, with many including myself beginning to have tears in our eyes. Lincoln's words resonated down the course of history into my spirit, reminding me of the great cost people had paid in order to establish the United States. These words also reminded me of the great power of leadership in the lives of people.

Many years later, I had a similar experience while walking through the Cabinet War Rooms in London. This museum reviews the leadership of Winston Churchill and the struggles of World War II. In various places throughout the museum you can hear the words of Churchill in some of his most famous speeches. I think Winston Churchill is one of the most quotable leaders in all of history. Speeches about fighting on the beaches, never surrendering, and victory at all costs inspired a nation and channeled all the tragedy and despair and anxiety of war into hope.

One might easily argue that it was the leadership of Winston Churchill during World War II that enabled Great Britain to endure the horrors of war and to achieve victory. It is no wonder that many consider Winston Churchill the greatest Briton who ever lived. Even today, Churchill still inspires people in the United Kingdom and around the world.

Leaders like Abraham Lincoln and Winston Churchill shape our imaginations. They certainly set the course of individual lives and might even set the course of nations. Around the world people recognize the vital importance of leadership for the well-being of society. Most societies consider leadership, in one form or another, the noblest of aspirations and callings.

THE ADVENTURE OF LEADERSHIP

When people become leaders, they begin an amazing adventure. It is an adventure into the unknown, without certainty of outcome or success. Most often the adventure feels like a crazy roller coaster ride, with dramatic ups and downs and spins. Yet it is the prospect of good outcomes, the prospect that perhaps we can change the world, and the prospect that lives might be better through our leadership that compels us onward.

As with most adventures, leadership may surprise and delight us. The potential rewards are great – not in terms of money but in terms of impact and satisfaction. However, as with most adventures, leadership will challenge and stretch us. We may often feel extremely uncomfortable. We may find the adventure highly painful.

Often, we are surprised by how difficult the adventure of leadership may become. We have heard the glory stories of yesteryear when it seemed that some people naturally led and others naturally followed in a mutually affirming and productive relationship of leadership. Yet the experiences of leaders today do not seem to measure up to these stories that have enlivened our imaginations and propelled us into leadership. We have a vague sense that leadership has become increasingly difficult, increasingly tough. Why?

LEADERSHIP QUESTIONS

Leadership is on the hearts and minds of people throughout the world today. Every year, hundreds of new books on leadership are published. The web contains thousands of sites that consider the issues of leadership. Hundreds of bloggers express their opinions on leadership. Aspiring leaders might choose from dozens of seminars, university courses, and other learning resources to help them grow in leadership effectiveness.

As Christians, we also value the importance of leadership. The Bible contains dozens of examples of great leaders. Jesus himself spoke a lot about leadership, as well as being a great leader himself. Many of the books, blogs, and resources about leadership are developed and published by Christians themselves. Overall there are probably more resources available today than ever before with regard to leadership.

Knowing the value people generally place on leadership and having access to such a varied array of resources for leadership development raise a number of questions. If we have so many resources then why is it so difficult to find great leaders? There seems to be this gnawing feeling in the gut of many people that good leaders are difficult to find, that we do not have many good leaders today, let alone great ones.

Another question: why is it so difficult to lead? We have the resources, we know how important it is, so why do we struggle to do it? We have a sense that there was a time when leadership was much easier than it is today. We have heard the stories where leaders lead and people follow. We know there was a time when leaders were held in high regard. But we also know that things have changed rather significantly – why?

The questions become even more difficult for us as Christians. We believe that Jesus is Lord. We believe that the Bible is God's Word. We know that God's way for humanity is the best. In light of this, we expect that Christian leaders should be great leaders. Yet our experience is rather different. Not only does it seem like Christian examples of leadership are few and far between in the marketplace, but it also seems like Christian examples of leadership are few and far between in the church. Because of this, many people have despaired of learning anything about leadership from the Bible or from churches, at least anything that has real-world applications.

Just in case you thought it was your imagination, we fully agree that leadership is tough – perhaps more difficult today than at any point in recent history. If we are to become effective leaders in the world today, then we must understand why leadership is so tough. We need to examine some of the characteristics of the world in which we live and of the lives of the people we lead so that we might become aware of some of the factors that seek to undermine our leadership continuously.

THE BIBLE'S PERSPECTIVE

In a strange sense, as Christians we should be encouraged by how tough leadership is today. We should be encouraged because the Bible actually predicted that leadership would become more and more difficult throughout the ages. The times in which we live have not surprised God. In fact, God anticipated them.

Paul observed in 2 Timothy 3:1–5 that "in the last days there will come times of difficulty". These times of difficulty would come because "people will be lovers of self, lovers of money, proud, arrogant, abusive, disobedient to their parents, ungrateful, unholy, heartless, unappeasable, slanderous, without self-control, brutal, not loving good, treacherous, reckless, swollen with conceit, lovers of pleasure rather than lovers of God, having the appearance of godliness, but denying its power." Paul was very much aware that these people would oppose good leadership, which is one of the reasons Paul was writing to Timothy about them. Surprisingly, Paul was not talking about people generally in this passage, but he was talking about those who would claim to be Christians! Paul probably expected that people who were not Christians would resist leadership even more.

Jesus himself told his disciples to expect these kinds of difficulties. In Matthew 24:12, Jesus told his followers that "because of lawlessness the love of many will grow cold". Jesus was also speaking about those who claim to be Christians, as well as those who are not Christians. Jesus was effectively saying that in the last days people would be undisciplined and unruly, resisting good leadership.

These passages and others indicate the challenges that leaders would face, especially in the last days. We believe that we are living in the times of difficulty predicted by Jesus and Paul. Building on what they have said, we can see a number of factors that work together to make leadership especially difficult.

OVERWHELMED

First, people are overwhelmed. We are living in times of unprecedented change, and the pace of change is increasing. Search for "unprecedented change" on the internet and depending on the day it will yield at least ten million results. Change is happening so rapidly that even the term "unprecedented change" has become a cliché. Two hundred years ago, one might have experienced a handful of life-changing or world-changing discoveries in the course of a lifetime. When I was a child, we might have seen five or ten life-changing or world-changing discoveries in the course of a year or two. Today, in any given month one might expect to see several major life-changing or world-changing discoveries.

The pace of change is so rapid that it is almost impossible for anyone to keep up. Even the most tech savvy people might struggle to incorporate, let alone understand, the various changes happening around them. The pace of change is overwhelming to most people, so much so that many people have simply tried to ignore the vastness of the changes happening around them.

We are also living in times of unprecedented challenges. It seems that almost every day some new challenge threatens the world. Terrorism has been around for centuries, yet the present face of terrorism is changing rapidly. In less than two decades terrorism has moved from being a state-sponsored activity, to being an activity sponsored by various nefarious organizations throughout the world, to becoming the spontaneous activity of a few radicalized individuals.

The global economy has occupied the thoughts of many people and leaders around the world. Since the great recession of 2008, the world has faced many economic challenges. The various governments of the world have tried many different strategies to boost their economies. Yet despite their best efforts, people have a general sense that the economy is struggling and may never again generate the prosperity that many had experienced previously. The sense of growing inequality between those who have and those who have not is generating unrest in many places of the world. Economic struggles always mean that governments will struggle. Yet even the best minds have not developed coherent solutions for the economic maladies that grip us.

These are just two examples of the many challenges that have arisen in recent years. We have not even fully considered things like urban poverty, new diseases, healthcare, climate change, wars, and natural disasters. We do not know how to address these challenges. We only know that they seem to get bigger and bigger every year.

We are also living in times of unprecedented choices. If you search a popular online retailer to find a new "Holy Bible", you would get more than 50,000 results. If you wanted to buy some new music, you might get over three million results. If you want to watch a bit of TV, you might turn on your Freesat and have over 150 channels from which to choose. If you decide to go to church, there might be dozens to choose from within a few minutes of your home. The dizzying array of choices overwhelms many people, leading them to make fewer and fewer choices.

The effect on leadership

When people feel terribly overwhelmed, they fail to think clearly and objectively. They begin to react instinctively and emotionally. Because they are so overwhelmed, they will struggle to choose the right leader. When they do choose a leader, they will struggle to follow that leader. They will resist good leadership. Instead, as Paul told Timothy, they will have "itching ears" that will lead them to accumulate leaders to suit their own passions (see 2 Timothy 4:3). People who are overwhelmed will make decisions about who to follow based on the perceived needs of the moment instead of wisdom for the future.

Leaders who are overwhelmed simply cannot lead. So many leaders spend so much of their time just keeping their heads above water, so to speak, that they cannot think creatively about how to lead more effectively. They may even become obsessed with the quest to find the latest technique or the latest gadget that will help them organize themselves and feel less overwhelmed. In the public realm, they may become so inundated with new laws, rules, regulations, and policies that they find it difficult to do anything else.

OVERLOADED AND CONFUSED

Not only are people overwhelmed, but they are also overloaded and confused. People generally seem to have lost the ability to think clearly. Good reasoning and problem-solving have become more and more challenging for people. At least four factors contribute to this problem.

First, people are flooded with so much information and sensory input that they can no longer process it all in order to make good choices. Alvin Toffler, the American writer and futurist, called this "information overload". We can see an analogy to this in the world of computing. From time to time, we hear stories of websites that have received so many requests that suddenly they crash. In some cases, an adversary might do this on purpose. This is a version of information overload. Just like computers, people can only ingest a certain amount of information and sensory input before they stop functioning properly.

This problem has become so endemic to modern society that it has led to a new mental health issue: information fatigue syndrome. In information fatigue syndrome, people expose themselves to so much information, media, and technology – not to mention other sensory inputs – that they become exhausted and unable to function properly. They may even develop health issues such as headaches, depression, and illness.

Second, people have so many choices today (as we saw above) that they experience what is called "choice overload". When people have too many choices they get stressed and feel paralyzed so they cannot make well-informed choices. About twenty years ago I met a man who had recently retired from a career as a missionary in an Asian nation. He told me about the time he and his wife first walked into a US supermarket. They had only just entered the supermarket before they became tremendously overloaded by the size of the place and the incredible number of choices they faced. Immediately, they turned around and left. It took weeks for them to adjust, after coming from a place that had very few choices when it came to food and other goods.

A third factor is something called "cognitive dissonance". This occurs when people try to accept and hold onto contradictory thoughts, beliefs, and values at the same time. People are exposed to many conflicting thoughts, ideas, beliefs, and details, many of which sound reasonable and acceptable. Over time, people will try to hold onto everything that sounded reasonable, whether or not it actually was. This leads them to embrace a variety of things that are mutually incompatible. When this happens, people become confused and unable to think clearly. The dissonance created by this becomes like background noise in the mind, not always obvious but influential. Enough of this background noise will overload someone's mind.

We encounter Christians who are suffering from cognitive dissonance all the time. For example, a couple begins to attend our church. Each person has chosen to surrender to Jesus Christ as

Lord of their lives. Each person claims that they believe the Bible is God's Word and that they have chosen to live in accordance with the Bible. Yet, this couple is living together and not married. They choose to live together, they accept it as appropriate, but at the same time they know that it is not something of which the Bible approves. This will create cognitive dissonance, and it will hinder their ability to live as followers of Jesus.

In the case of the final factor, "cultural dissonance", people become confused because the cultural environment around them is changing so rapidly. The standards and traditions of society are shifting seemingly overnight. People are exposed to more cultures and more opinions and more perspectives than ever before in history. In some cases, they may become surrounded by immigrants or people from other cultures in a way that creates a sense of disconnect with their own history and values. In other situations, they adopt an attitude that everyone must be right and so embrace highly conflicting ideas and perspectives. Cultural dissonance creates a sense of instability and the loss of a sense of "place" which is so important to people.

The effect on leadership

Being overloaded and confused inhibits the ability of people to follow leaders. Overloaded and confused people simply do not know who to follow. Because they are overloaded and confused, people make many mistakes and many wrong decisions. Sometimes they will not even become conscious of their mistakes for weeks and months, until it has become too late to change course.

Overloaded and confused leaders simply do not lead. They may be in a position of leadership, but they will not be capable of effective leadership. Instead, they will tend to follow whatever trend is emerging, whatever "wind" is blowing, whatever "good idea" might seem to work. We see this in the proliferation of opinion polls and similar instruments designed to measure popular opinion.

Eventually, they undermine the confidence of their followers in their leadership. Followers who do not abandon them will simply refuse to follow, thinking that their ideas are just as good as the leader's ideas – and they might be right.

UNFOCUSED

The third reason leaders find it so difficult to lead is that people are unfocused. All people need what we might call a filter, frame, and focus in their life. Without all three operating in a healthy manner, people will struggle in a variety of ways.

A filter is what we normally call a "worldview". A worldview is how people perceive and process the world around them. Worldviews help us process all the sensory input we receive. They suggest what we give our attention to and what we ignore. Thus, worldview serves as a filter for reality. Everyone has a worldview. The key issue is whether our worldview reflects reality, whether it is "true". For Christians, the Bible challenges and shapes our worldview as the Word of God and our objective standard for truth.

Our filter leads to a frame, which is the values and sense of integrity that help us determine our behavior and choices. Our frame helps us determine what is important in life and what choices might be appropriate for us. This frames how we live our lives, providing boundaries for what we perceive as acceptable and right.

Once we have a filter and frame, we need to use them to develop a focus – a clear sense of vision, mission, and goals in our life that precludes certain choices and activities. Our frame will help us to know what we can say "yes" to. Our focus helps us to say "no" to certain things, while emphasizing the really important things in our life and leadership. We must intentionally seek to develop and refine our focus. A focus does not develop naturally. It is easily deflected by everything else happening around us.

As the leader of a Christian charitable company, the Bible shapes my worldview to realize that God's purpose for us is to advance his kingdom in society as well as in the lives of individual people in the face of opposition from Satan who wants to keep society and people under his influence. This worldview helps me to create a values framework that embraces a diversity of issues, such as paying people a fair wage, not hosting events or activities that might undermine God's rulership in our lives, and giving good Christian hospitality to everyone who uses our services. This filter and frame then helps me to focus on what we need to do and, even more importantly, what we do not need to do. We will say "no" to things that might not promote God's kingdom. We will say "no" to things we cannot do well. We will say "no" to things that might actually harm people. My filter, frame, and focus operate every day.

The challenge is that if we do not have a strong filter, frame, and focus, we will follow the filters, frames, and focuses of other people. We will, in the words of the Bible, conform to the world (see Romans 12:2). In addition, we will not be able to process our sense of overload and confusion. We will not renew our minds with truth. If our filter, frame, and focus are not biblical, then we will become trapped in a cycle of worldliness and become subject to the spirit of the age.

For example, take the BBC. Personally, I appreciate the BBC, particularly the BBC news service. But every day, the BBC news shapes how people see the world. Editorial choices flow from the worldview of the editors. Because of this, the BBC does not report on how the Christian church is growing around the world. It seldom reports on Christian persecution in the world.

Based on its worldview, the BBC shapes the values that people have about what is happening in the world. The tone of the reporting suggests to people whether something is good, right or acceptable. One value of the BBC is that modern science determines what is "true". Another value is that God does not have much influence in the world today, unless it may happen to be a negative influence.

By choosing what to report on in the world, the BBC guides how people focus based on its filter and frame. The BBC's focus decides what it will *not* report on even more than what it will report on. The

BBC's focus suggests to people what is really important in the world and what they can safely ignore in the world.

In its filter, frame, and focus, the BBC is not guided by the Bible. It does not even consider the Bible. So the filter, frame, and focus the BBC promotes are not biblical. This means that if we as Christians do not have a strong filter, frame or focus of our own then the BBC gladly will determine them for us.

The effect on leadership

People without a healthy filter, frame, and focus will struggle to say "no". They will struggle to discern what is important. They will fail to set healthy limits and boundaries to protect themselves. At the same time, they will resist leaders who have a strong filter, frame, and focus. They will suspect the leader's confidence as arrogance or a self-seeking agenda. They will have no ability to discern a healthy leader from an unhealthy leader. Consequently, they will change leaders frequently, abandoning a leader at the first sign of problems.

Leaders without a holistic filter will fail to obtain the perspective necessary for healthy leadership. Those leaders will be subject to passing fads and the tyranny of the urgent. As leaders, we need to be aware of the broader implications of the decisions we make, such as how hiring a new employee might affect other employees and the organization generally. We need to be able to see how the trends in society might affect the work we do. We need to grasp the spiritual dynamics operating around us. We need to consider the long-term legacy our actions might have. All these things will flow from our filter.

Leaders without a sense of frame will not make the values-based decisions necessary to ensure that their organizations have the unity and cohesion necessary for fruitfulness. As leaders, we must ensure that our organizations operate according to good values so that we maintain the integrity and authenticity by which many people evaluate organizations today. Our values help us maintain our distinctiveness as leaders and as organizations.

Leaders without a focus will tend to say "yes" to everything, quickly becoming overloaded and dysfunctional. Great leadership is as much about determining what *not* to do as it is choosing what to do in the first place. Having a focus not only allows us to say "no" to things, but it also allows us to do so without guilt. It can free us from the gnawing sense that we are missing something important.

Leaders who do not have a filter, frame, and focus will fail to obtain a healthy vision for their leadership as well as for the people they lead. As Solomon observed, "Where there is no prophetic vision the people cast off restraint" (Proverbs 29:18). They become discouraged. They "perish", as it is often translated.

We need a filter, frame, and focus shaped by the Bible if we are to lead effectively as Christians. We often see Christian leaders who embrace the ideas and strategies of people around them, without realizing that those ideas and strategies might be contrary to the Bible. For example, I know of Christian business leaders who have adopted the strategy of paying their suppliers at the last possible minute even though they are fully capable of paying sooner. Yet Solomon said, "Do not withhold good from those to whom it is due, when it is in your power to do it" (Proverbs 3:27). For us to have authenticity as Christian leaders, we must seek to lead according to the Bible.

UNDISCIPLINED

Next, leadership is difficult because people are undisciplined – they do not exercise self-control and self-discipline. We have a modern-day version of the last verse of Judges where everyone does what is right in his or her own eyes. Many people do not discipline their thinking, leading to a loss of the ability to problem-solve and exercise good reason in the face of various challenges. Many people do not discipline their emotional reactions, leading to an emotional volatility that destroys relationships. Many people do not discipline their actions, leading to the failure to persevere in a way that overcomes problems.

There is a sense of lawlessness in the world today, where everything seems up for grabs. Many of the riots of the last decades around the world – even when triggered by a perceived injustice – have turned into manifestations of lawlessness leading to unbridled greed and theft. The various banking scandals of mis-selling payment protection insurance, manipulating the Libor banking rates, and fixing the foreign exchange rates show the lawlessness in parts of society. People view "austerity" as a punishment by the government instead of viewing it as the natural outcome of undisciplined spending and debt. Even governments get caught up in this lawlessness, as shown by rapidly and sometimes erratically changing rules, regulations, and laws.

We can see the lack of discipline in the shifting sense of ethical imperatives. People have a rapidly changing sense of morality which challenges the historic values on which much of Western society is built. A significant example of this is the redefinition of marriage to include same-sex marriage. Many have expressed shock at how quickly several nations have changed their views on morality and values. Such changes seem set to increase in the years ahead.

People show the undisciplined quality of life today in their spirituality as well. People might hold a variety of beliefs from a variety of religions without even noticing the contradictions. They embrace pluralism and tolerance – for everything except perceived intolerance. Even among Christians discipline has begun to wane. One of the most significant trends happening is the redefinition of active participation in a church from four Sundays a month to two to three Sundays a month.

The effect on leadership

Following a leader requires discipline. When people do not have discipline, they will change leaders whenever the leader begins to displease them. Without discipline, people will generally act in their own perceived best interests and have little ability to sacrifice for the best interests of others.

Without discipline, leaders will not lead. More and more, they will act in ways that benefit themselves, instead of focusing on what might benefit the people and organizations they lead. In recent years, an increasing number of leaders coming into organizations are demanding "Golden Handshakes" to give them incentive to come as well as "Golden Parachutes" to protect themselves in case things do not work out.

CONFLICTED

The fifth reason leadership is tough is that people are conflicted. They make contradictory demands and hold contradictory expectations. Someone might say, "I want to do as I please, but everything must be fair and equal", without realizing that perceived "fairness" and "equality" always involve restricting someone's freedom. Or someone might say, "I demand that we have good leaders, but I will only follow as long as the leaders do what I want", without understanding that really good leaders will often make difficult and unpopular decisions. Increasingly, people expect companies to act responsibly but assume that their own personal behavior is nobody's business. People often act in ways that are fundamentally selfish, but they are surprised when others act selfishly too.

One of the most ironic manifestations of this conflicted dynamic is how people seek "spirituality" without reference to God. Recent years have seen the establishing of atheist "churches" which have all the trappings of "church" without the belief in God. People do not seem to understand how without reference to the "divine" they become their own "god".

The effect on leadership

Conflicted people bind up leaders so that they cannot function effectively. They will make conflicting demands on leaders that are mutually exclusive. For example, in many churches pastors are expected to be great preachers, great pastoral care givers, great administrators, and fully knowledgeable about charity laws and good practice. Meeting all these demands not only requires more time than one person might have in a week but also requires a competing range of skills that one person seldom possesses.

Leaders feel disempowered by these conflicting demands. Trying to fulfill all these competing activities quickly wears down leaders. Since leaders cannot fulfill everyone's demands – and since these demands shift so rapidly – at any given time several followers will feel upset with the leader. This requires much conflict negotiation and resolution, something for which some leaders are not prepared.

UNEASY

People are living with a chronic sense of uneasiness. They feel like society is broken. They feel uneasy because of all the changes going on. Increasingly, people experience a lack of rootedness and stability. Whereas previous generations had hope that life would increasingly improve, expecting an improvement in areas such as living standards, many people now have lost hope that things will get better. Economic insecurity and uncertainty give people a sense that they may lose what "little" they perceive they have.

The effect on leadership

The uneasiness people experience leads to the avoidance of the risks necessary for progress to occur. They become fixated with health and safety. Instead of seeking leaders who might make difficult decisions and call people to sacrifice for the sake of others and of the future, people look for leaders who will give them a quick fix or bring them easy comfort. People seek "saviors" for themselves and for their organizations, but they quickly "crucify" them. This explains why there is such instability in key areas of society such as government and the church.

LEADERLESS

The consequence of all these factors is that people are leaderless. Many leaders today feel disempowered and demoralized. Many simply quit and retreat. In their place many surrogate leaders arise: technocrats, who are chosen because of their technical knowledge or expertise; autocrats, who lead by force and fiat; bureaucrats, who are experts at manipulating processes and rules; and plutocrats, who achieve positions of leadership because of their wealth. Being leaderless also gives rise to terrorists, extremists, and subversives who do not lead but seek to dominate and manipulate for their own advantage.

When leaders persevere and remain faithful to their leadership, they encounter a new set of struggles. When real leaders succeed some people will sabotage them. Often people will refuse to follow and then even withdraw from the leadership process. People will demand that the leaders make them feel good. When leaders tell them the truth, people often undermine the leaders.

THE LEADERSHIP DILEMMA

The challenges of leadership today make us wonder why anyone would want to be a leader. It reminds us of something Mark Twain said: "a man who carries a cat by the tail learns something he can learn in no other way". Leadership is difficult and painful, which sometimes makes us suspicious that the person seeking a leadership role either does not understand the real cost of leadership or does not know what it means to lead.

As leaders, we face many dilemmas. Dilemmas are issues

that have no clear and easy answers or solutions. We cannot solve dilemmas. We simply have to work through them as we lead.

This is the leadership dilemma of this chapter: true leadership is the only way we can resolve the great issues of our times whether they are personal, social, economic or global. Yet the very people who need true leadership are the ones who consciously or unconsciously undermine, attack, sabotage, and destroy leadership. So we need a greater vision for leadership.

Before we see that vision, let's see how leaders are tough.

2

THE TOUGH ADVENTURERS

There is no bad weather, only inappropriate clothing.

Attributed to many

The secret of a leader lies in the tests he has faced over the whole course of his life and the habit of action he develops in meeting those tests.

Gail Sheehy

Change does not roll in on the wheels of inevitability, but comes through continuous struggle. And so we must straighten our backs and work for our freedom.

Martin Luther King, Jr.

One of my favorite movie scenes is from David Lean's *Lawrence of Arabia*. In the scene, Lawrence has just extinguished a match between his thumb and forefinger. One of his colleagues, William Potter, tries to do the same thing. When he closes his thumb and forefinger around the flame of the match he calls out in pain. In response, Lawrence chuckles and explains that although it hurts, the key is to not mind that it hurts.

The scene reminds me that leadership often hurts, but the "trick" to success is not minding so much that it hurts.

The nature of our times demands leaders who will not shrink back at the first sign of difficulty. We need leaders who are willing to embrace the struggle of leadership in order to achieve the goals of leadership. Although we see how tough leadership really is, we have great confidence that leadership (particularly Christian leadership) might overcome all the challenges discussed in the previous chapter.

If we are to become leaders that might overcome the challenges to leadership today then we must overcome some of our common idealistic distortions about leadership. Some people seem to assume that leadership should be easy, that once one achieves the position of leadership then people should follow unquestioningly. Others expect people to hold all leaders in the highest esteem, giving them honor and deference.

Seldom today do people expect leadership to be as difficult, painful, and challenging as it really is. But if leaders are to survive the challenges of leadership and thrive in their leadership then leaders must be tough. In this sense, "tough" means durable and resilient.

We meet many leaders who are greatly discouraged. In our experience, this discouragement comes first because we have set unrealistic idealistic expectations for the leadership experience. Our initial excitement and enthusiasm about our leadership opportunity quickly fades when we encounter people who are uncooperative, indifferent or even hostile toward us as leaders. Sometimes even those who pledge to support our leadership turn against us or betray us.

We also become discouraged when things take longer than we expect. Someone said once that we tend to overestimate what we can accomplish in one year and underestimate what we can accomplish in five years. Yet sometimes the fruit of our leadership may even take longer than five years to emerge! In one sense this should not surprise us. Most people take much longer than five years to grow and mature, so we can expect that sometimes our leadership may take longer as well. What makes this challenge even more difficult is the fact that most leaders (and most groups) will not wait even five years to see major results, so many leaders quit (or get fired) before they ever see results.

A third factor that leads to discouragement is the relatively few but highly publicized amazing leadership success stories. In the business world, it is Steve Jobs who turns around Apple to become one of the largest companies in history or Jack Ma who builds Alibaba to become one of the world's largest retailers. What is often forgotten is how long and how difficult it was to achieve success or how dependent success was on a few key ideas at an important point in history (think "iPod"). In the church world, it is the stories of some pastor beginning with twenty-five people in his home and suddenly growing a church of 2,500 within a year or two. What is often forgotten is the unique set of circumstances that came together to enable such growth to occur in such a short amount of time.

The success stories would not be so discouraging if it were not for the books and seminars that follow suggesting that if we only apply the core strategies used by these amazing leaders then we would have the same results as these leaders. People want to reduce all the variables down to a few easily accessible and easily managed concepts so that they might "sell" these on to desperate leaders looking for a quick fix to their complex challenges. When it does not work for us – and almost never does it really produce the promised outcomes – then we compound our discouragement with disillusionment, while quickly looking for the next easy solution.

Wrestling through the discouragement, we have discovered that most genuinely transformative leadership in the world today does not involve the highly publicized, high-octane success stories but leaders who simply have the grit and determination to stay the course and lead no matter what obstacles might seek to hinder them. These are "normal" people, not superstars, who face their leadership challenges with endurance, allowing these challenges to toughen them up while refusing to shrink back.

The good news is that any person in leadership might become such a leader (which, after all, is the conviction and purpose of this book). The bad news is that most of these leaders will never grab the headlines. People will seldom hold them up as great examples of leadership, but it is these leaders who will truly change the world.

MY OWN LEADERSHIP JOURNEY

Unfortunately, I was one of those people who did not expect leadership to be tough and who consequently struggled with much discouragement. As I took a position as a church leader, I expected the people who so enthusiastically welcomed me would support and encourage me in my leadership. I expected people to honor their commitments to me and cooperate with my leadership. I learned quickly that leadership is tough and that if I was to survive then I must become tough as well.

In my own life, I have experienced the challenges of leadership both in the marketplace and in the church. In the remainder of this chapter, I want to give you a sense of what I have faced as a leader. For now, I will focus on my church experience.

THE FIRST CHURCH

In my career as a minister, I have served three different churches. Unbeknown to me, the first church had a forty-year history of conflict. When I was interviewing for the church, the people said that they wanted to grow the youth, to increase attendance, and to build a new educational wing for the church. Only one person in the church voted against me. He later said that it was not that he opposed me coming; it was just that he didn't think any minister should have a unanimous vote!

Within about eighteen months, everything that people had initially said they wanted had occurred or was in process. We had doubled the youth group, started a second worship service, and made plans for the new addition (which was completely paid off within six months of completion). Yet, some people in the church were very angry with me because these things did not happen in the way they had envisaged.

Throughout just over eight years in that church, we encountered an undercurrent of conflict, although it seldom flared up. I would do my best to placate those who were unhappy, but I discovered that I could really do nothing to make them happy. We experienced a lot of passive aggression, rumors, gossip and the like that would undermine our best leadership efforts. I read many books and attended many seminars to learn how to deal with these situations, but none of them really helped me all that much.

At the same time, we were seeing God change many lives. People were radically converted, becoming mature, moving into leadership and growing as disciples of Jesus. We experienced the power of God in many ways. I remember one youth camp when we had an encounter with the Holy Spirit that dramatically influenced the youth with the gospel, so much so that several of them are in church leadership almost twenty years later. We had a few people changed so dramatically for Christ that people who had known them before their conversion worried that perhaps they had joined a cult!

Looking back, I realize that the conflict we experienced was not really all that bad. At the time, I thought it was miserable! I certainly made many mistakes by focusing too much on the conflict and not focusing enough on the health of the church. I remember one year when I gave my annual report to the elders regarding the state of the church (rather like the US president's "State of the Union" address). I was almost completely negative in my assessment, due to the influence the conflict had on me. When I finished, everyone was quiet. Finally, one elder began to speak. Carefully and slowly he began to ask, "what about..." and then named something good that had occurred. After just a few minutes I realized that I had missed everything good that had been happening and that the good far outweighed what I had perceived as negative.

After almost nine years, I realized that it was time to leave, but my leaving had nothing to do with the conflict. I realized that we needed to leave because the healthy people were not rising up and taking the leadership as God was calling them to do. My presence was actually holding people back. When we got the call to move to our second church, making the decision to leave remains the single most difficult and painful decision I have ever made in leadership. Once I announced it to the church, I grieved so deeply and fully that I could hardly move for five days.

Sadly, once I left many of the young leaders also left because – as often happens – the conflict flared up in my absence. I tried to encourage people to stay and work it through but frankly I had not set a good example in my conflict management nor had I really prepared people for what would happen. In addition, I had left, so people wondered how I could encourage them to stay. However, almost all the people who left immediately took up leadership roles in the churches to which they went. One core group of leaders actually helped revitalize another dying congregation, building it into a thriving, healthy fellowship. People from our time in this church have remained dear friends over the years, supporting us personally and in prayer.

THE SECOND CHURCH

Before going to my second church, I wanted to ensure that it did not have the same kind of problems I had experienced in the first church. I spent a lot of time with people before going, discussing the style of ministry we would have and the goals we would have. I talked openly about the forty-year history of conflict in my first church and the people assured me that the second church did not have the same history. In fact, they had a *fifty-year* history of conflict!

The five years I spent in my second church were much more difficult than my first church. In that church, we began with two fairly productive years. The church grew. God ministered to many people, both within and outside the church. However, several people – many on the fringes of the life of the church – did not like the changes that were going on. Some people took offense at things I did, or did not, do. The disgruntled people began to make calls and visit others to stir up dissension. This resulted in a two-year period of extremely intense conflict.

During those two years of intense conflict, I received hate mail, prank phone calls, and many attempts to get rid of me. One of my elders affectionately dubbed the opposing group "the gang" because of some of the tactics they were using. Quite a number of people who had been very supportive initially became caught up in the divisive tactics used by the "gang". For some time, many of the healthy people in the church had no idea anything bad was happening. Then, some people in the "gang" began to call everyone in the church to spread negativity and dissension and seek supporters. This caused the healthy people to rally together in support of health in the church.

The turning point came at our annual congregational meeting one November, a time in which new elders are selected to serve the church. A month before this meeting, I felt that most likely my ministry at this church would be ending. I doubted I would survive this meeting. But the Lord seemed to assure me that everything would work out alright. At the meeting, a denominational executive chaired so that no doubt could be cast on the process. Those in opposition brought several nominations of people to serve as elders, but the church selected none of them. Instead, it selected a healthy, united eldership.

Foolishly, I thought this would decide the matter and that the church would move on in health. Instead, the gang began bringing complaints against the eldership (not me personally) in the higher governing bodies of the denomination. Although many on the commission to review these issues were openly sympathetic toward members of the gang, all the complaints had to be thrown out because either they did not have substance or because the eldership had resolved them immediately. The process to resolve these complaints should have taken thirty days; instead, it took over six months.

Although the commission could not sustain these complaints, they suggested that the presbytery (the body with oversight of the church) set up an administrative commission to review my ministry and that of the church because "where there's smoke there must be fire". Some in the presbytery were openly supportive of the gang, even though they had sown division and pain in the life of the church. After investigating the situation for several months, the commission gave its final report. Although acknowledging that mistakes had been made, the commission found a generally healthy and unified church and closed the matter.

The time in our second church was a time of very intense spiritual warfare. We felt it not only for us but also for many of the churches in our region. We engaged with this in prayer and worship. Thankfully the Lord brought us through that time and the church became healthy. Many churches in the region also experienced exceptional growth.

Although the church has experienced a few difficulties along the way since those years, it has become a reasonably healthy, growing church, having an impact far beyond its four walls. We have many wonderful friends from our time in this church as well who have continued to support and encourage us over the years. When God called us to London, we did not want to leave. We looked for any excuse to turn down the call. However, even people in the church reluctantly agreed that the call to London really was from God.

THE THIRD CHURCH

When we came to the third church we hoped that this church would not be like the first two. And it was not – it was much worse! My wife and I had spent a lot of time praying and preparing before we moved to London. God called us to the third church very clearly and strongly. We had built relationships with people at the church before we even arrived. We had even sought to build a common understanding of how we would do ministry together with the church after they issued the call. We received a number of prophetic words confirming the call.

Although there were a few hiccups, the first year went fairly well. However, what I call the "Cold War" began in October, just over a year after we arrived, when I received a letter from someone I thought was my friend. This letter accused me of many things, including trying to build my own kingdom. It felt crazy and confusing to me. But the situation seemed to pass quickly. What I did not realize at the time was that this letter marked the beginning of an undercurrent of conflict. This undercurrent of conflict ebbed and flowed for three years. Most of the time I did not recognize what was happening. During this time, I used all the leadership skills and techniques for conflict resolution that I had learned and studied over the previous thirteen years, all to no avail.

During the Cold War, it seemed we faced a constant stream of squabbles and problems. Our eldership team had meetings that lasted more than three or four hours, sometimes not even completing the modest agenda. We had a lot of miscommunications and misunderstandings – many more than one might expect. I felt under constant pressure and stress. We struggled to accomplish everything we did. Many factions and divisions seemed to arise in the life of the church.

The Cold War lasted until around December, just over three years later. At that time, an adherent of the church raised some questions at a church meeting, questions regarding financial management. (No one was ever accused of doing anything improper or illegal; these were just questions of good practice.) Unfortunately, a few people took this personally and thought I had encouraged him to raise the questions. They blamed me for the questions. This initiated what I call the "Hot War".

THE "HOT WAR"

The Hot War was a time of intense and sustained conflict, reaching the highest level of conflict referred to as "level five" conflict, where people may actually try to destroy others' reputations, relationships, livelihoods, and, occasionally, their lives. The conflict existed throughout the church although it was portrayed as a division between me and the rest of the elders. At the beginning of the Hot War, I felt the Lord tell me three things: "stand", "do not resign", and "remember this is not your fight". In the following months many people gave me the exact same words without realizing they were what the Lord had told me from the beginning.

After about seven months of the Hot War we brought in some mediators to help us. Unfortunately, they had not been trained in mediation so the process was largely unsuccessful at resolving anything. The outcome of three months of mediation was that my wife and I were forced to take what turned out to be a four-month sabbatical, during which time the elders were supposed to rebuild the governance of the church and bring health into the church. I agreed that if at the end of the sabbatical I could not agree with the new structure then I would resign. At the church meeting which agreed the sabbatical, I was forced to admit publicly that it was my own failure of leadership which had caused most of the problems.

Many people in the church rallied around me to offer support. Quite a number were very upset, feeling that I had not been treated fairly. However, I accepted the forced sabbatical and encouraged the church members to work with the elders to build a healthy church. I chose not to "fight" because of what the Lord had spoken to me.

Unfortunately, the conflict continued throughout my sabbatical. Efforts to get rid of me intensified. Two months into the sabbatical, at the end of a lengthy annual general meeting in December – under "any other business" and after taking an extended "comfort break" – the elders brought a surprise motion of "no confidence" in me as the minister. Unsurprisingly, the motion passed. However, when they told me about this, I remembered what God had told me: "do not resign". So, I said that I could not resign but I would willingly leave if the church meeting dismissed me formally. I subsequently learned that many people had left the meeting before the vote, not realizing what was going to happen.

The church meeting to consider whether or not to dismiss me occurred the following February. It was over six hours long. I spent about four hours answering questions from people in the church, many of whom had not realized fully what was happening and most of whom had never heard my perspectives. We had a good outside moderator for the meeting who ensured that I was able to speak without interruption.

After this, I left the room to wait in my office while the members of the church debated my future. The debate lasted more than ninety minutes. Apparently it was very intense, almost violent. Although I was in my office, I could sense the intensity of the spiritual warfare going on. The spiritual battle raged over the church. The weight of it was almost overwhelming to me personally. However, at 7:27 p.m. it broke. The intensity suddenly lifted from me. I said in my heart, "Doggone it! They've decided to keep me!" That was exactly what had happened at that moment. My wife and I resumed our ministry the very next day.

Although I was forced to take a sabbatical, I realize now it was a gift from God. I realize also that what I had admitted the previous October had been true: I *had* failed in my leadership. God had used the sabbatical to show me some of the ways I had failed in my leadership as well as to give me some new perspectives on leadership. When I returned to ministry many things inside me had shifted.

One would think that after the church voted to keep me things would have improved. But they actually became much, much worse. From that February until just over a year later in March the conflicts multiplied. I saw some of the worst things I have ever seen in ministry. There was another major attempt to remove me, the elders became very divided against me *again*, and there were many other problems that threatened to destroy the church – and that is not an overstatement.

By that March it had become so overwhelming that I felt like dying. I tried many things to correct the problems and improve the situation, but nothing helped. In desperation, I called a special church meeting at which I was going to reveal what had been happening – at least what I could properly and legally share – to the members of the church. On the Thursday morning before this Sunday church meeting, a man walked into the church and gave a prophetic word to our receptionist. He said, "The Lord woke me up in the night with a word for your church: there will be a final difficult time, a test, a clearing out, and then God is going to multiply the church." Honestly, I did not receive this as good news at the time. Exhausted, I did not think I could endure a "final difficult time". But God was true to his word.

The church meeting that Sunday was extremely intense. I was blocked in sharing what I had wanted to share. However, by the end of the meeting something significant had shifted. Our regularly scheduled church meeting was just two weeks later. Just before that meeting, all the elders except one resigned. The one who did not resign was the only one I knew I could still work with effectively. At that church meeting, the congregation welcomed many new members, some of whom had been waiting to join for more than a year. That day marked the end of the Hot War.

But the battle was not over yet.

MOPPING UP

The next two years are what I call the "mopping up period". During this time, there was a lot of work to rebuild the ministry of the church. We elected a new eldership, one which was positive and united. We had a tremendous amount of work to do. We exposed and repented of many sins – individually and corporately as an eldership and as a church. We worked through a number of challenges and disagreements, but we did so in a more healthy way.

Beginning with the March meeting and at other points during this period, over ten appeals were filed against the church meeting and the elders meeting with the denomination to which the church belonged. These appeals took two years to resolve. More on that in a minute.

In October that year, a lengthy complaint was filed against me using the disciplinary process for ministers in the denomination. A special mandated group was set up to investigate this complaint. It was actually more than seven months before I was even allowed to see or know what was in the complaint against me. The mandated group looked into a number of issues, not limiting themselves to those in the complaint itself. In the end, after investigating the situation thoroughly, the mandated group issued the ruling that not only was there no evidence that I had done something wrong, there was also no evidence that I *might* have done something wrong. It was a complete exoneration as far as the complaint went. I received the ruling verbally in November, just over a year after the original complaint had been filed. It was not until the following January that I received the ruling in writing.

Regarding the appeals, questions arose about them in the next highest governing body in the denomination, so the appeals had to be referred to the highest governing body in the denomination. This group formed a special commission which met with us in March, two years after the first appeals had been lodged. At that meeting, the commission dismissed or disallowed all but one of the appeals. For the last appeal, the commission simply wanted to know whether the procedure followed had been appropriate and fair. In the end, they determined that it had been. That day marked the end of the season of conflict at the church. In the end, the entire period of conflict had lasted for almost eight years. It took us another two years before we began to feel reasonably normal again.

Once the conflict was concluded, we had to continue rebuilding the ministry of the church. The church continued to face many significant challenges as it recovered from the conflict time and sought to minister in a complex urban environment. However, the days of conflict have become a distant memory for most as the church moves into the future God has for it.

FREED TO LEAD

Some people wonder how I have survived three such churches, especially considering the intensity of conflict at the third church. The key moment came for me in the middle of the conflict in my second church. The conflict had been very, very intense, wearing me down. I was at a conference where I was the worship leader. During a quiet moment, I had chosen to sit on the floor at the side of the room, quietly reflecting. The leader of the conference came to me and asked, "Are you OK?" I said reflexively, "Yes, I'm OK." That is when I realized that *I was OK.* At the deepest core of my being, no matter what I had endured, I was genuinely well. I was at peace.

Nothing in the struggles or the conflicts had fundamentally changed or altered who I was in Christ. I was still a "saint", a "holy one". I was still saved by grace through faith. I was still a "son" of God. Nothing any human being might do could touch me in this core of my being. I was truly free in Christ and freed to lead.

Around 1990 I had read *Victory over the Darkness* by Neil T. Anderson. This book had enabled me to see myself as a Christian in a fresh way, yet in a way fully grounded in the Bible as God's Word. The book really contained nothing new, just a renewed understanding of what the Bible had said – and many historical Christians had believed – all along.

In the following years, I used the material of *Victory over the Darkness* and *The Bondage Breaker* not only in my personal life but also in my first church. We saw many people changed and set free using the *Steps to Freedom in Christ.* We taught the material in our worship, Sunday school, youth ministry, membership classes, and marriage retreats. I personally had used the material to process through many painful memories of the past, and I found that others benefited as well.

By the time I got to my second church, I had integrated the teachings of Freedom in Christ into my entire ministry. These materials had become foundational to my leadership. Suddenly, I realized how they had grounded my identity and my leadership in Jesus to the extent that the conflicts of my church – as tremendously unpleasant as they were – could not change my being in Christ (unless I would allow them to do so).

Three themes of the Freedom in Christ materials were especially important for me during the times of conflict I endured.

KNOW AND BELIEVE WHO YOU ARE IN CHRIST

When I examined the Bible anew, I realized that Jesus had given me a new identity and met all my deepest needs because I was in him and he was in me. Nothing could change that identity because it was a gift of God's grace, not something that I had earned. This meant that I did not need to use my leadership role as a means to gain identity or to have my needs met. It reminded me of what Jesus told the disciples:

> A dispute also arose among them, as to which of them was to be regarded as the greatest. And he said to them, "The kings of the Gentiles exercise lordship over them, and those in authority over them are called benefactors. But not so with you. Rather, let the greatest among you become as the youngest, and the leader as one who serves. For who is the greater, one who reclines at table or one who serves? Is it not the one who reclines at table? But I am among you as the one who serves." (Luke 22:24–27)

Here the disciples were wanting to get their identity and sense of significance from being "the greatest", from others looking up to them. Perhaps they were debating who had the best ability to heal others or preach the kingdom, seeking a sense of importance from their abilities. They may have been arguing about who was closest to Jesus, seeking personal value from their relationships. Jesus inverted their concept of leadership, making it about serving from among people instead of dominating from above people. Jesus was implying that their true sense of identity and significance would come from relationship with him and not their "greatness". Leaders who are keen to be recognized as leaders are often just demonstrating their insecurity. The really secure leaders are those who, like Jesus, are simply there to serve.

As Christians, we need to know who we really are in Jesus – children of God loved by our heavenly Father and filled with his Spirit. If we do not get our sense of identity as a child of God, a holy one, we will invariably look to something else for our sense of significance, acceptance or security. If we are leaders in this situation, we may very well be trying to get these things from some aspect of leadership.

KNOW THE REALITY OF THE SPIRITUAL WORLD AND DEAL WITH IT BIBLICALLY

I had experienced the reality of the spiritual world as a very young Christian. I knew there were such things as angels and demons from personal experience. So I did not learn this from Freedom in Christ, but Freedom in Christ teachings helped me anchor my understanding of the spiritual world in the Bible as the Word of God rather than in some of the populist understandings of these things that had circulated among Christians.

Jesus reminded his disciples that the thief comes only to steal and kill and destroy. Jesus, in contrast, came that people may have life and have it abundantly. Jesus is the good shepherd who lays down his life for the sheep. Leaders who are hired hands and not shepherds, who do not love the sheep, see the wolf coming, leave the sheep, and flee. So the wolf snatches them and scatters them. These leaders flee because they are hired hands and care nothing for the sheep (see John 10:10–13).

The Bible reveals a spiritual reality where Satan comes to steal, kill, and destroy. He will do these things if he is allowed to. Leaders who are just hired hands will run away in fear when spiritual realities close in. Jesus, who is the good shepherd, did not fear a confrontation with Satan even though it meant suffering an agonizing death. Jesus did it all for those who follow him so he would give them abundant life.

As we lead, we need to be aware of the reality of the spiritual world and its influences. We have an enemy who wants to prevent our people living in that abundant spiritual life. The Bible gives us the perspectives and the strategies we need in order to deal with these spiritual realities in a healthy way. The more we understand how Satan works, the more we realize how powerless he is to hold people back as we help them take hold the truth.

THE BATTLE FOR YOUR MIND

We tend to think of power when we think of leadership. Even many Christian leaders try to frame the spiritual conflict we are in, as well as the whole task of leadership, in terms of power. We mistakenly believe that if we simply possess and exercise enough power then we will have the victory.

However, the Bible tends to frame these issues not in terms of "power" but in terms of "truth". The key is not possessing enough power but knowing and believing the truth. The power of God works itself through truth. The battle we are in is played out in our minds. It's a battle for truth and lies. (Of course, this involves the emotions and the will as well as the intellect, which we will examine in subsequent chapters.)

We don't necessarily believe what we think we believe. If we want to know what we – or anyone else – really believes, we must examine our actions. It is easy to think we believe what is in the Bible but then live our lives as if the Bible is not true. When it comes to looking at leadership, we can subconsciously favor secular principles we have learned over the Bible.

It is crucial that we discern where our thinking is not in line with God's truth. Then we can take steps to renew our minds which is, according to Paul, the thing that will lead to our transformation (see Romans 12:1–2).

Without fully being aware of it, these teachings had transformed me and my leadership, so that not only could I survive intense conflict I could also actually come out on the other side of it a better person. When I look at my life – although I would not want to go through it again and although I wish I had not had to go through it in the first place – I am grateful for the conflict that I have been through. What I endured as a leader had toughened me up in a way that no school or training course ever could. Through it all, I learned many important lessons. In the end, I know that I am a better person in Christ Jesus for what I suffered than I would have been otherwise.

Someone once asked me, "Does everyone have to suffer?" My immediate response was "probably yes". Then someone else suggested differently. She said, "We all must learn through suffering and pain; but perhaps God enables us to learn from the suffering and pain of others as well so that we do not have to suffer in the same way ourselves." Then, more recently, at a conference where I was presenting the material, a young man came up to thank me. He said, "Thank you for going through this so that I can learn from you in a way that I might not have to go through it myself."

Perhaps this expresses part of my desire concerning this book – that you might learn from my suffering and difficulty as a leader, becoming a tough leader taking on the tough challenge of leadership as a fruitful disciple of Jesus Christ and as a "son" (both men and women) of God.

THE LEADERSHIP DILEMMA

So here is our next leadership dilemma: in order to lead well as a healthy leader, leaders must be tough. As we face the challenges of leadership, they will toughen us up so that we might face even greater challenges with grace and perseverance, achieving God's purposes in our leadership. But our toughness as leaders does not depend on the external challenges we face. Our toughness as leaders comes from who we are inside and our gritty determination to stand and not resign, remembering that the greatest battles we seem to face are really God's battles to fight.

PART II

AUTHENTIC CHRISTIAN LEADERSHIP

Leadership is influence.

John Maxwell

The authority by which the Christian leader leads is not power but love, not force but example, not coercion but reasoned persuasion. Leaders have power, but power is safe only in the hands of those who humble themselves to serve.

John Stott

Jesus said several times, "Come, follow me." His was a program of "do what I do," rather than "do what I say." His innate brilliance would have permitted him to put on a dazzling display, but that would have left his followers far behind. He walked and worked with those he was to serve. His was not a long-distance leadership. He was not afraid of close friendships; he was not afraid that proximity to him would disappoint his followers. The leaven of true leadership cannot lift others unless we are with and serve those to be led.

Spencer W. Kimball

In the end, it is important to remember that we cannot become what we need to be by remaining what we are.

Max DePree

Any quick survey of the web will uncover a myriad of definitions of leadership. Here are just a few definitions of the thirty listed in an article on businessnewsdaily.com:

"Leadership is the ability to guide others without force into a direction or decision that leaves them still feeling empowered and accomplished." – Lisa Cash Hanson, CEO, Snuggwugg

"Effective leadership is providing the vision and motivation to a team so they work together toward the same goal, and then understanding the talents and temperaments of each individual and effectively motivating each person to contribute individually their best toward achieving the group goal." – Stan Kimer, president, Total Engagement Consulting by Kimer

"Leadership is the art of serving others by equipping them with training, tools and people as well as your time, energy and emotional intelligence so that they can realize their full potential, both personally and professionally." – Daphne Mallory, family business expert, The Daphne Mallory Company

"Leadership is influencing others by your character, humility and example. It is recognizable when others follow in word and deed without obligation or coercion." – Sonny Newman, president, EE Technologies[1]

We might consider these definitions as coming from more of a marketplace orientation. A downloadable document from the University of Warwick gives twenty other definitions from the scholarly literature regarding leadership. These include:

"Leadership may be considered as the process (act) of influencing the activities of an organized group in its efforts toward goal setting and goal achievement." – R. M. Stogdill

"Leadership is the process of influencing the activities of an individual or a group in efforts toward goal achievement in a given situation." – P. Hersey & K. Blanchard

"Leadership is the art of influencing others to their maximum performance to accomplish any task, objective or project." – W. A. Cohen

"Leadership is the art of mobilizing others to want to struggle for the shared aspirations." – J. M. Kouzes & B. Z. Posner2

As Christians, we might find many things in these definitions that resonate strongly with our Christian values. At the same time, we would perhaps find a few items that we might reject, or at least avoid, in our own leadership.

These definitions drive us to deeper questions about whether we need a uniquely Christian definition of leadership. Perhaps leadership is simply leadership, no matter who is leading and how they are leading. Perhaps what really matters are the results of leadership, no matter who is leading and how they are leading. Perhaps simply being a Christian who is leading determines what Christian leadership is, no matter what the results are or how they are leading.

We all have our perspectives of what it means to be a Christian in leadership. Generally, the perspectives people have shared with us about Christians in leadership tend to be a bit negative. "Oh, I knew a Christian boss once," someone might say. "He was a really nice guy but never could get anything done." Or, another might say, "I had a boss who claimed to be a Christian, but she was one of the meanest people I ever met!" The themes we hear are often a negative assessment of the Christian's character (being a "hypocrite") or a negative assessment of the Christian's effectiveness (not getting results).

All of this leads to a deep suspicion that someone cannot be both a sincere Christian and an effective leader. This suspicion causes many Christians to compromise their faith for the sake of effective worldly leadership principles, making faith a "private" affair that has no relevance to the "real world". I remember having lunch with a man in an Asian nation who was feeling deeply discouraged because he felt that in order to be a genuine Christian in the workplace he needed to stop exercising effective leadership. He felt that as a Christian he could not be strong, decisive, and direct; that somehow he needed to be a soft milquetoast. After a brief conversation, he left the table encouraged and strengthened in his faith, resolving to remain a strong marketplace leader who was also a strong Christian.

In this section, we will present our vision for Christian leadership. Although the heart of the Christian definition of leadership might share similarities with many other definitions of leadership, we believe that Christians might have a unique vision for leadership that is genuinely Christian. Not only that, we also have a commitment that uniquely Christian leadership is the leadership needed for the times in which we live.

3

DEFINING CHRISTIAN LEADERSHIP

Live so as to be missed when dead.

Robert Murray McCheyne

He is no fool who gives what he cannot keep to gain what he cannot lose.

Jim Elliot

The world sets the agenda for the professional man; God sets the agenda of the spiritual man.

John Piper

Wilhem was born in Zimbabwe of Scottish and German descent. When the economy collapsed in Zimbabwe he made the difficult decision to move to Manchester in the UK and start a new business. A committed Christian, he joined a local church with a big vision and quickly rose to become one of the elders. Although he enjoyed business, he loved his involvement in the church, so he considered his business simply as a way to make ends meet while he gave his best efforts to the church. Soon, many new people began to join the church, drawn by Wilhem's infectious smile and his big, "charismatic" personality. He and the minister seemed very close, although they had some different styles of doing things.

John was born of an affluent family in the Lake District of England. As he grew up, he discovered that he really loved to make money – and he certainly had a knack for it. He had some tumultuous times in his twenties, but while in his early thirties he had a dramatic conversion experience and became a committed Christian. Soon after, he moved to Manchester, starting a wealth management company and joining a local church. He quickly gained a reputation as an excellent wealth manager and a tough boss. He expected his people to work hard. He encouraged Christians in his company to have prayer meetings and Bible studies – as long as they did not interfere with their work. His company grew significantly. Although he participated regularly in the worship of the church, his business commitments meant that he had no time to serve on church committees or the church leadership team – although he was repeatedly asked to do so.

Looking at Wilhem and John, which one is exercising authentic Christian leadership?

We believe the times in which we live need authentic Christian leadership. We believe Christian leadership is not limited to the home and the church. If it is truly leadership, Christian leadership should apply in all contexts in all places all around the world. Such leadership must benefit everyone, not just Christians. Christian leadership is not some latest internet fad or self-help phenomenon; it is biblical, Christ-centered leadership. If it is genuinely Christian, Christian leadership will transform people, groups, and even societies while remaining faithful to the gospel. It will also transform leaders themselves.

Sadly, Christians have largely failed to discern and describe genuine Christian leadership. We have often settled for outward appearances, when God looks on the heart (see 1 Samuel 16:7). We have often focused on results, when God focuses on faithfulness (see 1 Corinthians 4:2). Let's return to Wilhem and John. Which one was exercising authentic Christian leadership?

After a couple years in his church, people began to notice that

Wilhem had accumulated quite a large group of people around him, people who were not very healthy personally and spiritually and who seemed to "need" Wilhem's strong personality and confidence. Wilhem seemed to thrive on the attention. At the same time, the people around him were not really becoming healthier emotionally and spiritually, even though they were becoming more committed to the church. Wilhem began to feel that the pastor was a bit weak, and perhaps not really suited to lead the church. Wilhem seemed the much better choice for lead elder. He began to undermine the pastor behind his back, while solidifying his followers. In the end, Wilhem's group forced the pastor to leave and assumed control of the church.

After ten years in his business – and just when the business seemed poised for even greater growth and profitability – John sold the business to a Christian friend who he felt would continue the growth. At his farewell party, several people testified to how John's integrity and presence in the company had encouraged them to become better people. Several had even become Christians. John used the profits from the sale of the business and the wealth he had already accumulated to form a charitable company to promote investment and job growth in developing nations. He encouraged his church to intercede for his new charitable company as well as for himself personally.

These two stories show how difficult it can be to discern authentic Christian leadership, especially since we tend to focus on outward indicators of effective leadership which may often deceive us – at least for a season. At the same time, we see how transformative Christian leadership can be – even Christian leadership in the marketplace. Although many might have criticized John for what might be perceived as a lack of commitment to his local church, in the end we discovered that John really exercised Christian leadership in a way that brought real change to people's lives. Although many might have praised Wilhem's commitment to his local church, in the end his leadership turned out to be unhealthy and destructive in a way that few might label "Christian".

BIBLICAL METAPHORS FOR LEADERSHIP

To understand Christian leadership, we need to keep in mind several biblical metaphors for leadership. None of these metaphors fully expresses leadership in itself, but each will inform our understanding of leadership. As with all metaphors, they have limitations, especially on their own, but taken together they give us a rich picture of the Bible's view of leadership.

Sent ones

As Christians, God has sent us into the world. God has sent us into the world in order to disciple the nations (see Matthew 28:18–20) and to be the ambassadors of his loving rulership (see 2 Corinthians 5:20). God sends us as leaders into the marketplace as well as the church. Whenever Paul would go into a new city, he would generally visit both the synagogue and the public marketplace, making an appeal for people to follow Christ in both places.

Many times Christians have wrongly assumed that those who work for the church are the genuine Christian leaders, while those who work in business simply exist to support the "real" Christian leaders. However, this is not the biblical perspective. Today, the marketplace is the front-line mission field for Christian leaders. Both those who lead in the church and those who lead in other spheres are equally important for the extension of God's loving rulership throughout society.

Stewards

As a young Christian, the only time I heard the word "stewardship" was when the church was having its annual drive to encourage people to give money to support the work of the church. Although we would agree that the Bible calls us to give money to support our churches, this view of stewardship is highly limited and rather reductionistic.

The Bible's concept of stewardship is much broader. Stewards are people who have been entrusted with certain resources to use and manage on behalf of the one who owns the resources and for the purposes of the one who owns the resources. Stewards in the Bible were not merely "managers" (as is often translated) but they were actually "leaders" with tremendous authority and responsibility. As leaders, they had accountability to the master or owner.

As Christians, we are stewards of the resources God has given us. We are stewards of our churches, homes, and businesses. We have been commissioned by God to manage these resources so as to bear fruit and to advance God's loving rulership into the world. We have been commissioned by God to lead in these areas in a way that honors God and his purposes.

Shepherds

In the Greek, "shepherd" is the same word as "pastor". One of the biblical roles of "shepherds" was caring for churches. Because of this, we can assume that the real biblical shepherds are the pastors of churches. However, all Christian leaders are also shepherds, caring for the people around them. Whenever a leader has any degree of responsibility for or supervision of people that leader is called to be a shepherd.

Shepherds look out for the well-being of the sheep, making sure they are fed and protected. Genuine shepherds have a commitment to the sheep, looking out for their welfare instead of using the sheep for their own benefit. Even in the marketplace, leaders must care for the people they lead, watching out for their best interests.

Servants

Many Christians define Christian leadership simply in terms of "servant leadership". Although there are many metaphors for Christian leadership, "servant leadership" is perhaps the most powerful. Christian leaders are called to serve. Jesus himself said he came into the world to serve. He said that anyone who wanted to be great in his kingdom would be the servant of all. True Christian leadership must serve others, seeking to achieve the good of others. True Christian leadership must not allow itself to become self-seeking.

In recent years, even the marketplace generally has come to recognize that the really great leaders, the ones who have the greatest effect, are those who put others or their company before themselves. Some people call this "servant leadership". Many writers and trainers point out the benefits and challenges of servant leadership.

One of the great challenges for Christians is to remember that servant leaders must *lead*. Sometimes our perspectives of servanthood suggest that servants are those who are totally submissive and passive. However, the biblical perspectives on servanthood suggest that servants are proactive and responsible.

Sons

As Christian leaders, we must recognize that we are also sons of God. We must recognize that our fundamental identity is not that of a slave but that of a son (see Galatians 4:7). Sons go into the world as leaders confident of their heavenly Father's support and encouragement. Sons realize they have their heavenly Father's resources. True sons of God (and this includes women!) make the best leaders.

Having our identity as sons of God has several implications for leadership. As sons, we must ensure that our leadership activities represent our Father. As sons, we must remember that our identity does not come from what we do as leaders but from the father–son relationship with the Father. As sons, we must embrace our wider family – especially our elder "brother" Jesus (our Lord) – as leaders, acknowledging that there are no self-sufficient sons.

CHRISTIAN LEADERSHIP DEFINED

With these metaphors in mind, we begin to identify the broad contours of authentic Christian leadership. We have developed this definition of Christian leadership:

> **Christian leadership is the interactive relational process of influencing people and people-systems toward beneficial outcomes through your identity, character, and calling in Christ, using your God-given strengths and spiritual gifts as well as your talents, skills, and knowledge.**

Obviously, there are many definitions of leadership out there. One of the simplest definitions comes from the leadership expert John Maxwell: "Leadership is influence." There are many different ways to understand leadership, and hundreds of thousands of books trying to explain those understandings. As we wrestled with understanding leadership, we wanted to get to the heart of leadership generally as well as asking specifically what makes leadership "Christian".

So let us look at each portion of this definition.

PROCESS

First, leadership is a process. It is not an event – something that happens once and is over. It is not a destination, as if we might achieve leadership one day if we keep trying. Process is something ongoing, something that is never fully completed. The process of leadership might be healthy or it might be dysfunctional. The process may have time and outcome limitations, or it may be ongoing.

When you are a leader, you can never say "Well, that's it; the job's done!" I knew of a leader who would repaint his vacation home every year, whether it needed it or not. He did this in order to have the satisfaction of finishing a job, something he never did as a leader.

RELATIONAL PROCESS

The leadership process is relational. It is always people centered. Leadership may never be merely task oriented. Although there are many things we do as leaders, we always do them in the context of relationships. Without relationship we have no leadership.

I had a minister friend who used to say, "Being a pastor would be a great job if it wasn't for all the people." Of course, there are many people in churches who might say, "This church would be great if it wasn't for the pastor." My pastor friend acknowledged both the essence and the challenge of leadership. Leadership cannot avoid relationship, yet those relationships will always challenge leadership.

INTERACTIVE RELATIONAL PROCESS

The relational leadership process always involves some degree of interaction between the leader and those being led. We sometimes embrace the myth that real leaders are these independent supermen (or women!) who lead others while remaining solitary and unchanged themselves. However, in the process of leading, leaders will change as much or more than the people they lead will change. If we are not willing to change then we should not be leaders.

One of the amazing benefits of leading a polycultural congregation such as City Temple is how that affects me as a leader. Over time, I have come to realize that as I interact with people from differing cultural, social, and ethnic backgrounds I begin to change because of the influence that my "followers" have on me as the leader. Although I was born and raised in the USA, many of my American friends have commented that I almost do not seem like an American anymore. As I am changed by those I lead, I become a more effective leader for them as well.

INFLUENCING PEOPLE AND PEOPLE-SYSTEMS

In one sense, John Maxwell (and many others) is correct. True leadership always involves influence. If we have no influence in the lives of others, we have no leadership.

Although leadership is influence, we can easily limit the perception of our influence to individual people. Most leaders focus primarily on how they are leading individual people around them. We can easily assume that if we lead individual people well then we will be successful in our leadership. However, we must realize that not only do we influence people through our leadership but we also influence the groups and organizations of which people are a part – what we call "people-systems". In fact, we would assert that our leadership *primarily* influences these "people-systems" and not just the individual people within those systems.

Over the years, I have spoken with many frustrated leaders who did not realize they needed to lead people-systems as well as individual people. This happens in churches all the time. A young pastor wants to introduce a new style of worship into his church. So he wisely meets with all the elders individually to discuss the change with them. One by one, the elders individually agree to the changes. Many of them seem very enthusiastic. So, when the day of the elders meeting arrives, the young pastor is confident that his motion will pass. After all, the elders lead the church. They are responsible for these decisions. The elders discuss the motion and vote it down strongly. The young pastor is stunned. Unfortunately, he had not accounted for several of the elders' spouses, who did not like the idea at all.

Christian leadership involves leading people-systems as well as people themselves. How we define and lead people-systems will be the focus of Part Three. For now, we might say that people-systems are the groups and organizations in which people cooperate together. Leaders influence these groups as well as individuals within these groups.

BENEFICIAL OUTCOMES

All leadership leads to something – whether it is change, stagnation, growth, prosperity, or disaster. Some leaders seek what is only good for themselves. Other leaders may have hidden agendas that are not good for the company. Most leaders genuinely want good things to happen, not only for themselves but also for those they lead.

Authentic Christian leadership always considers the outcomes of leadership.

Christian leaders do not lead simply for the sake of leading; they lead so that God's will might be done on earth as it is in heaven. Certainly, authentic Christian leaders do not want outcomes that are sinful, worldly or demonic. Another word for outcomes might be "fruit". Christian leaders want to bear good fruit.

This means that Christian leadership will create a positive direction toward beneficial outcomes. Christian leadership cannot be static; it must be moving somewhere positive. But this creates a dilemma: how do we know whether an outcome is beneficial or not?

Historically, business leaders have focused on achieving positive financial outcomes. After all, financial outcomes are the easiest outcomes to measure and the ones which generally ensure job security along with shareholder approval. However, over the past couple of decades the marketplace has begun to learn that simply making money is not enough. A company can make a lot of money doing very bad things. Some companies might make little money but have a positive contribution to society.

As we consider our outcomes, we believe there are at least five questions we need to ask in order to determine whether or not an outcome is beneficial. Each question has two aspects, one with narrower implications and one with broader implications. Additionally, we must answer each question both in terms of the people and people-systems (including society more generally) we are leading.

Is the outcome economically beneficial?

The first question includes the traditional "bottom line" – profit or surplus. Businesses need to make a profit in order to survive. Churches need to raise more than they spend, or at least ensure that they do not consistently spend more than people give. The Bible affirms that work should bring profit (see Proverbs 14:23). This is one measure of a good outcome.

This question is also about exercising good stewardship over all our resources – money, property, time, and the like. All leaders have a responsibility for the resources of the people and organizations they lead. Leaders need to help manage the resources of their organizations so that the organizations might remain productive.

A small church in the eastern US faced a consistent shortfall in its budget. The church had several options that may have produced economically beneficial outcomes. First, the church could have sought creative solutions for leadership. For example, it could have sought to bring in a retired minister to work part time and live in the church-owned house. Second, it could have made the necessary changes to reduce its costs and live within its means – even though some of those changes would have been painful – resolving to seek the Lord for a strategy to extend its ministry within its budget limits. Third, it could have decided to dissolve, selling its property to a new church plant that needed it or giving the money to a new church plant. In the end, the church decided to sell its house for the minister in order to supplement its budget for the next few years. This decision ensured that the church would not be able to afford another minister (because it could no longer afford the costs of housing the minister) and that the church would continue the process of decline until it was forced to close its doors with nothing left for other ministry.

In the end, the church failed to exercise good stewardship over the resource – in this case, the church-owned house – that would possibly have been the key to its rejuvenation and growth. Although the sale of the house enabled the church to maintain its financial bottom line, it also meant a failure to steward its resources in a healthy way. Thus, it would have failed to answer this first question positively.

Is the outcome socially beneficial?

The second question seeks to discern whether the outcome benefits people socially. The first aspect of this question is whether the outcome includes the promotion of healthy relationships. Some companies create an environment of unhealthy competition, pitting employees against one another in dog-eat-dog relationships. The competitive environment creates an atmosphere where people may lie to one another and cheat one another in order to get ahead. Other companies might create an environment of suspicion and mistrust, thinking that this might protect them from employees stealing from the company. In contrast to these companies, other companies might create games rooms, exercise facilities, and other such resources to promote healthy relationships among its employees.

The second aspect to this question is whether the outcome promotes a healthy society. One business may require its employees to work so many hours that marriages break down and families fall apart. Even if that business made lots of money, clearly its outcome would not be beneficial. Another company may provide nursery facilities on-site so that mothers may come to work in a way that promotes closeness to their children as well as the peace of mind that enables them to work more productively.

Is the outcome environmentally beneficial?

Over the past decade, people and organizations have awakened to the need to care for the environment. So the first aspect of this question applies to the physical environment in which we live. A business that pollutes the rivers so that people get sick, clearly is not achieving a beneficial outcome. A church seeking to minimize its carbon footprint may achieve a beneficial outcome in this regard.

But this question also applies to the spiritual environment, what the Bible often calls the "cosmos". We live in a spiritual reality, and our activities affect that spiritual reality as well as our physical reality. A business promoting prostitution is obviously affecting the spiritual environment negatively, but so would a business promoting corruption and greed. A bank promoting ethical investing as well as investing in the development of local communities might affect the spiritual environment positively. The church holding a street party affects the spiritual environment on that street, making people more open to the gospel. Prayer and worship effect a change in the spiritual environment, even if a leader might practice these things privately in the workplace. This bottom line reminds us that we must consider both physical and spiritual environmental issues in our leadership.

Is the outcome personally beneficial?

The fourth question reminds us that outcomes should benefit people personally and individually, not only collectively. The first aspect of this question involves things like promoting good health, stable income, and healthy lifestyles. Clearly, a business that worked people so hard that they died at forty of a heart attack would not be promoting a personally beneficial outcome. Similarly, churches that coerced people to spend so much time volunteering that they could not rest properly would not promote a beneficial outcome.

The second aspect of this question involves issues of character and maturity. Christian leaders empower people to take responsibility for themselves, becoming mature people. They enable people to grow up in terms of their character. Effective church leaders, for example, are those who help people learn how to pray for themselves and not to be dependent on the church leaders to pray for them all the time. Effective marketplace leaders might help people develop personally by giving time and resources for continuing education.

Is the outcome spiritually beneficial?

The first aspect of this question is whether the outcomes are ethically good. Christian leadership will promote outcomes that are ethically consistent with the Bible as God's Word. Christians have never believed that the ends could justify the means, so ethically suspect outcomes would not be beneficial.

The second aspect of this question asks whether the outcome is advancing God's loving rulership in the world. Outcomes that advance God's kingdom will be beneficial, even if people do not always perceive them as such. A Christian business leader that helps lift people out of poverty and enables them to become economically responsible for themselves would be promoting spiritually beneficial outcomes in this regard, even if the people did not become Christians. However, such beneficial outcomes might certainly help people become more open to following Jesus.

THROUGH YOUR IDENTITY, CHARACTER, AND CALLING IN CHRIST

Many of the leadership books available focus on what good leaders *do*. Christian leadership, however, focuses first on who good leaders *are*. This issue is so important that it will be the subject of the next chapter. For now, let us say that leadership primarily involves who you are. Christian leadership primarily involves who you are in Christ.

A key principle that we must understand, which applies to leadership in general and especially to Christian leadership, is this:

> **People will follow who you are and how you are before they will follow what you do or say.**

People will make the decision to follow you before they hear what you say or know what you might do.

This principle includes not only who you actually are but who people perceive you to be. If people perceive you to be a leader they will follow you – until they discover that you are not a leader. If people perceive that you are confident as a leader, then they will follow you – until they discover you have led them the wrong way!

We see this principle in action all the time. For example, notice how often people tend to follow the leadership of actors and actresses who are very popular. Making lots of money as an actor and actress simply shows that you are a good actor or actress – or that you have a really good agent, or that you are willing to take your clothes off for the camera. It shows nothing about your leadership or your good judgment. It certainly does not make you an expert in anything. The reason that people follow them as they make pronouncements about things as varied as climate change, world poverty or the right make-up to wear is because of their popularity, appeal, and attractiveness. They follow these people because of who they appear to be and how they appear to be.

Christian leadership recognizes that just as Jesus was the most compelling leader who ever lived, so too his followers remade in his image may become compelling leaders themselves. When our identity, character, and calling are grounded in Jesus Christ, any Christian may become an effective leader.

BORN OR MADE

This raises one of the biggest debates in leadership: can anyone be a leader, or is it reserved for a select few people? Are leaders born, or are they made? Personally, I have counselled dozens of leaders who felt completely ill-equipped for leadership because they did not perceive themselves as a natural-born leader. They did not think they fit the typical model of a leader. They found leadership to be a constant struggle. They assumed that if they were truly a leader then leadership certainly would not be so difficult.

If we are to thrive as Christians in leadership, then we must have some resolution to this debate. Are leaders born or are they made? The answer to this question is both!

Some people just have a propensity to lead. They lead because it is their natural disposition. We call these people "natural leaders". Natural leaders might lead naturally because they just seem to have the right mix of genetic material. Other natural leaders might lead naturally because they had the right blend of education and experience. Still more natural leaders might simply have found themselves at the perfect intersection of history and their personal strengths.

Not only do natural leaders come from a diversity of backgrounds, but natural leaders also have a diversity of personality styles, strengths, and weaknesses. Some natural leaders are extroverted. Other natural leaders are introverted. Some natural leaders lead by making decisive choices. Other natural leaders lead by building unity and agreement. The point is that we cannot develop one all-encompassing profile of a natural-born leader.

Other people lead because of their context and not because they are natural-born leaders. A man who does not like to lead may be promoted to a managerial role in his company. A woman who thinks of herself more as a servant may decide to start her own business. Although these people may not be natural leaders, they still must lead. We call these people "contextual leaders".

Finally, some people lead because of the needs of the moment. They see an accident occur and, instead of being a bystander, they rush in to help. The boss is off sick when a crisis occurs in the office and, instead of disturbing the boss, they make the decision. We call these people "situational leaders". They lead because the situation demands it.

The good news is that our definition of Christian leadership applies whether we are a natural leader, a contextual leader, or a situational leader. Although natural leaders lead as part of their natural disposition, this does not mean they are necessarily better leaders. Everyone needs to learn how to lead. Everyone can improve their leadership. So who we are as a leader is not determined by whether or not we are a natural leader. Christian leaders will lead whether or not they are natural leaders.

USING YOUR GOD-GIVEN STRENGTHS AND SPIRITUAL GIFTS AS WELL AS YOUR TALENTS, SKILLS, AND KNOWLEDGE

Of course, good leadership includes what you do. Leaders must lead after all. Every day leaders make choices and they respond to the situations around them. They use the skills they develop to help achieve beneficial outcomes. They may even develop areas of expertise. Our expertise is usually a combination of our knowledge and our abilities.

Every Christian leader has a unique mix of strengths. If we want to achieve excellence in leadership then we need to focus on what we might do better than most. Great leaders will discover what they do well and then do it to the best of their ability. What we do better than most results from the unique combination of our personal makeup, our skills, our knowledge, and our talents. These are our strengths. Effective leadership, including Christian leadership, requires that we focus on our strengths and not on our weaknesses.

Many leaders spend so much time trying to compensate for their weaknesses that they never use their strengths. Yet our strengths are what enable us to become great leaders. When we talk about weakness in this context, we are not talking about sin. We must repent of sin, not use it as an excuse for bad leadership. Weaknesses are simply those things we do not do well. Focusing on what we do not do well is a recipe for failure. Focusing on strengths is a key to successful leadership.

Christian leaders may also receive gifts of the Holy Spirit. We can use these spiritual gifts in the marketplace as well as the church. Many spiritual gifts have direct application in the marketplace context and might make us more effective leaders in that context.

For example, a woman had been promoted to lead a team in a large multinational corporation. Before she took the post, her boss told her that one woman on the team had caused a lot of problems for the previous team leader, but due to this woman's area of expertise the company did not feel it was appropriate to dismiss her. In her first encounter with the woman, the team leader felt the Holy Spirit reveal to her that this woman had been having marriage problems which had made her more critical and uncooperative in the workplace. Over coffee one day, the team leader simply asked the woman about her marriage – not saying anything about the Holy Spirit! It was as if a dam broke in the woman's heart as she talked about the problems in her relationship. After this, the woman became a productive member of the team, no longer causing any problems.

Leaders must lead, so what they do is very important. However, what leaders do is not nearly as important as we sometimes assume. As Christian leaders, we can never reduce our leadership to simple actions of leading. Our leadership always involves who we are and where we are going, not only what we are doing.

LEADERSHIP THAT IS TRULY CHRISTIAN

In closing this chapter, I want to emphasize those qualities that will make our leadership authentically Christian. Our relationship with God must influence everything in our leadership. We lead in the power of the Holy Spirit, as people redeemed by Jesus, to the glory of God our Father. If we fail to lead by allowing God to influence everything in our leadership, then we fail to exercise authentic Christian leadership.

Who we are as a leader must be grounded in the reality of who we are in Christ. What we do as a leader must be led by the Spirit of God, following the pattern of our leader Jesus Christ. Authentic Christian leadership is fundamentally an issue of discipleship.

As authentic Christian leaders, the Bible must govern everything in our leadership as the Word of God. The Bible offers us clear criteria to discern whether leadership pleases God. The Bible gives clear counsel regarding how to relate to those we are leading. The Bible provides the ultimate standards by which we determine whether or not an outcome is beneficial.

Finally, we must have the confidence that Christian leadership would benefit all people and all people-systems, whether or not they are "Christian". Christian leadership is good for everyone. Christian leadership would benefit society as it sees God's loving rulership permeate all the systems of society. In a sense, we are making a plea against the contemporary tendency simply to adopt secular leadership principles into the church. We have the confidence that people not only need authentic Christian leadership but that people truly want authentic Christian leadership and its benefits. They just do not realize it yet!

In the next chapters of this section, we are going to discover one of the most important dynamics that enables us to lead effectively. Understanding this dynamic may revolutionize our leadership ability and increase our leadership effectiveness.

4

BEING AND LEADERSHIP

Character is what you are in the dark.

Dwight L. Moody

Leadership is a potent combination of strategy and character. But if you must be without one, be without the strategy.

Norman Schwarzkopf

The supreme quality of leadership is integrity.

Dwight D. Eisenhower

n the last chapter, we defined authentic Christian leadership as "the interactive relational process of influencing people and systems toward beneficial outcomes through your identity, character, and calling in Christ, using your God-given strengths and spiritual gifts, as well as your talents, skills, and knowledge". This definition of leadership raises a twofold dynamic that we believe is at the heart of all leadership, but especially Christian leadership. Although many leadership materials show some awareness of this two-fold dynamic, few explore fully its implications for leadership. We believe that the Bible gives us some unique insights into this dynamic and its effects on leadership.

THE ANATOMY OF A LEADER

To understand this dynamic, let us look at the "anatomy" of a leader.

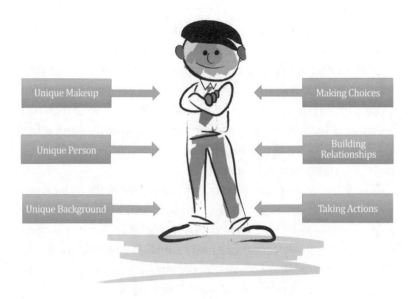

Every leader is a unique person. They have a mind, will, and emotions different from those of any other person. This person has a unique temperament. The leader might be an introvert, getting his energy from alone times of reflection and imagination. She might be an extrovert, getting her energy from being with people, finding her creative spark from interactions with others. The leader might be a strategic thinker and planner, or she might be someone who leads through her gut-feeling interaction with others.

Every leader has a unique background. We know that both men and women may become great leaders. However, we also know that men and women lead differently. One is not better than the other; they are simply different. We know that our cultural background shapes our worldview significantly. People from countries south of the equator have different perspectives from people north of the equator (not to mention whether you celebrate Christmas with a

BBQ while wearing your shorts or a roast turkey while wearing your parka!). Recent struggles in the European Union remind us again that northern Europeans and southern Europeans have different perspectives.

We know that each leader has a different upbringing. Whether your parents were disciplinarians or more permissive – and how you responded to this as you grew up – makes a difference in your leadership style. Leaders have had different educational experiences – some training in a world-class university, others never completing a degree. Even leaders who are remarkably similar in every other way will have had different experiences – and differing perspectives and opinions about those experiences.

Every leader also has a unique makeup. We all have our own natural abilities. My body size and shape – even when I was a slim young man – meant that I would most likely never become a long-distance runner. My center of gravity simply is not right for it. We all have our own strengths and weaknesses. I naturally do some things better than other people, but there are many more things that others do much better than I do. We all have our own hopes and dreams regarding the outcomes of our leadership, and these are in a continual process of development over time.

Although leaders have much that is unique to each person, leaders also have many things in common. Leaders make decisions and take actions. For example, all leaders must communicate. Without communication, there is no leadership, regardless of whether we are introverts or extroverts.

Leaders make choices. We are faced with various options and possibilities almost every minute of the day. Throughout the day, we make hundreds of choices that determine the effectiveness of our leadership. Some of these choices may seem minor, such as choosing to take your colleagues to coffee shop A or coffee shop B. Others will seem quite large, such as choosing a new personal assistant. However, small or large, our leadership will be determined by the choices we make.

All leaders build relationships. In order to influence people, leaders must have some kind of relationship with people. These might be close, personal relationships – such as the relationship that we might have with a staff member – or these might be more public relationships – such as the relationship a politician has with her constituency. Regardless of the closeness of the relationship, followers must have confidence that leaders are for them, having their best interests at heart.

BEING AND DOING

Looking at the anatomy of a leader, an important dynamic begins to emerge. This dynamic is the relationship between two aspects of leadership, what we call *being* and *doing*. This dynamic is present in every leader as well as every leadership context. Long-term, effective leadership requires that we understand and lead from this dynamic.

The personality, background, and makeup of every leader is unique. No two leaders are the same. These form what we call the leader's *being*. Although each one of us has a unique *being*, our *being* shapes our leadership – much more than most of us realize.

Our decisions, choices, and relationship building are part of what we call our *doing* as leaders. Leaders must lead. We must do something in order to be a leader. We make choices. We take action. We *do* stuff.

This *being* and *doing* dynamic operates in every leader. Once alerted to it, most of us recognize this intuitively. However, most people do not realize how important *being* is to leadership. Most of the time we think of *doing* as primary for leadership. We assume that our leadership is determined primarily by what we *do*. So, if I am going to be an effective manager, I need to *do* the right management things and perhaps not *do* the wrong things. If I am going to start an effective plumbing business, then I need to know how to *do* plumbing well and how to hire the right staff.

Although we would fully agree that *doing* is vitally important for leadership, and that without *doing* there would be no leadership, we have discovered that for long-term, effective leadership *being* takes primacy over *doing*. *Being* is much more important for leadership than most people realize. For the remainder of this chapter, we will focus on the *being* part of the leadership dynamic. In the next chapter, we will focus on the *doing* part of the leadership dynamic.

THE PRIMACY OF *BEING*

As we have talked with people around the world about leadership, we have noticed a cross-cultural pattern to which we referred earlier. People everywhere have a difficult time defining *leadership*. They know that it is very important. They feel they can recognize it. But they struggle to define what it is and even sometimes what it does.

At the same time, people everywhere have an easy time describing what makes a good *leader*. People around the world list a number of characteristics, almost all of which describe a leader's *being* – things like humility, servanthood, compassion, etc. People from various cultures will express these qualities differently, but the underlying qualities remain remarkably similar across cultures. Of all the qualities we hear, perhaps "lead by example" comes closest to describing *doing*; but, of course, we must *be* an example before we can lead by example.

Looking at our anatomy of a leader quickly reveals how vital *being* is to leadership. Leaders make choices, but these choices are conditioned by who we are. They are also conditioned by the context we are in at the time. A leader in London cannot simply choose to be a leader in Shanghai. The context restricts the choices.

Leaders take action, but these actions are governed by who we are and where we are. People simply will not consistently act in a way that is inconsistent with their *being*. If we are introverts then we cannot consistently pretend to be an extrovert. The context also determines the range of possible choices at any given time. We simply cannot be the president of the United States if we are Chinese and live in China.

Leaders build relationships of influence, but these relationships are determined by who we are. We simply will not make authentic relationships with people unless we are true to ourselves. If people perceive that we are trying to be something we are not, then they will not build a trusting relationship with us.

In leadership, *being* has primacy over *doing*.

One reason we have failed to notice this is that it is much easier to tackle issues of *doing* than issues of *being*. So most leadership books focus on what leaders *do*. Most Christian leadership training will focus on how to *do* things the right way, in accordance with the Bible. Or, we might talk about how Jesus *did* leadership so we can learn to *do* leadership the "Jesus way".

There is another reason we have failed to notice this. People are unsure how to address and resolve issues of *being*. Some people assume that either your *being* is "right" or it isn't, and there is nothing you can really do to "fix" it. Others will assume that talking about issues of *being* would lead into "fuzzy" concepts and "alternative" spiritualities not suitable for the workplace – and to some extent this may be true. Others struggle because addressing issues of *being* seems to lead to a place where we might be called to "judge" leaders – something most of us do privately but are loathe to do publicly. Still others are fearful that talking about *being* might lead us to a situation in which we are trying to make or remake everyone into the same leadership "mold", that all leaders should not only act the same way but they should also be the same kind of person.

DOING FLOWS THROUGH *BEING*

As we have seen, all leadership involves both who we are and what we do, our *being* and our *doing*. Our *being* involves our unique personhood, background, and makeup, what we might also call our identity, character, and calling. Our *doing* refers to our actions and choices. *Doing* is important, but will vary widely and situationally.

When we say that *being* has primacy over *doing*, we need to understand how the two parts of the leadership dynamic relate to one another. We are *not* setting up a contrast between *being* and *doing*, as if it is *being* versus *doing*. We are also *not* saying that it is one or the other, that some leaders focus on *being* while other leaders focus on *doing* and both approaches are equally valid. Further, we are not saying that it is *being* to the neglect of *doing*. We are not saying that if you work on your *being* as a leader, then your *doing* is not important or will not need any work.

We are saying that *both* our *being* and our *doing* are important for our leadership effectiveness. We must not neglect one in favor of the other. But we must also understand how the two relate to one another. This leads us to an important principle:

Our *doing* always flows from our *being*, always.

Effective leadership will flow from who we are, not primarily from what we do. If our *being* is not right, our *doing* will not lead in a healthy way. Our *doing* in a sense is a product of our *being*.

We see this example from the Pharisees of Jesus' day. The Pharisees were the pre-eminent leaders, not only religiously but in the community as a whole. Outwardly, they seemed righteous and good. They were doing all the kinds of things you would expect church leaders to do – tithing, memorizing Scripture, setting a "godly example", and giving money. Yet Jesus called them "white-washed tombs". The outcomes of their leadership were all negative according to Jesus (see Matthew 23:1ff.). Yet people still followed them, but to their own destruction. So we see clearly from the example of the Pharisees that it is not just what we do that is important; it is also who we are.

It is at this point that our Christian faith comes into play in a powerful way. The diagram above applies to any leader. But if we are

Christians, there is something fundamental that happened to our *being* when we first became Christians. Jesus made us spiritually alive in our *being.* As Christians, we understand that our relationship with Jesus Christ affects not primarily what we do but who we are. In other words, as Christians we become fundamentally new creations, with our beings restored and set free (see 2 Corinthians 5:17; John 8:31–32, 36). Living out this reality is at the heart of our understanding of Christian leadership. It is what makes authentically Christian leadership the leadership needed for the times in which we live.

BEING AND *DOING* IN CHRISTIAN LEADERSHIP

The *being* and *doing* dynamic is present in all leadership, whether Christian or not. All the principles we share will be true to some extent for everyone in a leadership role. However, the focus of our work is on *Christian* leadership. Although most leaders would benefit from this book, we are targeting Christian leaders. As Christians, how do we become effective leaders who are leading as authentic Christians? We must begin with three fundamental convictions.

First, for leadership to be authentically Christian our relationship with God – Father, Son, and Holy Spirit – must influence every aspect of leadership. Our *being* as a leader must flow from our relationship with God through Jesus Christ in the power of the Holy Spirit.

Our *doing* as a leader must flow from our lives as disciples of Jesus Christ, led by the Spirit as children of our heavenly Father.

Second, for leadership to be authentically Christian the Bible must govern everything in our leadership as the Word of God. We must allow the Bible to shape our worldview. The Bible must give us a healthy values framework which helps us to make decisions and choices. The Bible must also help direct our focus so that we can say "no" in healthy and productive ways. We are not talking here about "mining" the Bible for a set of leadership principles. Instead, we are talking about an active engagement with the Bible under the leadership of the Holy Spirit to discern God's will regarding our leadership.

Third, we must have the confidence that Christian leadership would benefit all people and organizations, whether or not they are "Christian". We must have confidence that if we use Christian leadership in our businesses, then they would become healthier and more productive. We must have the confidence that if we use Christian leadership in our work in politics, then it would benefit everyone we serve, not only Christians but also Muslims, Jews, and atheists.

As Christians, we often sell ourselves short and take a backseat when it comes to leadership. We have believed the lies that Christianity is good for our private lives but not for our public leadership. Because of this, many times when we have engaged with the world as Christians, the grounds of our engagement have been based on personal rights as opposed to public responsibility.

For example, we might sue our employer for our "right" to have a Bible publicly displayed on our desk. This may be a legitimate issue and an area in which our employer is discriminating against us. But this is a personal right, and focusing primarily on personal rights will always make us seem mean-spirited and narrow-minded. But as Christian leaders, we must use our leadership to call for and promote public responsibilities grounded in the Bible, such as paying workers a fair and suitable wage (see, for example, Luke 10:7).[1]

Authentic Christian leadership would benefit everyone in society. People of all faiths (or no faith) in the UK would be better off if there are godly Christians in leadership. If the government was full of authentic Christian leaders, everyone in the country would benefit. We must have this conviction: Christian leaders are what the world needs. We must have the confidence that if we have authentic Christian leadership, no matter what context it is in, our cities and nations will thrive.

BEING IN CHRIST

Grounded on the above convictions, we can begin to grow in our leadership effectiveness as Christians. Since our *doing* flows through our *being*, to grow in leadership effectiveness we must begin by becoming healthy in our *being*. Our *being* includes our identity, character, and calling, so we need to see how our relationship with God and the Bible influences each one of these aspects of *being*.

We begin by acknowledging an important reality. As Christians, God has *already* made our *being* alive in Christ Jesus. God has already given us his Holy Spirit. God has already given us all we need for life and godliness in Christ Jesus (see 2 Peter 1:3). We do not need to work for what we already have. We already have the grace of God working in our lives, preparing us for the good works God has planned for us to do (see Ephesians 2:10).

We make a basic mistake if we think we must work for these things. The key for us is to cooperate with what God is already doing in our lives (see Romans 8:5). Only as Christians do we have the ability to begin in a place where God has already made the core of our *being* right. We must simply believe and trust in what Jesus accomplished for us in the cross and the empty tomb.

We make a second basic mistake if we assume that simply because we are Christians then we are completely healthy in our *being* as a once and for all state. Jesus Christ has healed our *being* through the cross (see 1 Peter 2:24, for example), but that health must be maintained on a day by day basis. Just as if we do not maintain our physical health we may become ill or debilitated, so also if we do not maintain a healthy *being* we may become weaker or ill in our *being*. Every day we must continue to live by the grace of God in Jesus Christ.

A final mistake we often make is thinking that health is an all-or-nothing proposition. There are degrees of healthiness, both in our physical bodies as well as our *beings*. In a sense, we will never be completely whole until Jesus Christ comes again. Until that time, we will continue to struggle against sickness and brokenness in the world. Our goal is to become progressively healthier in our *being*, avoiding those things that bring sickness and death.

Being in Christ means that the life of Jesus Christ is continually flowing into our *being* by the grace of God in the power of the Holy Spirit. Being healthy in our *being* means having the quality of life in our *being* that Jesus had in his *being*. The gospel promises not only this possibility but also this reality through faith in Jesus Christ. The life of Jesus enlivens our unique personality, background, and makeup so that they might reach the potential for which God has created us. The life of Jesus in us transforms our identity, character, and calling so that we might become healthy in our *being*.

IDENTITY: CHRIST IN YOU

As Christians, our identity is formed by a twofold reality: Christ in you and you in Christ. First, we have Christ in us, the hope of glory (see Colossians 1:27). This is the great mystery of how we have been fundamentally changed in our *being* because Jesus Christ has united himself with us by the Spirit of God through faith. This also includes the reality that although we have been fundamentally changed in our *being* through our connection with Jesus Christ at the same time we remain the unique person God created us to be, shaped by our personality, background, and makeup.

Because Jesus Christ is in us, we have been intrinsically altered in the basic reality of who we are. In places such as Ephesians 1, the Bible presents a number of words that describe who we are as Christians at the very core of our *being*. The Bible says that we are now "saints", holy ones. We are also blessed with every spiritual blessing. We are redeemed, belonging now to the kingdom of God. We are chosen. We are "sons of God". We are forgiven, not just as something done in the past but as a present state of being. We have been and continue to be drenched in the grace of God. We are sealed with the Holy Spirit.

All of these words, and many others, describe how we have been fundamentally altered through our relationship with God in Jesus Christ by the power of the Holy Spirit. According to the Bible, we do not have to work to make these things part of our *being*. God has already made them part of our *being*. Our responsibility is to believe, to have faith in this reality of Christ in us.

Every day we must choose as Christians to believe that what the Bible says about us is true. All of these things are true because Jesus Christ is in us, whether we believe them or not. These qualities are part of our new birthright as children of God. The challenge for us is to make sure that our *being* is fully grounded or anchored in the reality of Christ in us and all that this means for us as people.

This leads us to two important principles regarding leadership:

To the degree that you base your identity in Jesus Christ in you as the hope of glory, you will be free to become healthy and effective as a leader.

To the degree that you base your identity in yourself as a leader, your leadership will be distorted, dysfunctional or less effective.

If you have confidence in your identity in Christ because you know that Jesus is in you and you know the benefits promised in God's Word are yours right now, then you will have freedom to lead. You will not be leading to show that you are a great or worthy person; you will know that you are already a great and worthy person because Jesus has made you a child of God. If you have confidence in your identity in Christ, then you will know that you are a "saint" who happens to sin and make mistakes. You will not see yourself as a miserable sinner trying to be a saint who then has to cover up failures and mistakes.

As a chosen child of God, we do not have to prove ourselves. We do not have to lead in order to show people that we are honorable human beings. Jesus has given us honor already. We still may not become effective leaders because there are many factors outside of our control that determine our effectiveness. However, we will have the *freedom to lead* as the people God has created us to be. The key is believing every day what God says is true.

At the same time, if we make our leadership – whether we are effective or not – the basis of our identity, then we will distort our leadership. For example, if I see myself as "Rod the Great Leader" then every day I will need to prove myself a great leader in order to protect my sense of identity. When I succeed, I will tend toward pride and arrogance. When I fail, I will tend toward despair and depression in myself or blaming and shaming others. Every day my core identity will be on the line since it is wrapped up in my leadership.

Most of the time when we see dysfunctional leadership in churches and ministries it is because we have leaders who do not really have their identity grounded in Christ. Certainly the fear of being exposed as an unworthy or incompetent person if they do not "succeed" in leadership drives many in the marketplace to use all sorts of manipulative tactics to prop up their identity in their leadership.

IDENTITY: YOU IN CHRIST

Not only do we have the benefits of Christ in us, but we also have the benefits of being in Christ as well. God created every single person with certain needs that could only be met fully in relationship with God. We all have a need to feel that our lives matter, that they count for something. We have a need to feel that we have a certain degree of power and influence in our lives. We have a need to feel safe and cared for. We have a need to know that people will embrace us for who we really are, without having to hide or disguise ourselves.

We see these needs being played out in the opening chapters of Genesis. God made Adam and Eve companions and told them to be fruitful and multiply, to fill the earth and subdue it. He gave them an important purpose. They had an unhindered relationship of full openness and acceptance with God and also with one another. God had created them with needs that God chose to meet in himself.

They enjoyed all these benefits, experienced the fulfillment of all these intrinsic needs, until the point that they sinned. At that point, they died – not physically, but spiritually. This spiritual death meant in part that they would continue to experience these needs but would no longer have the relationship with God essential to the fulfillment of these needs. Consequently, they began to look to other things to provide the fulfillment of these needs. Ultimately, these things would become idols, objects of worship because of their perceived ability to meet these fundamental needs outside of the one true living God.

Various counselors and scholars describe these needs in different ways, but we can summarize all of them with three words: significance, security, and acceptance. Neil Anderson used these words to identify these needs in his groundbreaking books, *Victory over the Darkness* and *The Bondage Breaker*. Since then, they have been used by Freedom in Christ Ministries around the world to describe the benefits of being in Christ.

Not only is Christ in us, but the Bible indicates that also we are in Christ (see Romans 8:1–2 and 1 Corinthians 1:30). Because we are in Christ, we have life abundantly (see John 10:10). An important part of this abundant life is the fulfillment of these fundamental needs in Christ.

Because we are in Christ, we are significant. God has made us important for his kingdom advancement. God has given us power, love, and self-control (see 2 Timothy 1:7). We have gifts of the Spirit by which we can serve others (see 1 Corinthians 12).

Because we are in Christ, we are secure. God will never leave us or forsake us (see Deuteronomy 31:6). God protects us even in the midst of very difficult times in our lives (see Psalm 91).

Because we are in Christ, we are accepted. We are now called God's adopted "sons" (see Galatians 3:23ff.). We have been forgiven. We have been set free.

The above represents just a few of the many Scriptures that show how God meets all these fundamental needs in our lives through relationship with him in Christ Jesus by the power of the Holy Spirit. This leads us to two more important principles regarding leadership:

> **To the degree that you have your needs for significance, security, and acceptance met in Christ by faith, you will be free to become healthy and effective as a leader.**

> **To the degree that you seek or find your significance, security or acceptance in yourself as a leader (or anything other than Jesus), your leadership will be distorted, dysfunctional or less effective.**

Many people look to their leadership responsibilities in order to find a sense of significance, security or acceptance. However, realizing that these needs have already been met and continue to be met in Christ gives us the freedom to lead without any agenda other than serving the best interests of the people and groups that we lead. Trying to find significance, security or acceptance in a leadership role places an incredible burden not only on the leadership role, but also on the people we lead. Having these needs met in Christ, and choosing to believe and find this every day, allows us to lead freely, not based on what we might receive but based on how others might benefit from our leadership. We will have the freedom to lead with our basic needs already met through a vibrant relationship with Jesus.

Wherever we find distorted or dysfunctional leadership, we will often find leaders who are trying to have these basic needs met through their leadership. We see this played out in the church and marketplace every single day. Let us consider a few examples.

John has just been promoted to team leader in one department of a large multinational corporation. John had been working and hoping for this promotion for years. He was tired of working for people he felt were incompetent. He felt very proud of this promotion. It made him feel important. In other words, John was getting his sense of significance from this new leadership role.

Soon after starting his new role, things began to go wrong. Several members of the team had ideas that were very different from John's ideas. Initially, the team performed poorly – largely due to plans the previous leader had put into place – which deflated John's enthusiasm. John began to engage in behaviors that were controlling and manipulative. The poor relationships and poor team performance threatened John's sense of significance so, without even realizing what he was doing, John began to behave in ways that were very unhealthy. His leadership was distorted by his quest for significance.

Ore started a small, urban congregation in London. He grew the congregation to about seventy-five adults, just enough to pay the bills and give Ore a decent salary to support his family. One day, one of his strongest givers came to Ore to say that he and his wife felt they had a call from God to move to a different part of London and plant a church. To the surprise of this church member, Ore responded very strongly against the idea. He said he thought that the member should pray about it more, that the member wasn't really ready to start a church and that the member should commit to Ore's church for at least another year or two before venturing out. What Ore did not fully realize is that having one of his strongest givers think about leaving threatened Ore's sense of security. He was getting his sense of security from having just the right number of people to support him and the ministry financially.

Everyone had good things to say about Sally as a boss. She was extremely kind and considerate. She really enjoyed it when people liked her and liked the way she led. One of Sally's team, Sam, was a perennial under-performer and a bit of a troublemaker. He would manipulate others with hard-luck stories from his past and stories of how his parents had abused him verbally. Unfortunately, because Sally was looking to her leadership role for a sense of acceptance, she could never bring herself to deal with Sam and address his behavior. She struggled with the thought that Sam might reject her or find her unfair or unkind in her leadership. Consequently, the workplace suffered.

Over the years, I have counseled and coached many people in the marketplace and in the church. Sometimes people will tell me stories of personal and spiritual abuse – not the kind that would land someone in jail but very real nonetheless. I have learned always to read between the lines and ask difficult questions, because often the problem lies with the person telling me the story and not with the leader in question. However, whenever there has been a genuine complaint to answer, it has been because the leaders had been looking to their leadership roles to meet their needs for significance, security or acceptance.

When people have these needs met in Christ, through their relationship with God, they find freedom to lead in a more healthy way. One challenge is that most people have unrealistic and idealistic notions of Christian leadership. They believe that Christian leaders should be "nice", that they should do things that make others "happy", that they will never put any pressure on you. But authentic Christian leaders are not pushovers. Jesus was not nice, nor was he focused on our happiness. He confronted people rather strongly when needed.

So let us consider a few other examples.

Clare is a vice-president of a major multinational corporation, heading up a division. She knows who she is in Christ, so she does not get any of her sense of significance from her job or her achievements. She only remains in the job because God specifically told her not to leave the job. As a boss, she is known to be very tough and plain spoken, but extremely fair and scrupulously honest. Because of this, she continues to thrive in a male-dominated company where many often fail or quit.

Brian leads a small church in a major city. They have a constant influx and outflow of people, sometimes seeming more "out" than "in". A few years ago, Brian began to ask people who were feeling led to another church, another ministry or another city to let him know so that the church could pray for them and bless them as they left. Since then, the church has prayed for many people in its worship service who were leaving the church so they could send them out with a blessing. Brian's security comes from Christ, not from the number of people in his church.

Robert has a high-profile public leadership position. A few years ago, he made a major mistake that could have deeply injured his organization. However, with his sense of acceptance grounded in Christ, he did not feel that he needed to cover up the mistake in order to protect his relationships. He did not fear the rejection of people. Of course, he did not like rejection, but he did not fear it. So he openly and quickly admitted his error. Surprisingly, not only did the people he was leading not reject him as their leader, his admittance led to a deeper sense of trust in his leadership. They perceived the health in his leadership, so they allowed him to correct the mistake and continue leading.

In all the examples above, we see how having our identity anchored in Christ as opposed to our leadership allows us to lead with greater freedom and effectiveness. Of course, the stories of those who have their identity in Christ do not always have a happy ending. Sometimes people with their identity in Christ lose their jobs, close their businesses, and leave their churches. However, having our identity anchored in Christ enables us to learn from these experiences and continue to grow in our leadership effectiveness. It enables us to evaluate our leadership more objectively and move on to the next leadership challenge.

CHARACTER

The second aspect of our *being* is our character. Character is the essential quality of our personality. It is our moral fiber, our sense of internal fortitude and uprightness. Overall, it is the personal and moral qualities that we have as individuals. As a Christian, our character develops from three factors: maturity, sanctification, and integrity.

Maturity is the willingness and ability to take responsibility for our own mind, will, and emotions. This includes our decisions, choices, and opinions. Mature people have the ability and self-control to express themselves in a way that is healthy and proper. When they make mistakes, they take ownership of those mistakes because they recognize their responsibility in making the mistakes in the first place.

When children are three years old, we expect them to throw temper tantrums every now and then. The reason is that very young children do not yet have the language skills and self-control to express their deepest emotions responsibly. When children are four years old, we do not expect them to be able to choose the right doctor, house or insurance policy. Again, the reason is that they do not yet have the reasoning power to make these decisions. This is one reason why most societies require someone to be of a certain age before that person might sign a contract.

As we get older, society expects us to take responsibility for our thoughts, actions, and feelings. God has this expectation for us as well. As mature people, we must exercise self-control and take responsibility to do the things that God tells us to do and not do the things that he tells us not to do. We can be said to have good character only to the extent that we display this kind of maturity.

Character also includes what the Bible calls sanctification. Sanctification relates to holiness, or moral uprightness. When we come into relationship with Jesus Christ, Jesus sanctifies us – sets us apart for God and cleanses us from our sin. However, throughout our lives, we also undergo a process of sanctification, whereby we become more and more like Jesus in our character.

The standard by which we can observe and measure our ongoing sanctification is something called the "fruit of the Spirit":

But the fruit of the Spirit is love, joy, peace, patience, kindness, goodness, faithfulness, gentleness, self-control; against such things there is no law. (Galatians 5:22–23)

The fruit of the Spirit is not something we work to attain, any more than a fruit tree works to produce its fruit. The fruit of the Spirit is the product of our ongoing relationship with God through the Holy Spirit, the struggles we face in our lives, and the unrighteous or unhelpful things we prune away from our lives. When we observe the fruit in increasing measure, we know that we are developing good character in our relationship with God.

The third aspect of character is integrity. We often think of integrity as having strong moral principles, and certainly the word would include this meaning. But in terms of our character, integrity is actually referring to our wholeness, or the lack of division between our inner self and our outer self. In other words, people with integrity are the same on the outside as they are on the inside.

People with integrity practice openness and transparency. This does not mean "letting it all hang out", which is not really appropriate. This means being a person with nothing to hide, who is not a hypocrite who says one thing and does another. People with integrity have and show a consistency between the internal and external.

As leaders we need to understand the role of suffering and brokenness in developing our character. Many parts of the church express an unrealistic sense of triumphalism in our Christian faith. Certainly, victory is an important part of our reality, but so is suffering. Part of God's preparation of our character as Christian leaders is brokenness.

In part, God uses suffering to help us remain in a place of dependence upon him, relying on his leadership and reminding us that apart from him we can do nothing (see John 15:5). We may often find ourselves in a place where we feel overwhelmed and unable to cope. But it is in these moments that we can experience the power of God and grow in our character as never before.

Paul's life is a study in suffering and brokenness. In 2 Corinthians, he talks about a thorn in the flesh that he prayed for God to take away. But God refused, simply reminding Paul that "My grace is sufficient for you, for my power is made perfect in weakness." So Paul responded, "Therefore I will boast all the more gladly of my weaknesses, so that the power of Christ may rest upon me" (see 2 Corinthians 12:7–9).

For us, our "thorns" and struggles may take many shapes, but we can have the confidence that God will work in all these things for our good (see Romans 8:28). We may face loss of reputation, personal conflict, injustice, health issues or financial difficulties. However, God will work through all the situations we face to develop our character and further ground our *being* in Jesus Christ.

God is deeply concerned with our character. Much of the Christian life is about developing and maintaining a healthy character. God has designed many of the activities he has given us as Christians – including things like worship, prayer, fasting, Bible study, fellowship with other Christians – to develop our character in a way that conforms to Jesus' character.

CALLING

The final aspect of our *being* is our calling. Unfortunately, much of the language used by Christians has confused our understanding of calling. For some, calling refers only to our decision to go into paid or unpaid Christian ministry – such as becoming a missionary. For others, calling is something that we receive once in our life, signifying a lifetime vocation. For still others, calling is something mysterious that God must convey to us by mystical means. However, what we discover is that calling most of the time is not a once-in-a-lifetime permanent experience, but something that happens frequently and changes from time to time.

We need to note that calling does not always refer to what we do in life, such as a particular job. For example, I might have a calling to be an entrepreneur, but that does not tell me what business to start. I might have a calling to pastoral ministry, but that does not tell me whether I will serve primarily through preaching or through counseling and pastoral care. Someone may feel called to be a mother, but that does not tell her how many children she should have – or even whether she should give birth to children or adopt children. Calling engages our *being* before it engages our *doing*.

Calling is based on the interplay of three questions:

- **Who are you?**
- **Where are you?**
- **Who are you where you are?**

The first question is "who are you?" This question refers to your unique personality, background, and makeup as a human being. God generally does not call men to be "mothers" for the obvious reason that their makeup as a male is not suited to giving birth to children. As I look over my life, I realize that there are many things I could have done, but just as many that I could not have done because I simply was not suited for it, either physically, mentally, or temperamentally.

In order to know our calling, we need first to know ourselves – Socrates' famous dictum. Many people lead unexamined lives in which they never find a sense of calling. Various personality tests and tools might help. Certainly looking at ourselves through the mirror of Scripture will help. Talking to others might give us many insights into ourselves. However, we must strive to answer the first question.

The second question is "where are you?" This might seem obvious, but it is amazing how often we forget to ask this question. The answer to this question might include the sphere of influence God has given you (see 2 Corinthians 10:13–18). If I have not trained as a lawyer and been given a license to practice law, then the law is not my sphere. If I am living in London and speaking English, then I will find it difficult to be a leader in Shanghai speaking Chinese.

The answer to this question will always include our context – things like the city in which we live, our area of training and experience, and our workplace. If I am the minister in a church in London then I will find it difficult to be the leader of a major technology firm in Silicon Valley. Sometimes God might change my placement, but my calling will always involve a solid understanding of where God has placed me.

The third question is "who are you where you are?" To begin with, answering this question involves our sense of vision and mission, our passion and our values. Most often, God is working to develop these things within us in order to achieve his purposes (see Philippians 2:13). Our calling will often grow out of these very things that God has grown in our lives.

Another aspect of answering this question involves our relationships. Our sense of self and purpose often grows out of our relationships with others. God has created us as inherently social beings. These relationships include our assigned roles – what our group has assigned to us. I could not be a minister except that a group of people had chosen me to be their minister and to lead them as a group. Often, we find that the people around us know our calling before we do.

The answers to these three questions work together to give us our sense of calling. The Holy Spirit will work with us as well and guide us in this process. Obviously, our calling will change from time to time as the answers to the questions change. It is important that we frequently review these questions to maintain a healthy sense of calling.

GROUNDED IN CHRIST

Our identity, character, and calling in Christ work together with our unique personality, background, and makeup to give us a healthy *being*. Long-term, effective leadership flows from this healthy *being* grounded in Christ. If our *being* is not right, then our *doing* will not lead effectively. Even more, when our *being* is not healthy, then our *doing* will not be truly healthy either.

It is at this point that most of us want a top ten list of things we could *do* in order to get our *being* in the right place. Fortunately, there is no such list – otherwise we would be back to *doing*. But we can give some guidance.

Developing a healthy *being* that is grounded in Jesus Christ is a journey of relationship with God. As with any long journey, there is a beginning and a few signposts along the way. The end of the journey is the end of our lives, so perhaps we should not want to rush along too quickly. As with any journey involving a relationship, there are ways of relating that help us connect to one another. In the journey of developing a healthy *being* grounded in Christ, there are ways of relating to God that will help us connect with God more fully. The deeper that connection, the healthier our *being* will likely become.

The journey begins by surrendering ourselves to Jesus Christ as the one who leads our lives and deals with our sin issues. Jesus died on the cross so that we would have forgiveness of sins and new life with God. As we surrender to him in faith, he reconnects us with God the Father and fills us with God the Holy Spirit. As we believe that God truly raised Jesus from the dead, we are connected with the reality of that resurrection and its victory over sin, death, and hell. This is where every journey to a healthy *being* grounded in Christ must begin. God initiates that journey with us in our hearts by inviting us to respond in prayer to receive the invitation and surrender to the leadership of Jesus.

The journey continues every day as we continually surrender to the leadership of Jesus. Part of this surrender is choosing to believe every day that what the Bible says about us is true, that we are new creations in Christ Jesus, that we are saints, that we have a new identity in Christ, and so on. We also must choose to believe that what the Bible says about God is true as well. The Bible gives us a picture of the Father, Son, and Holy Spirit that we must trust and believe.

In this sense, every day we will face a battle for our mind. Driving along the highway in the US, we encounter many different billboards advertising many different products. The goal of these billboards is to persuade us to leave the journey and make some stop in order to spend our money. Resisting these advertisements can be a battle sometimes, especially if there are children in the car. In a similar way, there are many distractions and temptations that we face that try to persuade us to end or delay the journey. We must learn to resist these things.

Another aspect of our relationship in this journey is repenting when we do wrong and forgiving when others hurt us. Our sin hurts others, but it also hurts Jesus. Repentance means that we confess that what we did was wrong and decide to move in the opposite direction. When others hurt us, we must release them to God just as God has released us from the consequences of when we hurt him through wrongdoing. When we fail to repent and forgive, we inhibit the relationship with Jesus in the Holy Spirit that will help us develop the healthy *being* grounded in Christ.

All relationships and all good journeys require communication. In this journey, the means of communication are prayer and worship. We must engage with God through Jesus. The Spirit helps us to engage appropriately. The Father joyfully receives this communication through Jesus. We must avoid trying to reduce this relational communication to a few principles. It is not about principles but about healthy interaction with God according to God's preferences revealed in the Bible.

One final note is important about this relational journey. We travel *daily*. This is not a journey for "Sunday drivers". It is actually not a journey for drivers at all, since Jesus is the driver and leader of the journey. If we are to journey to the place where we have our *being* firmly grounded in Christ, we must travel with Jesus every day. In the end, Jesus will bring us to the place where we realize that our *being* has become healthy, reflecting the image of Christ in our lives.

THE LEADERSHIP DILEMMA

Every person has a unique *being*, which means that every leader has a unique contribution to make. Our dilemma is that we can spend a lot of time trying to imitate someone else – doing what they do – without realizing that our key to successful leadership already lies within us, in the *being* that we already have.

Our dilemma grows when, as Christians, we begin to think that becoming a great leader involves mastering complex theories and techniques of leadership instead of remaining connected to and grounded in a living relationship with God through Jesus Christ so that our *being* will become stronger and healthier. We are the people whom God has created. Through Jesus Christ in us we may become fully the leaders God intended.

5

DOING AND LEADERSHIP

If your actions inspire others to dream more, learn more, do more and become more, you are a leader.

John Quincy Adams

You gain strength, courage and confidence by every experience in which you really stop to look fear in the face. You must do the thing you think you cannot do.

Eleanor Roosevelt

Become the kind of leader that people would follow voluntarily; even if you had no title or position.

Brian Tracy

Placing such a strong emphasis on the *being* of a leader may lead people to assume that what a leader does is less important or not at all important. The idea of just *being* as a leader and having people naturally follow your "karma" or "aura" is an attractive one for some. The reality is that leadership is hard work. It takes effort. It requires personal discipline. It demands action. This is where *doing* comes in.

When we say that *being* takes precedence over *doing*, we are not saying that *doing* is unimportant or less important than *being*. *Doing* is as important as *being* for leadership effectiveness. It is just that *being* comes before *doing*; or, *doing* flows through *being*. If we fail to do anything, then we will not be leaders.

THE DEFINITION OF CHRISTIAN LEADERSHIP

In our definition of Christian leadership, *doing* was an integral part of leadership. Our skills, activities, and knowledge focus our strengths and spiritual gifts and flow through our identity, character, and calling in order to influence people and systems toward the beneficial outcomes. We need to use our skills, activities, and knowledge – *doing* – to direct our strengths and spiritual gifts – *doing* also – which flow through our *being*. Without putting our skills, activities, knowledge, strengths, and spiritual gifts into action we cannot lead.

As a minister and a business leader I have developed certain skills. I have preached, taught, prayed, used spiritual disciplines, developed knowledge of the Bible, and integrated them into my thought processes. I have also learned how to manage staff, to hire and fire, to deal with various legal responsibilities and the like. These and many other skills and abilities are common to most leaders in the church and in business. However, what is different is that all these things flow through my unique *being* grounded in Christ.

I am not like any other leader. We have similarities, but we are different people and therefore lead differently. We all have different *beings* which may be grounded in Christ. As Christians, we will act (choosing and responding) on the basis of our character and calling. We will act in a manner informed by biblical values. We will act according to the needs of our context. But all our actions will filter through and flow through our *being*.

Because of this relationship between *being* and *doing*, in which what we do flows through who we are, anything we do as leaders is profoundly influenced by our *being*. Clean water that flows through a dirty conduit will become dirty itself. In the same way, doing the right things will become corrupted or distorted as they flow through an unhealthy *being*. At the same time, if *no* water is flowing through a clean conduit then it does not even matter that the conduit is clean. It is of no use unless something is flowing through it according to its purpose. When our *being* is generally healthy and grounded in Christ, our *doing* flows more naturally and freely.

DOING EFFECTIVE LEADERSHIP

So obviously, *doing* is essential to any leadership. You can be a good person but a very poor leader because you do not do the right things in your leadership. You can know your identity in Christ but fail to lead others because you are not *doing* the things that influence others. We cannot simply sit on some proverbial leadership mountaintop and expect people to come to us in order to receive our amazing leadership, like some leadership guru. We cannot expect people to become enthralled with our *being* to the extent that they merely respond to our presence and do the right things.

With leadership, *doing* is more consequential that just *knowing* what to do. We can know everything there is to know about leadership, but if we actually do not do anything we will never lead. I have met some people who have said they knew how to lead but who never did anything and who never had any real leadership. I have also met other people who have claimed not to know anything about leading – or claimed not even to be a leader! – yet who were some of the best leaders I have met.

With leadership, *doing* at the right time determines whether or not something we do actually leads anyone. The timing of our actions as leaders affects our ability to influence people and lead well. We often use the phrase "too little – too late" to describe the actions of a leader that simply had the wrong timing. People will often perceive leaders who do not act quickly enough as weak and ineffective. They will often perceive leaders who act too soon as aggressive and controlling. Timing may not be everything, but it is very important.

Doing in the right way, with the right morals, regulates the impact our leadership will have. For most people, the *how* of our leadership means much more than our intentions or our results. The closer we are to leaders relationally the more important the morals and values of leaders seem to be for us. Of course, when we talk about "morals", as Christians we understand that the morals of people in the world might be very different from the standards of the Bible. However, people still have standards and expectations for leaders and their *doing.*

With leadership, *doing* with an outcome in mind makes a greater difference than *doing* for the sake of doing something. The famous exclamation – "Just *do* something!" – can have disastrous consequences when it comes to leadership. *Doing* may become counterproductive, undermining leadership effectiveness. Without an outcome in mind, we will have difficulty discerning *doing* that is leadership from *doing* that is not leading anyone and even from *doing* that is harmful.

So, although *doing* is essential for leadership, we can never reduce leadership to simple *doing*, as if that was the extent of real leadership. We might do all the right things but at the wrong time and in the wrong way so that we fail to lead. We might also be busy doing many things but fail to do the right things to lead. In addition, while there are certain things we might do that will always lead others, they might not always have long-term beneficial effects. We are all aware of people who did all the things necessary to lead others well, only later to have it revealed that the people were "leading" others to their destruction.

When I lead a conference, I like to ask people who they think was the most effective political leader of the twentieth century. Then I tell them about the person who was arguably the most effective political leader of the twentieth century. This was a leader who when he came to office promised to rebuild the nation, turn around a disastrous economy, bring a renewed sense of national unity, make people proud of themselves as a nation again, and give people a common sense of purpose. This leader was well-liked and charming, an artist who loved children and made people feel special. Within a few years of coming to power, this leader achieved everything he had promised – and more. Yet, few people today who study his leadership would

121

consider him a good leader, let alone a great one. This is because his name is Adolf Hitler.

The example of Adolf Hitler leads us to question what makes truly "effective" leadership, what decides whether we are *doing* effective leadership. On one hand, even an evil person can lead people in a way that seems effective by doing the "right" things. Most people tend to feel that leadership is effective when it gets "results", but many wicked leaders throughout history have achieved "results" – often to the great harm of others.

We believe the solution to these dilemmas lies in the word "beneficial" from our definition of Christian leadership. We may describe something as "beneficial" when it represents something good, advantageous or favorable. Something beneficial promotes well-being, wholeness, and genuine satisfaction. Something beneficial profits others, helps others, advances the best interests of others, adds value to the lives of others.

For some, this will raise a further, vital issue: how do we determine what is beneficial, especially since the benefit of something may only emerge after much time? Some things we do bring immediate positive results. With other things, it may take some time to see positive results – as in raising children well. With still other things, we may feel the immediate results are positive only to discover much later that the results were not good after all (think "Hitler").

Once again, Christians have an advantage. We have the Bible which gives us a coherent worldview along with a values framework by which we may begin to discern what is beneficial. The Bible clearly shows that some things may seem good but in the end prove harmful. It reminds us that some difficult things that do not seem very good will bring us life and wholeness. It is the Bible that leads us to assert that there are at least five determinants of whether an outcome or result is beneficial, that we cannot simply look at the financial bottom line to know whether something is good.

For us, the word "beneficial" defines effective leadership. We might say that leadership is effective only if it is leadership that genuinely benefits people, bringing about beneficial outcomes. We might only say that our *doing* is effective when it brings good in a way consistent with God's good plan for humanity as revealed in his Word, the Bible.

We must evaluate leadership effectiveness in terms of whether the timing, the morality, and the outcomes of the *doing* are beneficial. If we are not leading people toward beneficial outcomes at a beneficial time and in a beneficial way, then it is difficult to say that we are genuinely effective leaders. Healthy *being* and beneficial *doing* make effective leadership. Our *doing* becomes more assured and leads more effectively when it flows from our healthy *being* with the confidence that what we are *doing* will benefit the people we lead.

Using the word beneficial does not imply that our *doing* will always satisfy people or shield them from suffering. The Bible shows us that there are ways that seem right and satisfying but are not beneficial (see Proverbs 14:12). The Bible indicates that there is suffering that produces something very beneficial (see, for example, 1 Peter 4:14). We must discern carefully, in light of the Bible, what we might call "beneficial".

WHAT LEADERS DO

Beneficial *doing* will determine leadership effectiveness, but not everything a leader might "do" qualifies as leadership. When we look at the *doing* of leadership, we can break down the activities of leadership into a number of categories. We must take care not to reduce leadership to these categories. It is always more than these categories. It involves the interplay of these categories with one another and with the *being* of the leader.

By examining the categories of leadership *doing*, we both free leadership from a nebulous, mysterious concept and enable leaders to improve their leadership. All leaders do remarkably similar things. All leaders may improve the quality of their *doing*. Identifying these categories enables us to determine what we do well, what we do not do well and how we might improve.

We must also recognize that what we do as leaders, represented by these categories, occurs in the context of relationships. We do not include building relationships as a separate category because everything we do as leaders involves relationships. Without healthy relationships in the process of leadership, all the things we do as leaders will not have the impact that we hope for.

DECIDING

Leaders make hundreds of decisions every day, many related to their leadership responsibilities. Most of these decisions seem relatively small, but we all live with the realization that sometimes small decisions make big differences. We all like to think that we make these decisions based on cold, hard facts and pure logic. However, recent scientific studies have demonstrated that human decision-making is a very complex process, rarely based on "facts" and "logic".[1]

Leaders face dozens of choices every day. Often, we struggle to know what to choose and how to choose well. Our choices may seem overwhelming. As leaders, we all need a values framework to enable us to make positive choices. We also need a clear focus that will enable us to say "no" wisely and constructively.

As leaders, we all act in faith. No one knows the ultimate outcomes of our decisions – no one except God, that is. Even atheist leaders make decisions based on faith. Although it may not be faith in something they identify as "god", it will be faith in themselves, in science, in reason, and many other things. As Christians who are leaders, we need faith in God and, to an extent, faith in ourselves (or who Christ is in us) in order to make good decisions.

We can grow in our ability to make good decisions. In recent years, people have done much research in how we make decisions and how we might improve our decision-making process. Many insights coming from research resonate with the Bible's view of humanity. From a biblical perspective, making good decisions is called "wisdom". Much of the Bible deals with wisdom. Books such as Proverbs and Ecclesiastes give much insight into how we can improve our decision-making.

DISCERNING

Discernment involves recognizing God's best for ourselves, the people, and the groups that we lead. As leaders, we have more things to do than we can possibly do in the time we have, so we need to discern what are the best things we can do. We need to identify the core "business" we are in and stick with the activities that promote that core business. Many problems arise when we fail to maintain our core business as leaders. For example, some would argue that part of the cause of the 2008 financial crisis was bankers failing to recognize their core business in their pursuit of ever higher levels of personal wealth.

Four areas especially require discernment. The SWOT analysis tool used by many leaders accurately identifies these four areas: strengths, weaknesses, opportunities, and threats. We can review these areas for ourselves as leaders as well as for our leadership contexts.

Strengths involve things we do well or the resources we have at our disposal. As leaders, we need to maximize our strengths. Weaknesses include things we do not do well, resources that we lack, and other contextual challenges.

Opportunities represent the timing and circumstances that make it possible to do something. Perhaps there is a service needed by the marketplace that no one else provides. Perhaps there is a basic human need that one might be able to meet. In the United Kingdom, John Kirkby recognized the burden of debt many people carried, so he established Christians Against Poverty to help address that need. CAP has grown to become one of the best debt help services in the world.[2]

Threats include anything that might hinder or harm us or our leadership contexts. We face many different kinds of threats – financial threats, relational threats, and threats from competition, to name a few. One threat we face often goes unrecognized – spiritual threats. As leaders, we must be aware that we have a spiritual enemy who wants us to fail in our leadership. We need to discern these threats alongside the others.

Cultivating a biblical worldview is one of the best ways to grow in our discernment. The Bible alerts us to the real nature of strengths, weaknesses, opportunities, and threats. For example, we might consider hiring a highly effective salesman for our staff team. However, in the interview we notice that this man is very proud and arrogant, and seems ultra-competitive. Having a biblical worldview would alert us that although this man might achieve stellar sales he would also threaten the unity and mutual cooperation of our sales team in a way that would harm our business.

Another way to grow in our discernment is expecting and allowing for failure. We do not mean approving of wrongdoing, but acknowledging that we will not succeed at everything we do. We are not perfect, but too often we expect ourselves to be. However, when we expect to fail from time to time, we make failure into a learning opportunity that will increase our ability to discern in the future.

DIRECTING

Many people think of leadership primarily in terms of directing. They think that the leader is the one who is the "boss", the one who gives the orders that the followers must obey. While this may work in the military, the real picture of directing in leadership is seldom like this. People refuse to follow blindly in today's marketplace. Today's followers – whether in church or the marketplace – are more like volunteers than employees. They certainly will not respond to being treated as slaves.

Directing in leadership begins with giving vision and mission. We need to give people a picture of where we are leading them. Followers need a sense that leaders know where they are going. If people perceive that where we are going is beneficial, and if they connect with our healthy *being*, people will follow. This is the core of vision.

Mission involves what we do as we go on the journey to the vision. Mission focuses our various activities, enabling us to give a strong "no" to the things that do not advance the mission. Knowing the questions for determining beneficial outcomes helps us understand that often mission is more layered than we might realize at first.

For example, say our core business is the manufacturing of widgets. So, one layer of our mission would be making the best widgets possible. However, we also realize that in order to make the best widgets possible, we need a highly motivated workforce. So we decide to give our entire workforce important responsibility for quality control, to the extent that anyone could stop production instantly if they noticed any flaws in the widgets. We also decide to give a learning grant to all workers so that they might take courses for self-improvement paid for by the firm. These actions fall under the rubric of "Is it personally beneficial?" So we recognize that whereas the core business is making widgets, our mission is to make the best widgets possible while enabling our workers to become the best people possible.

Directing also incorporates keeping our eye on the big picture. Leaders must have a "global" perspective when it comes to their people and their organizations. We need to understand how all the various pieces fit together and why various things are important. If we lead complex organizations, we cannot expect our followers to know and understand fully the larger perspective. We need to share this larger perspective with the people we lead and help them understand how they fit within it – how important they are. We also must help people see the potential beneficial outcomes toward which we are moving.

Once we give vision and mission, and as we keep an eye on the big picture, we may begin to direct the people we lead. In order to follow our directing, people need to know that our directing flows from a healthy *being* in a way consistent with that healthy *being*. The style of our directing must be consistent with our values. They need to know how their contributions fit within the big picture and how that big picture is truly beneficial. Our directing must help people focus in their responsibilities, learning how to say "no" to the things that might become a waste of time or energy.

DEVELOPING

Developing comprises building healthy people, healthy processes, and healthy organizations. All leaders have the responsibility to help develop healthy people. For the church, this includes "making disciples". We often think of a disciple simply as one who does the right things. However, a true disciple is one who becomes healthy as Jesus was healthy in his *being*. We fail as leaders if we build great, "successful" businesses in such a way that we destroy the health of people in the process. The example of how miners were treated in nineteenth-century Britain is an example of this, but so is how some firms exploit cheap labor in developing nations.

As leaders, we need to develop healthy processes by which people relate and through which we accomplish our vision and mission. How we do things together is as important as the outcomes we might achieve. We must beware of the tendency to add more and more processes leading to more and more bureaucracy which may actually destroy the health of people and organizations. However, healthy processes – from human resource processes, to financial processes, to management processes – will help promote healthy people and healthy organizations.

Healthy organizations function in a healthy way and naturally achieve healthy, beneficial outcomes. Churches often make the mistake of thinking that adding the latest bit of technology will help them grow, even when they fail to address unhealthy relationship issues within the church. Technology will not save an unhealthy organization. However, a healthy leader might help lead an organization to health, in which case the organization may begin to have healthy outcomes.

As Jesus observed, "Every healthy tree bears good fruit, but the diseased tree bears bad fruit. A healthy tree cannot bear bad fruit, nor can a diseased tree bear good fruit" (Matthew 7:17–18). We cannot expect fundamentally unhealthy people, processes or organizations to produce healthy, beneficial outcomes. Health determines outcomes more than we would like to accept. We often fail to recognize how vital promoting health is to effective leadership.

DELEGATING

We often view delegating as passing on to others those things we do not want to do ourselves. Many leaders "delegate" the difficult and thankless responsibilities to others so that they can focus on what is easier, more pleasant or more personally satisfying. However, this is not what we mean by delegation.

True delegation involves sharing authority with responsibility. When we delegate, we give people something to do, but we also give them the authority to make decisions and fulfill their responsibility in the best way possible. When someone is untested, we may begin by sharing a smaller responsibility, but we must always give them the authority that accompanies that responsibility. Otherwise, we end up micromanaging the person, taking more time to complete the task than if we had done it ourselves.

Delegating effectively requires that we believe in people as God believes in people. Of course, we know that people struggle with sin and are very imperfect. But God knows this as well. Yet he also gives to people the responsibilities of being fruitful and multiplying, filling the earth and subduing it in accordance with his will (see Genesis 1–2). God entrusts parents with the responsibility of raising their children, and elders with the responsibility of guarding the flock. Clearly, God maintains a high view of the people he created, and so must leaders if we are to delegate effectively.

Delegating also reminds us that leadership is a team effort, not a solo journey. Delegating communicates to people that they form a vital part of the team and that we depend on them. Healthy people will rise to the challenge of delegating as described here. Delegating will also help to promote health in less healthy people, by enabling them to take personal responsibility. At the least, delegating invites people into the process of learning, as we allow them to make mistakes as they grow to fulfill the responsibilities they have received.

DISCIPLINING

We often respond negatively to the word "discipline" because so often "discipline" connotes "punishment". However, from a biblical perspective, discipline and punishment are different concepts. Punishment involves retribution for wrongful or harmful behavior. In punishment, there is no attempt to set wrong things right. Instead, punishment seeks to penalize the persons and perhaps require them to do some sort of penance.

Discipline, on the other hand, entails putting things in order, making the wrong things right. Discipline includes training and instruction. Sometimes discipline will correct wrongful behavior, but it does so in a way that trains the other to become better and healthier.

As leaders, we discipline both people and organizations. With regard to people, we must think of discipline as training with a focus, and that focus as leading people toward beneficial outcomes. Effective leaders do not seek to punish people. However, as leaders we will often have to correct behavior. We can do this effectively only when we do not regard it as punishment.

As a leader, I have regretfully had to dismiss people from employment. (In the US, we would call that "firing people".) Over the years, I have developed a question that I ask myself before I will dismiss anyone: have we done everything within our ability to help the person succeed in their employment? This is another way of asking whether we have exercised appropriate training or discipline. When the answer to the question is yes, then I know it is time to dismiss the person. I realize that we do not have the ability to bring them to a place of health within the organization. When I meet with the person to terminate their employment, I always have this focus in mind. Over the years, I have had employees thank me for firing them because they recognized that it was not only in the best interest of the organization but also in their own best interest that I had dismissed them. This happened because we maintained a focus on discipline, not punishment.

For organizations, discipline is about creating shape and form in the organization. Discipline includes helping the organization stay true to its mission and vision. Discipline also involves pruning away things that no longer promote or produce health, no matter how much we like those things. The core of discipline includes training people so that they work toward the beneficial outcomes. When we focus on training as the core of our discipline – as opposed to "punishment" and its cognates – then people will often (not always) respond in healthier ways.

We must note that discipline is not pleasant, even at the best of times. Discipline takes us out of our comfort zone. It stretches and challenges us. We must remind ourselves and the people we lead of the discomfort involved in discipline. We must also remind ourselves and the people we lead that if we persist with discipline, it will produce good fruit in our lives and our organizations.

DEMOLISHING

When thinking about our activity of "demolishing", we must distinguish this from "destroying" (compare John 10:10 with 2 Corinthians 10:5). Destroying something is about ruining it, making it unusable and worthless. When we destroy something, we try to make a complete end of it so that it may never be used again. So destroying someone's reputation includes making it so that no one would ever trust that person again. Destroying a business would involve forcing that business to close down so that it could never redevelop. Destruction in this sense is the work of the devil.

Demolishing involves something completely different. Demolishing seeks to clear the way so that something new might emerge. So if we demolish a building, our purpose is to build a new and better building in its place. If we demolish strongholds (see 2 Corinthians 10:5), then we want to build healthy thought processes in their place.

Building ourselves as leaders requires that we demolish our own strongholds, which includes our own habits and thought processes that are not healthy. We may also be forced to demolish old ways of doing things that, although not sinful, are not the best way to do things in the present context. Building people requires that we help them take responsibility for themselves and demolish their own strongholds and past ways of doing things. Building healthy organizations requires an ongoing process of demolishing those things that are no longer effective, that no longer move toward beneficial outcomes, in favor of those things that will promote healthy outcomes.

Building something healthy and vital always requires some level of demolishing. The Bible helps provide a framework for knowing some of the things that need demolishing. The questions for determining healthy outcomes may also help reveal things that need demolishing. Demolishing works best when the people we lead may become involved in the demolition process. We must help them see how what we are demolishing together might be replaced by something more beautiful, healthier, and leading toward beneficial outcomes.

All of these are things that all leaders do to some extent. The good news is that we can study, improve, and develop our skills in all these things. Having this framework enables us to see the things that perhaps we have failed to do as leaders, as well as the things that we do well. However, we have to remember that our *being* influences the health and effectiveness of all these *doing* areas.

A few quick examples of how our *being* affects our *doing* in these areas may suffice. If we are trying to find our sense of significance in our leadership role, then we will often make the vision about us and our need for importance rather than about God's best for our organization. If we are looking for our identity in our leadership, then we may fire the person who raises legitimate challenges to our leadership, seeing the person as attacking our identity when all they were doing is raising appropriate concerns about how the business was going. If we are looking to our leadership for our sense of security, then we will have a tendency to destroy people who want to promote positive change rather than see the things that need to be demolished in order that something better might emerge.

DOING WITH EXCELLENCE

In order to achieve effective leadership, we must do the above things with excellence. Over the years, "excellence" has become a buzz word in business circles, and this has influenced churches as well. For some, the concept of excellence has liberated them into cycles of continuous improvement in their leadership and its contexts. For others, "excellence" has become a club with which they beat themselves or others, ultimately leading to discouragement and despair regarding their leadership context. They become encumbered with the thought that no matter how good they might become, they will never be as good as someone else on their minds.

Our *doing* as leaders must have excellence, but we need to reframe how we understand excellence. Too often, we frame excellence in reference to others. So we think we are excellent when we perceive that our *doing* is better or of a higher quality than the *doing* of other people. However, to define excellence in this way always brings about discouragement and failure. We will always be able to find people and organizations who are better than we are and worse than we are.

We need to frame excellence in reference to ourselves, our context, and the Bible. The Bible gives us a sense of excellence in terms of our behavior as human beings. The Bible shows us behaviors that are beneficial and behaviors that are harmful. The Bible also presents a vision for a beneficial society.

Regarding ourselves and our context, we can first understand excellence as doing the best we can possibly do with the resources at our disposal in the context where we find ourselves. All of our *doing* involves the unique person we are. We all have certain limited resources with which we work. We can only engage in *doing* where we are at any given time. Excellence involves doing our absolute best within these limitations. Excellence refers to these three dynamics – self, resources, circumstances. To achieve excellence, we need only to do our best regarding these three dynamics.

London has some of the best hospitals and doctors in the world. Medical excellence in London implies world-class treatment. When someone gets an infection or has complications during a routine surgery, there is an outcry and an investigation. Such things cannot be tolerated. In a developing nation, the closest hospital for remote areas may be hours away. Because of the limitations of training and resources, infections and complications are common. One or two doctors might serve the entire hospital population, while dozens might serve one hospital in London. Although every doctor will work to give patients the best possible care, the definition of excellence will be different in the developing nation. Excellence for the doctor with limited resources will look different than excellence for the doctor with seemingly unlimited resources.

I have been playing guitar for many years. I usually lead worship several times per week using my guitar. Excellence for me is playing to the best of my ability while seeking always to improve as much as possible. I know some people who have only been playing guitar for a year or two. They do not have the opportunity to play several times a week. But if they play to the best of their ability and seek to improve, they will play with excellence. The challenge is that their "excellence" will look different from my "excellence". As a leader, I must learn to acknowledge their excellence. I have another young friend who is pursuing a degree in music, playing the guitar. Although much younger than me, he is a much better guitar player from a worldly standard than I am. His "failure" as a guitarist would likely look much better than my "excellence".

The definition of excellence will always involve our unique person, our finite resources, and our circumstances. While we can use the examples of others in different circumstances to motivate us and give us a vision for what is possible, those examples do not in themselves define excellence. Of course, we can always use global benchmarks in order to achieve higher standards, but genuine excellence in a particular place is not the same thing. For leaders, this is good news, because it means that we may all achieve excellence in our own way.

Regarding ourselves and our context, we can also understand excellence from the perspectives of our strengths. As leaders, we often work on our weaknesses rather than focusing on the strengths that God has given us. Yet focusing our efforts on eliminating our weaknesses will never bring about excellence. It will often trap us in a downward spiral of trying to eliminate weakness while neglecting our strength.[3]

Doing leadership effectively requires that we discover what we do well, even what we might do better than most. What we do better than most results from the unique combination of our skills, knowledge, strengths, and spiritual gifts. If we want to achieve excellence, we focus on improving our strengths continuously, while seeking out people and resources that may help compensate for our weaknesses. Those who do leadership excellently focus on doing what they do better than most.

LEADERSHIP STYLES AND THEORIES

Whenever we discuss leadership, the question of what style of leadership we use often comes up. For some people, style is everything. Some will focus on various theories of leadership and adopting various leadership techniques in order to make themselves good leaders. Quite often, changing leadership styles, techniques or approaches achieves nothing other than alienating and confusing the people we lead.

In our understanding of Christian leadership, the particular theory or style of leadership is not as important as the leaders themselves. We have found that there are many different approaches to leadership and many different styles of leadership which are highly effective in their given context. We have also found that while there may be some *wrong* or *ineffective* styles of leadership there is seldom a *right* or *perfect* style of leadership.

We may choose to adopt a particular style or approach based on several criteria. As we become familiar with these criteria, we may find that we could have several styles and techniques for leading in our leadership toolbox, all of which we might learn to apply effectively. The key is having the right criteria with which to discern the appropriate style in the appropriate context.

Is it consistent with the Bible?

The first criteria is whether the style or approach to leadership is consistent with the Bible. Someone might lead by abusing or manipulating another person or group, but that would not be an appropriate leadership approach. We might try to lead by adopting a lot of rules and regulations people must follow, but that would resemble the leadership of the Pharisees which Jesus roundly condemned.

Asking this question does not mean that we should try to find some "proof text" in the Bible for everything we do as leaders. We will not find many of the specific challenges we face in the Bible – such as what computer to purchase and where to locate our company – but we will find much wisdom for facing these challenges. Our leadership style should be broadly consistent with the revelation of God's will in the Bible, exemplifying the same characteristics as the leadership of Jesus.

Does it flow from the leader's being?

People value authenticity in a leader very highly. People will not follow leaders they perceive to be false or inauthentic. When we ask whether a leadership style flows from the leader's *being*, we are asking whether that leadership style is authentic to the leader. If we operate more as a consensus-building leader, then trying to lead like a military commander will not seem appropriate. If we are a "charismatic" up-front leader, then trying to lead "behind the scenes" will seem like we are playing politics – not a favorable quality when it comes to people's perceptions of leadership.

Leading authentically requires that we embrace fully who we are, especially who we are in Christ. It requires that we seek to ground our *being* in Jesus Christ, while affirming the uniqueness of our personality, background, and makeup and its effects on our leadership. Saying this does not give license for us to just do what we feel like doing, no matter what the consequences. However, if our *being* is becoming healthier, then it will naturally moderate our styles of leadership and help ensure the style we choose resonates with who we are.

Is it appropriate and beneficial for the context?

This question forces us to consider the overall context of our leadership at any given moment. We need to understand that the appropriateness of any style of leadership depends largely on the context. We must ask whether our style of leadership in any given context will lead toward beneficial outcomes. No matter how palatable the style of leadership might be for people, if the style is not appropriate and beneficial for the context then it is not good for that situation.

For example, when I am coaching the managing director of a company, it is generally not appropriate for me to yell at the managing director during the coaching appointment. My leadership style is more that of a friend on a journey, with the managing director setting the overall direction and me asking questions to help him determine the best way to go. Yet, if I was in a meeting with that same managing director and a fire erupted in the building, then it would be appropriate for me to raise my voice over the fire alarm in order to give the managing director suitable instructions for evacuating the building safely.

The context helps determine the appropriate leadership style. Most of the time when leaders make mistakes regarding this question, it is because they chose the wrong leadership style for the context. Over time, most of us learn how to answer this question almost instinctively – providing we have learned to ask it in the first place.

Is it wise?

The final question is more of a question for reflection. Jesus said that "wisdom is justified by all her children" (Luke 7:35). This means that sometimes we will only understand what is wise in retrospect, after whatever we have done bears some fruit. This question leads us to discern what the potential impact of any given leadership style might be on those we lead. It also helps us avoid the tendency to do anything as long as we do something. We all face the tyranny of the urgent. We all have people insisting that we act immediately in the way they demand. This question forces us to slow down and think before we act. This question leads us to examine our thoughts, emotions, and motives carefully, before we adopt a particular style or approach.

SUBVERTING OUR LEADERSHIP

As Christians, we have a daily struggle against three forces identified by the Bible: the flesh, the world, and the devil. All three have real power to subvert our leadership by undermining the health in our *being* and polluting the purity of our *doing*. We include these in this section because they primarily affect our *doing* once we become Christians and our *being* is made alive in Christ Jesus.

The flesh

The flesh is that sinful aspect of our humanity that draws us away from God and God's will. Although we have been made alive in Christ Jesus and set free from the power of sin, we can still choose to act in accordance with our sin tendencies as opposed to God's will. We can practically live as a non-Christian, even though we fully acknowledge Jesus Christ as Lord and Savior.

Sometimes we try to lead from our own strength and abilities, and according to our own wisdom. We can begin to think that if we work hard enough then we will become a great leader. We may become angry, irritable or frustrated. All these are indicators of the flesh at work.

One of the strongest temptations we face as leaders is to manipulate and dominate others, trying to force them to do what we want them to do, what we think is best. Rather than doing the difficult work of relating to and persuading others, we try to take short cuts toward beneficial outcomes. This also suggests the flesh at work.

Sometimes we can get stuck in sinful patterns of thinking, feeling, and behaving. We all can develop broken ways of thinking and feeling. These patterns may become strongholds in our lives that will begin to predetermine our behaviors and reactions. We must learn to identify and demolish these strongholds. Freedom in Christ Ministries provides a number of resources for this, including a "Stronghold Busting" exercise.[4]

The world

Every day the world around us bombards us with its ideas about what constitutes good leadership. Advertising gives us the picture of perfect leaders. Movies and TV create compelling fictional stories of leadership that have little intersection with reality. The church often cooperates with this by creating its own superstar mentality when it comes to leaders. The examples held up by the world – both inside and outside the church – create a picture of leadership that only includes an amazing few people and excludes the vast majority of leaders changing the world every day.

The world promotes a number of values when it comes to leadership. The world's view of leadership is that it is quick and easy. Even when a movie tells the story of a lifelong leadership struggle, it does so in the space of a couple hours, giving the impression that it was quick, even if it did not seem easy.

In the world's view of leadership, leaders get results – no matter what. The successes of leaders are emphasized while the costs those same leaders inflicted on the lives of others are generally ignored. Leaders are often portrayed as lone heroes, succeeding by themselves in spite of overwhelming odds. All these are fictions.

With the world, leaders always seem to conform to the fad *du jour*. The world rewrites history so that all our leaders seem strangely modern and strangely conformist to the values promoted by the world at any given time. Leaders as portrayed by the world are seldom people of faith, and if they have faith then that faith is marginalized.

Many leaders find it difficult to withstand the onslaught from the world. Christian leaders often surrender to the idea that our Christian faith is a private matter, having no place in the public world of leadership. The world suggests that it is our *doing* that matters as leaders. Often, we only learn too late that the world is wrong and that *being* is much more important than we thought.

The devil

We give the devil too much credit, often blaming him for problems that actually stem from our flesh, not from some demonic activity. However, the devil – and by that we mean the spiritual forces of wickedness at work in the world around us – does seek to undermine effective leadership. When we sin, we give the devil an opportunity to work in our lives (see Ephesians 4:26–27). Literally, this means a base from which to operate in our lives. However, God has given us the gift of repentance so that we might turn away from the sin and remove this foothold.

We need to recognize that we live in a world that is both physical and spiritual. It is never just one or the other. The spiritual forces of wickedness operate in this world – sowing discord among people, tempting people, accusing people, and deceiving people. The good news is that Jesus Christ came to destroy the works of the devil (see 1 John 3:8). Through faith in Jesus we can overcome all the efforts of the devil to undermine our leadership.

We must learn to identify when evil spiritual forces are operating in our leadership context. Sudden, intense disagreements might emerge among friends. Resources seem to dwindle. Technology suddenly ceases to function properly. A sharp sickness erupts without warning. We feel overwhelmingly depressed and discouraged. All these might indicate the work of spiritual forces.

Combat!

We combat these three enemies in the same way. First, we need to maintain the health of our *being*, grounded in Christ Jesus. Most of the time when I see unhealthy leaders who are capitulating to the flesh, the world or the devil it is because those leaders have failed to maintain their *being* with their identity in Jesus Christ. Consequently, they are trying to get from their leadership what they can only really get from Jesus Christ. This corrupts the *doing* of their leadership.

141

When our *being* is healthy, we are more naturally able to recognize and resist the activities of the flesh, the world or the devil in our lives. Part of maintaining a healthy *being* involves choosing to know and believe the truth on a daily basis. The flesh, world, and devil tell us lies and give us wrong perspectives. Knowing and believing the truth enables us to expose the lies and choose the truth.

Second, we cooperate with the Holy Spirit working in our lives. The Holy Spirit seeks to produce the fruit of the Spirit in our lives (see Galatians 5:22–23). The Holy Spirit will convict us when we sin (see John 16:8). The Holy Spirit leads us into all truth (see John 16:13). By the Holy Spirit we can come to a place where our natural tendency is to know and choose to obey God's will (see Ezekiel 36:26–27). When we cooperate with the Holy Spirit, he alerts us to the activity of the flesh, the world, and the devil – plus he will give us strategies to resist and overcome them.

Third, we nurture our faith in God – Father, Son, and Holy Spirit. Our connection with God the Father through Jesus in the power of the Holy Spirit enables health and life to flow into our *being*. Faith does not come from some rigorous intellectual exercise, nor does it come from positive thinking. Faith flows from a living relationship with God whereby we come to know God and his ways. The better we know God as he reveals himself in the Bible, the better we may resist the counterfeits of God in the flesh, the world, and the devil.

THE LEADERSHIP DILEMMA

We often spend considerable time and energy to improve our *doing* as leaders while neglecting our *being* as leaders. This creates a leadership dilemma, undermining our own leadership effectiveness. Recognizing that our *doing* flows through our *being* as leaders will help liberate us from the seemingly endless cycle of leadership crazes and fads, on which we spend considerable time and money often without seeing any tangible results except that we feel a bit better about ourselves because at least we are doing *something*.

When our *being* is not healthy, we can realize that the pathway to greater leadership effectiveness and impact (better leadership *doing*) rests with us right now, not in finding some new technique, unlocking some mystery, or forcing people to cooperate with our leadership, but in affirming who God has made us to be and grounding ourselves in Jesus Christ. When our *being* is healthy, we can learn to trust ourselves more fully in the decisions and choices we make, releasing us from the expectations others try to force on us and from the second-guessing to which all leaders are prone to some degree. Our leadership *doing* will then lead people more authentically to the beneficial outcomes.

PART III
THE CONTEXTS OF LEADERSHIP

The greatest leader is not necessarily the one who does the greatest things. He is the one that gets the people to do the greatest things.

Ronald Reagan

Whenever you see a successful business, someone once made a courageous decision.

Peter Drucker

To lead people, walk beside them... As for the best leaders, the people do not notice their existence... When the best leader's work is done the people say, "We did it ourselves!"

Lao-tsu

eadership never occurs in a vacuum. One of the greatest mistakes many leaders make is to assume that the success or failure of any venture depends on the quality of their leadership. Many other factors determine our leadership effectiveness. The experienced captain of a ship at sea understands that although he might command men, he cannot command the winds and waves and weather.

Sir John Franklin (1786–1847) had served in the Royal Navy since he was fifteen years old. Rising to the rank of captain, he led a ship in the great battle of Trafalgar and became a well-liked and highly effective captain. He led four explorations of the Arctic, mapping hundreds of miles of coastland. People respected and admired him greatly, with many volunteering to serve with him. Yet in spite of his effectiveness as a leader and many successes, his last voyage to discover the Northwest Passage resulted in total failure and the deaths of Franklin and every sailor with him. In the end, he was undone by the weather, by lead poisoning in their food, and by disease.[1]

We can never really control or determine the effectiveness or "success" of our leadership. One of my favorite leadership quotes comes from Ecclesiastes:

> Again I saw that under the sun the race is not to the swift, nor the battle to the strong, nor bread to the wise, nor riches to the intelligent, nor favor to those with knowledge, but time and chance happen to them all. For man does not know his time. Like fish that are taken in an evil net, and like birds that are caught in a snare, so the children of man are snared at an evil time, when it suddenly falls upon them. (9:11–12)

Solomon realized that we as leaders could not master many of the variables that determine the outcomes of our leadership. We can be the fastest, strongest, wisest, most intelligent, and knowledgeable person who ever lived and yet still fail utterly as a leader. Time and chance – circumstances, in other words – govern our leadership more than we understand or want to admit.

Fred was a highly effective salesman, having worked his way up from the ground to become vice president in a major multinational corporation. As Fred reached his mid-fifties, he was challenged by a friend to change businesses. The friend realized that Fred's skills would be a major advantage for starting a new business. So with his usual enthusiasm, Fred joined the new business. Yet, after several years of intense effort, using the same skills that made Fred a vice president, the business failed. Fred's best efforts could not save it.

We see this story replayed almost every day in a variety of ways. A highly successful person moves to a new business, a new church or a new community and suddenly fails. Or, sometimes it happens in reverse. Someone who utterly failed in one place moves to another place and succeeds spectacularly.

What makes the difference is one of the most overlooked variables affecting leadership: the context of leadership. We don't lead in isolation. Leadership always operates in a context. Although leadership is relational, it is never simply the relationship of solitary individuals. Those relationships always have a context. The context of leadership will determine our leadership effectiveness as much as our actions as leaders. One of the great delusions many leaders have is that they can function effectively no matter where they are.

We will look at three contexts that help shape the outcomes of our leadership: systems, situations, and spheres. Although these contexts exert enormous influence on our leadership, we are not simply helpless in the face of them. We will discover that our *being* and *doing* as leaders shape and direct these contexts more than we might realize at first.

6

LEADING PEOPLE-SYSTEMS

*The way a team plays as a whole determines its success.
You may have the greatest bunch of individual stars in the
world, but if they don't play together, the club won't be
worth a dime.*

Babe Ruth

*I prefer to win titles with the team ahead of individual
awards or scoring more goals than anyone else. I'm more
worried about being a good person than being the best
football player in the world. When all this is over, what are
you left with? When I retire, I hope I am remembered for
being a decent guy.*

Lionel Messi

*No institution can possibly survive if it needs geniuses or
supermen to manage it. It must be organized in such a way
as to be able to get along under a leadership composed of
average human beings.*

Peter Drucker

When we think of the concept of "systems", our first thoughts often relate to something completely different than what we are talking about here. We often think of the "establishment", the "authorities", bureaucracy or the ruling class. However, these colloquial meanings do not relate to the real understanding of "system" as we describe it. That is why we have chosen the phrase "people-system".[1]

We actually use the word "system" in a variety of ways that relate to the real definition of a system. We might say that a system is a set of things working together as parts of a mechanism or an interconnecting network. It is a complex whole. Or, we might say that a system is a set of principles or procedures according to which something is done, like an organized scheme or method. System also may refer to a set of rules used in measurement or classification. The one thing all these ideas have in common is that a system is a *set* of something.

A computer system is a set of electrical components connected together to form a complex whole, such as a laptop computer. The digestive system is a set of organs and processes that work together as a complex whole to enable the body to process food. A belief system is a set of values and beliefs that we connect in our minds which work together to shape our thinking processes.

PEOPLE-SYSTEM DEFINED

In light of these perspectives, we can offer our definition of a people-system: *any set (group) of people with a connectedness from which its own identity and forms emerge.* As people connect together in groups, they naturally begin to develop a common sense of identity and certain ways of doing things. Very quickly this group begins to have a life of its own, becoming a complex unit with an existence distinct from its individual members. Consciously or unconsciously, the group will develop its own forms – ways of operating, procedures, "rules", and other such things. In time, this group's life will become so strong that it would continue even though individual members might leave the group.

The most basic people-system is the human family. However, wherever people connect together in groups they form a people-system. This is a natural and automatic tendency among all human beings. God created us this way. We are inherently social beings.

Two sets of dynamics shape the life of people-systems. First, people-systems can be temporary or stable. Temporary people-systems are those that form for a determined or relatively short period of time. For example, a number of years ago I attended a week-long training for coaching. During that week, the group became rather close as we shared our lives, our experiences, and even some meals together. We created a bond that was very real and became a people-system. However, although we had all the dynamics of a people-system, we only existed for a week. We were a temporary people-system.

Stable people-systems are those whose existence becomes more enduring or long-lasting. Usually, stable systems outlive the departure of the original members or the original leaders. For example, Thomas moves back to his home country after some time away. He gathers with a group of people who are united by a common mistrust of the "establishment" as well as a desire to worship God and study the Bible. He becomes the leader, recognized for his preaching skill. Over the next few years, more and more people begin to join in with this group, especially since religious persecution has lessened in their country. Some people leave the group from time to time as well. After ten years with this group, Thomas receives an appointment as president of a college. So he resigns as leader of the group. However, the group continues to meet together, selecting a new leader. Three hundred seventy-five years later, the people-system called City Temple continues to live.

The more stable a people-system becomes, the more influence it will exert on leaders and the more difficult it will be to change. However, leaders may also have greater influence and impact the more stable a people-system becomes. This greater influence applies both to the people-system and the people within the system. The longer the tenure of the leader, the more lasting this influence will become.

The second dynamic is that people-systems may be simple

or complex. We may call a people-system "simple" when it is a relatively small and limited group of people – not because it is easy or uncomplicated. A family or a small group at church are examples of simple people-systems. These groups are simple in the sense that a single-cell organism is simple – not because they are easy to deal with, as anyone in a family would know! Obviously, the ways that simple systems function may be quite complicated and difficult at times.

Complex people-systems are composed of many different people-systems working together. A multinational corporation or a large church might be examples of complex people-systems. When dealing with complex people-systems, we must remember that there are a number of different people-systems affecting how the whole operates. A multinational corporation will have various divisions and teams operating within it. As we have seen with various financial crises in recent years, one team or division (one people-system) within the whole company might cause the whole system to stop functioning properly.

Simple people-systems respond more quickly to leadership stimuli. The leader of the small group at church has only to get agreement from a small group of people in order to effect major change. Complex systems require leadership that patiently builds healthy processes while focusing on what is healthy within that complex system in order to effect change.

Often leaders make the mistake of trying to fix what is unhealthy in a people-system rather than building on what is healthy. But focusing on health is the key to bringing about change. Effective CEOs will often return ailing companies to their "core business", or what that company has historically done well, instead of trying to fix everything that is wrong. They will jettison underperforming divisions in favor of those who have produced well.

Whether they are temporary or stable, simple or complex, people-systems determine leadership effectiveness much more than we would like to admit. Effective leaders are always leaders of people-systems.

PEOPLE-SYSTEMS IN THE BIBLE

Although the phrase "people-system" might be new to some, the concept is very biblical. In the New Testament, the concept of "household" is an example of a people-system. In the Bible, "household" can refer to a family (see Genesis 7:1), a business (see Proverbs 15:27 and Matthew 24:45), or even the church itself (see 1 Timothy 3:15). All these examples function as a people-system.

In the Old Testament prophets, God often referred to whole nations as one large people-system by using a singular name, such as Ephraim, Edom or Egypt (see Hosea 5:3, for example). The first three chapters of Amos has God calling out the sins of nations as if they were the sins of individuals. This suggests that nations had the same characteristics as people-systems.

Paul himself even compares the church as people-system to another well-known system: the human body. In 1 Corinthians 12, Paul mentions that the church has a variety of people connected together in a variety of ways with its own sense of leadership and identity. It is interesting that almost 2,000 years before systems theory developed formally Paul had already discovered the importance of people-systems.

WHY PEOPLE-SYSTEMS

We need to understand people-systems because God designed people as essentially social beings. We naturally and automatically group ourselves together. These groups quickly become a living entity, as people spontaneously organize themselves with a discernible identity and forms of relating.

Once they have formed, people begin to get their sense of personal identity from these groups. One example of this is how in many cultures the wife will take the name of her husband. The woman's literal identity changes as she changes her name on her papers, such as her passport. When they have children, the people-system – the family – into which they are born also shapes their identities as they receive a first name and surname.

Another example is how joining a church at one time changed a person's sense of identity. People became "baptists", "presbyterians" or "nondenominationals" based on the church they joined. At one point, when people relocated to another town they would naturally join the same type of church that they had come from because that church had influenced their sense of identity.

As they connect in systems, people begin to receive their own sense of personal satisfaction and meaning from their association with these people-systems. We can see how this happens with sports teams. Growing up in St. Louis, I could not help but become a baseball fan, especially the St. Louis Cardinals. Over the years, I have received much joy – and considerable heartbreak! – through my association with the Cardinals. Although I live in a big city with no baseball team – London – I still follow the Cardinals during the baseball season. Even something relatively trivial as my association with a sports team – a people-system – significantly influences me. Such influence becomes ever deeper when the association involves a significant people-system such as a church, a company, a city or a nation.

Once people become part of a particular people-system, they will tend to conform their behavior to what is acceptable to the people-system. People-systems always influence the behaviors of the people within them. When they are healthy, people-systems will influence people toward behavior that is good and virtuous. When they are unhealthy, people-systems will influence people toward behavior that is destructive or harmful.

We can see the negative influence of people-systems in the example of how some Christians in Nazi Germany willingly gave over their Jewish neighbors even though such behavior was contrary to the Bible and Christian morality. This influence did not take away individual responsibility, but it was very real. Paul reminds us, "Do not be deceived: 'Bad company ruins good morals'" (1 Corinthians 15:33).

We can see the positive influence of people-systems in some schools. My third-grade classroom and teacher in the US influenced me deeply as I was growing up. Although I do not remember much of what I learned during that year, I do remember how something in that year awakened my desire to learn, to take risks, and to lead. That people-system changed the course of my life. Throughout my life I have connected with many such people-systems which have shaped me profoundly.

The dynamics of people-systems will influence people within those systems more than they influence the systems themselves. One misconception many people have, especially people in the West, is that we are the "masters of our fate" and we determine our own behavior and make our own choices. We would call this individualism – that we are self-reliant and independent individuals who make our own choices and determine our own destiny. The nature and power of people-systems contradict this misconception. Although we might think we are independent individuals, we always conform our behavior to the people-systems of which we are part.

Although people-systems wield much influence, people must cooperate with one another and with the system they are in for the people-system to continue and thrive. However, once we are in a people-system, our natural human tendency is to work together with others in the system and with the established norms of the system in order to allow and even encourage the people-system to operate well. This is one reason we must choose the people-systems to which we belong carefully – once we are in one we tend to remain in it and continue to be shaped by it, even if it no longer functions as it should.

When we consider how people-systems function, we can understand why God has chosen the church as the locus of discipleship and kingdom activity. Paul discerned the church as a people-system as he compared the church with a human body, another complex system. As a people-system, the church has tremendous influence over the behaviors and beliefs of the people within it. Thus, the church by its very nature as a people-system innately molds people as disciples. Our challenge is to ensure that the church is making disciples of *Jesus*, not disciples of a particular leader or particular denomination.

LEADERS OF PEOPLE-SYSTEMS

All people-systems have leaders. Leaderless people-systems do not exist. Some form of leadership hierarchy will always emerge in the people-system.[2] Leadership does not come from our position, job description, role or status within the system. We become leaders based on one or both of two factors: how we are behaving within the system or how people perceive us within the system.

If we are behaving like a leader and people are following us, then we are a leader within the people-system. This is true whether or not we have a "position" of leader. Old Man Jenkins had been a member of First Baptist Church for forty-seven years. During that time, he had seen seventeen pastors (church "leaders") come and go. Jenkins had never served as a deacon in the church, but he had visited people in the hospital, welcomed new members with a supper in his home, and preached on several occasions when the pastors were away. Ted, the current pastor, noticed early on that whenever he proposed a new ministry or a change in the life of the church people would sneak a furtive glance over to Old Man Jenkins. If Jenkins was nodding his head affirmatively or smiling, then everyone would approve the proposal. If Jenkins looked disappointed or just sat quietly, then the proposal would fail. So Ted wisely realized that he was not the leader of the church; Old Man Jenkins was the leader because everyone was following him. Ted learned that if he took everything to Jenkins and persuaded him, then all his proposals would receive the approval of the people-system.

We also become a leader when people in the people-system perceive us to be a leader. When people perceive us as a leader, they expect us to lead. Ruth worked as a nurse alongside five other nurses, three doctors, three partners (senior doctors), and seven support staff in a medical practice in a large city. Ruth performed her duties with excellence, as well as being very personable and compassionate. Although she was not a doctor or even the senior nurse on staff, she began to notice that other nurses and staff members began to come to her for advice, not only advice regarding work but also advice regarding their personal lives. She noticed that people would listen to her carefully and generally report back to her as her advice produced good results. Ruth could never understand why people were coming to her instead of the senior nurse or one of the partners. Even a couple of the younger doctors began to come to her. She had not realized that the people in her people-system had begun to see her as a leader and treat her like a leader. She had become a leader in the practice because the people had intuitively and spontaneously assigned leadership to her.

When we become leaders in a people-system, the people-system will largely determine our effectiveness as leaders more than any of the individual choices that we make or the things we do. Healthy people-systems will normally produce healthy leadership. Unhealthy people-systems will often produce unhealthy leaders or cause healthy leaders to become dysfunctional – unless the leader's *being* has a robust health that enables the leader to withstand the unhealthiness in the people-system.

At this point, we can begin to see the advantage of being a Christian leader. When our *being* is grounded in Christ – when we are receiving our identity and our sense of significance, security, and acceptance from Jesus – we will naturally have a healthier and more robust *being*. This means if our people-system is healthy, then the health of our *being* will add to that health. But if our people-system is not healthy, then we will have a greater ability to withstand the sickness and dysfunction of our people-system. This will give us greater effectiveness in leading that people-system toward health.

If our *being* is not healthy and grounded in Christ, then we would tend to drain away some of the health of a healthy people-system. In an unhealthy people-system, we would tend to absorb more of the dysfunction into our own leadership, making our leadership less effective and more liable to burnout.

We can see how people-systems affect leadership effectiveness in the story of Tom. Tom served as part of the leadership team in a medium-sized church, alongside three other leaders. Tom led the outreach efforts of the church. The church grew significantly while Tom was part of the team. As a healthy people-system, the church grew and became very good at making disciples of Jesus Christ.

After five years, a small group of people in a larger city in the same general area of the country invited Tom to come plant a new church. The group had met together for a few years, but struggled to grow. Soon after Tom arrived, the new church trebled in size. They found a new meeting place and developed an excellent worship team. Then several problems began to emerge. The initial group resented their loss of control and influence in the new church. The initial group had not grown because the people in it were rather self-centered and comfortable. Although Tom was a great evangelist, he was a terrible pastor, lacking a number of the skills necessary to manage the people dynamics. Yet although he was a terrible pastor, he would not let others step in and help. Without realizing it, Tom had begun to get his sense of significance from having a growing church instead of from his relationship with Jesus. In the end, the church stopped growing and functioning well, mired in in-fighting and lack of pastoral leadership. In both churches, the people-system determined Tom's leadership effectiveness.

Tom's story also points to another important insight about leadership in people-systems. In healthy systems, leadership will rotate among various people depending on the needs of the people-system at any given moment. Healthy people-systems will assign different people to lead at different times based on the person's leadership style, personal strengths, and spiritual gifts.

People in healthy systems recognize this dynamic and cooperate with it. People in unhealthy systems resist this dynamic, leading to increasing levels of frustration and dysfunction.

PEOPLE-SYSTEM LEADERS IN THE BIBLE

In the Bible, leaders of people-systems were called "stewards". Stewards were leaders with authority, not just "managers" as is often translated in passages such as Luke 16. Every household would have a lead steward, to whom the master of the household gave the responsibility and authority to lead the household in accordance with the master's general instructions. Since many masters often traveled on business, the lead steward would have to make decisions and exercise good judgment regarding the day-to-day operations of the household. A good lead steward would seek to anticipate how his master would run the household and then act accordingly. As leaders of the people-systems, these lead stewards made the difference to determine whether or not the master would be successful.

As people-system stewards, leaders have a responsibility within the people-system to lead well and to promote good outcomes. However, they must remember two things. Stewards are not "owners". They are simply custodians and caretakers. Leaders never own the people-system they lead; they simply care for it and oversee it for a season. Second, stewards are never fully in control of a people-system or its people. They influence. They seek to promote good outcomes. But they must never seek to dominate the people or the people-system. As stewards, they are there to serve.

LEADERS AS BRAINS

In people-systems, leaders function much like brains function in the human body.[3] The human body experiences the brain throughout the entire body at all times. The very connection between the brain and body means that the brain is always influencing the body, whether or not we are conscious of that influence. In the same way, the very connection between a people-system and a leader means that the leader continually influences the people-system, even when people are not conscious of it.

We can see this by returning to the story of Old Man Jenkins. Tom had first realized Old Man Jenkins was the leader at a deacons' meeting in his church. Tom had planned to propose a fairly radical change in the church. So he spent time meeting with each of the deacons before the meeting. Individually, they had all agreed to the change, believing it was best for the church. When the day of the meeting came, the deacons discussed the proposal briefly. Everyone seemed to be in agreement. Tom proposed that they vote. Just as they were ready to agree, someone said, "You know, I wonder what Mr. Jenkins would think of this?" Immediately, the atmosphere changed. Another said, "You're right; I wouldn't want to do anything without knowing what Mr. Jenkins thought about it." Another said, "That's settled then; we'll postpone the decision until we can talk to Mr. Jenkins." That was it. All Tom's efforts were undone by the influence of Mr. Jenkins, the real leader of the church who was not even at the meeting and to whom no one had spoken before the meeting.

The longer we are present in a people-system as a leader, the greater our influence over the people-system will become, even when we are not present. I have served as senior minister of my current church for almost fourteen years (as of this writing). When making decisions, my staff just naturally consider what my opinion might be before implementing the decision. It is not because they fear what I might do if I disagree with their decision. It is a natural phenomenon in any people-system.

The brain influences the human body through autonomic activities and somatic activities. Autonomic activities happen automatically and continuously, without much thought. This roughly corresponds to our understanding of *being*. The leader's *being* influences the people-system often without much thought or intention. The integrity of our *being* automatically promotes the integrity of our people-system. The peace and calmness of our *being* naturally flows into our people-system, promoting peace and calmness there. All this suggests that having a healthy *being* as a leader has more ramifications than we often perceive and understand.

Somatic activities happen by choice and intention. This roughly corresponds to our understanding of *doing*. The leader chooses to take actions that influence the people system, much as the brain chooses to take actions that stimulate the activity of the body. With this dynamic, we can see more clearly how our *doing* flows from our *being*. Just as the brain influences the body, the *being* of the leader influences the general well-being and functioning of the people-system, while the *doing* of the leader affects the specific functioning of the people-system.

PEOPLE-SYSTEMS AS "PERSONS"

If leaders function in a way similar to the human brain, then we might see how a people-system is similar to a human person. This brings us back to Paul's discussion of the church as a people-system using the analogy of the human body. In 1 Corinthians 12, Paul describes the church as a body with many parts. This gives us great insights not only into the life of the church as a people-system but also into all people-systems. In his description, Paul talks about people as various parts of the body, working together for the health of the body as a whole.

In light of this observation, we would contend that a people-system is roughly analogous to an individual human person. Each person has a spirit, a soul, and a body. The soul includes the emotions, the mind, and the will. Each people-system has all these characteristics as well. Because of this, people-systems are relatively subject to the same life principles that a human person might be. In addition, people-systems are relatively subject to the same biblical principles that a person might be.

Leaders influence all these characteristics of people-systems through their *being* and their *doing*. However, the *being* of the leader influences these characteristics more deeply than the *doing* of the leader, just as the autonomic activities of the human brain influence more deeply the healthy functioning of the human body. We can see this in the following story.

Barney had worked for many years as a senior manager in a transportation company. Approaching his sixtieth birthday, he decided that he was tired of the stress and hassle of his job. He also had begun to feel his job (life?) was meaningless, so he decided to take a senior post at a small charity. His skills and strengths seemed a very good match with the needs of the charity. A part of him wanted to coast into retirement with a more rewarding and stress-free job.

Once he arrived at the charity, Barney realized that he had to work with a number of very strong personalities. He also discovered a number of big challenges. Although he tried to do his best, his *being* was not healthy. He was personally tired and avoided confrontation. His lack of effectiveness undermined the sense of significance that he was trying to get from the post. The staff could sense his heart was not in the job, so some tried to manipulate him while others simply ignored him. He left the job after a couple years of completely ineffective work. His somatic (*doing*) activities as a leader could not overcome his autonomic (*being*) unhealthiness.

People-system leaders influence the spirit, soul, and body of people-systems primarily through their *being* but also through their *doing*. However, people-systems respond more deeply to the leader's *being*. This means that if our *being* is not healthy then our *doing* will not lead consistently and effectively. We will examine how leaders influence the spirit, soul, and bodies of people-systems.

THE SPIRIT OF A PEOPLE-SYSTEM

People-systems have what we might call a "spirit". By this we do not mean something that is strange or weirdly mystical. Instead, the spirit of a people-system is an invisible spiritual dynamic that emanates from the people-system much like a gravitational field emanates from a planet. We do not see gravity itself, but we can certainly see gravity at work in things such as the tides of an ocean or how planets revolve around the sun. Another analogy might be that of an electromagnetic field. Two magnets will wield an influence on each other even if they never touch. Both a gravitational field and an electromagnetic field influence things around them, causing discernible changes and effects. Both are invisible, yet both are real.

The spirit of a people-system is the range of the system's powerful effective influence on people. The spirit of a people-system affects people spiritually. It may help or hinder the ability of people to connect with God, even in a "secular" workplace. It will influence people socially, in their interactions with one another both inside and outside the people-system. It will influence people's morality, whether or not the choices they make are righteous.

Almost everyone has noticed the effects of the spirit of a people-system. For example, we might walk into a church and suddenly sense that this church is a joyful, faith-filled place. When the church begins to worship, we almost cannot help being caught up in the positive atmosphere. We go away feeling good and upbeat.

Another example: we might visit someone in their home. We walk in the door and suddenly feel uncomfortable. Everything seems awkward. We do not realize that a few hours earlier the husband and wife had been having a strong argument. This argument was the latest in a long line of arguments. The atmosphere was charged with tension.

In another example, we might pass from one neighborhood into another. Suddenly, we feel depressed or discouraged because of the oppressive atmosphere. We later discover that the neighborhood is impoverished with much family breakdown. All these examples point to the spirit of a system.

Because it is a spiritual reality, the spirit of a people-system operates in accordance with spiritual principles. As a spiritual reality, the spirit of a system may be influenced by the Holy Spirit, angels or demons. The spirit of a people-system may become charged by holiness or charged by the demonic.

Paul is very aware of this spiritual reality. In Colossians 2, Paul cautions the church about the elemental spirits of the world that may influence them corporately. In Ephesians 6, Paul tells us that we are not struggling against flesh and blood but we are wrestling against principalities and powers – spiritual forces that are influencing people-systems. In Ephesians 4, Paul tells the church to remember they are all members of one body and so they should not give the devil a foothold.

As a spiritual reality, the spirit of a people-system may also be influenced by spiritual activities such as prayer, worship, Bible reading, and thanksgiving. Youth With A Mission's (YWAM) Megacities Initiative based in Perth, Australia, targets one of the world's megacities every two years. Teams locate in various neighborhoods of the city to work alongside churches to reach people in that neighborhood. They have developed a practice that when a team goes into a neighborhood they will often begin by simply reading the Bible out loud continuously from beginning to end. They feel that the public reading of Scripture affects the spiritual atmosphere of a neighborhood, enabling them to minister more effectively. This is just one example of how spiritual activities can influence the spirit of a people-system.

People with problems in their workplace – such as strife and dissension – have reported to us that if they come early to work (when no one else is present) and spend time praying for each of their co-workers at the person's desk then over time they will often experience a discernible change in the behavior of people, with people becoming more pleasant and more cooperative.

The spirit of a people-system has a discernible influence on the people in and around that people-system. Understanding the effect of the spirit of a system might explain a number of "mysteries" about various people-systems, such as why one church or business thrives while a similar church or business struggles. Effective leaders will consider the spirit of their system as they seek to lead well.

THE PRESENT PAST

In Exodus, as God gives the Ten Commandments, he makes a statement that has startled many people:

> "I the Lord your God am a jealous God, visiting the
> iniquity of the fathers on the children to the third
> and the fourth generation of those who hate me, but
> showing steadfast love to the thousandth generation
> of those who love me and keep my commandments."
> (Exodus 20:5-6)

The word "iniquity" in this passage suggests the brokenness that comes from sin generally, not active, culpable transgression. However one might finesse this passage, the general message seems to be that sin and its brokenness have consequences, not only in the present but also into the future. In addition, the passage suggests that righteousness has consequences, not only in the present but also into the future. Neither the consequences of sin nor the consequences of righteousness affect the future in some fatalistic sense, but they do have tangible influence. This leads us to an important observation regarding people-systems.

Because of the spiritual dynamic of people-systems, the past continuously influences the present in the people-system. The good legacy of the past will influence the people-system toward beneficial outcomes. The sin of the past will influence the system in ways contrary to God's will. Much like stepping into a river and being caught in the force of the stream, people who step into a people-system will naturally experience the influence of the stream flowing from the past.

We experienced this dynamic in the life of City Temple. City Temple has strong evangelical foundations, based on the Bible as

God's Word, the ministry of the people, and the work of the Holy Spirit. From 1640 to 1903, this righteous past influenced the direction of City Temple positively. In 1903, a liberal minister became the leader of City Temple. He rejected the evangelical history of the past in favor of what was called the "New Theology". Liberalism more or less diverted the flow of City Temple away from evangelicalism. However, after just over seventy years, a new minister came who was in the flow of City Temple's heritage. City Temple naturally began to re-join with its past, a past that had never completely left it. Today City Temple once again has a life based on the Bible as God's Word, the ministry of the people, and the work of the Holy Spirit. City Temple boldly proclaims Jesus Christ as the crucified and resurrected Lord and calls all people to surrender to Jesus as Lord and Savior.

When leaders start a people-system – whether it is a church, business or charity – leaders must carefully establish a healthy flow for the people-system, one which will come from the leader's healthy *being* first. When we as leaders step into the flow of a people-system that has existed for some time, we must learn the past of the people-system because that past will influence the present continuously in ways that we might not perceive at first. We must realize that people-systems with unhealthy beginnings, or unhealthy roots, often resist positive change. We also must realize that it is very difficult – and often impossible – to divert fully the flow of a people-system from its past.

Saying all this does not mean that we are helpless regarding the past of our people-systems. It also does not mean that we will automatically experience the benefits of the past. Two spiritual activities become essential – one to counteract the negative effects of the iniquity of the past and one to align ourselves and our people-systems to the positive heritage of the past.

The first spiritual activity is repentance. When we discover iniquity in the past of our people-system, then we need to repent both as leaders and as a people-system. Saying we need to repent does not mean that we as leaders or the people of our system have committed the same sins as those in the past. Sometimes the people are doing the same things, but often they are not.

Repentance involves two things. First, we must confess the wrongdoing or the brokenness. We must acknowledge fully that it was wrong and inappropriate. We must do this without trying to justify the wrongdoing or explain it away. Second, we must renounce the wrongdoing or brokenness. We must indicate that we reject the behavior and reject the past in this regard. We make a decision not to continue the wrongdoing into the future. This is not necessarily an admission of personal culpability on our part. It is simply a clear turning away from the wrongdoing of the past.

We can practice repentance even in the workplace. We do not need to use religious language. Sally took over a senior role in a financial services company. As she examined the records, she learned that her predecessor had not been fully open with his clients. Looking further back, she discovered that the past three people in her post, including the one who started the position, had done the same kinds of things. The practices were not technically illegal, but they did not represent best practice and the kind of honesty that Sally wanted to bring to the post.

Sally began by taking this information to the three partners in the company. She showed them the records and stated forthrightly that she did not feel this behavior had been appropriate and she refused to do these things. The partners agreed, registering some disappointment that they had occurred in the first place. She then went to her clients and set forth her intention to deal with them openly and honestly, describing the kind of behaviors (without exposing or putting blame on her predecessors) that she would not engage in. In the process, she regained a client who had left the company because she had suspected that something was not entirely right with Sally's predecessors. In her process, Sally had practiced repentance without ever using religious language.

The second spiritual activity is thanksgiving. Thanksgiving enables us to celebrate and take hold of the good of the past.

Thanksgiving involves telling the good stories from the heritage of the people-system. This enables people in the system to identify with the past and embrace the good practices of the past. Thanksgiving also acknowledges the good contributions made by various people in the system throughout its history. Thanksgiving brings the positive heritage of a people-system to life.

LEADING THE SPIRIT OF A PEOPLE-SYSTEM

Leaders first influence the spirit of their people-system through their *being*. Our personal spiritual health and integrity as leaders naturally promotes spiritual health and integrity in the system. Most people desire a sense of spiritual well-being, even when they are not aware of it. When we as leaders have a sense of spiritual well-being, people in our system will instinctively perceive this and naturally move toward it. Having a living relationship with God in our *being* helps the people-system connect with God, although we may never use religious language or even speak openly about our relationship with God. The life of Jesus flows through our *being* into the life of the people-system.

Leaders also influence the spirit of the system through their *doing*. When we as leaders engage in activities such as prayer, worship, repentance, forgiveness, and thanksgiving – on our own and with others – we influence the spirit of the people-system. This happens even when we do these things in the marketplace. When we resolve the iniquity of the past through repentance and when we embrace the positive heritage of the past through thanksgiving, we shape the spirit of the people-system.

When people perceive a healthy spirit in their people-system, they tend to have greater satisfaction in their people-system. They will tend to cooperate more freely. They will also tend to be more open and honest. It helps people feel more optimistic about the future. It also enables people to endure times of difficulty and stress more effectively.

167

THE SOUL OF A PEOPLE-SYSTEM: EMOTIONS

The soul of a people-system has three parts: emotions, mind, and will. Each one has different dynamics operating, so we will deal with each one separately.

The emotions of a people-system are what we call "emotional processes". These emotional processes are constantly active in people-systems. We define emotional processes as "the complex interplay of our impressions, feelings (especially of liking or disliking something), and inclinations in combination with our automatic mental activities of perceiving things around us and remembering experiences from the past which leads us to reflexive thoughts, emotions, and choices".[4] These emotional processes come from everyone present in the people-system at any given time. They continuously influence the emotions and emotional interactions of people within the people-system. Like our human emotions, emotional processes happen automatically.

We are constantly receiving ideas, feelings, and opinions about people and things happening around us. These impressions occur without any conscious thought or consideration. Occasionally, the strength of these impressions causes us to take note of something, but most often they just come and go without any consideration.

We also have a tendency to sense immediately whether we like or dislike something. We meet someone in the shop and we feel like they could be a good friend, but we have no idea why. We walk into a crowded room and we immediately do not like it because there are too many people. This liking and disliking happens to us before we are conscious of it. Other feelings happen as well, such as feeling happy or unhappy, peaceful or disturbed.

We have instinctive inclinations, some of which are natural and others of which are learned. My instinctive inclination is to avoid conflict and crowds. I have sought to develop an instinctive inclination to avoid looking at inappropriate images and to focus on the person I am speaking with at any given time. These inclinations kick in before I realize it.

We automatically perceive things with our senses, some of which we recognize but most of which we filter out. As I sit writing, I have music on in the background; I hear children outside playing; I have the blinds on my window open, so I notice the difference between the light of the sun and the lights in my office; I am sitting in a certain way, which is only partially comfortable; and I am subtly aware of many other sensory inputs. We normally filter out most of these sensory inputs, but we are still aware of them whether or not we realize it consciously. These inputs continuously affect our emotions.

As people, our memories automatically engage with any number of external stimuli. The smell of strawberries immediately invokes thoughts of early summer and my wife (who loves strawberries). Throughout my day, I may suddenly sing part of some obscure song from my past because the thought of the song had somehow been stimulated by something I was doing at the time, as if my life had a soundtrack. Most of the time, I could not identify the specific memory. My memories just trigger automatically. This influences how I am feeling about anything at any given time.

All of these factors work together in us as individuals, as well as in us connected together in a people-system, to stimulate reflexive emotions, choices, and thoughts. These then govern how we interact with others. How we interact with others affects their own reflexive emotions, choices, and thoughts, which in turn affects others as well as us. These emotional processes are occurring whenever people gather, especially when they are part of a people-system.

For example, Jacob walks into a small office party with his friend Ben. Suddenly, Jacob hears Fred's voice, slightly standing out from the quiet roar of the conversations in the room. Jacob remembers how Fred complained about him to their boss, even though Jacob did not feel he had done anything wrong. Although the complaint was not upheld, Jacob still felt those negative memories. Without saying anything, Ben senses his friend beginning to grow tense. Ben remembers how his wife used to have that response whenever she thought Ben was doing something wrong. Ben immediately begins to get annoyed with Jacob because he is wondering what Jacob thinks he (Ben) has done wrong. Fred notices that Jacob and Ben have walked into the room and immediately turns away because he is embarrassed about his complaint about Jacob since he realizes now that Jacob had done nothing wrong. But he has never apologized. Fred excuses himself to get a refill on his drink, causing the woman to whom he was talking to feel that she must have been boring Fred with her conversation. These interactions happen within a matter of seconds, changing the overall interactions throughout the room.

Emotional processes like this are happening continuously in any people-system when people are together. They influence how people function within our people-systems. Whether the emotional processes are positive or negative determines how well people respond to our leadership, even whether we are able to lead at all. We often will not fully realize what is going on. We must seek to become aware of them at any given time in our people-system. The following story illustrates how emotional processes affect our leadership.

Sarah prepared a two-hour motivational training for her staff team. When Phil arrived, she noticed that he seemed a bit down but decided not to pry. The first hour of the training was like walking through treacle. Phil's attitude was gruff and uncooperative. Sarah told the team to take a break. She gently asked Phil how he was doing and discovered that the night before Phil had learned that his wife had cancer. She encouraged Phil and then told Phil to take the rest of the day off to be with his wife. Phil gave her permission to share his news with the team. When the team came back from break, she told them what had happened and then cancelled the remainder of the training. Two weeks later, the training went very well and even Phil seemed engaged.

LEADING THE EMOTIONAL PROCESSES
OF A PEOPLE-SYSTEM

Although emotional processes will shape the effectiveness of our leadership, as leaders we have great power to shape the emotional process of our people-system. In fact, our *being* will affect the emotional processes of our people-system whether or not we want it to. If we are feeling depressed and discouraged as a leader, the people in our people-system will instinctively and often unconsciously discern it. Our discouragement will change the emotional processes in the people we lead, along with their attitudes and behaviors. If we feel positive and hopeful about our people-system, the people will also perceive it. Even if we try to lie to ourselves, the people-system will pick up on it and change the emotional processes.

Because of this, it is essential that our *being* is healthy and grounded in Christ. People perceive when our *being* is grounded in Christ and the health of who we are in Christ brings health to emotional processes. We need to develop good emotional intelligence and awareness about ourselves, becoming aware of our own emotional processes and the impact they are having on others. We also need a realistic assessment of our people-system – its strengths, weaknesses, opportunities, and threats. Such an assessment will enable us to respond in healthy ways to the various emotional stimuli we encounter.

When our being is grounded in Christ, we can maintain a calm and steady presence in our people-system. When extreme or intense emotional processes try to subvert the healthy emotional process of the people-system, our calm and measured response will govern the response of the people-system. Just as a gentle answer turns away wrath and a harsh word stirs up anger (Proverbs 15:1), so also the gentle response of the leader shapes the response of the people-system. How you react emotionally to things going on will help determine how other people react.

171

As leaders, our *doing* also influences the emotional processes of the people-system. If our communications are positive and set a hopeful tone – even when things are difficult – we will enable people in our system to respond more positively. We can choose to emphasize the good and wholesome things in our people-system, which produces joy. We can express appropriate humor, choosing to laugh at ourselves. Taking great care as to how we express anger or frustration makes a significant difference in how the people-system deals with this emotional issue. These things are examples of the many ways leaders can influence emotional processes in a healthy direction through their *doing*.

SOUL OF A PEOPLE-SYSTEM: MIND

Have you ever noticed how people who spend a lot of time together begin to think alike? Over time, people in the same people-system begin to have the same attitudes and the same perspectives. We see this principle at work in the marketplace as well as the church. This tendency to think alike affects our perspectives, attitudes, ideas, and thought processes. We call this tendency for people in a people-system to think alike the people-system "mind".

When people-systems respect and honor the individuality and integrity of the people in the system, this dynamic may shape our values, worldviews, and behaviors in healthy ways. When people-systems exert pressure for conformity and consensus among its members, this dynamic may lead to "groupthink". Groupthink forces the members of the people-system to think in the same way, even when the thinking process is irrational or dysfunctional. In extremely unhealthy situations, this dynamic may lead to brainwashing. Whether healthy or unhealthy, this dynamic is the "mind" of the people-system.

Like individual persons, people-systems tend to have a mind of their own. This is a natural and healthy phenomenon. It is also biblical. In places like Philippians 2:5, 1 Peter 3:8, and Romans 12:1–2, the Bible uses the singular word "mind" in a collective sense.

So when Paul tells Christians to have the "mind of Christ", Paul is telling us together as one people-system to have the mind of Christ. In this case, Paul wants the mind of Jesus Christ as represented in his life and ministry to shape our collective thinking so that we grow together to spiritual maturity as measured by the standard of Jesus (see Ephesians 4:13).

Like individual persons, the primary way to bring transformation is by renewing the mind of the people-system. We can renew the mind of the people-system by discerning and focusing on truth. We can renew the mind of the people-system by testing our common perceptions and perspectives, seeking new and fresh perspectives whenever possible. We can renew the mind of the people-system by considering our people-system with sober judgment (see Romans 12:1–3).

Just as with us individually, the primary spiritual battle for our people-system is a battle for the mind of the people-system. This is one reason that the Bible warns so strongly against false teachers and false prophets. False teachers, prophets, and leaders might do much damage to how the mind of a system functions. People-systems also may develop mental strongholds that influence them in ways contrary to the will of God. One might see examples of this in various contexts.

A photography business might become so focused on producing the best film possible for cameras that it misses the digital revolution and the fact that more people are using phones to take pictures than cameras. A church may become so engaged with eradicating poverty that it fails to tell people about the saving grace of Jesus. A nation may become so convinced that another nation is the great Satan that it refuses to negotiate with that nation in productive ways.

We always find changing the mind of a people-system a daunting prospect. But leaders can shape and change the mind of a people-system. The mind of a people-system will always shape the thinking of those in the people-system, so we must promote healthy thought processes throughout the people-system. Over time, these processes will affect the mind of the people-system in healthy ways.

LEADING THE MIND OF A PEOPLE-SYSTEM

As leaders, we influence the mind of our people-systems through our *being*. What you think about and focus on as a leader will determine the thinking and focus of your people-system. This is one reason, for example, why church leaders who want their church to focus on outreach must focus on outreach themselves. If they want a praying church, then they must become praying leaders. If we as leaders value the Bible and ensure that the Bible conditions how we think, then the people we lead will naturally begin to do the same. If the business leader wants financial integrity in her business, then she must ensure she has financial integrity in her personal life.

This explains why vision is so important for leaders. As author and researcher George Barna defines it, vision "is a clear mental image of a preferable future imparted by God to his chosen servants and is based on an accurate understanding of God, self and circumstances".[5] If we have a vision and keep ourselves focused on that vision then our vision will naturally influence the vision of our people-system. The influence of a leader's *being* means that having a vision is as important as the vision itself. People will sense whether we have a vision and positive direction which will then help them decide whether to follow us.

Our *doing* as leaders also shapes the mind of our people-systems. The mind of people-systems will share many similarities with the minds of their leaders. The sermons we preach – or, in the case of the marketplace, the messages we send – and the perspectives we communicate influence the mind of the system. How people see us publicly engage in thinking and reasoning will influence the mind of our system. The people in our system must know how we think and how we come to the conclusions that we do. If we honor people, they will honor people. If we show grace and mercy, they will show grace and mercy.

SOUL OF A PEOPLE-SYSTEM: WILL

People-systems also have a will. They make corporate choices and decisions. These choices will involve what to do and what not to do. They will involve who will or will not be leaders in the people-system. Voting is a common way that many people-systems express their will. The choices and decisions of the people-system will reflect the true values of that system.

How people-systems exercise their collective will tells us a lot about the people-system. For example, all churches will tell us that outreach and prayer are very important, perhaps the most important activities of churches. But many of these churches do very little outreach or prayer. A company may say that they exist to enrich its clients. But if the only ones who get rich are the top executives then that people-system shows its real will.

People-systems may tell us what they value, but what they actually do shows us what they value. In these situations, the spirit, emotions or mind of the people-system will be influencing the will of the system. So if we try to change the will of the system before we change the spirit, emotions or mind of the system, then we will almost always fail. People-systems will do what they have been spiritually, emotionally, and mentally conditioned to do. This is as true of a small group meeting in a home as it is a nation.

When a people-system experiences volitional gridlock – where it is difficult or impossible for the people-system to make decisions and take actions due to conflict within the people-system – it suggests that the people-system has dysfunction or disease due to disunity or lack of discipline. In such cases, people-systems will struggle to choose good leadership and, when it has good leadership, will tend to undermine the leaders. Such conditions will often take a long time to resolve. It involves managing the emotional processes of the people-system so that we might guide the mind of the people-system to new perspectives and ways of thinking. It will often involve influencing the spirit of the people-system as well.

LEADING THE WILL OF THE PEOPLE-SYSTEM

In order to lead the will of our people-system, our *being* must remain well connected to the people-system. People in the system must know and believe that our destiny as the leader is fully connected to the destiny of the people-system. If we are double-minded in our *being,* such as hoping that everything turns out alright but making plans to leave, then our people-system will not have the courage to make difficult choices and decisions. We must be determined to persevere when people in the people-system do not do what we think they should right away.

Our *doing* as leaders must model healthy choices and healthy relationships. We must be able to say "no" even more than we say "yes". We have to embrace the reality that some of the choices and decisions we make will disappoint and even upset people. How we respond to people when they are disappointed and upset will determine how the people-system responds when it has to make difficult choices that disappoint or upset people. We must seek good outcomes, but refuse to appease those who will not cooperate with the people-system or those who seek to disrupt the people-system.

If we expect our people-system to make difficult choices, then we must first make difficult choices ourselves, ones that benefit the people-system. If we want people to sacrifice for the common good, then we must model healthy sacrifice for the common good. If we want our people-system to anchor its choices in the Bible, then we must visibly anchor our choices in the Bible and show people how we do this.

As the soul of a people-system, the emotions, mind, and will of the people-system are constantly interacting with one another. They influence each other continuously even as they influence each other in an individual human being. For the soul of a people-system to be healthy, life must flow from the spirit of the people-system.

THE BODY OF A PEOPLE-SYSTEM

People-systems also have what we might call a "body". However, because the concept of "body" has different connotations in places like 1 Corinthians 12, we will also call this aspect of the people-system its "flesh and bones". The flesh and bones of a people-system includes things like the structures created by the people-system (such as buildings), the policies and procedures they develop (such as a constitution), the ways the people-system portrays itself to the world (such as a website), and how the members of the people-system interface with one another (such as workplace teams and small groups in church).

The flesh and bones of a people-system – what some people have called the "corporate culture" of the people-system, although over the years that phrase has taken on a broader meaning – is an expression of the interplay of the spirit, soul, and leadership of the people-system. The flesh and bones of a people-system tends to grow as the people-system ages, just as the flesh and bones of a human tends to grow as we get older. At some point in the life of every people-system, the flesh and bones will mature and take specific shape. Once this happens, the flesh and bones will begin to influence the spirit, soul, and leadership of the people-system in increasingly greater degrees.

We must take care as we shape the flesh and bones of our people-system because eventually the flesh and bones will shape us. For example, the sanctuaries of many historic churches were built using fixed wooden pews. Those pews face forward toward the two pulpits at the front of the sanctuary. This may create the impression that Christian worship is a spectator event much like a theatrical production. Yet most church leaders would say that worship should engage people with God and with one another. I know other churches that were built in the round, with worshipers on three or four sides of a central platform. This creates a different feel for the worship service. In this situation, the building – part of the flesh and bones

177

– affects the spirit and soul of the people-system, perhaps in ways contrary to our preferences.

When I was setting up my office at the church I considered the influence of a flesh and bones issue – the placement of my desk. Instead of placing my desk in the middle of the room opposite the door with my chair on the side away from the door I decided to place my desk against the wall with my chair between the desk and the door. This way, whenever someone came into my office I was able to greet them personally without anything between us. My desire was to create a sense of openness and approachability. In a recent reordering of my office, I put my desk in a side cupboard and created a meeting space in the main room. In this way, people do not interact with my desk at all. People who come into my office say they feel comfortable and at home – precisely what I wanted to create with part of the flesh and bones of my people-system.

The influence of the flesh and bones occurs not only in the physical structures of a people-system, but in the other structures such as policies, procedures, websites, and the like. How a church orders its worship service is a flesh and bones issue that determines how people perceive and experience the church. How a business leader develops his staff policies shapes how the staff will interact with that leader and with one another.

Many people make the mistake of assuming that the flesh and bones of a people-system is a bad thing, that having unmistakable and solid flesh and bones means a lack of freedom and much bureaucracy. However, without flesh and bones, life as we know it cannot exist. A human being without flesh and bones would be an ill-defined and unrecognizable mess. The same is true with people-systems. In order for people-systems to thrive and persevere, they must have flesh and bones.

Problems only come when the flesh and bones of the people-system either becomes too fat or ossified. Too much flesh on our bones – too many programs and procedures, unwanted buildings, and the like – becomes a drag on the health of a people-system.

Healthy people-systems must trim down to the bare minimum. If our bones become hardened and inflexible – if our policies become set in stone and difficult to change as needed – then we will risk the breakdown of the people-system. At the least, it will not have the ability to function well.

LEADING THE BODY OF A PEOPLE-SYSTEM

One of the greatest mistakes leaders make is assuming that they can lead by changing the flesh and bones of a people-system. We assume if we have the right structure in place then people will naturally conform to it. People-systems do not function this way. The histories of churches, businesses, and nations are filled with stories of leaders who failed because they tried to lead by first changing the flesh and bones of their church, business or nation.

Leaders begin to shape the flesh and bones of their people-systems by understanding and respecting the flesh and bones of the people-system. Leaders must become aware of the areas of consistency and inconsistency between their own *being* as leaders and the flesh and bones of the people-system. For example, some leaders thrive in a highly regimented context, while others prefer a context that offers them great freedom. If people who prize freedom and free expression become leaders of people-systems that have strong rules and procedures, then they will inevitably experience a conflict between their *being* and the reality of the people-system. Leaders may only begin to change the flesh and bones once they have a healthy sense of *being* grounded in Christ that allows them to evaluate the flesh and bones of a people-system calmly and respectfully, showing appropriate appreciation for what exists.

David had served as the minister of an independent charismatic church for a number of years when he was called to become the minister of a charismatic church led by a group of elders. In his previous church, David made all the major decisions by himself, consulting with church members and various professionals only as needed. His new church had a consultative form of governance in which no action was taken unless agreed amongst all the elders. At first, David failed to recognize the differences between the two governance structures. He often acted unilaterally, not respecting the leadership of the other elders. After a few confrontations, David decided to re-examine his own presuppositions and to try to understand better the leadership structure of his new church. Once the other elders felt David's respect and willingness to change personally, they began a conversation with David about how they all could lead more effectively. This led to a change in some policies and procedures that gave David more freedom in certain areas and defined more clearly those areas on which the eldership needed to agree before action was taken. The church grew healthier because of this new arrangement.

Leaders who want to bring change to the flesh and bones of a people-system must begin by promoting health in the spirit and soul of the people-system. Then leaders must enable the people-system to see areas of consistency and inconsistency between the spirit and soul of the people-system and how that is manifested in the flesh and bones of the people-system. People in a system will often respond more positively to change in the flesh and bones when they see the change as a better demonstration of the spirit and soul of the people-system.

The flesh and bones of a people-system carries the spirit and soul of the people-system, allowing the spirit and soul to interact more effectively with the world around it. When the flesh and bones are congruent with the spirit and soul, people will perceive that the people-system has authenticity and integrity. When the flesh and bones are incongruent with the spirit and soul, people will sense that the people-system is hypocritical and untrustworthy. Leaders have a major responsibility for ensuring the congruency between these aspects of the people-system.

The spirit, soul, and body of a people-system constantly influence the people within that system. They enable people-systems to become agents of transformation in people's lives – for better or for worse. Our major influence as leaders will be to influence the spirit and soul of our people-systems through our *being*, not just our *doing*. That is why healthy leadership is essential for a healthy people-system. Having our *being* grounded in Christ becomes a major advantage as it anchors our *being* in the life of Jesus and allows us to seek the welfare of our people-system without any selfish agenda on our part.

HEALTHY PEOPLE-SYSTEMS

Healthy people-systems naturally promote healthy people. Healthy people-systems help build a healthy and stable society. However, with all the diversity of people-systems in the world, how do we know when a people-system is healthy? We have found that healthy people-systems have three characteristics, no matter whether they are churches, businesses or governments.

Mutual submission

The first characteristic is mutual submission among its members and between its leadership and its members (Ephesians 5:21). Unfortunately, most people do not understand the biblical concept of "submission". Submission is not blind obedience. Submission is not doing the bidding of another. Submission is not allowing someone else to control or manipulate us. Submission is not tolerating and cooperating with sin.

Submission is the spirit of cooperation with one another so that we become the best we can be, individually and corporately, and together we achieve beneficial outcomes.[6] To have mutual submission, we must seek God's best for each other and for our people-system. When this happens, we will experience the benefits together. When we submit to one another, we want the other person to be the best they can be, knowing that if the other person is their best then that will benefit everyone.

David leads a small conference center in the city with eight staff members. Each staff member has their own area of responsibility, but all staff members must help one another as needed. They also must practice consultation at all levels, meaning they must consult with one another (and occasionally David) before making significant decisions, especially if those decisions affect anyone else. When they are all working together, the leadership rotates among them based on the area of responsibility. So, when Rebecca has a major catering job to prepare, everyone might work together in the kitchen for a time. When that happens, even David follows Rebecca's directions. When Tom, the building supervisor, needs help to set up the rooms for clients, everyone responds to Tom's directions. They help each other and work together for the conference center to thrive. Each person's success, including David's, depends on everyone else. Cooperation – or mutual submission – benefits everyone.

Mutual submission does not imply tolerating sin or wrongdoing. Continuing with the example, David has a policy that if any staff member perceives that he is making a mistake or doing something wrong but fails to tell him then that staff member would be guilty of gross misconduct and subject to dismissal. David encourages staff members to work out their issues with one another, and there are healthy processes in place when intransigent problems arise.

With mutual submission, leaders must win the cooperation of their followers instead of forcing obedience through institutional or personal power structures. This begins with leaders having a healthy *being* that others trust. People must respond to our character and integrity in a way that gives them the desire to follow. David treats everyone in his people-system as a volunteer, even when they are paid staff. He shows appreciation and respect for each person and that person's contribution to the whole. He has discovered that if he begins to feel that he has to command obedience then it is likely that the staff member needs to move on.

Unity

The second characteristic of a healthy people-system is unity (Psalm 133; Ephesians 4:3). Unity is a sense of cohesiveness and coherence. Cohesion means people are committed to one another as a united whole. People work together in solidarity. Coherence means that people have consistency and orderliness. They are committed to working together in an orderly and focused way.

Unity arises from four things in a people-system. First, unity comes from a commitment to excellence throughout the people-system. Excellence is doing our best with the resources at our disposal as the people God has made us to be. We must promote excellence in every facet of our people-system.

Second, unity comes from a compelling vision leaders communicate to the people-system. In order for unity to occur, we must communicate the vision repeatedly and consistently. The people-system must also embrace the vision that the leader communicates.

Third, unity comes through a clear mission or purpose for the people-system. Vision answers the question "Where are we going?" Mission answers the question "What are we going to do as we get there?" People in the system need to know the core business or primary purpose of the people-system. Having realistic goals and coherent strategies will help in this regard.

Fourth, unity flows from healthy leadership. When the *being* of the leader is strong and healthy, the leader will naturally draw people closer together as they grow closer to the leader. This does not mean that the leader must be everyone's "best friend" or spend an equal amount of time with everyone. This means that people must sense the health of our *being* as leaders so that they trust and respect us. Our integrity as leaders brings integrity into our people-systems.

Love

The third characteristic of healthy people-systems is love (Colossians 3:14). Love is a selfless concern for the well-being of others. It is a sense of altruism, working for the good of everyone. Love does not mean some sense of romance or sentimentality. It is not soft. Love involves a sacrificial giving of ourselves to see God's best accomplished in the lives of other people.

People-systems must have genuine love. In the marketplace, love involves actively seeking the beneficial outcomes as discerned by the five questions for beneficial outcomes. Historically, many businesses started with a genuine desire to benefit people, including their employees, instead of simply a desire to make money. Cadbury, Rowntree, Guinness – these are just some names of people who began businesses to benefit society. Even today, many entrepreneurs launch businesses because they have an idea how to make life better for people. Of course, businesses need to make money in order to survive and benefit their employees, but for many money is only one motivator.

Leaders who show love become compelling leaders that people want to follow. When we have love for our people-system and the people we lead – as well as the people we serve or benefit – people will give us more grace and trust us more fully when we go through difficult situations. Love requires us to seek the benefit of our people and people-system, even if it costs us personally – as often it will.

When systems embody these characteristics they are healthy. They will have a positive influence on other people. They will naturally tend to promote beneficial outcomes.

SICK PEOPLE-SYSTEMS

People-systems may also become sick. There are three characteristics of sick people-systems.

Rebelliousness

The first is rebelliousness, where people refuse to cooperate with one another. People make demands for themselves and seek their own advantage. They try to impose their will on everyone else.

In order to recognize rebellion, we need to know the distinction between rebellion and immaturity. As leaders, we need to realize that rebellion and immaturity may initially look the same, but they are very different. Immaturity describes people who do not take responsibility for their own mind, will, and emotions. Immaturity may also describe people who have not become familiar with the culture of a new people-system they have joined. Each people-system has different ways of doing things which new members must learn. New employees need time to learn the expectations and requirements of their employers. This is why most businesses have a probationary period.

Rebellion describes a stubborn refusal to cooperate, insisting on one's own way. It takes time to distinguish rebellion from immaturity, because it takes time for people to "grow up". People who are immature have a genuine desire to become mature, and will respond quickly to healthy leadership. Rebellious people will not improve their behavior over time. They might seem better for a season, but they will always regress into their rebellion.

Leaders can help immature people through training and personal coaching. Unfortunately, there is no real cure for rebellion – at least in a natural sense, because only Jesus can heal our rebellious hearts! – so leaders will often have to remove rebellious people from the people-system. As leaders we must realize that rebellion, as with many sicknesses, is highly contagious, so simply tolerating or isolating it will never heal a people-system.

Factionalism

The second characteristic of sick people-systems is factionalism. In factionalism, people form sub-groups within the people-system that are opposed to others within the system. This opposition may be directed against other individuals, other groups or leaders. In factionalism, each person or group seeks their own advantage or their own benefit. The people-system becomes highly political, with people playing various power games in order to gain the upper hand.

One of the clearest indicators of factionalism is secrets, gossip, and rumor-mongering. People hoard information for themselves. They share information and misinformation with a select few. One will often hear two very different versions of the same story coming from the same person. People will also frequently use some form of the phrase, "People are saying..." When pressed to give a name, they will be unable or unwilling to do so.

As leaders, we must expose factionalism for the evil that it is. Whether it exists in the church or the marketplace, factionalism destroys people-systems. One reason many governments are completely ineffective is that they have tolerated, and even endorsed, some form of factionalism.[7] We must not tolerate those who set themselves up in opposing groups. We also must not tolerate any form of anonymous communication. Anonymous communication allows people and groups to do much damage without taking any personal responsibility.

Selfism

The third characteristic of unhealthy people-systems is selfism. Selfism entails a radical sense of selfishness – self-centeredness, self-promotion, self-aggrandizement – in the people-system. Whereas love focuses on the benefit to others, selfism seeks the benefit of oneself, with little reference to others.

People-systems express selfism in two ways. First, the people-system may have a corporate selfishness. One example of this might be the banking crisis of 2008, where it seemed that many financial institutions had so focused on making money for themselves and their employees that they had forgotten their duty to their account holders and society in general. Another example would be the church that has become more of a social club, benefiting the members but ignoring its community.

Second, people-systems may tolerate or even encourage personal selfishness. When a people-system has a number of its members seeking their own personal perception of good – or their faction's perception of good – that people-system is bound up in selfism. Employees in a small business may start working simply for the paycheck, not seeking to contribute to the productivity of the business. Church members may demand the time and attention of the minister, diverting him from working with others. Selfism in people generally promotes factionalism and rebelliousness.

Leaders can reframe the challenges and issues of a people-system in a way that inhibits selfism. For example, some churches may ask the more self-oriented question, "how can we get more members?" Leaders may reframe this as "how can we make disciples more effectively?" or "how can we serve the people in our community better?" Such reframing will often help people-systems think more creatively.

Leaders need to set the example of self-giving and resisting selfism. At the same time, we must appreciate that many of our attempts at self-giving are actually selfishness in disguise. A business leader may cover her employee's mistakes seemingly as an act of self-sacrifice and concern for the employee when actually she simply does not want to look bad personally or she does not want to do the difficult task of dismissing the employee. A pastor may rush to respond to every cry for help seemingly as an act of self-giving love when actually he gets his personal sense of significance from being needed by everyone. In order to set an example of self-giving, we must ensure our *being* is grounded in the self-giving love of Jesus Christ.

We need to challenge selfism as leaders – in ourselves, our followers, and our people-system. Challenging selfism directly will often reinforce it by driving people into self-defense. However, we can challenge selfism indirectly by asking good, reflective questions that help people consider others more fully. We can also challenge selfism indirectly by upholding examples of loving behavior publicly and privately.

Whenever a people-system has one or more of these characteristics it will be dysfunctional. If we fail to address and resolve these symptoms as leaders, eventually our people-system might die altogether.

BUILDING A HEALTHY PEOPLE-SYSTEM

Although people-systems greatly influence our leadership effectiveness, for good or for ill, as leaders we have a tremendous ability from God to influence our people-systems. In fact, one of the highest responsibilities of leadership is to help create and build healthy people-systems. Healthy people-systems will help build healthy people and help create a healthy society. The failure to see the need for healthy people-systems and then work diligently and sacrificially to create those healthy people-systems is one of the great leadership failures of our time.

As leaders, we have great power to influence our people-systems. But the power we have is primarily about who we are, not what we do. So many leaders waste time trying to find the right thing to do when actually our focus needs to be on becoming a healthy person with our *being* grounded in Jesus Christ. With our *being* grounded in Jesus Christ, we will naturally become leaders who influence our system to become healthy and to stay healthy.

Our *being*, more than anything we do, helps to set the mood and tone of our people-system. Our *being* grounded in Jesus Christ will naturally regulate in a positive way the spiritual, emotional, and rational processes of our people-systems — much as the autonomic processes of a healthy brain naturally regulate the functioning of the body.

Of course, our influence depends on our own spiritual health and how well we are connected to our people-systems. If we are not healthy and grounded in Jesus Christ, finding our significance, security, and acceptance in him, then we will be hindered in promoting a healthy people-system. If we are not genuinely and authentically connected to our people-system, having a tangible, loving presence in their midst and a strong commitment to remain connected, then we cannot influence it to become a healthy people-system.

Healthy leaders enable people-systems to connect with God's sovereign purpose for them (1 Peter 2:4–10). Healthy leaders will enable people-systems to identify and repent of corporate wrongdoing (Nehemiah 1:6). Healthy leaders enable systems to stand against the devil's schemes (2 Corinthians 2:11). Because of our influence on our people-system, we have been given the power and authority to help resolve issues in our people-systems — helping the system to choose to believe the truth, helping people in the system to repent personally and corporately, and helping the system submit to God and resist the devil.

THE LEADERSHIP DILEMMA

But we have another leadership dilemma. As healthy leaders, we might shape and transform the people-system until the people-system becomes healthy also. But only if we survive long enough! Unhealthy systems will often expel healthy leaders before they complete the task. I have heard it said that no pastor or boss can be said to be really effective unless they have been fired at least once. While this may not be true, it is true that leading people-systems has become more difficult today than ever before, for many of the reasons shared in the first chapter.

This means that our leadership context will determine our leadership effectiveness far more than we as leaders will realize or want to admit. This will help keep us humble and grounded in Jesus Christ as leaders. To paraphrase the words of Solomon quoted earlier: "Again, I saw that no matter where you are the race is not to the swift, nor the battle to the strong, nor bread to the wise, nor riches to the intelligent, nor favor to those with knowledge, but time, and chance, and people-systems happen to us all."

7

LEADING IN SITUATIONS

The nation will find it very hard to look up to the leaders who are keeping their ears to the ground.

Sir Winston Churchill

The ultimate measure of a man is not where he stands in moments of comfort and convenience, but where he stands at times of challenge and controversy.

Martin Luther King, Jr.

Not the cry, but the flight of a wild duck, leads the flock to fly and follow.

Chinese Proverb

Sue hated difficult conversations. She liked to be everyone's "best friend". She practiced management by walking around, stopping by people's work stations on a regular basis to check in, problem solve, and give whatever guidance might be needed. So, when she scheduled a meeting with Steve in her office, she dreaded having to give him a written warning for his poor job performance. As they began the conversation, she knew she would have problems when Steve showed little awareness of his poor performance – although she had discussed these issues with him before. Immediately, he became very defensive, almost aggressive toward Sue. But Sue responded calmly yet firmly. Steve quickly settled down and then fully engaged in the conversation. He finally acknowledged the problems and owned his responsibility for failing to work to the expected standards. They agreed an action plan for correcting poor performance, with a follow-up meeting scheduled in two weeks. Sue decided to withhold the written warning in order to give Steve more time for improvement. Steve left in an upbeat mood. Sue was exhausted, but felt good that the meeting had gone well.

The story of Sue and Steve involves the second context of leadership: situations. When we think about leadership, we normally think about leadership in the context of the various situations of life. Most everything written about leadership involves this context of leadership. The many leadership books on subjects as varied as time management, financial management, people management, human resources, conflict resolution, and others are usually focused on how we address these issues in the context of the situations we face throughout our day and our week as leaders.

SITUATIONS DEFINED

Situations are simply the episodes of life. They are the combination of circumstances at any given moment and in a given environment. Situations arise in the midst of various people-systems. Situations shape the course of our lives even as we live from one situation to the next. People-systems, situations, and people are in a state of constant interaction and mutual influence.

We were having lunch with a couple on our staff who are good friends as well. Sitting next to the front window of the restaurant enabled us to enjoy the sunshine, the traffic passing by, and our shared meal. Suddenly, my wife jerked to attention as a car and a cyclist had a minor collision on the opposite side of the road. Our natural instinct was to get up and go to the accident, but we noticed that several passersby had already stopped to assist the cyclist, who was lying on the ground at first but indicating that he was OK. The car had stopped as well. We saw people seemingly calling the police and ambulance services.

We relaxed and carried on with our conversation and meal, although the events unfolding outside continued to draw our attention. Soon the ambulance arrived to assist the cyclist. Immediately, the people who had stopped to help stepped aside to allow the paramedics space to work. Eventually, the police arrived as well, with one officer speaking to the driver of the car and another interviewing others and making notes. When questioned by the police, almost everyone stood up straighter and seemed to become even more sober in their body language. In the end, everyone seemed fine and went their own ways. The whole episode unfolded over the course of twenty minutes or so.

We can easily see in this episode how people, people-systems, and minute-by-minute changes in the situation continually influenced one another. We see how the introduction of authority figures changed the situation. We see how leadership influenced the way the situation unfolded. My leadership influenced those with me: if I would have run out to the accident, then my lunch companions would have joined me. When I relaxed, they relaxed. We have the leadership of the first passerby who immediately stopped to help the cyclist. We have the leadership of the paramedics and the police. Each leader influenced how the situation unfolded. All these dynamics – and many more – worked together to create the situation and determine its outcome.

Leadership always occurs in the situations of life, within the context of various people-systems. Much of the training and writing of leadership involves how to lead in situations. So instead of focusing on what others have covered well, in this chapter we want to alert you to a number of issues we often miss regarding leadership in situations. We will also discuss how the *being* and *doing* dynamic governs our leadership in situations.[1]

PEOPLE IN SITUATIONS

Most of us share a common delusion. This delusion blinds us to many powerful influences that determine our behavior every day. Failing to recognize the power of this delusion makes us victims of it automatically. For many, the failure to recognize this delusion leads to feelings of guilt, failure, weakness, and despair. Allowing this delusion to remain in our lives might actually put us in a place where God opposes us – even as Christians.

Our delusion is that we are powerful individuals who are stronger than the situational forces operating in the episodes of our lives. All people tend to believe that they make logical and rational choices and decisions independently of other factors operating at any given time. We think that we are in control of our lives, at least of our decision-making processes. We see ourselves as sovereign individuals, "captains of our fate", who steer our "ships" through the tumultuous seas of life unhindered by the crashing waves and the driving winds.

This delusion drives us to a place of pride and self-sufficiency. We see a report about a police officer's grievous actions on the evening news and think if we were in that situation we would never do what the police officer did. But we are not in that situation. We have no idea what we would do. We just assume we are above such behavior and surely would exercise better self-control. In this way, this delusion brings us to a place where even God has to oppose us. As the Bible says, "God opposes the proud but gives grace to the humble" (see James 4:6).

If we reflect, even for a moment, we would quickly notice the delusional nature of our sense of invulnerability to situational forces. Certainly, advertising agencies understand how influenced we are by the ads we encounter in the episodes of life. Supermarkets understand that where they place products on the shelf will guide how consumers buy the products. Salespersons know that there are certain techniques they can use to persuade us to buy products, even products that we do not want or need. Drug dealers know how peer-pressure leads people to try drugs. Young engaged couples committed to sexual purity before marriage often discover – to their great shame and sadness – that being alone in a private place "making out" may lead to the defeat of their strongest moral commitments.

Ironically, the delusion that we are invulnerable to situational forces makes us more vulnerable to situational forces. Thinking that we may easily resist situational forces, or even failing to consider they exist at all, blinds us to their reality and to their influence over us. However, our blindness does not negate their influence. Instead, it gives their influence free reign in our lives.

At this point, what we have said might lead us to assume that situational forces are inherently bad or evil. After all, most of the examples we think of regarding the power of situational forces are negative.[2] However, situational forces may just as easily lead toward behavior that is good and virtuous, especially within the context of a healthy people-system.

For example, in our opening story, it was situational forces at work that led Steve to calm down and engage with Sue in a positive manner after an angry start. When I have played golf in the past, it was situational forces that enabled me to exercise self-control and not swear when I made a really poor shot. Situational forces at work during a time of worship lead people to engage in worship in a positive manner. Every day, situational forces promote behavior that is good and virtuous.

Any healthy people-system depends on situational forces to help it function well. In a healthy people-system, situational forces lead us toward cohesiveness. They help persuade us to cooperate with one another harmoniously. They make us tend to follow good leadership. They can promote a sense of altruism.

Obviously, unhealthy people-systems magnify the power of situational forces to produce bad outcomes, or even evil ones. A Christian student traveling home with non-Christian friends gets sucked in as the non-Christians begin to harass a teenager with a mental disability. Afterwards, he feels ashamed of himself – realizing his sin – and wonders how he could possibly do something so against his principles and values. It was not the absence of values – or even the weakness of his values – it was the power of situational forces. As Paul says, "Bad company ruins good morals" (1 Corinthians 15:33).

So situational forces may work for good or for evil, but these forces are always stronger than individual forces. These forces are so strong that they may bring about significant character change, as in my example above. However, understanding the power of situational forces does not excuse anyone from personal responsibility for their behaviors and attitudes. Situational forces do not remove our culpability. People are not helpless victims to these forces. We can act responsibly and powerfully in the face of situational forces. As leaders, we may even shape and change situational forces through our leadership.

TWO KEY PRINCIPLES

People can alter the impact of situational forces with both their *being* and their *doing*, but generally not without recognizing the power of these forces. Recognizing the power and influence of situational forces leads us to two important principles:

> **Personal influences are weaker than we assume.**

> **Situational influences are stronger than we assume.**[3]

We must begin by admitting the truth of both these principles if we are to learn how to resist the negative influences of situational forces. We also need to affirm both these principles if we are to learn how to lead in light of the power of situational forces.

We must begin by admitting fully that we are weaker than we

would like to think. We must set aside our illusion of power and embrace our weakness. We might think that if we heard a woman crying out for help because she was getting beat up by a group of thugs then we would run to her rescue, but experience tells us that most people would not respond. We might like to think that if we came into a group of people who were gossiping and saying all manner of evil against another person then we would quickly step in and ask people to stop, telling them that gossip was sin. However, experience reveals that most of us would just listen and say nothing.

Acknowledging our weakness has two benefits. First, it allows us to take a sober assessment of ourselves as required by Scripture (see Romans 12:3, for example). Such an assessment allows us to make important adjustments in our thinking and behavior. Second, it leads us to invite God to come and meet us at our point of need. The power of God comes into our situation and we can discover along with Paul that when we are weak, he is strong, for his power is perfected in weakness (see 2 Corinthians 12:9–10).

By "personal influences" in our principle above, we mean all the things within our *being* that we might normally have at our disposal. This includes our values, our upbringing, our natural disposition, and our culture. These influences shape us over the course of our lives, but in the urgency and demands of the situational moment they often fail us.

This leads us to the second principle, that situation influences are stronger than we assume. We will discuss four of these situational influences below, but there are others. Daniel Kahneman's work referenced earlier shows the power these situational forces have to direct our decision-making processes. These forces exert much more influence than we would ever realize without examining them.

Becoming aware of the power of these forces does not mean that we must fear these situational forces. Just as we would not fear electricity but respect it and take care regarding its use, so we need not fear situational forces as long as we respect them and take care regarding them. Becoming aware of their power also will generally not lead us to feel helpless or victimized by situational forces. Such awareness may lead us to learn how to overcome their power and influence for bad and use their power and influence for good.

In a forest fire, good firefighters will respect the power of the fire and understand the damage it might do not only to the forest but also to them personally if they are trapped in the middle of the fire. The goal of firefighters will be to extinguish the fire so that it does as little damage as possible. At the same time, firefighters may have to start little fires in order to create a firebreak that keeps the main fire from spreading. Firefighters realize that we can often fight fire with fire and that sometimes fires are healthy for a forest in that they allow forests to replenish their life.

SITUATIONAL FORCES

Every situation we encounter in leadership has at least four powerful situational forces operating. Although there are many more, these four give a good perspective on the power of situational forces – for good or for evil. They also help us see how our leadership can neutralize or overcome the power of these forces for evil and promote the power of these forces for good.

We might use the illustration of an airplane to see the various forces at work. Airplanes have to deal with many competing forces influencing them. We have the power of gravity at work, ensuring that if they stop flying they will certainly crash. We have the power of aerodynamics, manifesting both on the flow of air over the wings as well as through turbulence. We have the second law of thermodynamics, which means that the plane will eventually burn up all its fuel. Some of these influences compete against one another, such as gravity and aerodynamics. However, as humans we have generally learned how to minimize some influences and maximize some others. We deal with situational forces in similar ways.

THE POWER OF THE SPIRITUAL

Spiritual forces are the first situational forces working in every situation. Some of these forces are evil (see Ephesians 6:12, for example) and some of these forces are beneficial. These forces exert such a great influence that Paul reminds us in the Ephesians passage that wrestling with these evil forces becomes one of our greatest struggles. We can see how the spiritual influences situations in the following examples.

Alan arrived to the board meeting late again. He resented David's leadership of the board. A "little voice" seemed to tell him from time to time that David was destroying the company, not moving quickly enough to take advantage of various market forces that seemed to be in their favor. Alan had a talent for saying seemingly "innocent" and funny things that subtly undermined and poked fun at other people. He had frequently used this tactic to disempower Marge, one of David's closest allies. Whenever Alan walked into the room, the atmosphere seemed to change. People became negative and uncooperative. The meetings took twice as long as needed. David's best efforts seemed ineffective. People felt David was simply a poor leader.

Julie had not liked "religious" things ever since her mother forced her to attend church as a child. As an adult now, she felt miserable about her life. Nothing seemed to work. Every relationship she had seemed to fail. So when her friend, Anna, invited her to church, she resisted strongly. Eventually, Anna's kind approach won her over – reluctantly. Julie entered the church building determined not to like anything. She thought it was too cold, the coffee was terrible, the people shallow. Yet, as the people began to sing songs of worship, Julie began to feel her resistance melting away. Instead, she felt as if she was surrounded by a "blanket of love". She could not explain it, but she felt her heart soften and change. When the pastor eventually invited people who wanted to become Christians to respond, to Anna's surprise (and Julie's!) Julie was the first person who went forward.

The spiritual exerts a subtle force, often not perceived. The spiritual used Alan to create dysfunction in the boardroom. His "little voice" was demonic – and he did not even realize it. The spiritual induced a change in Julie that made her consider the claims of Christ and respond to a sense of God's love. Most leaders fail to consider the power of the spiritual as a force operating in their situations. We often only consider this dynamic as an afterthought, if at all.

THE POWER OF RULES

We all have a natural tendency to obey rules[4] – whether good or bad, useful or useless. Put a "do not walk on the grass" sign in a park where people are normally allowed to walk on the grass and most people will follow the sign. Even if they decide not to obey the rule, you will see that people have a natural tendency to obey which forces them to stop and consider before they violate the rule. God seems to have hard-wired our brains to follow rules, most likely for our safety and security.

People will tend to obey rules even if the rule is nonsensical or harmful. We heard of a pub that set a rule that no bottles could be passed over the bar by the wait staff. A Bible-affirming church passed a rule that no one could raise their hands in worship – although that is clearly in the Bible (see Psalm 28:2, for example) – and that anyone doing so should be asked to stop or be removed from the church. A bank refused to close a dead person's credit card account even though they had access to the obituary, forcing the family to go through a laborious process during their time of grieving. The rules disempowered the staff from acting compassionately, instead leading the staff to act heartlessly in a time of mourning. (Another company closed a similar account in two minutes, even waiving the repayment of the balance on the card.)

Some of the rules we obey are written down and clearly expressed, such as laws, policies, and procedures. Other rules are unwritten, unofficial or verbally expressed, such as the unwritten rules about how people should dress in social situations. Sometimes people make up rules on the fly – such as when a council decides not to hold a parade due to some nebulous and incorrect appeal to "health and safety". No matter how the rules are expressed and communicated, people tend to follow them without much question.

When we choose not to follow a rule, we tend to do so as an act of rebellion as opposed to an act of ignorance or neglect. People see the "do not play ball games" sign and choose to do it anyway. We know the rule that people should get in line, but then decide to jump to the head of the line. We see the "do not remove this label" on our mattresses and decide to remove it anyway – just because we can. These responses to rules demonstrate the power of rules to shape our behavior.

Healthy people-systems and healthy leaders will review and evaluate rules (including policies and procedures) periodically to ensure that the rules guide behavior in ways that are healthy. Just as the rules of the Pharisees created an oppressive environment that disempowered and enslaved people (see Matthew 23), so too many rules or the wrong rules will cause a people-system and its people to become less effective, less satisfied, and less free to function as God intended.

THE POWER OF ROLES

Not only do people respond instinctively to rules, but they also respond instinctively to roles. Every people-system has various roles: leaders, court jesters, police, teachers, and so on. People both inhabit these roles and respond to these roles based on their place within the people-system and the perception of others within the system.

Roles carry enormous influence as well as unique responsibilities. We have already seen how "leaders" will influence a people-system. "Court jesters" are the comedians who allow us to poke fun at ourselves while exposing our inconsistencies. "Police" monitor our compliance to our own rules and procedures and hand out "penalties" when rules are violated. "Teachers" work to see that everyone understands the basic "doctrines" of the people-system. Every role has its "job".

In situations, people often respond to these various roles automatically – whether for good or for bad. Court jesters may imperceptibly slip from poking fun to humiliation. Police may keep the peace or they may arrest the troublemakers and the innocent alike. What is important for us as leaders is to realize the power of the various roles, including our own, operating in any given situation.

We see the power of roles in how people quickly obey someone wearing a uniform – even if that person has no official capacity or influence other than wearing a particular hat or safety vest. Most people find it excessively difficult not to obey someone in a perceived role of leadership.

Healthy systems require certain roles in order to function effectively. The actual police do "protect and serve" more often than not. Politicians do want the best for their country. We need the ability to laugh at ourselves. Leaders may use their influence in healthy ways, seeking beneficial outcomes not only in the long term but also in the moment-by-moment nature of situations.

THE POWER OF SOCIAL APPROVAL

Most of us think of ourselves as influencers, that we influence others at least as much as others influence us. We would like to think that we make up our own minds and that what everyone else does would not affect us much. What we discover is quite different. Social approval wields enormous power in our lives.

Consider the UK expertise of "queuing" or "lining up". It is a social value in the UK that people should queue in an orderly fashion. People who fail to queue meet strong disapproval and furtive distasteful glances. Although most people and organizations have no rules to enforce queuing, people do it rather naturally because of the dynamic of social approval.

The power of social approval leads people toward conformity with the behavior of others. The power of social approval will cause people to dress alike, think alike, and act alike. People will make the same choices. They will support the same political parties as their families. The dynamic of social approval may give people the illusion of independent action, but it is only an illusion. (Think of how any group of teenagers tends to dress alike and act alike even though they might insist they are individualists!)

Not receiving social approval, or even receiving social disapproval, is highly painful. When we do not have social approval, everyone feels uncomfortable and we begin to feel very alone. Social approval makes nonconformity very difficult.

As with the other situational forces, social approval may work for good or evil. Social approval may lead citizens to surrender their Jewish neighbors to the gas chambers, or it may provide a solid base from which people might pursue new ideas and strategies for developing a healthy society. In churches, social approval may become an aid to discipleship, reinforcing healthy discipleship practices and attitudes while supporting people in their personal struggle with the flesh. In businesses, social approval may help new employees adapt to their job and build a sense of camaraderie more quickly.

Leaders benefit from the power of social approval in that it enables them to influence people in their leadership situations toward behaviors that might lead to beneficial outcomes. People will try new discipleship practices – such as new ways of worshiping and praying – because the leader encourages them and others join in. Personally, it was the power of social approval that gave me freedom to raise my hands in worship for the first time.

This chapter considers just a few of the many situational forces operating at any given time in any situation. The forces we have examined briefly here may serve positively or negatively. Some situational forces are generally negative, such as the power of self-serving biases that tend to cause individuals and groups to overlook problems and overemphasize their strengths. However, many work either way. Whatever situational forces inhabit any given moment, we have to remember that we are not merely victims of these forces. We can shape these forces by our *being* and our *doing*, especially as leaders.

SITUATIONAL LEADERSHIP

Situations present some difficult leadership challenges because it is in the midst of situations that we are most prone to surrender our leadership and allow the situational forces to hold sway. Situations have a complex interchange of influences that affect the behaviors and attitudes of people in the situations, including us as leaders. However, we know that we can learn to lead more effectively in our situations.

Unlike leading our people-systems, where our *being* influences the system even when we are not present, situational leadership requires that we are embedded in a situation in order to understand it and influence it. We cannot become "armchair quarterbacks" where we try to influence the direction of the game from the sidelines. This simply will not work in situational leadership.

Leading effectively in situations involves our *doing* as leaders primarily. That is why most leadership training focuses on what we are calling situations and focuses on what to do in various situations. However, as we have seen, *doing* in a healthy way flows from a healthy *being.* For this to happen, we must embrace humility and grace in our situations, recognizing our own weaknesses and vulnerabilities.

Being and situational leadership

Our *being* influences our *doing* in situations in two important ways. First, having a healthy *being* grounded in Christ Jesus enables us to resist situational forces more effectively. They will still have influence in our lives and our leadership, but our *being* can mitigate that influence.

For example, when our *being* is grounded in Christ we will be more sensitive to the Holy Spirit prompting us to recognize that something is wrong. Deborah was meeting with a group of co-workers after work for drinks. As they met, the co-workers began to speak about another person in a highly negative way, deriding the person behind his back. No one had noticed the shift in the conversation but Deborah, who had begun to feel increasingly uncomfortable. Grounded in Christ, Deborah resisted the force of social approval and simply mentioned that she did not think it was good to speak about another person in this way. To her surprise, everyone instantly agreed and the topic changed.

Second, having a healthy *being* grounded in Christ will enable us to use situational forces positively to promote healthy responses in people. For example, when people use our church building inappropriately, we have often found it helpful simply to mention the rule governing appropriate behavior and the good reasons for it. People usually comply quickly. In situations requiring immediate leadership, I find that all I need to do is speak more directly and forcefully for people to respond well because they know that I am the leader.

At the same time, we must take care about people with an unhealthy *being*. Having an unhealthy *being* causes us to tend toward manipulation and control with regard to situational forces. Situational forces influence us because they tap into our need for identity, significance, security, and acceptance. People who have an unhealthy *being* may try to use situational forces to prop up their own sense of identity or significance by manipulating (as opposed to leading) others. I have seen Christian leaders use the power of social approval, for example, as a tactic to induce people to give more money. We rightly resist and expose such practices.

Doing and situational leadership

We might do many things to lead in situations, but we want to consider three. First, we must practice awareness and discernment. In order to lead, we must become aware of the various influences operating in any given situation. We need to look below the surface of what is happening – the details of the situation – and notice what other forces are guiding people's behaviors. Then we need to discern whether or not these forces are beneficial or harmful.

Practicing awareness and discernment means that we must expose the negative situational forces at work. When we see the power of social approval influencing people toward negative behavior, we need to share our observation and the visible effect it is having. When people are following rules that are unnecessary, nonsensical or harmful, we need to expose this and encourage people to see whether these particular rules really are the best approach.

A few years ago the doctor ordered me to the hospital for what he suspected might be a perforated ulcer. The hospital admitted me for a few days so that the doctors could examine me and run a number of tests. (Thankfully, they found nothing seriously wrong.) During that time, various nurses sought to give me a variety of medicines, some of which seemed unnecessary. When we asked why they were giving certain medications, the response was "it is the protocol" – in other words, the rules. We would then ask whether it was really necessary. In almost every instance, the nurse looked surprised, thought about it a moment, and then said that it was probably not necessary. I avoided several unnecessary medications during my stay this way.

Practicing awareness and discernment also means that we become self-aware in the midst of situations. We become aware of where we do not have the skills or knowledge to lead. We become aware of how we are feeling in any given moment. We become aware of how the situational forces are shaping us. This enables us to follow the counsel of Paul, who tells Christians to "stand firm" (see Ephesians 6:13).

Second, we need to learn what I call "deliberate *doing*". In the urgency and clamor of any situation, before we do anything we must learn to stop – to take a pause and cease from any activity. Even if it is only for a few seconds, we must take a break.

Then, we need to slow down our activity. Great athletes perform well when they learn to work in "slow motion". They envision themselves moving more slowly and gracefully – even when they are in a high-energy situation. In those moments, they seek to filter out all extraneous noise and activity in order to focus on the task at hand.

Next, we act deliberately and purposefully. We know what we are doing and why we are doing it. We choose our actions, attitudes, and responses carefully. Deliberate *doing* gives us poise and enables us to exercise self-control – even with powerful situational forces driving at us.

Third, we need to embrace continual training. Soldiers practice drills day after day. They understand these drills may save their lives in the heat of battle. Firefighters practice fighting fires in live-action training grounds, so that they might survive the heat of the flames. Virtuoso musicians practice hours every day – playing scales, doing exercises, and the like. Anyone who wants to succeed in any area of life must have and cooperate with training. By engaging in continual training, people get the ability to respond effectively in an instant, without much conscious thought.

As leaders, we must train ourselves in the same way. We need to become continual learners, using every challenge or success as a learning opportunity. We need to become masters of our areas of service. We must push ourselves beyond our perceived limits, remembering that if we do not do this then God will do it for us. Whatever our field, we strive to become the best we can possibly be, to reach our own standards of excellence.

This is true for our discipleship as well. We practice spiritual disciplines such as prayer, Bible study, fellowship, worship, giving, fasting, and many others. We practice these disciplines not because they make us closer to God (we are already God's children), not because we get God's approval by doing these things (we already have that), and not because they are necessary religious observances, but because these disciplines help prepare us for the situations of life. Continual training in and practice of the spiritual disciplines enables us to respond effectively and immediately, maximizing the opportunities that God has revealed or minimizing the power of the situational forces arrayed against us.

THE LEADERSHIP DILEMMA

We have already suggested our leadership dilemma: we can easily think we are leading in the situations of our lives only to discover that the situational forces have been leading us. Leadership requires humility and alertness if we are to minimize the impact of situational forces and maximize the influence of our leadership – leadership which ironically has influence because of situational forces.

We all may grow in our situational leadership effectiveness. With our *being* anchored in Christ, we can receive training to magnify our strengths and help compensate for our weaknesses. We can learn how to direct and delegate more effectively. In the end, we will discover that in our situations, although people respond to our leadership *doing*, they will perceive our leadership *being*, which will lead them to a greater sense of confidence and a deeper sense of participation in the situation for the good of all involved.

8

LEADING IN SPHERES

You are not here merely to make a living. You are here in order to enable the world to live more amply, with greater vision, with a finer spirit of hope and achievement. You are here to enrich the world, and you impoverish yourself if you forget the errand.

Woodrow Wilson

If you want to build a ship, don't drum up the men to gather wood, divide the work, and give orders. Instead, teach them to yearn for the vast and endless sea.

Antoine de Saint-Exupéry

A man who wants to lead the orchestra must turn his back on the crowd.

Max Lucado

My brother-in-law is an excellent police officer. He has an easy-going nature that puts people at ease – unless they are violating the law. Then, he has a huge presence (meaning that he is a really big man!) that would put healthy fear in the heart of any sane person. He protects and serves the people in a suburb of a major US city. One day he hopes to visit me in London. When he does, I know a number of things he will bring, such as shaving kit, clothes, and – best of all – my sister. I also know a number of things he will not bring – his uniform, his gun, and his badge. For although my brother-in-law serves the people of his city well, he has no right or responsibility to serve the people of London in the same way. In fact, if he tried to do so it would likely result in a longer stay in the UK than he had intended – in one of the nation's prisons.

Few people would fail to see immediately that my brother-in-law could not serve as a police officer in London. However, most of us have never considered why. This illustration alerts us to the third context of leadership: spheres.

SPHERES DEFINED

Your leadership sphere is the total range of your effectual leadership influence. Wherever you have a legitimate leadership influence – your family, your work, your church – falls within your sphere. One Bible passage stands out in reference to this concept of sphere:

> But we will not boast beyond limits, but will boast only with regard to **the area of influence God assigned to us,** to reach even to you. For we are not overextending ourselves, as though we did not reach you. For we were the first to come all the way to you with the gospel of Christ. We do not boast **beyond limit** in the labors of others. But our hope is that as your faith increases, **our area of influence among you** may be greatly enlarged, so that we may preach the gospel in lands beyond you, without boasting of work already done in another's **area of influence.** "Let the one who boasts, boast in the Lord." For it is not the one who commends himself who is approved, but the one whom the Lord commends. (2 Corinthians 10:13–18, emphases added)

In this passage, Paul references his "area of influence". The two Greek words used here are "measure" and "canon", which indicated a rod used to measure things such as areas of land. So another way to express "area of influence" might be the area measured out by God. Our sphere is the area of influence given to us by God.

We have some degree of authority in all the various people-systems and situations in which we are involved, regardless of whether we are leaders. This authority comprises a right and responsibility to act in ways that bring about well-being. The people and the people-system essentially delegate that authority to us by choosing to have a relationship with us and by allowing our presence within the people-system. We may use this authority to act in ways that promote health and beneficial outcomes in all these people-systems and situations. The degree of authority we have comes from a number of factors, such as our position within the people-system, how people perceive us, and our knowledge and skills. However, authority alone does not determine our sphere.

Our sphere emerges when we use that authority to influence people and systems toward beneficial outcomes and consequently see positive impacts from using that authority. We actually influence others so that they, and the people-system involved, respond to that influence and follow us as leaders. Our influence begins to bear good fruit and people experience beneficial outcomes. Everywhere we exercise this positive and effectual influence becomes part of our sphere. As we step into our sphere, our leadership influence increases along with our authority to build people up (see 2 Corinthians 13:10).

THE GRACE-GIFT OF A SPHERE

From our Christian perspective, God assigns our spheres as a gift of God's grace. God determines our spheres for our own benefit and for the benefit of society. God orders the times and seasons for our leadership, setting up leaders and removing leaders (see Daniel 2:21).

In Ephesians 2, Paul discusses how we have been saved by grace through faith. Then Paul tells us that we are God's workmanship who have been created in Jesus to do good works that God has prepared beforehand for us (see 2:10). God has created us in Christ Jesus for certain activities under his loving rulership. The total range of effect for those good works becomes our sphere. Our salvation as well as our good works come by the grace of God. They are a gift.

We can use the concept of stewardship as another way to describe spheres as a gift. Every steward receives a stewardship from the master of the household. The master requires that the steward exercise leadership over his stewardship, leading that stewardship in a manner that conforms to the master's will and values (see Luke 12:41ff.). The steward is called to lead within his stewardship, not simply manage the stewardship. The area of stewardship is the steward's sphere.

Our sphere then is the area of our God-given stewardship. Wherever God has given us a stewardship – our family, job, church – becomes part of the sphere from God. We then have a responsibility to exercise influence within that area so that we do the will of God according to the ways of God.

We must emphasize that a sphere is a gift of God's grace. We do not earn our sphere, nor can we take it by force. We do not receive a sphere because we are a natural leader as opposed to a contextual leader. God assigns our sphere, but that assignment is not based on our value to him, our holiness, our Bible knowledge or whether God thinks we are more competent than others. It comes from his grace.

At the same time, just as we must walk in the good works God has prepared for us (Ephesians 2:10) we must also step up into our sphere. Although the Promised Land was given to Israel by God, they still had to walk into that Promised Land. As leaders we must step up into the sphere assigned to us by God. We have a responsibility and we need to take the responsibility seriously. Jesus had some harsh words for those who failed to exercise faithfully the stewardship the master had given (see Luke 12:45–46).

ENLARGING OUR SPHERE

Once we step into our sphere, we can enlarge our sphere through faithfulness and fruitfulness. Paul reminds us that the Master requires faithfulness from us as stewards (see 1 Corinthians 4:2). Faithfulness is the primary responsibility of stewards. If stewards were faithful, then masters would reward them accordingly. The masters understood that stewards could not always make a profit or have success because of the variables of life and business. But they did demand faithfulness.

Although a master might not dismiss a steward for lack of success, fruitfulness was still important. Masters expected a return on their business. Jesus' parable shows that the fruitful exercise of our stewardship brings enlargement (Luke 19:15ff.). (It is important to note in the parable that the third steward was judged based on a lack of faithfulness, not a lack of fruitfulness.) As we are faithful and fruitful in our stewardship within our spheres – as we use our leadership influence to promote outcomes pleasing to our Master – God will expand our spheres.

STEPPING INTO OUR SPHERES

As we have said, although spheres are a gift of God's grace, we must step into those spheres as leaders. We must assume our responsibilities within our spheres. Awareness of our spheres often unfolds gradually, step by step. The development of our spheres often begins in seemingly small ways. As we are faithful in the small things, God will begin to enlarge our spheres accordingly (see Matthew 25:21). If we are not faithful, we may lose what little we have (see Matthew 13:12).

As our spheres develop, God also works to develop our *being*. When our spheres enlarge, we might become more prone to find our identity or our sense of significance, security or acceptance in our spheres rather than in Jesus. This would lead to all sorts of distortions of our leadership, as we saw in Part Two. Our *being* allows us to maintain our spheres in wholeness, reminding us that it is not the sphere that makes us who we are.

In creating spheres, God's plan is to bless the world and extend his kingdom through his people, particularly through us as leaders. God calls us to use the full range of our effectual influence to reshape our world in accordance with God's will and God's ways. By his grace, God works in partnership with us as leaders to see his kingdom come and his will be done.

We generally step into our spheres in one of four ways. Once we step into our spheres and lead faithfully, our spheres will expand in these same four ways. As our spheres expand, we must maintain our faithfulness in order to maintain our spheres. We also need to keep our *being* healthy and grounded in Jesus.

Acknowledged assignment

The first way we step into a sphere is by "acknowledged assignment". God assigns us a sphere which the people or people-systems within that sphere acknowledge and affirm. We will often use the language of "calling" to express God's assignment.

An example of acknowledged assignment would be the person who feels called to be the pastor of a particular church. The church would need to acknowledge that assignment by hiring or calling the person as its pastor. Without such acknowledgment, the potential pastor would not have the church as part of his sphere.

Although we might use semi-religious language to describe it, acknowledged assignment occurs in the marketplace as well as the church. Henry might feel God has assigned him to be a manager in a major restaurant chain, but the human resources department still has to choose to hire him. If the firm does not choose to hire him, then it is not part of his sphere and Henry needs to reconsider the situation.

Acknowledged assignment often begins with our sense that God has assigned us a sphere. The sense of God's assignment may unfold gradually. We might receive it through a prophetic word or something similar. Or, we might hear it through the voice of other people speaking into our life. We must receive and affirm the assignment.

Once we understand the assignment, the people or people-systems must confirm it. The new business has to hire us as a leader. The people must elect us to serve in government. When we receive the acknowledgment, the confirmation, we know that we have a sphere. Then our sphere might continue to grow in the same way, with God giving us more assignments that are in turn acknowledged by the people and people-systems.

Relationships

The second way we step into our spheres is through relationships. Relationships are a major doorway to any people-system, whether it be a business, church or government. Spheres are fundamentally relational, so it is no surprise that relationships would enable us to step into our spheres. God has an amazing way of connecting people together in a massive relational web by his sovereignty. He will then often use these relational connections as a way to step into a sphere.

I see this in my own life. While ministering in the US, I became part of a renewal organization. Some people from the church I serve came to conferences offered by the organization, which is how we connected to the church in the first place. This led to the church calling me to serve as its minister. The church and this organization sponsored some conferences in the UK. While at one of the conference venues I discovered a flyer for Freedom in Christ Ministries in the UK. I had already been using FIC materials for over a decade at that time, having already met Neil Anderson in the US, so I made the connection with Freedom in Christ UK. This led to me becoming a board member of Freedom in Christ UK as well as developing *Freed to Lead* as a Freedom in Christ Ministry. This represents a very small strand in the relational web God has used to provide a way for not only stepping into my sphere but also having my sphere enlarged.

The wider our web of relationships, the larger our sphere may become as we influence more and more people through our leadership. We could never know at the beginning of any relationship where that relationship may take us. However, if we will listen to the Holy Spirit, he will connect us to people in some marvelous ways.

This process is not the same as networking. Networking enables us to connect with people who may benefit us, either through providing us some goods or services or creating opportunities for us to provide goods or services to others. Networking helps many people develop mutually beneficial professional relationships. God may use networking to help us step into a sphere, but that is not the primary reason for networking.

We must beware any temptation to exploit relationships to enlarge our sphere. We do not advocate seeking out relationships simply for the purpose of increasing our sphere. Our *being* must remain healthy and grounded in Jesus so that we might resist the tendency to use people and relationships for our own benefit. This would violate the principles of Christian leadership we have presented.

Instead, we have to allow our relationships to develop organically. We have to allow our spheres to expand organically. Even so, we still have to cultivate and nurture our relationships, which is really the only way relationships develop in a healthy way. We would encourage people to have an intentionality about their relationships, seeking healthy relationships with as many people as possible. Although we do not exploit relationships, we never know which relationships God may use to expand our spheres of leadership.

Expertise

Solomon reminds us that "a man's gift makes room for him and brings him before the great" (Proverbs 18:16). The basic meaning of gift in this context is "present". However, we may legitimately extend the meaning of the word to include anything that we have to offer or give. Whatever we have to offer in terms of personal skills and resources that has qualities of excellence and worth to others may become our gift. We might use the word "expertise" to describe our gift in this way.

Our expertise often makes room for us to step into our spheres. Expertise includes areas of recognized excellence in our skills, knowledge, spiritual gifts, and abilities. Any area of high competency or proficiency in our lives might serve as an area of expertise. Our expertise represents what we might offer to our people-systems in order to achieve beneficial outcomes.

Regarding spheres, our expertise must have at least three characteristics. First, our expertise must be recognized, acknowledged by others – especially those within our people-system and our sphere. We might have musical virtuosity, but if our sphere is accountancy our virtuosity will have little influence in our sphere. We may play the guitar well, but if no one ever hears us play guitar then it will not affect our sphere.

Second, our expertise should represent genuine mastery of some skill or knowledge. It should stack up to established standards whenever possible. Most often, this means that it will represent our strengths, not a shoring up of our weaknesses. Mastery requires much effort and study. True mastery does not lead to pride but a sense of humility.

Third, our expertise must be communal. It applies to and benefits the wider people-system, not just us. Expertise that is private or expertise that helps only us personally will not make room for us in our sphere.

Paying the cost

A fourth way we step into or enlarge our sphere comes when we "pay the cost" for our sphere. Paying the cost involves sacrifice and suffering for the sake of our spheres. Sometimes leadership seems to come easily. We have good experiences and everyone seems to respond well to our influence. More often, leadership may become a struggle, with much opposition. It will require real personal sacrifice in order to bring about the beneficial outcomes.

Some of the greatest leadership challenges in the world today will require much personal sacrifice in order to overcome. We may likely not experience quick results. Resolving issues like terrorism or the breakdown of society will take great commitment and stamina. We need to count the cost (Luke 14:28) and be prepared to pay the cost.

When we persevere in our leadership, embracing pain and difficulty in the adventure of leadership, we pay the cost for our spheres. When we sacrifice ourselves for the good of our people-system – not because of some martyr complex but because we really desire the best for our people-system – we pay the cost for our people-system. Paying the cost for our people-system may involve many varieties of sacrifice, but it always involves giving ourselves for the best of others.

THE CONTOURS OF SPHERES

As we step into our spheres, we need to know how to map out our spheres. Their boundaries are often very fluid and their shapes ill-defined. So it is helpful to think of spheres having contours, like the boundary lines and geographical features on a map.

Spheres may have many different contours. They may be geographical spheres, encompassing communities, cities, regions, or nations. A member of the British Parliament has a geographical sphere. A police officer often has a geographical sphere. A parish priest has a geographical parish which is his sphere.

Spheres may include our occupations in government, health, finance, education, entertainment or any other area of the marketplace. A teacher has an occupational sphere. A banker will have a sphere in a bank.

Spheres may have a cultural dynamic. We might be called to serve a particular culture, people group, age group, social group or other demographic. A missionary to a people group in Uganda has a cultural sphere. A youth worker in an urban center might have a social sphere in a particular age group.

Our spheres may encompass our social relationships. Our families are always part of our sphere, but this may also include our friends and other general relationships. Pastors and church elders have a sphere that comprises a particular church. Mutual friends share a sphere of influence with one another.

Finally, spheres may cover the spiritual. We might be one of the ministers described in Ephesians 4:11 – apostle, prophet, evangelist, pastor or teacher. We might have a particular ministry. Our sphere may even incorporate areas where God has given us a burden to intercede. If God calls us to pray consistently for North Korea, for example, this might indicate North Korea is part of our sphere, even if we never travel to North Korea.

Spheres may encompass many, if not all, of these contours. We must not limit them but allow God to unfold them for us. If we are unclear, we might ask God to reveal the contours of our sphere. If we do not have clear influence in a particular area then that area is not likely part of our sphere.

SPECIFYING OUR SPHERE

As we map out our spheres, we then need to describe or specify our leadership sphere. We have to do this at regular intervals in our lives since our spheres will expand – and occasionally contract – from time to time. Their contours change. So we need to write down clearly and succinctly our specific sphere, using the contours suggested above. We might include whatever sense of vision or mission God has given for our leadership. We might also include all the people-systems covered in our sphere.

In the passage from 2 Corinthians quoted earlier, Paul suggests several benefits of specifying our spheres. First, identifying our spheres enables us to know our limits, which will often bring greater creativity and passion. Little children generally have a greater sense of confidence and freedom when they play within a well-defined area instead of a large undefined space. Specifying our spheres will bring that same sense of confidence and freedom for our *doing* within our spheres.

Second, specifying our spheres helps prevent us from overextending ourselves. Two common leadership problems are that we have too much to do and that we often struggle to say no. Operating within a specified sphere gives better definition of our responsibilities. We can learn to say no with a greater sense of peace in our *being* that we are doing what we need to do. As a leader, I receive many unsolicited pleas for help from various leaders in nations around the world. Knowing my sphere enables me to decline those not within my sphere without feeling guilty or regretful.

Third, specifying our spheres helps ensure that we do not intrude into other leaders' spheres, which often causes conflict and competition. It also reminds us that we need to practice mutual submission – the spirit of cooperation – with those who share our spheres or whose spheres overlap with ours. Church leaders in a city, for example, would become stronger if they acknowledged one another's individual spheres – their churches – as well as the sphere they share – their city. They would cooperate more fully, honor one another more deeply, and even seek to help one another without a sense of the competition that often plagues church leaders.

Fourth, specifying our spheres enables us to remain humble. It reminds us that not everything is within our spheres, so we depend on others from different spheres. The business leader, for example, recognizes that she needs someone with a sphere that includes accountancy and a sphere that includes the law so that she can operate her pastry shop with excellence. She realizes that she cannot do everything herself. Such humility allows her to focus on her business. Remaining humble also helps us acknowledge when we are not the leader who is supposed to do a certain task or fulfill a certain need.

We encourage people to take some time regularly to discern their sphere and how they might become even more effective in their sphere. Time away nurtures our *being*, which improves our *doing*. Reflecting on our spheres, and our mission and vision within our spheres, will bring a greater sense of confidence to our leadership. Specifying our sphere will also enable us to lead out of rest.

LEADING OUT OF REST

Over the years, I have heard many teachers in Christian circles talk about leading from a place of rest, or leading out of rest. For most leaders, this often sounds ludicrous. Any leader knows that often rest is fleeting. Our lives are crazy. How could we possibly "rest"? Even more, how could we possibly lead and rest at the same time?

We frequently find ourselves longing for rest. We might dream of ourselves on some beach somewhere with no responsibilities whatsoever except eating and drinking. We might fantasize about some adventure holiday, windsurfing, scuba diving, and the like. Or we might think of hiking in the mountains, surrounded by the glory of God's creation. For most leaders such notions of rest become nothing more than a fleeting daydream. However, these notions are not "rest"; they are holidays.

For many, saying that we have to lead from a place of rest suggests that we should get more sleep. It frequently leads us to feel guilty, thinking that we are not eating right, sleeping right or exercising right (and most often we are not doing these things!). So leading out of rest might suggest that we do fewer things and sleep better.

Rest – at least in this context – is not about getting more sleep, relaxing more, taking more vacations or doing less at work. These things are good, but they do not define "rest". To understand "rest" and how to lead out of rest, we need to consider an important Bible passage:

Therefore, as the Holy Spirit says, "Today, if you hear his voice, do not harden your hearts as in the rebellion... As I swore in my wrath, 'They shall not enter my rest.'"

Take care, brothers, lest there be in any of you an evil, unbelieving heart, leading you to fall away from the living God... As it is said, "Today, if you hear his voice, do not harden your hearts as in the rebellion."

For who were those who heard and yet rebelled? Was it not all those who left Egypt led by Moses? And with whom was he provoked for forty years? Was it not with those who sinned, whose bodies fell in the wilderness? And to whom did he swear that they would not enter his rest, but to those who were disobedient? So we see that they were unable to enter because of unbelief.

Therefore, while the promise of entering his rest still stands, let us fear lest any of you should seem to have failed to reach it. For good news came to us just as to them, but the message they heard did not benefit them, because they were not united by faith with those who listened.

For we who have believed enter that rest, as he has said, "As I swore in my wrath, 'They shall not enter my rest,'" although his works were finished from the foundation of the world. For he has somewhere spoken of the seventh day in this way: "And God rested on the seventh day from all his works." And again in this passage he said, "They shall not enter my rest."

Since therefore it remains for some to enter it, and those who formerly received the good news failed to enter because of disobedience, again he appoints a certain day, "Today," saying through David so long afterward, in the words already quoted, "Today, if you hear his voice, do not harden your hearts."

> For if Joshua had given them rest, God would not
> have spoken of another day later on. So then, there
> remains a sabbath rest for the people of God, for
> whoever has entered God's rest has also rested from
> his works as God did from his.
> Let us therefore strive to enter that rest, so that
> no one may fall by the same sort of disobedience.
> (Hebrews 3:7 – 4:11)

In this passage, the writer uses the Hebrews as an example of people who did not enter God's "rest". The failure to enter God's rest occurred when the Hebrews refused to enter the Promised Land (see Numbers 14:1ff.). They refused to believe God, hardened their hearts, and became disobedient. Consequently, they refused to enter the Promised Land. God resolved that they would not enter his rest.

From this passage, we see that "rest" is not the absence of activity or a reclined position. Rest is the release from striving for what we already have and for what God has already promised us. Such rest has two aspects.

The first aspect, implicit in our concept of *being*, involves who we are in Christ. We do not have to strive for identity, significance, security or acceptance because we have already been given these things in Christ. God has made us new creations in Christ Jesus.

The second aspect of rest involves entering the "land" promised to us by God. Rest comes from being in, affirming, and remaining in our "Promised Land". Our leadership sphere is our own "Promised Land". As God gave the Promised Land of the Old Testament, so also God gives us our spheres as a gift of grace, going before us to prepare the way.

We lead out of rest – or we could say out of a "place" of rest – when we are leading in our Promised Land, our sphere, from a faith-filled obedience to God. To rest we must know and fully embrace what God has already given us – identity, significance, security, acceptance – and we must know and believe that we have received what God has already promised us. We must enter our sphere with the faith that God goes with us, giving us the "ground" by his grace.

THE PROMISED LAND OF REST

Our Promised Land is the place of God's blessing over our leadership. Our Promised Land is the place God has called us to and promised to give us. For Isaac, that place was called "Rehoboth", for God had made room for him so that he could be fruitful in that place (see Genesis 26:22). For David, the boundary lines had fallen in pleasant places so that he had a beautiful inheritance (see Psalm 16:6). Our Promised Land as leaders is our sphere.

God has prepared the Promised Land – our sphere – for us (see, for example, Ephesians 2:10) in advance. God has designed us especially for fruitfulness in our sphere. Thus, our sphere is a gift of God's grace. It is part of our inheritance in God's kingdom. From this we can see why knowing our spheres make such a difference in our leadership effectiveness.

God gave his people the weekly sabbath day not because they needed to have a "day off" each week. God gave his people the sabbath to remind us that everything good we have comes from God as a gift of grace. It is not a product of our strong effort, or willpower, or intelligence. God has given us everything good, including our sphere. We have a sabbath, in part, to remind us that we neither created our sphere nor earned our sphere. The sabbath reminds us that we do not maintain our sphere or expand our sphere by our own good efforts. Knowing that our sphere is a grace-gift enables us to rest, knowing that what God has given no one can take away. So we can have peace.

Rest comes as we enter and remain in our sphere, working and leading from that place in a faith-filled obedience to God. This is what we mean when we say "lead out of rest" or "lead from a place of rest". When we know that we are in our sphere, our *being* becomes grounded in the reality that our identity does not come from being

223

in or maintaining our sphere, but from being connected with the life of Jesus. When we know that we are in our sphere, our *being* recognizes that our significance, security, and acceptance come from a healthy relationship with the God who gave us our sphere and not from anything within our sphere – or even the sphere itself, its size or its perceived importance. This gives us the freedom to lead more effectively within the sphere.

When we enter our place of rest, we rest from our efforts, our works, to gain a "place" in the world that God has already given us. We recognize that our skills, abilities, efforts, strategies, and everything else regarding our leadership have no real influence outside God's intentions for us and the Promised Land God has already provided for us to enter.

RESTING IN CONFLICT

Rest does not mean the absence of struggle, conflict or difficulty. When the Israelites finally entered the Promised Land, they had many battles to fight (see Joshua – the whole thing!). They had to contend for their God-given sphere. God required that they do so in the ways he prescribed and according to the values he set forth. His people had to honor him as they entered and remained in their rest, their Promised Land. For Joshua and company, rest meant that God's people could engage in these struggles, experience these difficulties, with the confidence that God had given them the land. It gave them a position of strength and influence because of their connection with God.

In the same way for us as leaders, rest does not mean that we will not experience various difficulties in and around our leadership. We can actually expect these things to happen. Rest means that we face these difficulties with the knowledge that our God has already given us our sphere, so we can be strong and courageous, *doing* the things God has called us to in the way God has outlined we should do them with our *being* grounded in our relationship with him (see Joshua 1:7).

Not looking to our sphere for our identity and not fearing the loss of our sphere enables us to lead freely and confidently in our sphere. Even if we do seem to lose our sphere or part of our sphere, we have confidence that God will lead us to a new Promised Land of rest. When we face conflict and challenges, we can do so with a heart to serve others instead of the desire to prove ourselves that so often leads to conflicts of will and people-system breakdown. We will begin to realize that conflict and challenges are a normal part of leadership, no matter the sphere.

ENTERING BY FAITH

We enter our place of rest by faith. We must choose to believe that God has given us our sphere. We must choose to believe daily what the Bible says about us is really true – that we are "sons" of God (men and women!) and the bride of Christ (men and women!); that we have our deepest needs for significance, security, and acceptance met only in Jesus; that God has created us all as significant, valuable, unique, and beautiful human beings. We must choose to believe that the God who has given us our sphere, our place of rest, is the God who will keep us in our sphere – or lead us into another as needed. Entering and remaining in our sphere requires the daily exercise of faith.

Faith requires us to believe that God intends good things for us in our sphere. Faith in God's intention for good becomes especially important in the midst of suffering. When we are suffering, we can be tempted to believe God is punishing us or that we are failures. However, suffering is a normal part of living. Without suffering in some degree we could not become the people God intends. We must trust that God can work in all things for our good, and that he certainly intends to do so in our spheres (see Romans 8:28).

As with the Israelites, unbelief and disobedience prevent us from entering and remaining in our spheres. If we refuse to believe

God, then we will destine ourselves to wander in the proverbial wilderness of frustration and dissatisfaction. If we refuse to obey God, God will not – indeed cannot – bless us and make us fruitful in our spheres. Only our own unbelief and disobedience will keep us out of our spheres, which means that entering our place of rest is largely up to us. God has given us everything we need otherwise (2 Peter 1:3).

Sam had faced many disappointments. Now in his fifties, he had never married and never had children. He had failed in his chosen career. He had struggled with sickness in the past, but had fought to become generally healthy. In spite of all his problems, Sam had a good place to live. He was surrounded by a church family who loved him. He had many Christian ministry opportunities, which is what he really desired to do. He had longed for a certain kind of Christian ministry for many years, and the church had given him the freedom to pursue this ministry. Yet Sam completely focused on his disappointments. He could not see all the blessings and the possibilities. He refused to see the sphere God had given him. He would not believe, so he continued to struggle and never gained fruitfulness. Although his friends could see what God had provided, Sam refused to believe – even denying the encouragement of his friends. In the end, his behavior caused much relational breakdown which prevented him even more from entering his sphere.

Understanding that the church I serve is part of my own sphere provides some great advantages to me as I minister. I feel no need to prove myself as a minister. I do not evaluate myself based on "results" – such as massive numbers of new members and lots of money – because I have learned how fleeting these things can be. Instead, I seek faithfulness. This allows me to focus on my strengths and what God has called me to do. It also means that when people challenge me or criticize me I do not generally respond with anger or defensiveness. If I do feel angry or defensive, I recognize it as a problem within me, not with the person who is criticizing me. I know who I am in Christ, so I do not use my ministry to gain a sense of identity or a sense of importance. All this comes by faith, allowing me to enter and remain in the sphere God has assigned me.

STRIVING TO REST

The writer to the Hebrews concludes this passage with a strange instruction in light of what we have learned about the place of rest. He tells us to "strive to enter that rest". It seems like a contradiction. How could we possibly *strive* to enter *rest*, especially when that place of rest is a place where we *cease* from striving and come to peace? How could we strive to enter our sphere when our sphere by its nature is a gift of God's grace – something we cannot earn?

We strive to enter God's rest – our sphere or our Promised Land – in a number of ways. First, we must *choose to be strong and courageous* (Joshua 1:9). We must resist fear and the sense of intimidation that we often feel when we face great challenges. Fear and unbelief kept the Israelites out of God's rest, and we have seen the same happen time and again with God's people today. We can never eliminate fear altogether, but we can choose to be strong in the Lord and very courageous – feeling our fear and leading anyway.

Second, we have to *take the next step.* We have to step forward deliberately into our sphere, the place of God's rest. We have encountered so many Christians who just wait for things to happen to them. They have a sense of God's call for their lives. They might know what their sphere is supposed to be. God has given them a vision. But they do nothing. They just sit by and expect things to be handed to them quickly and easily. In some cases, they wait their entire lifetime only to experience disappointment after disappointment.

In Joshua's situation, the waters of the Jordan River did not part until they stepped out into the water (see Joshua 3:8ff.). After they stepped into the water God then stopped the Jordan so they could walk across on dry land. Striving to enter God's rest means that we must take the next step. We have to move forward. We cannot sit back and wait for it to come. God will often not open the way until we have taken the step.

Third, God requires our *obedience*. We must obey God, not only in things directly related to our sphere and our leadership but also in the daily issues of living as a disciple of Jesus. God requires our obedience as an act of love toward him and others (see 1 John 5:2–3). God requires obedience not only for us to enter our sphere but also for us to enlarge our sphere. In each place Joshua went, God gave him new instructions about how to gain the Promised Land. God will do the same for us.

Fourth, we must *choose to have confidence in God* in order to enter our place of rest. In the story of Joshua, we think many misunderstand the promise that God gave to Joshua, saying that "every place the sole of your foot will tread I have given you" (see Joshua 1:3). Many read this as a mandate to go anywhere they desire – take any sphere they want – and God will give that to them. However, this is not the sense of the passage.

A better way to understand God's promise might be this: "Josh, everywhere I am going to take you, everywhere your foot will step, I will have already given to you; it is part of my plan that you have this land." God is promising Joshua, and we believe us as well who are Christians and leaders, that he will lead Joshua into his sphere and give him his sphere as he goes there. God wants Joshua to have confidence in God's leadership even as Joshua exercises his leadership. With confidence in God, we can move forward into our sphere. We may also see our sphere expand.

Finally, we have to *prepare ourselves* to enter our place of rest. We need to receive training. We have to engage in continual learning. The time of preparation may seem very long. For Joshua, it was over forty years of preparation. For me, entering my current sphere required over twenty-five years of training and preparation. This included getting a seminary degree and a doctoral degree. It also included many different learning experiences. I had many previous spheres that helped me to get ready for this one. As I look back, I can see how God has skillfully woven the different strands of my life together as preparation for my own place of rest.

The process of preparation will differ greatly for every leader. Along the way, we encourage leaders to take every opportunity to grow and improve. One of my favorite foreign words is the Japanese word *"kaizen"*, which apparently means little steps of continuous improvement. We have so many little things we can do that might make a great difference in how we come into our place of rest.

THE LEADERSHIP DILEMMA

Knowing that our spheres are a gift of God's grace and at the same time knowing that we must step into those spheres creates our leadership dilemma. Balancing our faith in God with our responsibilities as leaders requires much prayer, humility, passion, and willingness to take risks. We must obey God while continuing to listen for how God might speak and direct us.

Coming into our place of rest begins with our *being* becoming healthy and grounded in Christ. As long as we are looking to our leadership for any sense of identity or significance, security or acceptance, we can never fully enter our rest. Unless met in Christ, we will always strive to meet our deepest needs in our *doing*, including our leadership. We may even try to meet our needs by expanding our own sphere in our own way. When that is happening, we cannot enter the place of rest – nor can we lead effectively.

Once we enter the place of rest (our sphere) through faith, our *being* enables us to remain in rest so that our *doing* becomes more natural, more authentic, and more graceful. Our leadership influence grows as do our spheres. We do not try to force them to grow. We do not strive for them to grow. We simply remain faithful. God then gives the growth and increases our fruitfulness. We become more freed to lead.

PART IV

ANXIETY – THE BANE OF LEADERSHIP

Now is the age of anxiety.

W. H. Auden

What would life be if we had no courage to attempt anything?

Vincent van Gogh

Anxiety does not empty tomorrow of its sorrows, but only empties today of its strength.

Charles Spurgeon

Every tomorrow has two handles. We can take hold of it with the handle of anxiety or the handle of faith.

Henry Ward Beecher

As a kid, I would often watch old black and white films broadcast on Saturday afternoons. I remember watching a few scary films (although they did not have the violence and profanity of many more recent films). *The Wolf Man* was one of my favorite films of this genre. The thought of a brave man trying to rescue someone and getting bitten by a werewolf so that he himself would become a werewolf engrossed me. The tragedy and sadness of it all stuck with me. It was in this film that I first heard of wolfsbane, a flower that when in bloom signaled the possibility that even the best of people could tragically become werewolves. I later learned that wolfsbane supposedly would ward off werewolves as well.

When I was thinking about the topic of this section, wolfsbane came to my mind. In the mythology of werewolves, wolfsbane not only opened the way for the best of people to become completely transformed, but it also disempowered what was supposed to be a superhuman creature. It occurred to me that it was exactly this that happened when anxiety was present – even the best of people could be transformed by its power into something tragic, and even the best of leaders could become completely disempowered.

Then I wondered whether the word "bane" might apply as well. A "bane" is anything that might cause great distress or annoyance, perhaps even death. Immediately, I realized how anxiety really served as the "bane" of leadership. Anxiety causes great distress, annoyance, and sickness in leaders, people, and people-systems.

Like most people, I had thought of anxiety as little more than a common annoyance, a normal nervousness and worry that afflicted most everyone at some point. I saw it as basically harmless – as long as we listened to the Bible and cast these little annoyances on God. I knew that some people suffered from anxiety disorders, but I also knew that counseling and drugs might help those people. I thought of anxiety as sin, but not one of those "big" sins.

I had no idea how wrong I really was.

I have discovered that in our experience at our third church, anxiety was the major corrosive element for my leadership. The people-system that we call the church was completely bound up in anxiety. A few of the leaders, without realizing it, were using anxiety to help them get and then manipulate followers. Anxiety had become such a powerful force in me personally that I had even abdicated my leadership responsibilities. This was my failure of leadership.

Although anxiety was operating so powerfully at the church, nobody realized what was happening. No one understood it. In fact, some people had even found ways to make their anxiety seem biblical and appropriate. It was not until I went on my forced sabbatical that I began to realize what was happening. God had taken me out of the context of the church in order to show me what was happening both in the church and in my own life.

Around that time I came across a profound book which began to help me see things from a new perspective. The book is called *A Failure of Nerve*, by Edwin Friedman. Friedman wrote the book in the late 1990s but he could have been writing it just yesterday. Friedman introduced me to the concept of anxiety and the effect that it had on people and people-systems, as well as leaders.[1] Friedman gave me a framework by which I could decipher some of the mysteries of leadership.

Once I saw the effect that anxiety was having on the church, and once the Lord began the process of resolving anxiety in my own life, I was able to lead much more effectively so that the church might become a healthy church. It took some time, but as I continued resolving anxiety in my own life others in our fellowship also began resolving anxiety in their lives. I saw how people responded to the way I handled anxiety, even though most people did not understand what was happening. Occasionally, anxiety-ridden people would come to me – or come at me! However, I found that if I did not react in an anxious or defensive way then the anxiety in most people would quickly drain away.

The church had experienced such a deep wounding and devastation during the conflict years that many people doubted whether we would survive. Not only did we have the issues of the conflict years, but we had issues that had accumulated over the previous forty plus years in the life of the church. People knew how fragile and vulnerable the church was. We had a financial mountain to climb and limited resources. Although the major conflicts were over, we still had to contend with normal church conflicts and issues. All these issues sought to create anxiety in us.

Although I wrestled with all these issues, God gave me a supernatural faith that the church would make it through the difficulties and eventually thrive. I knew that God had not brought the church through 370 years of history only for her to perish after one of the most difficult seasons in her history. God gave me a vision for how we would move forward as a congregation. The vision included a number of "signposts" along the way so that people could see our progress.

We saw God do some amazing things during this time. God revealed a number of spiritual issues from our past that he wanted the church to resolve through forgiveness and repentance. God provided for us financially so that, even though we never had much, we always seemed to have enough. God brought reconciliation to relationships. He rebuilt the ministry of the church. We celebrated as we passed most of the signposts we had indicated.

As I confronted anxiety, both in myself and in the church as a people-system, my leadership changed. It became healthier and more secure. People responded to me differently. I experienced a deeper sense of God's peace. I became more patient to allow God's processes in people's lives to take their course so that people could become mature followers of Jesus.

I also began to notice more and more how anxiety was at work in people's lives. I discovered that anxiety pervades most of the people-systems in society. We witnessed how anxiety destroys relationships, disempowers people at work, causes medical problems, and undermines leadership. We witnessed how anxiety disheartens and devitalizes leaders, even leaders in the churches. We learned that we could explain so much of the dysfunction in society by looking at how anxiety lurks and exercises a destructive influence. We noticed how common and "normal" anxiety seemed to be. Most people seemed to have learned to adjust to anxiety like a limp that we do not even pay attention to anymore because it is just an expected part of life.

Most importantly, we learned that we do not have to tolerate or accept anxiety as a normal part of life. We discovered that – although anxiety might be tenacious and stubborn and although we might never completely eliminate it – we could overcome it. We also found that the single most important factor for overcoming anxiety – whether in people or people-systems – is healthy leadership, particularly Christian leadership. And we discovered, as with most things, that the Bible had showed us how all along.

9

UNDERSTANDING ANXIETY

People become attached to their burdens sometimes more than the burdens are attached to them.

George Bernard Shaw

I am an old man and have known a great many troubles, but most of them never happened.

Mark Twain

In almost everything that touches our everyday life on earth, God is pleased when we're pleased. He wills that we be as free as birds to soar and sing our maker's praise without anxiety.

A. W. Tozer

Getting the call to lead a team at a major multinational corporation felt like one of the best days of Lee's life. Although he knew it would be very challenging, he felt this could set him on a path for future promotions in his career. The team had been underperforming for many years. The last team leader had been dismissed because of the lack of results. Almost immediately, Lee realized that he was a little out of his depth. So he decided that he would attend some leadership seminars to learn how to lead more effectively. Every seminar was teaching something new that he would dutifully bring back to his team. Each seminar would mean major changes for his team, none of which really made much difference.

Lee's team dreaded these seminars. Each one meant further disruptions to their work. Every change seemed to put them further and further behind. David, a member of Lee's team, really felt that he should have been the leader of the team. He was concerned that Lee's lack of leadership would cause all of them to be dismissed. So David would often talk behind Lee's back, trying to convince the other team members that Lee should be replaced. He made a number of "confidential" complaints to Lee's supervisor. Rather than working together, each team member began working to save his or her own job. The team continued its underperformance.

Aisha had been a highly competent PA for more than twenty years. She had a passion to see her bosses succeed. She worked in a number of major corporations, in high-stress positions. When she landed the job at a small company focusing on innovations in medicine, she felt she had found her dream job. She was assigned to be the PA for Barbara, the operations director of the company. Barbara's last PA had been a complete disaster. He had made multiple mistakes that cost Barbara considerably. This made Barbara wonder whether she could trust any PA.

It only took a month for things to begin to break down. Aisha began to feel that Barbara did not like her. Barbara would not allow Aisha to manage her diary. Barbara would review everything Aisha did, micromanaging her every activity. Aisha became more and more nervous, more and more insecure, feeling that she could lose her job at any minute. Barbara, on the other hand, was very pleased with Aisha's performance. She loved working with Aisha. But Barbara was determined not to have another mess to clean up. In the end, Aisha applied for a new job in the company.

John had been serving his first church for a year when the congregation realized that they really needed a new educational building. At the same time, the church did not have a large congregation. The people realized that they would have a difficult time paying for a new building. The idea of a large mortgage caused considerable apprehension among the people. When the idea of building a new educational wing was presented to the congregation, although many were in favor of it, most people resisted it.

John listened intently to the concerns people raised. Then he calmly suggested a way forward. Since they already had bought a basic architect's design for the new educational wing, John suggested that they invite contractors to bid on the project. This would cost the church nothing and enable them to see whether they could finance the new building. Since this did not obligate the church in any way, the people agreed.

On the day the bids were opened, one bid was 50 percent less than all the others. One woman in the church remarked that it was as if God had just paid for half of the building himself. Confident and excited, the church agreed to proceed with the building. They were able to acquire a construction loan so the work could proceed, and four months after the work was completed the church had repaid the loan in full.

In all three stories, one dynamic was at work to undermine the efforts both of leaders and followers. In none of the stories did anyone recognize the dynamic at work. In the first two stories, the leaders and followers never overcame this dynamic. In the last story, the leader overcame this dynamic without really understanding what was happening.

This dynamic was the *anxiety* we introduced you to in the opening of this section.

ANXIETY REVEALED

Many people have no idea how pervasive anxiety actually is. Anxiety is endemic in the world today. It is the unavoidable byproduct of the times in which we live. Everything we discussed in the first section produces anxiety. Whenever people feel overloaded and confused, they will struggle with anxiety. Whenever people have too many choices, they will struggle with anxiety. If people feel that their people-systems – whether it is their churches, their businesses or their government – do not have the leadership they need, then people will struggle with anxiety.

Anxiety may cause many forms of physical illness, from stomach ulcers to high blood pressure. Anxiety may lead to all sorts of mental illness, including depression and various phobias. People who are bound up in anxiety will struggle to be healthy.

Anxiety is one of the major reasons for the breakdown of many families. When a family struggles to pay its bills, it will be subject to anxiety. When husbands and wives have unresolved disagreements, they will open themselves to anxiety. Sadly, I frequently see parents yelling at their children, screaming at the kids for no apparent reason other than they are kids. Whenever I see this, I know that the parents are struggling with anxiety. Anxious parents frequently lose their temper with their children and struggle to bring good, healthy discipline in the family.

Anxiety is one of the major reasons for the breakdown of many churches. Many Western churches are declining rapidly, losing essential people and resources. The pace of change in the world leaves traditional churches confused and always trying to catch up. This situation leaves many churches bound up in anxiety. Churches look for superstar leaders who might help them overcome these obstacles, only to fire these leaders when either they do not get the desired results or they bring about too much change. This condemns many churches and church leaders to a perpetual circle of anxiety.

Anxiety is partly responsible for the dysfunction that we see in our governments. The highly adversarial and uncooperative nature of party politics in nations such as the United Kingdom and the United States leads to governments that cease to function effectively. Each party tries to make people feel that if the other party is in power then the country will fall apart. Each party undermines the other to the extent that nobody knows whom to trust. The parties effectively are seeking to govern based on whether or not they can generate enough anxiety in the country. Yet anxiety undermines good governance, creating an environment of mistrust and bitter rivalry.

We can see anxiety at work in many other people-systems within our society. Take healthcare, for example. In the United States, the highly litigious system – where people may bring malpractice lawsuits against physicians to win big, lottery-like paydays – creates a climate of anxiety in the medical community that may often lead physicians to perform totally unnecessary tests simply as a way to protect themselves. In the United Kingdom, the tendency of politicians to tinker with both the budgets and the operations of the National Health Service – when most often they know nothing about either one – leads to anxiety among healthcare professionals and a breakdown of trust within the system. The tendency to use the NHS as a political football in order to gain favor with constituencies increases this anxiety.

Media and technology tend to increase our levels of anxiety. They bring us face-to-face in real time with the great crises in the world today – from the terrorist attacks in various cities and nations, to the persecution of Christians beheaded by radical Islamists, to the rogue nations seeking to develop nuclear weapons, to the natural disasters that claim the lives of thousands, to the financial crises that affect the lives of millions. All these things unfold before us on our screens, generating anxiety. In addition, instead of helping us to manage information well, technology floods us with information so that we struggle to make choices and struggle to determine what is true and what is false.

In the end, it is not just the presence of anxiety that creates the problems. After all, anxiety has affected people throughout the millennia. It is a combination of two factors that makes people so susceptible to the influence of anxiety. Most of the time, anxiety operates silently and secretly in the background of our lives. We simply do not realize it is there and so we take no action to resolve it. In addition, we have generally lost our ability to cope with and resolve anxiety. In our anxiety, we have weakened and undermined the people and people-systems who have helped us resolve anxiety effectively in the past.

ANXIETY DEFINED

So what do we mean by "anxiety"? We have a simple definition that we use:

> **Anxiety is the painful and disturbing unease or apprehension that stems from inappropriate concern about something uncertain.**

Anxiety makes us uncomfortable. It causes us pain. It disturbs us and disrupts our ability to live well. In spite of the fact that it is painful and disturbing, people can often become so used to anxiety that they no longer seem to notice it. However, even if we do not notice it, anxiety influences us.

The pain of anxiety flows from inappropriate concern about something uncertain. We will distinguish appropriate concern from inappropriate concern below. This concern arises from uncertainty – about change, the prospect of change, the future, our current crisis, and so on. When something is uncertain, it may lead to anxiety.

Often, anxiety is episodic — it comes up when we face a certain crisis or difficult situation. As soon as the crisis is over, the anxiety goes away. That is fairly normal for everyone. We call this "acute" anxiety. For example, if I have to take an exam – even if I know the subject very well – I will likely experience a certain degree of anxiety. I might manage this anxiety by making sure I prepare properly for the exam. I might also manage anxiety by putting the exam in its proper context – for instance that if I fail the exam it does not mean the end of life as I know it! These strategies and more will enable me to overcome the anxiety and perform to my best on the exam. As soon as the exam is over (or when I get the results) the anxiety will go away.

For many people today, anxiety becomes an ongoing part of life. It becomes almost habitual, affecting us continually. We call this "chronic" anxiety. It is this chronic anxiety that has such a destructive influence on people and people-systems. It never really stops or lets up; it just continues to function in the background of our lives, rather like static noise.

ANXIETY IN THE BIBLE

The Bible has quite a lot to say about anxiety. In 2 Timothy 1:7, Paul tells Timothy that God has not given us a spirit of fear. The word translated as "fear" is difficult to translate accurately. The word might be more accurately understood as "a cowardice, timidity or failure of nerve that comes from anxiety". Paul tells Timothy that when we feel the tendency to withdraw from our leadership and not do what is required at the time, this indicates the presence of anxiety. Anxiety creates a sense of cowardice that entices us to retreat from our responsibilities. Such anxiety does not come from God. Rather, God has given us the spirit of power, love, and self-control necessary for overcoming anxiety. In other words, as Christians we *already* have what we need to have victory over anxiety.

In Proverbs, Solomon observes how anxiety can become a terrible burden for a person. He says that anxiety in our hearts – in our *being* – weighs us down (see Proverbs 12:25). The psalmist reminds us that incessant, anxious toil is empty unless the Lord is at work as well (see Psalm 127:2).

In Matthew, Jesus encourages us not to be anxious but to seek first the kingdom of God and his righteousness (see Matthew 6:25–34). Jesus reminds us that each day will have enough anxiety as it is, so do not have anxiety about tomorrow.

In 1 Peter 5:7–8, Peter points out the connection between anxiety and the demonic. Peter urges us to cast our anxieties on God. Then he reminds us that Satan is prowling around like a lion to find someone to devour. The implication is that anxiety makes Christians susceptible to demonic attack. Clearly, anxiety is a big issue for the Bible.

BIBLICAL WORD FOR ANXIETY

In the Greek, the word often translated as "anxiety" actually has a range of meanings. The word can be translated as "anxiety", or the word can be translated as "concern". In the Greek, this word has the same range of meaning as the word "care" does in English. So when Paul talks about his daily pressure of concern for all the churches (2 Corinthians 11:28), he is not saying that he is anxious about the churches – as in some translations – but that he has a healthy care for all the churches. But when Paul tells the Philippians not to be anxious about anything (Philippians 4:6), although he is using the same Greek word, he is clearly talking about something different. He is telling the Philippians not to have an unhealthy care about things. In the first passage, "concern" would be the proper translation of the Greek word, but in the second passage "anxiety" would be the proper translation. Whether the word is translated as "concern" or "anxiety" most often depends on the context.

Concern or anxiety describes an emotional state that causes us to attach importance to something. In both cases, we "care" about something. When we are concerned about something, we believe it is important. When we are anxious about something, that too indicates it is important to us. Caring is a natural human emotion. Like anger, the emotion of caring indicates something that needs to be addressed.

To care about something in a healthy way or to be anxious about something in a sinful way are both emotional states that lead to certain responses. Many times, what concerns us or what makes us anxious involves our sense of significance, security or acceptance. If the boss suddenly calls me into his office, then I might feel anxious because of my sense of (job) security. If we walk into a room and the people suddenly stop talking, we may become anxious that they were talking about us because of our sense of acceptance.

243

Whether something concerns us or makes us anxious, the primary issue is truth. In the examples above, what causes anxiety is not the fact that we are called into the boss's office, but our suspicions of why the boss has called us in the first place. The truth of why the boss called us makes all the difference. When the people stopped talking as we entered the room, the truth may be that they stopped because they wanted to greet us and involve us in the conversation. The truth makes all the difference. Taking a caring action or resolving anxiety both require a truth-filled assessment and response in obedience to God's Word.

ROOTS OF ANXIETY

In order to understand and resolve anxiety, it is helpful to know why people become so anxious. Anxiety seems rather like a weed at times. Weeds often have very deep and strong root systems. We might think that simply cutting off the visible part of a weed will eliminate the weed. However, if we fail to deal with the root of the weed, the weed will likely come back, and may even multiply. Just cutting off the top of the weed may make the situation worse. So we need to deal with the roots of anxiety if we are to resolve anxiety.

As a weed, the roots of anxiety attach to our *being*. Anxiety attacks our identity and our sense of significance, security, and acceptance. The behaviors that result from anxiety are only the flowers of the weed. The real influence of anxiety lies much deeper. This means that our *doing* will only ever show a small portion of the full weed of anxiety in our *being*.

People who are lost and ungrounded in their sense of identity and integrity will tend to experience anxiety. If we do not have a clear sense of our *being* – even as non-Christians – we will more likely encounter anxiety. The ancient Greek aphorism "Know thyself" has great relevance to resolving anxiety. Having a healthy *being*, especially a *being* grounded in Jesus, will help us become anxiety resistant.

People who do not have a sense of confidence in themselves will have difficulty with anxiety. How we think about ourselves – whether we perceive ourselves as helpless, hopeful, competent or incapable – affects our ability to deal with anxiety. This gives Christians an advantage regarding anxiety, as long as we know and choose to believe who the Bible says we are in Jesus Christ. When our relationship with God through Jesus shapes our identity in line with biblical truth we will become much stronger for working through anxiety.

As mentioned earlier, when people are overloaded and confused, they will struggle with anxiety. Having a flood of information overwhelming us makes us wonder whether we are missing something important. That sense of possibly missing something creates anxiety. When people have too many options available to them so that they feel paralyzed from making a good choice, they will experience anxiety. This anxiety will lead them not to choose until they are forced to do so. They will feel anxious about making the wrong choice or making what seems to be a decent choice but one that prevents them from making a better choice in the future.

People who face the possibility of loss will feel anxious. We call this "loss aversion". All people are motivated more by what they might lose than what they might gain. Many in society today feel anxious because they are concerned their future will not be as good as their present. They are concerned for their children's future and the possibility that they have a poorer standard of life. Such uncertainty raises anxiety in our hearts.

People who place their trust in people and things that are not God will inevitably suffer from anxiety. The Bible calls this "idolatry". In many respects, the anxiety that results will be very subtle. We may even deny it. But the feeling will be there nonetheless. It is similar to the experience we might have if we stood on the top rung of a ladder. We have a certain degree of confidence that the ladder might hold us but realize at any moment it might tip over and cause us to crash to the ground. Idols always cause anxiety, because in our spirits we realize that an idol can never fully support us.

245

People who fail to take responsibility for something which they are responsible for will struggle with anxiety. If we do not pay our bills, even if we stick them in a drawer somewhere so they are completely out of our sight and our conscious mind, then we will suffer from anxiety. No matter how much we struggle to ignore it, we cannot evade it. Our failure to take appropriate responsibility makes us vulnerable.

Likewise, if we try to take responsibility for something that is not our responsibility, then we will struggle with anxiety. I was speaking to a group of cell leaders. One of them spoke to me about his struggles because two marriages in his cell group were having trouble. He felt that it was his responsibility as their leader to help them stay together. Consequently, he was suffering with major anxiety. Once I showed him that the marriages of other people were not his responsibility, almost immediately the anxiety lifted from him.

Finally, if we believe lies about ourselves, our situations, our people-systems or God, then we will wrestle with anxiety. If we think that we are incapable of dealing with the issues of life, then we will feel anxious. If we think our boss is out to get us, then no matter how much the boss may like us we will suffer with anxiety. (Ironically, this anxiety may actually cause a breakdown in our relationship with our boss!) If we see God as an angry deity who desires to punish everyone, then we will feel anxiety. As I mentioned, anxiety is primarily an issue of truth.

FEATURES OF ANXIETY

As leaders, we need to recognize five important features of anxiety if we are to correctly discern and overcome anxiety. Anxiety always has these five features, no matter how it manifests in our lives or our people-systems. Many times we may not perceive these features, but we need to know they are present whether or not we perceive them.

Infectious

First, anxiety is *infectious*. I mentioned the nature of anxiety as an illness. It resembles the common cold or similar viruses. Most of the time, as a virus anxiety simply makes us and our people-systems sick. Sometimes it becomes a chronic illness in which we go from one infection to another. Sometimes it may even kill us or our people-systems, physically or spiritually. Regardless, it is highly infectious. Whoever comes into contact with anxiety in people or people-systems risks becoming infected themselves. As with all viral infections, the best "cure" is to become healthy and therefore naturally resistant to viruses.

We can partly understand why anxiety is so infectious by understanding how God has wired our brains. We all have mirror neurons that fire in our brains. These mirror neurons cause us to reflect the behaviors and attitudes of others. They help us learn from others. They help us engage socially with others.

To see the effects of mirror neurons, stand on a street corner and look up – and keep on looking up. Notice how many other people look up when they walk past you. That is partly the influence of mirror neurons. Because of this, when one person in a people-system has anxiety, that anxiety may spread to many other people in the system. The more intense the anxiety the more likely it is to spread. Anxiety has a social dynamic that we often fail to recognize.

Over the years, I have experienced several situations where I was leading a course and a highly anxious person walked in. Perhaps a course member had just received some bad news or had an especially difficult day at work. Occasionally, a troubled person might wander into the course. I have learned that even if that person never said a word, their anxiety would affect everyone. People would become fidgety and inattentive. So in those situations I will now stop what I am doing, identify what is happening, minister briefly to the anxious person, and then resume the course. If I try to ignore it, then I will only perpetuate anxiety's influence.

Understanding the infectious nature of anxiety makes us more alert when anxiety is present. This will enable us to take precautions so that we do not become infected ourselves. When cold and flu season comes around each year, we tend to take more precautions in order to keep ourselves from getting sick – such as washing our hands, getting better rest, and eating well. When we recognize the presence of anxiety, we can also take more precautions to resist anxiety in our own lives.

Disguised

Second, anxiety always hides itself. In my experience, most people have little awareness of how much anxiety is working at any given moment. Most leaders have no idea how pervasive anxiety might be in their people-system. Although I teach this stuff and have lived through a highly anxious time in my church, I often find that I miss the work of anxiety in various situations.

A number of years ago, I took part in a meeting in the US to develop some new ministry resources. Most of us knew each other reasonably well, and we were familiar with the ministry's normally healthy style of working together. But the leader had decided to invite a couple of people not really known to the others, who were not as familiar with the ministry's style. These people were also not fully grounded in the vision and values of the ministry.

One woman had some strong opinions and was not afraid to express them strongly. The leader did not like to interfere with group process, believing people should work things out among themselves without much direction from the leader, so he just let her talk – to the point that she was effectively taking over the meeting. Two of my friends and I began to feel very agitated with the whole situation. One of my friends tried to express her concerns in the group, but the leader clearly thought that my friend was the problem and seemed to attack her. Effectively, anxiety had gripped the group but I got caught up in it and failed to recognize it.

It was only during an extended break that my friends and I got together and prayed. We began to realize how anxiety was affecting everything happening. Following the break, we tried to approach the situation differently. I also alerted the leader to what was happening. He adjusted his leadership approach. I sought to engage the opinionated woman positively and directly, seeking to establish a good rapport with her.

In the end, we never fully overcame the anxiety, but we were able to resolve it enough to continue the meeting. We had some good outcomes, although sadly not what we had anticipated. The important point to take away is that at the beginning I had not realized how anxiety was working to undermine the meeting.

When anxiety cannot hide itself, it will disguise itself as something else. It is amazing how much people will deny that they are anxious. Some people will disguise their anxiety as an appropriate level of concern. I have seen Christian parents disguise their unhealthy worry for the well-being of their children as "good parenting". The problem is that if parents allow anxiety to enter their relationship with their children, the children will perceive this as lack of trust and respect. In turn, the children will often react by engaging in rebellious behaviors that increase and seem to justify the anxiety of their parents. The cycle may continue until there is a major breakdown of relationships.

We have to expose anxiety if we are to deal with it. We have found that simply identifying where anxiety is operating often empowers people to resist it. If people know that pickpockets are in the area then they will take greater care over their wallets. Exposing anxiety is often the first step to resolving anxiety.

Distorting

Third, anxiety has a distorting influence on everything in a person and people-system. Anxiety distorts a person's perspectives, communications, and perceptions of reality. To the degree that anxiety is present, we cannot trust any of our perceptions fully. The greater the level of anxiety the greater the level of distortion will be.

A few years ago researchers at Ohio State University conducted an experiment with spiders. They exposed volunteers who said they had a fear of spiders to variously sized tarantulas in an open-top glass tank. They measured the level of the participants' distress as they encountered the spiders. Afterwards they asked the people to estimate the size of the spiders while no longer being able to see them. We can guess the outcome. The greater the sense of distress the more likely people were to overestimate the size of the spider.[1] Anxiety distorts everything.

When anxiety is present, we cannot trust our perceptions. When anxiety is present, we cannot trust that we are communicating accurately or that we are hearing others accurately. When anxiety is present, we cannot trust either our emotions or our instincts. The presence of anxiety signals that we need to re-evaluate all our perceptions, communications, emotions, and choices to ensure that they reflect the truth.

Molly serves as the pastor to women in a large congregation. One woman under her care, Susan, had recently begun to come out of a long struggle with ME. As her health improved, Susan began to act aggressively and abusively in her relationships with others. Susan wanted to serve as a deacon, but her lack of emotional maturity and personal awareness, along with her still weakened state, led the church leaders to decide that it would not be in the best interests of Susan or the congregation for her to serve as a deacon. Susan responded angrily to the elders. Molly decided to meet with Susan to encourage her.

They spent a couple hours together over coffee. Molly affirmed Susan's ministry gifts. She explained how the leadership based its decision on a concern for Susan's well-being. She let Susan know that she was continuing to pray for God's healing in her life. She also encouraged Susan to use the time to build healthy relationships. After the meeting, Susan complained about Molly to another leader in the church. She said that Molly told her that she did not have the gifts to be a deacon. Susan felt angry because she thought Molly had said that God had given Susan ME because she did not have healthy relationships.

The accusations of Susan stunned Molly. As she debriefed with a close friend in leadership at another church, the friend suggested that the problem was that Molly had failed to take into account Susan's anxiety – as well as her own. Molly immediately realized that Susan's anxiety had distorted her perception of everything Molly had said. By failing to recognize the presence of anxiety, both Molly and Susan had become victims to anxiety's distorting influences.

Weakens defenses

Fourth, anxiety weakens the natural defenses of both people and people-systems. Anxiety makes people and systems susceptible to the influence of outside forces. Anxious people and people-systems are highly suggestible, especially if they become overloaded with information and choices.

For example, much advertising depends on influencing anxious people to buy things they do not need. Salespeople convince people to purchase extended warranties by generating anxiety that the product might break down. Ironically, they will sell people on the idea that the product is high quality, then sell the warranty based on the remote chance that it could break down. The price of the warranty might approach the cost of the product itself. Generating anxiety has become one of the primary advertising techniques throughout the industry.

We can see this operating at the level of people-systems as well. Over the past decade, political parties have sought to win elections not only by promoting their ideas but also by trying to make people feel anxious that if their opponents got into power then they would make things worse. Hitler's propaganda in Germany succeeded by generating anxiety among people that groups such as the Jews were the source of all the nation's problems. In such an anxiety-ridden system it became easier to convince people to do things they would never have done otherwise.

Resistible

Finally, and most importantly, anxiety is resistible. Peter tells us to cast all our anxieties on God because he is the one who cares for us. Healthy people in healthy people-systems can resist and resolve anxiety as they renew their minds with truth, demolish strongholds that stand against truth, take appropriate responsibility for themselves, and maintain healthy processes. As we have said, the primary issue to resolve anxiety is truth. We need the confidence that we can resist and resolve anxiety in ourselves and in our people-systems.

ANXIETY AND THE DEMONIC

As we seek to resolve anxiety, we must recognize that anxiety is a spiritual dynamic as well as an emotional dynamic. Demons, including principalities and powers, seek to use anxiety in people and people-systems in order to control them. As we said, anxiety makes people highly susceptible to outside influences.

First, demons will try to produce anxiety. I have had meetings with people who came into the meeting with a high level of anxiety – much higher than we would expect from the content of the meeting. The meeting would often begin with some tension, but I would put the person at ease and we would generally have a good meeting. At the end of the meeting, very often I would hear a comment like: "I'm not sure why I was so worried about this meeting. We always have good meetings together. It was *as if something told me* before the meeting that if I told the truth then you would not like me anymore." We recognize this as the work of the demonic.

This happens on a people-system-wide level as well. I have seen churches split because two groups began to believe lies about one another and then to "demonize" each other, forgetting that our struggle is not against flesh and blood people (see Ephesians 6:12). A common tactic of the demonic in societies is to cause people to focus on various minorities or misunderstood groups as the source of a society's problems – economic problems, crime, unemployment, and the like.

Second, demons will try to magnify the anxiety that is already present. When people in a church have disagreements – which by their nature produce some level of anxiety – demons will insert thoughts into people's minds that question the integrity and the motives of the people with whom we are disagreeing. When we question the motives of others we will not trust them and we are less likely to want to work with them, which increases anxiety. Demons may deceive us into thinking that problems are greater than they actually are, which produces anxiety.

Third, demons will manipulate anxiety, anxious people, and anxious systems to produce their own ends. We may attribute much social breakdown to how the demonic manipulates anxiety. For example, all marriage relationships have disagreements from time to time, sometimes very strong disagreements. These disagreements always produce anxiety. I have seen marriages break down not because of the severity of the disagreement but because demons began to speak lies into one or both spouses' minds. These lies include "good marriages never have disagreements", "the marriage is over", "I'm not happy anymore", and many others. When spouses begin to believe these lies, the anxiety intensifies, making it more difficult to resolve the issues. In the end, unless the spouses choose to know and believe the truth – not only the truth about each other but also the truth of the Bible and what it has to say about marriage – demons will manipulate their anxiety in order to effect a divorce.

Left unresolved, anxiety will give a foothold for the demonic in any person or people-system. This means that leaders must confront the spiritual aspects of anxiety in order to resolve anxiety. The next chapter will give leaders some insights into how to confront anxiety and resist the demonic in our own lives. The following chapter will talk about how to resolve anxiety in our people-systems.

TOP TEN SYMPTOMS OF ANXIETY

As leaders, we need to learn how to recognize when anxiety is at work. Good medical doctors become familiar with the symptoms of various diseases in order to identify them correctly. Healthy leadership will also learn the symptoms of sicknesses like anxiety so that people and people-systems will be able to recognize and then resist anxiety. Only when we identify it correctly will we then be able to confront it for what it is. So here is my top ten list of the symptoms of anxiety in people:

- **Loss of imagination**
- **Struggling to reason**
- **Struggling to choose**
- **Emotional volatility**
- **Distorted communication**
- **Defensiveness**
- **"Too much" syndrome**
- **Seeking quick fixes**
- **Restlessness**
- **Helplessness**

Loss of imagination

Anxious people struggle to imagine a way out of their perceived problems. They also begin to lose a sense of their hopes and dreams. Instead, they become locked into a sense that things will never change. They cannot see a better future.

Struggling to reason

Anxious people lose their ability to think clearly. Normally, people are able to think rationally. They can weigh up options. They can recognize when others are lying to them or when what they say does not make sense. However, when anxiety takes hold of people, they lose their ability to problem solve. They lose their sense of reason. They believe lies more easily.

Struggling to choose

Anxious people have difficulty making good choices. Often the "tyranny of the urgent" will dominate them, drawing them away from a focus on what is really important. They will tend to make choices reflexively, often regretting those choices. When they do choose, they will tend to make choices based more on what other people are doing (or their perception of what other people are doing) rather than on what has the best outcomes.

Emotional volatility

Anxiety produces high levels of emotions in people. These emotions range from "falling in love" quickly to anger and rage. The intensity of the emotions drives people toward unhealthy or unhelpful choices. It makes people feel like they have to *do* something, no matter what it is. Whenever we see high emotionality we can know that anxiety is working.

Distorted communication

We can see anxiety's distorting influence most clearly in communication. So whenever we see consistent patterns of distorted communication we need immediately to suspect the work of anxiety. When people hear us say something completely different than we intended, or vice versa, we know that anxiety has affected the communication. The distortion includes written communications, such as emails. We know of many situations where people have misread emails. On occasion, I have had to sit down with someone and review an email almost word by word in order to help that person understand the email. Distorted communication almost always suggests anxiety.

255

Defensiveness

Anxious people tend to respond defensively. If we need to discuss a problem with an anxious person – say the resolution of a disagreement at work – and the person responds quickly with things like "That wasn't my fault" or some other defensive posture, we know that anxiety lurks. Whenever we feel defensive, we can know that we are struggling with anxiety ourselves.

"Too much" syndrome

Anxious people will try to medicate their anxiety, often leading to the "too much" syndrome. People may drink too much, eat too much, talk too much, watch too much TV, shop too much, surf the internet too much. Whenever we see the too much syndrome at work we need to suspect anxiety.

Seeking quick fixes

Anxiety drives people to find quick fixes to eliminate the anxiety. People will try to propose easy solutions to complex problems. They may try to identify issues as black and white, without allowing for any grey, any subtlety. They will often underestimate how long it takes to resolve some issues. Some people would even prefer a return to a difficult or dysfunctional situation rather than do the difficult work of resolving issues and confronting anxiety.

Restlessness

Anxious people have trouble resting. They will often surround themselves with a flurry of activity. Intense, unrelenting movement has a way of masking anxiety, giving the illusion that it is not present. Anxiety may actually provoke people to do more, engage in even more activity, thinking it might be the solution to anxiety. Busyness nearly always increases anxiety. Restlessness will nearly always generate more anxiety.

Helplessness

Anxious people often feel helpless. They begin to believe that they are the victims of circumstances and situations, without any real control over their lives or their selves. Such helplessness either leads people to do what they have always done, assuming it will get different results, or it leads people to stop doing anything and just try to survive. Both responses increase anxiety.

So let's get the picture here: Anxiety wears down our mind, will, and emotions, interfering with our ability to communicate. We begin to feel helpless and defensive, making us very restless. We try to alleviate these symptoms by seeking quick fixes and engaging in the "too much" syndrome. The more anxiety we have, the worse these effects are.

TOP FIVE SYMPTOMS OF CHRONIC ANXIETY

The longer anxiety lasts, the more intense the above symptoms might become. Eventually, anxiety becomes chronic and people become even less aware of its influences. When chronic anxiety takes hold, you can add five more big symptoms:

- **Willfulness**
- **Self-centeredness**
- **Fault-finding and criticism**
- **Blame shifting**
- **Harmful behaviors**

Willfulness

Chronically anxious people tend stubbornly to insist on their own way. They refuse to cooperate with others, especially leaders. They often find themselves in overly intense arguments and contests of will, where negotiation becomes impossible and the only goal is to win the argument at all costs.

Self-centeredness

Chronically anxious people will become increasingly self-centered. Everything seems to become about them – their pain, their pleasure, their opinion. Chronically anxious people will even turn things about other people toward themselves. It is the old story of the man on a date who, after talking about himself for two hours, says: "OK. That's enough about me. Let's talk about you. What do you think of me?" The attitude is often one of "I cannot possibly help others until I've dealt with all my own problems." However, with anxious people there will always be yet another personal problem for them to resolve.

Fault-finding and criticism

Chronically anxious people tend to find fault with everything and everyone. They often have a highly critical attitude toward others. Because of the painful nature of anxiety, they have difficulty seeing the positive in anything. Instead, the anxiety makes them pessimistic perfectionists. Even when they try to speak positively about something, they will end up turning the positive into a negative.

Blame shifting

Chronically anxious people always shift the blame for their present condition – and their anxiety – onto something or someone else. They struggle, or even refuse, to take responsibility for their own mind, will, and emotions. Instead, they feel that other people and things have caused their problems and their anxiety.

We can see one of the clearest examples of this in the language of "offense". It seems that people take offense more often and more easily than ever before. If someone accidentally uses an emotionally charged word, then suddenly millions of people cry out in the Twittersphere that they have been deeply offended by this language. If someone fails to greet us in church, then we claim to have been deeply offended by the person.

The problem with the language of offense is that in order to be offended we must choose to *take* offense. In other words, nobody can offend us unless *we allow them* to offend us. Nothing that anyone can say to me can possibly offend me unless I choose to let it offend me. If I blame someone else for my offense, then I am only showing my own failure to take responsibility for my own mind, will, and emotions. In other words, I am shifting the blame for my offense to the other person.

Harmful behaviors

Chronically anxious people more easily engage in behaviors that are harmful to others. We must carefully distinguish harm from "pain". Not every behavior that causes pain is the result of a harmful behavior. Pain is necessary for health and life. Harm takes away health and life.

Harmful behaviors by their nature cause real injury, damage or evil to others. They normally have some sense of culpability associated with them. Some of the key harmful behaviors found in anxious people are rumors, gossip, personal attacks, and bullying.

Anxious people spread rumors about others, often based on some truth but including some major distortions. They will often attack people personally. Instead of focusing on different opinions about something, they may suggest that the other person is too stupid to know what is right. They will also bully other people, trying to intimidate them through difficult behavior. These and many other behaviors cause harm to others.

In summary, when people are caught up in chronic anxiety, they can become extremely stubborn, selfish, and very critical. They take no responsibility for problems, instead blaming everyone else, no matter how irrationally. They might even begin engaging in highly destructive behaviors, such as rumors, personal attacks, and bullying. Like a volcano, these behaviors may seem dormant much of the time but they will erupt suddenly from time to time to create havoc and cause damage.

TOP TEN SYMPTOMS OF ANXIETY FOR PEOPLE-SYSTEMS

As we have seen, people-systems function much like individual persons. Since people-systems have a mind and emotions of their own, they also have their own symptoms of anxiety. Again, here are my top ten symptoms of anxiety in people-systems:

- Intolerance of pain
- Tolerating immaturity and irresponsibility
- Preoccupation with comfort and convenience
- Fad issues and cures
- Corporate self-centeredness
- Focusing on rights
- Obsession with rules
- Exaggeration
- Vague, ill-defined complaints
- Groupthink

Intolerance of pain

Anxious people-systems cannot endure pain and discomfort. Instead, they will seek anything that will relieve pain or discomfort, even if it is not healthy for them. They will struggle to allow difficult processes to achieve beneficial outcomes. For example, an anxious church will more likely fire its pastor – even if he is not the source of the problem – than work at repairing and rebuilding relationships in the church. An anxious business will more likely replace its managing director than make the systemic changes necessary to build a healthy business model.

Tolerating immaturity and irresponsibility

Anxious people-systems tend to tolerate – and even adjust to – people who are immature and irresponsible in the people-system rather than expect those people to become mature and responsible. For example, imagine a church board that has one member who is chronically late to meetings. If that church board is anxious, then most likely the church board will tolerate the chronic lateness rather than either starting the meetings on time or challenging the late member to improve his behavior. Failing to address the problem of lateness allows one person to control the meeting – at least when it starts. This shows how immature and irresponsible people might easily dominate anxious people-systems.

Preoccupation with comfort and convenience

Anxious people-systems crave comfort and convenience. They want things that require as little effort and commitment as possible. For example, if an anxious church has to decide a new time for worship, the discussion will likely focus on what time is most convenient for the present members and attenders of the church – even if that time is not the best for other people in the community. Anxious businesses will tend to develop policies and procedures that focus on what the staff finds most comfortable, instead of developing policies and procedures that focus on the well-being of its customers.

Fad issues and cures

Chronically anxious people-systems continually seek what is new and novel. They will usually get caught up in the latest fads. For anxious businesses, this means that they will bring in one consultant after another to tell them how to improve their business. For anxious churches, this means that they will often try to get the latest technology – think overhead projectors in the 1980s – or embrace the latest self-help craze – think codependency in the 1980s – to make them more effective at reaching people with the gospel. However, the fad issues and cures never fully bring about the promised results. In addition, they often increase anxiety.

Corporate self-centeredness

People-systems may become selfish just as people are selfish. The political parties might easily put their own policy goals and serving their own constituencies ahead of the well-being of the nation. Churches might talk about reaching out with the gospel but in reality focus primarily on the preferences and desires of their members. Bankers may become more focused on earning money for themselves than on sharing their profits with account holders. Corporate selfishness exists in many different ways, but generally signals the presence of anxiety in the people-system.

Focusing on rights

People in chronically anxious systems focus on their rights instead of their responsibilities. The language of rights in turn generally increases anxiety in people-systems. John F. Kennedy famously said, "Ask not what your country can do for you; ask what you can do for your country." Chronically anxious people-systems always reverse this statement.

Obsession with rules

Whenever you see a people-system obsessed with making and keeping rules, you are witnessing a chronically anxious people-system. One of the most common ways that people try to respond to anxiety is by creating more rules. So the business leader who is anxious that people might be wasting resources will create a new rule or a new form that people must follow or fill out in order to access needed resources. The church that is struggling with internal conflict might try to create a new constitution to bring order to the conflict. Rules never resolve anxiety; they simply increase it.

Exaggeration

People and anxious people-systems are prone to exaggeration. They will exaggerate the nature of problems. They will exaggerate the weaknesses of people. They will exaggerate negative perceptions of other people's behaviors. They tend to magnify issues. Anxiety distorts everything.

Vague, ill-defined complaints

Anxious people-systems know that something is wrong, but they struggle to define what it is. So we will tend to hear a number of vague, ill-defined complaints. When pressed to define the complaints further, people will struggle to do so. Instead, they will try to emphasize the complaints by becoming louder, more passionate, or more insistent that something be done. We will often hear attacks on leaders or other people in the system that seem to lack any substance. These attacks will tend to focus on perceived character flaws rather than on clearly defined behavior.

One way to expose these vague, ill-defined complaints is to keep pressing for more details. As leaders, we must resist the temptation to react quickly. Instead, we must take time to gather information. We must always focus on clear, definable behaviors rather than unclear, accusatory character flaws.

Groupthink

Groupthink happens when people in a people-system begin to think alike to the point that they begin to draw irrational conclusions and choose unhelpful, difficult or harmful behavior. One example of groupthink is the tendency to blame one category of people for the ills of society. In many nations today, that category of people is "immigrants". For some churches today, that category of people might be "liberals". Whenever it occurs, groupthink often signifies the presence of anxiety in a people-system.

So let us see how anxiety influences a people-system: when a people-system is struggling with anxiety, people run away from any kind of difficulty and tolerate all sorts of immaturity and poor behavior. The people-system will try any fad that comes along, as long as it is easy and helps them feel better by giving them a sense they are doing *something*. The system loses its sense of mission, becoming inwardly focused. People harp about rights and rules, exaggerating any issue that might arise. People are always complaining, but their complaints have little substance. They also struggle to work out their issues rationally.

TOP FIVE SYMPTOMS OF CHRONIC ANXIETY IN SYSTEMS

As anxiety becomes more entrenched in a people-system we will begin to observe a number of other symptoms:

- **Fixating on what's wrong**
- **Forming factions**
- **Fixating on health and safety**
- **Unrealistic expectations**
- **Personal attacks, especially on leaders**

Fixating on what's wrong

Chronically anxious people-systems struggle to focus on what is good and right. They struggle to have a positive outlook. Instead, they tend to acquire a pessimistic focus on what is perceived to be wrong. This pessimistic focus does not come from truth but from perceptions of reality that more often than not are incorrect or inappropriate. Remember how anxiety distorts all our perceptions.

Forming factions

Factionalism both results from and creates anxiety. Highly anxious people-systems will see people form into increasingly more adversarial groups that refuse to cooperate for the benefit of the people-system. Instead, they will strive for their own perceptions of what is good – perceptions that again will be distorted and unhealthy. This will lead to increasing levels of breakdown in the people-system.

Fixating on health and safety

In the opening pages of *A Failure of Nerve*, Friedman referred to this phenomenon as the "seatbelt society".[2] People-systems bound up in anxiety will always focus on health and safety. They will find themselves increasingly unable to take the risks necessary in order to overcome their problems and conquer their anxiety. In the name of health and safety, people-systems will undermine courage, restrict leadership, and disempower the best efforts of its people.

Unrealistic expectations

Chronically anxious people-systems will develop and insist on unrealistic expectations of the people-system and its leaders. For example, many people expected national leadership to overcome the problems of the financial crisis of 2008 very quickly. They refused to acknowledge that the problems in the financial system had developed over many years and would take many years to repair. People expected to maintain the same standard of living based on borrowing while being able to pay down national debt at the same time. Such expectations were not realistic.

Personal attacks, especially on leaders

Anxious people-systems will always attack their leaders for any number of reasons, some legitimate but most not. Chronically anxious systems will make those attacks personal. They will attack the personality of the leader, the leader's family, and the leader's friends. They will also extend these personal attacks to one another. These *ad hominem* attacks will achieve nothing but decreasing trust in the people-system and increasing anxiety.

In summary, when the people-system's anxiety becomes chronic, people tend to fixate on what they perceive to be the problem, and then they tend to gather in factions with others who think or feel the same way. They fixate on peripheral issues like health and safety. They begin to develop totally unrealistic expectations, but refuse to consider these rationally. They ultimately begin attacking one another personally, especially leaders, using all sorts of ugly language.

If we think through the above symptoms, we might quickly identify quite a number of people-systems caught up into anxiety – the health community, the police service, political parties, perhaps even our own business or church. It is essential that we recognize and expose the work of anxiety so that we might overcome it.

ANXIETY AFFECTS LEADERSHIP

Obviously, all this chronic anxiety has a corrosive effect on leadership. Anxiety inhibits real leadership. We have three principles regarding the effect of anxiety on leadership:

> **To the degree that a leader has unmanaged or unresolved anxiety that person cannot lead effectively.**

> **Anxiety in the leader always produces or magnifies anxiety in the people-system.**

> **To the degree that a people-system has unmanaged or unresolved anxiety that people-system will resist leadership.**

If we as leaders have unresolved anxiety, that anxiety will distort our leadership as it distorts everything else. We simply cannot lead effectively. Our anxiety will deceive us into thinking that we are more effective than we actually are. We will find it difficult to think creatively and lovingly about our leadership context.

If we as leaders have anxiety in ourselves, then our anxiety will be multiplied in the system that we lead. Anxiety in the leader always produces or magnifies anxiety in the system. This principle is true whether or not we are aware of our anxiety. It is true whether or not we think we have hidden or disguised our anxiety. This will lead to dysfunction in the people-system.

When people-systems are anxious, they always resist leadership. Sometimes, they will do everything they can to remove the leader. Unrealistic expectations and demands will sidetrack or undermine leadership, causing the leaders to focus on meeting felt needs and incessant demands rather than looking to the best for the people-system.

THE LEADERSHIP DILEMMA

So this leaves us with our leadership dilemma.

True leadership is the only way we have of resolving anxiety, whether in people or people-systems. Yet true leadership often intensifies anxiety before leading people and systems out of anxiety. Things can seem to get much worse before they get better. We will need to recognize the presence of anxiety before we can resolve it. We will need to help our people-system endure anxiety once recognized before we can overcome it.

Anxious people who need to experience true leadership will be the ones who consciously or unconsciously seek to undermine, attack, sabotage, and destroy true leadership. This means that leadership requires love that hurts – especially us as leaders. What we need is anxiety-resistant leaders fully connected with their people-systems in love who are actively seeking to resolve their own anxiety while helping their people-system to resolve its anxiety.

10

OVERCOMING PERSONAL ANXIETY

*If you are distressed by anything external, the pain is not
due to the thing itself, but to your estimate of it; and this you
have the power to revoke at any moment.*

Marcus Aurelius

*Sometimes people let the same problem make them
miserable for years when they could just say, "So what?"
That's one of my favorite things to say. "So what?"*

Andy Warhol

*Character cannot be developed in ease and quiet. Only
through experience of trial and suffering can the soul be
strengthened, ambition inspired, and success achieved.*

Helen Keller

Sam manages a conference center in West London. One day, a client came in who was rushed, stressed, and late. The client treated Sam and his staff brusquely and rudely. Sam became offended by the rough treatment and explained to the client rather forcefully that such treatment will not be tolerated. The client immediately backed down from the behavior, but was clearly not happy.

During the lunch service, Sam's team forgot to prepare the gluten-free option requested in advance by one of the client's delegates. The client became enraged at Sam for his poor service and spoke to him loudly in front of several members of the group as well as Sam's staff. In response, Sam turned and spoke sternly to his staff in front of the others, rebuking the staff for this terrible oversight. The delegate, a bit embarrassed by the exchange, decided to make do with a few bits of salad for lunch. Following the event, the client demanded compensation, so Sam felt obligated to give a 20 percent discount to the booking for the mistakes. The client never booked with Sam again.

Deborah manages a conference center in East London. One day, a client came in who was rushed, stressed, and late. The client treated Deborah and her staff rudely. However, Deborah – refusing to take offense and having trained her staff to do likewise – recognized that the client was acting out of his anxiety about his event. So Deborah spoke calmly with the client, assuring him that all the preparations had been made. The client immediately experienced a sense of relief and calm. Deborah's staff calmly came alongside the client and ensured him that everything was ready, even helping the client with a few extra things.

During the lunch service, Deborah's team forgot to prepare the gluten-free option requested in advance by one of the client's delegates. The client spoke to Deborah about this sharply in front of several members of the group as well as Deborah's staff. Deborah apologized for the mistake, taking responsibility for the oversight and shielding her staff from the criticism of the client. Both the client and the delegate calmed down measurably. At that moment, one of the catering staff had a creative idea and was able to prepare a gluten-free option in minutes, so that the delegate was served late but still in time for the lunch break. The delegate enjoyed the option, which pleased the client. When Deborah's staff made yet another mistake in the afternoon, the client responded calmly and the mistake was corrected in moments. Following the event, the client gave a good review of the day, pleased with how everything seemed to go perfectly. He did not even mention the problems in his review. The client later booked three more conferences with Deborah.

These two stories show how anxiety affects many of the situations and relationships in our daily lives. At the same time, they show how leaders might manage their personal anxiety so that they might lead more effectively. When we resist and resolve anxiety in ourselves as leaders, we will experience greater leadership freedom.

ANXIETY AND THE *BEING/DOING* DYNAMIC

Anxiety rests in our *being.* As long as it rests securely in our *being* without challenge, it will distort everything in our *being* to a greater or lesser degree. We will find our sense of identity weakening as we begin to focus on what we perceive to be wrong with us instead of on our strengths. We will find our confidence eroding as we begin to worry whether or not people might accept us. We may try to ignore or deny our anxiety, but that will only push it deeper into our *being.* If we are to overcome anxiety, we must resist it in our *being.*

Because anxiety attaches to our *being,* it influences our *doing* rather profoundly. Anxiety begins by trying to deceive us about the true nature of our *doing.* When we have unmanaged anxiety, we will try to compensate for it or relieve it by our *doing.* Yet as leaders we know that to do something in leadership simply to compensate for our own anxiety would violate the integrity of our leadership in some way. So we work to develop other excuses for what we are doing rather than just trying to compensate for our own unmanaged anxiety. We may even find evidence that supports what we are doing as some good leadership practice, often developed by other anxiety-ridden people.

Jane's consulting business employed ten staff members full-time. Because they had limited office space, Jane allowed seven of her staff members to work from home. Everyone seemed to enjoy this arrangement very much. It saved Jane considerable money on office space plus gave her employees a greater sense of satisfaction in their jobs.

Jane began to suspect that two of her staff members were not putting in a full week's work. However, Jane really did not like to confront people. It made her unsettled inside (read *anxious*). So instead of speaking directly with the two people she suspected, she decided to create a new rule that everyone had to check in when they arrived at their desktop each morning. She also required people to fill out weekly time sheets. She justified this as good business practice and making things fair for everyone. However, it simply masked her anxiety.

Instead of helping Jane deal with her suspicions, the new policies upset all ten of her staff members. They felt that Jane's policies were a sign of mistrust. One of her most loyal staff members assumed that the policies were a direct attack against her, since she would come in at 7:30 a.m. each morning and work for seventy-five minutes before taking her daughter to school at 8:45–9:15 a.m. Since the sign in time was 9:00 a.m., this disrupted her usual routine. Jane also failed to realize that if employees were cheating her then they would find ways to get around the new rules. In the end, the whole situation only magnified anxiety – both in Jane and in her business.

ANXIETY AND *BEING* IN CHRIST

As Christian leaders, having our *being* grounded in Jesus Christ will give us a great advantage when resisting and resolving anxiety. The more we know and embrace who we are in Jesus Christ, the more we can resist anxiety when it comes to us. Once we know that in Christ we are significant, secure, and accepted, we can resolve the anxiety that attacks us more effectively.

Having our *being* grounded in Jesus Christ is so important to dealing with anxiety that we have developed three important propositions:

> **To the degree that we fail to know and fully embrace our identity in Jesus Christ we will be susceptible to and struggle with anxiety.**

271

> To the degree that we try to found our identity on something or someone other than Jesus, we will be susceptible to and struggle with anxiety.
>
> To the degree that we try to find our sense of significance, security or acceptance in something or someone other than Jesus, we will be susceptible to and struggle with anxiety.

If we do not know and believe who we are in Jesus Christ, then anxiety will always result. We will not have the sense of stability needed to overcome anxiety consistently. If we are trying to get our identity from our leadership, then we will always be anxious that we might lose our leadership and therefore our sense of identity. If we are trying to find our sense of significance, security or acceptance in our jobs or families or possessions, then we will always struggle with the anxious thought that we might lose these things and therefore lose our significance, security or acceptance.

Having our *being* fully grounded in Christ provides one of the best ways of resisting anxiety. Just as the best way to resist the annual cold virus is to promote health in ourselves – healthy rest, healthy diet, healthy hygiene – so also the best way to resist the virus of anxiety is to promote health in our *being*. A healthy *being* flowing from a dynamic relationship with God through Jesus Christ becomes the best way of resisting anxiety.

STRATEGIES TO PROMOTE HEALTHY *BEING*

Although anxiety attaches to our *being*, we can do certain things to promote a healthy, anxiety-resistant *being*. These things would fall under the rubric of "disciplines", with some of them being called "spiritual disciplines". Certain disciplines enable us to resist and resolve anxiety.

In order to practice disciplines in a way that will promote a healthy *being*, we must not see them as ritualistic or legalistic practices. Spiritual disciplines are not some empty rituals that we practice in order to make God happy with us. Spiritual disciplines do not work like some talisman that wards off anxiety. Practicing disciplines does not allow us to achieve greater favor with God in order to force God to do our bidding.

Disciplines enable us to train our *being* so that we remain focused on health and grounded in Jesus. As with all successful training, we must practice these disciplines on a daily basis. We must develop the disciplines until they shape the natural response of our being to the anxiety-inducing stimuli around us. These disciplines must become second nature to us, so that we do not even have to think about them before we do them.

In the military, soldiers train relentlessly day after day. They repeat the same tasks over and over until they can do them swiftly and thoughtlessly. They develop their bodies to respond in certain ways. They become fully knowledgeable about the issues that they might face as a soldier. For much of the time, the training might seem meaningless and useless. However, the soldier understands that all this discipline prepares the soldier for perhaps the one moment in time when he will depend on all that training and discipline to protect himself and his fellow soldiers. Being ready for that one moment makes all the difference.

We also must understand spiritual disciplines as inherently relational. These disciplines must flow from a dynamic relationship with God through Jesus Christ and the power of the Holy Spirit. Every successful marriage practices some sort of personal "disciplines". For example, husbands and wives tend to sleep on the same side of the bed each night. They each tend to have their own chores about the house. They may each have their own responsibilities regarding their social calendar. Having such disciplines does not indicate that these marriages are lifeless and dull. In fact, these disciplines allow for spontaneity and stability in the relationship.

In the remainder of this chapter, we will focus on a number of vital strategies, key disciplines, that will enable us to resist and resolve our personal anxiety. However, all the strategies have a biblical basis. Practicing these disciplines will enable us to develop a strong, healthy *being* grounded in a relationship with Jesus Christ.

THE ANXIETY PASSAGE

One passage of the Bible presents a number of vital strategies for resisting and resolving personal anxiety. As leaders, we need to master the spiritual disciplines that emerge from this passage in order to mitigate the effects of anxiety in our leadership.

> Rejoice in the Lord always; again I will say, rejoice. Let your reasonableness be known to everyone. The Lord is at hand; do not be anxious about anything, but in everything by prayer and supplication with thanksgiving let your requests be made known to God. And the peace of God, which surpasses all understanding, will guard your hearts and your minds in Christ Jesus. Finally, brothers, whatever is true, whatever is honorable, whatever is just, whatever is pure, whatever is lovely, whatever is commendable, if there is any excellence, if there is anything worthy of praise, think about these things. What you have learned and received and heard and seen in me – practice these things, and the God of peace will be with you. (Philippians 4:4–9)

Implementing the strategies in this passage will bring victory over anxiety. Paul promises this when he says that the "peace of God will guard your hearts and minds" and when he says that "the God of peace will be with you". This twofold mention of peace indicates the overcoming of anxiety as well as the resistance to anxiety.

We might marvel that Paul seems to address the issue of anxiety so directly. Or, we might wonder whether this was Paul's intention at all. One might suspect that Paul's writing about anxiety was only incidental to his letter. We might take this view until we understand the context.

Paul actually begins this section of his letter with an interesting instruction to the church in Philippi:

> I entreat Euodia and I entreat Syntyche to agree in the Lord. Yes, I ask you also, true companion, help these women, who have labored side by side with me in the gospel together with Clement and the rest of my fellow workers, whose names are in the book of life. (Philippians 4:2–3)

Apparently, two key women in the church at Philippi were having some major disagreements. We assume that they were probably leaders of some sort. However, they most certainly were influential. We do not know the nature of their disagreements, but we can assume they disagreed strongly. They had not been able to work through the disagreement themselves. Paul urges his faithful companion to work with them to help them resolve their conflicts, remembering that they are both written in the book of life.

Whenever a people-system has people within that system who disagree so strongly with one another, anxiety will come up in the system. This will always happen. We cannot avoid it. When those people are recognized leaders in the people-system – or at least they are important to the people-system – their disagreement will magnify and intensify anxiety.

Paul is effectively writing this passage to help the Christians in Philippi to resolve their personal anxiety as well as anxiety within their people-system. Paul's instructions speak to the roots of anxiety in our lives. The disciplines he introduces in this passage have particular reference for anxiety. These are not all the spiritual disciplines found in the Bible, but ones that have special usefulness for tackling anxiety.

Let us examine each of these disciplines in turn.

REJOICE IN THE LORD ALWAYS

Joy or sorrow comes from what we pay attention to. Imagine eating an ice cream cone with three scoops. If we pay attention to how good the ice cream tastes, the flavors in our mouths and perhaps the people with whom we are enjoying the ice cream, then most likely eating the ice cream cone will bring joy. If we pay attention to all the fat and calories in the ice cream, how we need to lose 10 kilos of weight and that the person next to us seems to be able to eat anything and not gain weight, then we will most likely experience sorrow.

To rejoice in someone or something means that we choose to pay attention to those qualities that produce delight or a sense of satisfaction. Although joy has an emotional aspect that we do not fully control, rejoicing involves a conscious choice that most often leads to this emotional aspect. We can choose to rejoice in almost anything. For example, I normally rejoice in my car. It is nothing fancy but it is fun to drive and practical. I choose to focus on the good qualities in my car. At the same time, I could choose to focus on the squeaky brakes, the road noise on the highway, and its age, which would produce dissatisfaction. So my joy comes from how I pay attention to my car.

To rejoice in the Lord means that we pay attention to the Lord, celebrating his qualities such as goodness, mercy, grace, beauty, and truth. We choose to pay attention to the great works God has done. We choose to pay attention to God's promises that will be fulfilled in Jesus. Paul challenges us continually to pay attention to the wonders of God and his love for us. God has no bad qualities, so focusing on him according to the truth of the Bible will always bring joy. We can rejoice in the Lord. Always.

We can see the importance of this discipline in all areas of life, not just anxiety. I have noticed when I have spiritual conversations with people who are on the edge of Christianity that often they will immediately raise objections such as suffering and tragedy in the world. They are paying attention to things that produce sorrow. However, I have found that by directing their attention to the obvious goodness of God – the beauty of the world, how God did not create evil and brokenness, the blessings we have as people – I will almost always change the direction of the conversation. Instead of sorrow, people begin to experience joy.

We rejoice in the Lord always because God's goodness and beauty never fades. I can imagine with my car there would come a time when the things that produce sorrow outweigh the things that produce joy. Not so with God. We can never exhaust the wonders of God in which to take joy. Rejoicing – paying attention to the good – confronts anxiety directly. For anxiety to flourish, we must pay attention to the things that produce anxiety. When we rejoice, anxiety cannot continue.

BE OBVIOUSLY MAGNANIMOUS

The second spiritual discipline presents some translation difficulties. Each Bible translator seems to have their own preferences. I have chosen the phrase "be obviously magnanimous". Magnanimity involves being openly gracious and generous to others. It includes the idea that we will be forgiving toward others when they hurt us. When we are magnanimous, we give grace generously to others. We give them the benefit of the doubt. We do not expect them to be perfect. We forgive their faults.

Paul tells us to be obviously magnanimous. We must make this quality evident to all around us. Our behaviors and attitudes must have the quality of generosity and graciousness. Effectively, this is an invitation for us to be open and transparent to others. Many people experience anxiety because they close themselves off from others, holding grudges and refusing to forgive. When we do this, we cannot resist anxiety.

REMEMBER THE LORD'S PRESENCE

Next, Paul reminds us that "the Lord is at hand". I phrase this discipline as "remember the Lord's presence". We need to remind ourselves all the time that the Lord is with us and the Lord is for us through his Son Jesus. Anxiety often comes because we feel alone and on our own. But this discipline reminds us that we are never left alone by God.

Three things may help us remember the Lord's presence. First, we have the Bible. As we have emphasized, we must know and choose to believe what the Bible says is true. Second, we have prophetic words and promises that the Lord may have given us. Third, we have the Body of Christ, the church. Our brothers and sisters in Christ help us remember the Lord's presence as they encourage and challenge us.

RESIST ANXIETY

The fourth discipline directs us actively and intentionally to resist anxiety. Paul commands us not to be anxious about anything. We do not have to tolerate anxiety in our lives. We can resist it. However, we must make a conscious, daily choice to resist anxiety. Anxiety lurks everywhere in our society today. The only way to remain at peace is to oppose anxiety. The choice to resist anxiety involves the other disciplines in the passage, but especially the next three.

PRAY

Paul tells us that in everything we are to pray. The word here is a general word for prayer, indicating every type of prayer that we might think of. This would include worship, meditation,[1] silence, praying in one's prayer language, praying the Scriptures, and the like. Prayer in all its forms provides a way to overcome the power of anxiety.

SUPPLICATE

Supplication involves presenting specific requests based on perceived needs. When we supplicate, we ask God for particular answers to the issues in our lives. Many people think of supplication as the entirety of prayer, but it is only a part of the overall dynamic of prayer. Other people seem to suggest that it is not right for a Christian to make specific requests or demands of God in prayer. However, Paul tells us that God approves of making clear and direct appeals to God for certain outcomes. For anxiety, this means that we focus on the issues we perceive are generating anxiety in our lives.

GIVE THANKS

Thanksgiving is one of the most powerful spiritual disciplines for overcoming anxiety. We simply cannot remain anxious while we are actively giving thanks to God. Thanksgiving forces us to focus on the blessings that we have received from the hand of God. Thanksgiving also enables us to find the good in even the worst of circumstances. When we give thanks to God, we acknowledge God's presence even in the most difficult circumstances of our lives.

We like to give people the "Five-Minute Thanksgiving Challenge". We encourage people to stand up and for five minutes do nothing but give thanks to God. We tell people to thank God for specific blessings in their lives. To challenge them, we tell them that they cannot repeat any blessing during the five minutes. For those who want a greater challenge, we tell them to focus their thanksgiving on just one area. For example, I will often spend the five minutes just thanking God for different things about my wife or my church. The Five-Minute Thanksgiving Challenge is a practical way to exercise this spiritual discipline.

INTERLUDE: THE PEACE OF GOD

At this point, Paul provides an interlude on the peace of God. Paul promises that if we persist in practicing these disciplines then the peace of God will come into our *being*. This peace will guard – or set up a fortress around – our hearts and minds as they are grounded in Christ Jesus. "Hearts and minds" is one biblical way of expressing our concept of *being*. "In Christ Jesus" refers to everything we have said about finding our identity and our sense of significance, security, and acceptance in Jesus Christ.

When we experience the peace of God in our *being*, we can know that we have successfully integrated these disciplines into our lives. Peace and anxiety oppose one another, so they cannot exist simultaneously in a person's *being*. When we do not experience the peace of God, we can know that anxiety is working in us. The lack of peace leads us back to the disciplines Paul gives us in this passage.

CHOOSE YOUR FOCUS

Most people take the first peace interlude as the conclusion of Paul's instructions. However, we see two more disciplines in this passage, leading up to the "God of peace" conclusion. These two disciplines are essential for overcoming anxiety.

The next discipline is in verse 8: "whatever is true, whatever is honorable, whatever is just, whatever is pure, whatever is lovely, whatever is commendable, if there is any excellence, if there is anything worthy of praise, think about these things". Paul tells the Philippians to think and keep on thinking about the things that have the qualities he has listed. We would call this discipline "choose your focus".

To understand the importance of this spiritual discipline, we need to understand something of how the human brain works. Our expectations and preconceptions actually shape our experience of reality. We tend to see what we expect to see. We tend to find evidence that confirms our preconceptions. We tend to find what we are looking for. So if we're looking for things that are good, we will tend to find things that are good. This is not because of the "power of positive thinking", but because our expectations and preconceptions shape the way our brains function.

Focusing our brains creates chemical and physical reactions in the brain. Repeated and purposeful focus actually changes the way our brains function. We create new neural pathways in the brain that then predispose us to thinking and acting in certain ways. So if we continually focus our attention on things that meet the requirements set out by Paul in verse 8, then we will actually change our brains – how they think and what they perceive. Choosing our focus is key to achieving long-lasting personal transformation.

Anxiety tries to get us to focus on the things that produce anxiety, such as uncertainty, change, and painful situations. If we allow anxiety to choose our focus then we will predispose our brains to feeling anxious. If we choose to focus on that which is true, honorable, just, pure, lovely, commendable, and excellent then we direct our brains away from anxiety and toward things that create a sense of peace.

For us as leaders, choosing our focus has important ramifications for the people-systems we lead. The focus of leaders naturally influences the focus of their people-systems. People-systems influence and direct the focus of their people naturally and automatically. Compelling vision and strategic goals help create healthy focus. Mirror neurons will lead people naturally to reflect the focus of the leader. So how we choose our focus will help determine how the people in our people-system choose their focus.

Because focus is so important, we need to ensure that we are focusing on truth. Ideas that have our attention change the way our minds and our people-systems operate. In a sense, we live in a mental world, so whether we focus on and choose to believe the truth makes all the difference. We are transformed by the renewal of our minds in truth. We must actively seek truth.

As Christians, the Bible is our objective standard for truth. In order to choose our focus in a healthy way, we have to seek a biblical worldview that will enable us to choose our focus well. Strongholds in our minds and our people-systems result from not focusing on truth or from focusing on that which is not true. Strongholds are patterns of thought not consistent with God's Word which assume a controlling power in the minds of people. Strongholds direct our focus away from those things mentioned by Paul and toward those things that produce anxiety.

We can choose our focus. Sometimes, the world, the flesh, and the devil work hard to deflect our focus away from truth and away from those things mentioned by Paul. However, Jesus Christ has overcome all the power of the world, the flesh, and the devil. Jesus has given us the ability choose God's focus for our lives and for people-systems. Choosing our focus well helps us to resist and resolve anxiety.

PRACTICE YOUR FAITH

Paul concludes this section of Philippians with one last discipline and a promise. I call this last discipline "practice your faith". Basically, Paul is telling us to put our faith into practice. Paul reminds us that Christian faith – and by that we mean the totality of our lives in Jesus Christ – is not an intellectual exercise but an all-consuming lifestyle. The language Paul uses here suggests that practicing our faith is an ongoing discipline. We must do it every single day.

Practicing our faith involves four things. First, Paul tells us to practice what we have learned. We need to do the godly discipleship practices that we have already integrated in our lives. For example, we need to keep on praying and keep on reading our Bibles.

Second, Paul tells us to practice what we have received. We need to continue to follow the godly traditions and practices that have been passed down to us. This might include things such as baptism and the Lord's Supper. It may also include things such as some of the great worship music that Christians have written over the centuries.

Third, Paul tells us to practice what we have heard. We need to integrate the godly teaching we have received into our lives. We need to learn from the stories of the great heroes of faith from across the centuries.

Fourth, Paul tells us to practice what we have seen. We need to follow those godly examples of living as a Christian that we have witnessed with our own eyes. We need to learn from our leaders and other mature Christians. Practicing our faith includes all four of these activities.

CONCLUDING PROMISE

Paul concludes the section on spiritual disciplines with a second promise related to peace. Paul promises that as we continue these disciplines the God of peace would be with us. In the first promise, the peace of God protects our hearts and our minds. In the second promise, the very presence of the God of peace also protects us, especially against anxiety.

We need to understand the importance of these promises. They are *promises*, which means God guarantees these assurances. Because of this guarantee, the promise of peace becomes the standard by which we can measure whether or not we have actually integrated these disciplines into our lives. If the peace of God is not present, then we know that we need to practice the disciplines more faithfully and consistently so our *being* becomes healthier and stronger. If the peace of God is present, then we know that we are integrating these disciplines more fully into our lives as Christians, supporting and encouraging health in our *being*.

CHOOSE TO RESPOND

In addition to those outlined by Paul in Philippians, we have found four other disciplines that help us to resist and resolve anxiety. We may not refer to them as "spiritual" disciplines, but they still have value for overcoming anxiety. Four verses from Proverbs point us toward the next discipline:

> Whoever is slow to anger has great understanding,
> but he who has a hasty temper exalts folly. (Proverbs 14:29)
>
> Desire without knowledge is not good, and whoever makes haste with his feet misses his way. (Proverbs 19:2)
>
> The plans of the diligent lead surely to abundance, but everyone who is hasty comes only to poverty. (Proverbs 21:5)
>
> Do you see a man who is hasty in his words? There is more hope for a fool than for him. (Proverbs 29:20)

The clue to understanding this discipline rests in the word "hasty". Those who act or react in a hasty manner create problems for themselves. So instead of reacting in haste we have to "choose to respond".

Choosing to respond involves making principled, determined choices. Choosing to respond forces us to pause, take stock, and then determine the best choice that might lead to a preferable outcome. We spend most of our day making intuitive, and often reactionary, choices driven by emotions and instinct. These instinctive choices often cause us to miss our way and say things we regret.

When we choose to respond, we can ensure that our response reflects our worldview, our values, and our focus. As Christians, our choice to respond will involve the Holy Spirit, the value and dignity of people created in God's image and for whom Christ died, and the genuine needs of the situation and the people-system. Choosing to respond will lead others, especially as our choice flows from our *being.*

We need to remember that it is not what happens to us that makes the difference in our lives but how we respond to what happens. Our choice to respond includes what we choose to believe about what happens, along with what we choose to believe about ourselves and about God.

When we do not choose to respond but instead react instinctively, we subject ourselves to anxiety. Failing to choose our response allows anxiety – both the anxiety in us and the anxiety in others – to influence our choices and reactions. This in turn increases anxiety in us and in others. Simply pausing to choose our response often disempowers anxiety so that we might make non-anxious choices.

Choosing to respond also includes choosing our expectations. Unmet or unfulfilled expectations lead to both anger and anxiety. Most people live with a whole set of expectations that they have never examined or evaluated to determine whether or not they are legitimate. Many times, we react instinctively when people do things that violate our expectations, such as cutting in line in the supermarket. Unfortunately, most of our expectations involve things much more important to us than standing in line.

Our expectations involve how we expect to be treated, how we expect people to listen to us, how we expect others to behave, what we expect out of government, and what we expect out of church – just to name a few. These expectations determine how we react to many of the things that happen to us on a daily basis. If we change our expectations, we change our reactions.

The problem comes when we hold expectations that are not legitimate. In order to be legitimate, an expectation has to meet at least two criteria. First, an expectation must be realistic. If I expect the government to give me a good job, a house, and enough money to feed my family without having to do anything in return, then I would suggest that perhaps that is an unrealistic expectation. If I expect my wife to be faithful to me just as she has promised, then I would suggest that is a realistic expectation.

Expectations must also be agreed when they involve other people. If I expect my wife to do the dishes every night, then that expectation is only legitimate if my wife has actually agreed to do the dishes every night. If I expect someone not to cut in line in front of me, then that expectation is only legitimate if the person could reasonably know that it is not appropriate to cut in line. When I travel to a culture that does not have the expectation that people will queue in an orderly manner, then my expectation that everyone queue in an orderly manner would not be legitimate.

One of the most effective things to determine our choice to respond is to set and reset our expectations to ensure they are legitimate. As a young leader, I expected people to respect and honor me, even people who were older than me. As you can imagine, I would often find myself bound up in anxiety when people did not treat me as I expected. After reading the Bible and learning from the life of Jesus, I decided to reset my expectations so that I expected people to treat me as they often treated Jesus and his disciples. Simply changing my expectation to one where people might hate me and exclude me and revile me and spurn my name as evil (see Luke 6:22) changed the way I responded.

Choosing to respond helps us resist and resolve anxiety in our lives. By choosing to respond we take control of ourselves and our mind, will, and emotions. As we choose to respond, we realize that we have power over the forces of anxiety. Choosing to respond helps anchor our *being* in peace as we recognize the authority given to us by God over our lives.

Choosing to respond also brings another important benefit to us as leaders. When we choose to respond, we enable the people in our people-system to choose to respond also. Because of who we are as a leader in our people-system, people will naturally follow our example. We give people in our people-system hope that just as God is working in us so also God might work in them. As with all these things, the choice to respond applies both in the marketplace and in the church.

EMBRACE PAIN

Nobody really likes the next discipline but it is one of the most powerful for resisting and resolving anxiety. I call this discipline "embrace pain". Anxiety is painful. Pain also produces anxiety. So if we are to overcome anxiety then we must learn how to deal with pain, especially pain that is ongoing. Otherwise, the anxiety caused by painful situations will overwhelm us. Three Bible passages point toward this discipline:

> Remove vexation from your heart, and put away pain from your body, for youth and the dawn of life are vanity. (Ecclesiastes 11:10)

> Share in suffering as a good soldier of Christ Jesus. (2 Timothy 2:3)

> But if when you do good and suffer for it you endure, this is a gracious thing in the sight of God. (1 Peter 2:20)

We can easily misunderstand Solomon's words in Ecclesiastes. It could almost sound as if Solomon was advocating the use of drugs or other forms of escape from our pain. But Solomon is telling us not to focus on the sense of anger and frustration that we might have. He is telling us to pass over the pain in our body so that it does not become our all-encompassing reality. Essentially, Solomon tells us to acknowledge our pain without allowing our pain to define us. In other words, he suggests we "embrace" our pain.

Paul echoes this theme in another way. He commands Timothy to share in suffering in the way a soldier suffers. The training undergone by soldiers causes pain. It is difficult. It is not pleasant. Yet, in order to become a great soldier one must endure this suffering. We also experience our own training and growth as something painful and difficult at times. We need to embrace this pain in order for our training to bear fruit.

In the third passage, Peter reminds us that sometimes even doing good might cause us pain. So when we experience the pain of doing good we must endure this pain – embrace it. Such endurance brings about grace in our lives. As leaders, we will often find ourselves in situations where doing good, the right thing, causes pain for us and for others. In these situations, we must embrace the pain and resolve to continue doing good even though it is painful.

From time to time as a leader I have had to bring correction to someone under my care. Perhaps a staff member has a pattern of behavior that contravenes good practice. I always experience these meetings as personally painful. I never enjoy them. Most often, the people whom I am correcting also do not experience the process as pleasant. I have found that if I choose to embrace the pain of this encounter and continue to relate to the person in love then we will most likely achieve a good outcome together. I have also found that if I fail to embrace the pain and avoid such meetings then I will actually prolong the pain and even increase it.

To embrace pain we must raise our threshold for personal pain by determining to get on with our lives, even in the midst of pain.[2] We must also raise our threshold for the pain that other people are experiencing. We often respond to people in pain by trying to stop the pain they are feeling. By doing so, we might short-circuit what God is trying to accomplish through the painful situation.

When it comes to embracing the pain, we must refuse to do three things that we tend to do instinctively. First, we must refuse to "rescue" people. So often we find people in pain and our first response is to try to help them so that the pain will go away. As leaders, our responsibility in these situations is not to save people from the pain they are experiencing – unless of course that pain is from something harmful or destructive – but to help them endure the painful situation until they achieve beneficial outcomes from the pain in their lives.

Second, we must refuse to "medicate" people. When we see people in pain, our first instinct is to make the pain go away, to try and help them feel better. This often causes much more pain for the person. For example, I have spoken with many people grieving the death of a loved one who have told me about asinine things others have said to them which have made their pain much worse. One person might say, "I guess God needed another angel." Another person might say, "God never gives us anything we can't handle." These and many other similar statements are said by well-meaning people who are trying to take away the pain of others. Most often they are also trying to resolve their own anxiety that is caused by the pain others are experiencing.

Third, we must refuse to take responsibility for others. Many people in pain want us to take away their pain by taking responsibility for something they themselves are responsible for. They want us to do for them what they should do for themselves. Many times Christians fall into this trap and accept the responsibility. Not only will this not resolve anxiety but it will also create much more anxiety for the person as well as for ourselves.

Over the years, I have often had people come up to me for prayer. I consider praying for people one of the great privileges of ministry. However, I have noticed that some people want me to pray for something that according to the Bible is their own responsibility. Someone might ask me to pray that God would take away the demon that has been attacking them. Someone else might ask me to pray that God would help them to give money faithfully. The Bible tells us that it is our responsibility to submit to God and resist the devil so that the devil will flee (see James 4:7). The Bible tells us that it is our responsibility to decide in our hearts what we should give and then give it faithfully (see 2 Corinthians 9:6–8). I can pray for these people but I will serve them better if I help them see their responsibility, know that God has already given them everything they need to fulfill their responsibilities (see 2 Peter 1:3), and then encourage them to act in faith.

How people deal with pain is one indicator of their level of maturity. Immature people like young children struggle to process pain in a healthy way. Mature people evaluate pain and then choose an appropriate course of action in response to the pain. As we become more mature in our *being*, we will find it much easier to embrace pain and allow pain to accomplish its purpose in our lives.

As leaders we must remember that how painful a situation feels does not indicate whether things are getting better or worse. Sometimes when things seem to be getting more painful our people-system may be adapting for the better. Sometimes when things seem to be getting less painful, it may indicate that we are avoiding the pain or masking the pain with things such as alcohol, food, activities or media. This shows one reason why we need to help ourselves and our people-system to embrace the pain. It enables us to discern more clearly and cooperate with God more fully until we can achieve the beneficial outcomes and the resolution of the pain.

In order to embrace the pain properly, we must distinguish pain from harm. Not all pain is harmful but much harm is painful. We see this clearly in the pain caused by a surgeon. Surgery almost always causes us pain but a successful surgery protects our body from harm. We sometimes need surgery, and the pain it causes, in order to bring healing. We can also see where a person might be harmed but not experience pain at the time. The one-night stand that leads to guilt and disease might be an example of this.

Although we need to embrace the pain, we must never tolerate harm. Harm in this sense is more than subjective. It is something that causes genuine damage, destruction, debilitation or injury. We base our discernment of harm on objective criteria, not on the subjective experience of pain. We might find one set of criteria for harm in the Bible. Using objective criteria helps us realize that someone is not necessarily harmed simply because they feel harmed.

Because of this, we must take great care regarding harm-based language such as the word "abuse". Over the years, I have sadly counseled with many men and women who decided to divorce their spouses. One very common reason given to justify the divorce has been that "my spouse is abusing me". When I have explored this accusation with the people, I have often not uncovered what I would expect to be called abuse – physical assault, verbal insults, yelling and screaming, deprivation, and similar things. What has often constituted abuse for these people have been things like: "My spouse doesn't spend enough time with me"; "We haven't had a date in years"; and "She doesn't pay attention to me." Although I would not deny the painfulness or the legitimacy of these complaints, in themselves they simply do not constitute genuine abuse. We overuse the language of abuse, which often makes genuine abuse more difficult to discern and correct.

We can learn to embrace pain as well as to distinguish pain that might bring good outcomes from pain that comes from something harmful. Choosing to embrace pain almost immediately begins to lessen anxiety, not only in ourselves but also in the people and people-systems we are leading. By embracing pain in people and people-systems, we actually help them to embrace their own pain and look beyond the pain in a way that brings hope to their situation. As we respond to pain calmly and peacefully, we bring anxiety-resistant peace into our systems and situations.

MANAGE YOUR RESPONSE TO STRESS

Everyone experiences stress. We believe that stress is normal and essential for life. Most often, the stress itself is not what causes us problems; it is how we deal with stress. So as a discipline we must manage our response to stress. In one sense, the Bible really does not consider the issue of stress as many would understand it today. The closest we might get is Paul's comment in 2 Corinthians 11:28 about the daily pressure he felt because of his concern for all the churches. In another sense, we might say that entire books such as Ecclesiastes address the issue of stress, albeit in an indirect way.

We learn to manage our stress in a number of ways. We must take responsibility for ourselves and the controllable aspects of our situations. Self-control is a fruit of the Holy Spirit and really the only biblical form of control. God has ordained that some things are our responsibility, so if we fail to maintain these responsibilities we will experience stress and anxiety.

We also manage our stress by surrendering what we cannot control to God. Prayer helps us do this, as does remembering that God is in control of the universe. Trying to control people, situations, and our people-systems will always cause stress and anxiety. Other people and people-systems simply are not subject to our control.

Third, we manage our stress by distinguishing godly goals from godly desires.[3] Confusing godly goals with godly desires always causes stress. It also creates anxiety as we try to force ourselves or others to achieve what we want.

For us, godly goals are goals that people or circumstances cannot thwart. In other words, they are godly goals because they are goals that we can achieve no matter what happens with the strength God supplies. For example I might have a godly goal of becoming the best preacher I can be. No one can prevent me from achieving this goal. My own *being* and *doing* will determine whether I achieve the goal.

Godly desires are outcomes that we would like to achieve but depend upon other people and circumstances for us to achieve them. Other people and circumstances might easily thwart the accomplishment of these godly desires. For example, I might have a godly desire of doubling the size of my congregation in one year. In order to achieve this desire, I need the cooperation not only of the people within my church and the circumstances around my church but also of the people whom I would like to attract to the church.

Fourth, we can learn to manage our stress by clarifying our expectations. We mentioned earlier that unmet expectations cause much of our anger and frustration. Unmet expectations also cause great stress in our lives. So we need to learn to clarify our expectations using the two criteria mentioned above: realistic and agreed.

Next, we manage stress by remembering that anything worthwhile always takes longer to achieve than we think it should. Trying to hurry something along always causes stress and anxiety. I remember hearing that we often overestimate what we can accomplish in one year and underestimate what we can accomplish in five years. Trying to accomplish too much too soon often generates stress and anxiety.

Sixth, we can manage our stress by refusing to take responsibility for other people and their problems and responsibilities. We need to understand that the more impatient we are to see that something is done the less motivated other people will be to do it. In addition, the more impatient we are to see that something is done the less likely it will be that other people will take leadership.

We simply cannot will people to do things that we want them to do. They have to make their own choices and decisions. We need to accept that this means sometimes things we believe are important simply will not get done. Sometimes important things will fall away. However, we all have enough responsibilities of our own without taking on the responsibilities of others.

Finally, we manage stress by eating, exercising, and resting properly. This is fairly common advice. It also leads us into our final discipline.

REMEMBER THE SABBATH

This discipline includes several things under the rubric "remember the sabbath". Incessant activity almost always magnifies anxiety. The more anxious we are the busier we will become. Our busyness will fuel our anxiety and spread our anxiety to others. Therefore, appropriate rest is essential for overcoming anxiety. Rest in this instance involves a cluster of concepts related to the biblical idea of sabbath.

First, rest requires that we follow the biblical injunction to "remember the sabbath". For the Bible, the sabbath is not some random "day off" that we might take whenever we feel like it. It is also not some legalistic observance required of us as Christians. The sabbath is a day each week set apart to honor God by withdrawing from our labors and our striving. For the Jews, the sabbath began at sundown on Friday and continued until sundown on Saturday. For Christians, the sabbath moved to the first day of the week on which they celebrated the resurrection of Jesus.

Regardless of the date chosen for sabbath observance, the sabbath is our privilege and a blessing. It reminds us of the sabbath rest that we spoke about when we talked about our sphere of leadership. Most often, the sabbath is the day we set aside for corporate worship and fellowship with other Christians. We choose to cease from our incessant activity on the sabbath and choose the way of peace. It is not a day to catch up with the various other projects and activities that we have not been able to do during the rest of the week.

Second, rest requires that we seek to take a weekly day off that is not the sabbath. People who advocate only one day off per week often quote the Bible as saying on six days we are to do our labor. While this is true, labor for the people of the Old Testament included all of the business of life – business dealings, household chores, home improvements, and so on. If we spend six days doing our professional jobs we will not have time for the other things that we must do in order to survive, such as buying food and cleaning the house.

We encourage people to rest by setting aside a second day each week on which we can shop, work on our do-it-yourself projects, engage in social activities, and catch up on our sleep. This is an important catch-up day during the week on which we can accomplish all the various bits and pieces that we could not accomplish the rest of the week.

Observing both the sabbath and a weekly day off may require some creativity. Sometimes our jobs require us to work strange hours or long hours. Some people work swing shifts, where their times rotate on a regular basis. In these situations, we must seek God for how to implement the sabbath day and our weekly day off. We may have to divide our weekly day off into two. Or we may have to program both our weekly day off and our sabbath day on a month-by-month basis depending on our work schedule. However we accomplish this, we need to get appropriate rest on a weekly basis if we are to overcome anxiety.

A third concept for achieving rest is to take our holidays. We must take all the holiday to which we are entitled. We must beware the tendency to take our holiday just in bits and pieces. A proper holiday normally requires at least a week off from work. We must also beware of what is called "worlidays". Worlidays are working holidays to which we take all that is needed to work on the side while we are taking our holiday.

Fourth, in order to rest we encourage people to take regular retreats. A retreat is different from a holiday. Retreats are planned times away with God, during which we seek God's vision and God's will for our lives. Retreats can take many different forms, from a relaxed time away with your family to a silent retreat in a monastery. Some retreats involve nothing but personal reflection while other retreats might include the guidance of a spiritual leader. Having a retreat might include an inspirational conference of some sort, or it might involve quiet time for reading the books we have on our reading list.

For retreats to be effective they should have several qualities. They need to involve time away from our normal activities and from the places in which those activities occur – such as our homes and our workplaces. They need to have some sense of purpose, some intentionality. They normally need to include at least one full day. And they should invite us into an encounter with the living God.

Appropriate rest protects us from the constant onslaught of

anxiety. Like all disciplines, it does not happen easily or naturally. We must choose rest actively and intentionally. When we rest, we not only help protect ourselves from anxiety but we also become more effective at helping our people-systems resolve anxiety.

RESISTING PERSONAL ANXIETY: ADDITIONAL CONSIDERATIONS

The disciplines described in this chapter will help us resist and resolve our personal anxiety. However, there are a few other strategies we can keep in mind as well. These are more like discipleship reminders than they are disciplines, although they might require some discipline to carry out.

We cannot emphasize strongly enough how vital it is for us to maintain a healthy *being* grounded in Jesus Christ. Knowing who we are in Christ and how Christ has met our most fundamental needs as human beings helps insulate us against anxiety. It not only helps us to resist our own anxiety but also to resist the anxiety of others.

An important part of our *being* involves getting over our need for approval and acceptance from other people. People pleasers will always experience anxiety. Leaders who are looking to the approval of other people cannot properly orient themselves to Jesus Christ. They will not rest in the approval of God – which is a gift of God's grace through Jesus. Being a people pleaser always leads us to experience more anxiety as we subject ourselves to the ever changing whims of other people.

In order to resist anxiety, we must continue to serve from our strengths. When we spend time and energy trying to overcome our weaknesses, we will subject ourselves to anxiety. (It is important to note that weaknesses and "sins" are not the same here. Weaknesses are simply things we do not do well.) Of course, we may often need to find someone who can help us in our weaknesses, but the best we will normally do regarding our weaknesses is learn to compensate for them.

Serving from our strengths while accepting our weaknesses generates confidence and creativity in our leadership. When we feel confident we are more able to resist anxiety. When we are creative, we can imagine new possibilities that enable us to overcome the anxiety of the present situation. Serving from our strengths often draws together others who are also serving from their strengths to help us form a team, or a people-system, that may achieve many beneficial outcomes.

We need to understand that anxiety left unchecked will produce strongholds in our minds. These strongholds are patterns of thinking that are contrary to God's will and God's Word. So as we resist anxiety on a daily basis we would encourage people to practice the stronghold busting that is part of the *Freedom in Christ Discipleship Course.* We would also encourage people to pray through the *Steps to Freedom in Christ* on their own or with a partner on a regular basis. These discipleship practices will help us overcome strongholds.

Finally, we encourage people to practice forgiveness daily. Unforgiveness in our lives always magnifies anxiety. It will also create anxiety in our relationships, even when the unforgiveness involves a completely different relationship. We need to practice forgiveness every day and preferably at the instant we experience hurt or wounding.

We often mistake forgiveness as only relating to wrongdoing that has been done to us. We feel that before we can forgive we need to determine that what someone has done was sinful or wrong. However, forgiveness primarily involves *pain* that we have experienced, not just wrongdoing. We need to forgive every time someone does or says something to us that causes us pain, even when what they have done was not wrong.

If we think about it we can easily see how forgiveness involves pain and not just wrongdoing. For example, if I am sitting in a chair and someone walks past me and accidentally steps on my foot, they have caused me pain but they may not have done anything sinful. I will need to forgive the person, but I do not have to judge their action as sinful in order to forgive them. I simply need to know that they have caused me pain. If I have experienced pain, then I need to forgive.[4]

In order to forgive it helps us to remember that the root meaning of the word "forgive" is to release something. In the case of forgiveness, we are releasing the pain that the actions or words of another have caused us to God. Forgiveness in this situation is a form of prayer, and it is prayer that we direct to God, not to another person. So when we forgive we are releasing the pain to God, choosing not to cause pain in return and choosing not to hold onto our pain.

In Freedom in Christ Ministries, we use a simple prayer to help us forgive: "Lord I choose to forgive (name the person) for (describe what was said or done) which made me feel (describe the pain)." This prayer helps people learn to forgive quickly. We have found that most people can learn this prayer easily and use it daily.

If we practice the above strategies every day we can help our *being* become anxiety resistant. We can learn to resolve anxiety as soon as we begin to experience it. We will also discover that we become much more sensitive to the presence of anxiety not only in ourselves but also in other people and in our people-systems.

THE LEADERSHIP DILEMMA

We close this chapter with yet another leadership dilemma. As the blind cannot lead the blind (see Matthew 15:14), so an anxious person cannot effectively lead anxious people and anxious people-systems. At the same time, the contagious nature of anxiety means that if our people and our people-systems are bound up in anxiety then we will tend to face anxiety on a daily basis.

Because anxiety always hides or disguises itself, we may not be aware as leaders of how anxious we really are and how that influences everything in our leadership. Furthermore, the presence of anxiety undermines the self-control and renewing of the mind with truth that are essential for leaders to overcome anxiety. In other words, we may easily become blinded to the activity of anxiety and how it is influencing everything in our leadership.

Simply resisting and resolving anxiety in our own lives alone will help increase our freedom for leadership. Once we are resolving anxiety in our own life, we will begin to see anxiety at work in the people and people-systems around us. We will not only become much more confident in ourselves, but also others will become much more confident in us as leaders as they sense our ability to resist anxiety. However, we will not always see anxiety at work. Anxiety is, after all, sneaky and shifty.

Because anxiety is so prevalent in our society, we must assume that anxiety is at work even if we do not perceive it. We must protect ourselves daily from the infection of anxiety. We can only do this as we refuse to focus on anxiety while practicing the disciplines that will enable us to become anxiety resistant in our *being*. Once we become anxiety resistant in our *being*, we can help our people-systems overcome their anxiety as well.

11

OVERCOMING SYSTEMIC ANXIETY

All of the great leaders have had one characteristic in common: it was the willingness to confront unequivocally the major anxiety of their people in their time. This, and not much else, is the essence of leadership.

John Kenneth Galbraith

A crust eaten in peace is better than a banquet partaken in anxiety.

Aesop

Courage is grace under pressure.

Ernest Hemingway

From October 1 to October 17, 2013, the United States Government shut down. The US Congress refused to pass a spending bill to meet the budget unless President Obama worked to repeal the changes to the US health system known as "Obamacare". In order to gain the upper hand, Republicans in the US Congress sought to magnify the anxiety of people concerning the changes to the medical system. The President, on the other hand, sought to magnify the anxiety of the American people by presenting the worst-case scenarios regarding the shutdown. Not only was the entirety of the United States bound up in anxiety for a time but also anxiety rippled around the world as people in many nations wondered whether the economic shutdown of the United States might cause global financial problems.

In the end, the United States had no winners in this contest, only losers. The Republicans lost a lot of respect and popularity among the American people. President Obama lost favor and respect among his fellow Democrats. The American people and others in the world lost a little more of the battle with anxiety. We might frame the entire story from the perspective of anxiety and its effects on the people-systems of society.

THE ANXIETY EPIDEMIC

Anxiety has infected the people-systems of society – including churches. Once Friedman opened my eyes through *A Failure of Nerve* I began to see the influence of anxiety all around me. For me, this did not mean that I saw the proverbial demon behind every proverbial bush. It simply meant that I began to notice the influence of anxiety much in the same way as I might notice how many people are sick with a cold during the cold season.

I also began to wonder why anxiety had become such a major issue in the world today. Why had I not noticed anxiety in the same way in the 1980s? Why had not anxiety featured more prominently in the stories that my mother told me of the Great Depression in the 1930s? Why had the people of World War II London banded together so strongly to resist and overcome the anxiety caused by the war? As I reflected on these questions I began to notice the nature of the anxiety epidemic.

Anxiety often escalates when a people-system is overwhelmed by the quantity and speed of information and change.[1] We have access to more information than ever before. We are experiencing more change in society than ever before. Not only can individuals be overloaded and confused, but also whole people-systems – and even society itself – can become overloaded and confused.

Anxiety escalates when the institutions and individuals that normally absorb and resolve the anxiety are no longer available to do so.[2] There was a time when the presence of police actually helped to decrease anxiety in people. Recent controversies and scandals regarding allegations of police malpractice have undermined the ability of the police to help absorb and drain away anxiety.

There was a time when the political leaders helped resolve anxiety in a nation. We can see this with Winston Churchill during World War II. However, the increasingly adversarial and contentious nature of party politics in many nations today actually increases anxiety in the nation. We see few leaders in the world today who can rise up and help drain away anxiety from the people.

There was a time when the strength and stability of the neighborhood church, along with that of the "parish priest", gave people a sense of hope, comfort, and security. When a community was struggling it often turned to the parish priest to help them overcome anxiety. However, churches today are often so full of anxiety themselves based on declining numbers and declining revenues that they cannot help their surrounding communities resolve their anxiety.

Technological advancements tend to empower anxiety. One hundred years ago during World War I, a person may have had to wait days for information concerning the war. Today, because of the internet and social networking, we can experience the horrors of war almost as they are happening. We can see terrorist attacks even as they are unfolding. We can witness the ravages of epidemic diseases, counting the bodies even as they fall.

The anxiety epidemic has given rise to all sorts of technical, technological, and managerial attempts to resolve anxiety. We only have to think of the proliferation of leadership books and computer programs! These things may help alleviate the symptoms of anxiety, but they will not resolve anxiety itself. In some situations, these attempts to resolve anxiety may actually increase anxiety as people try to learn new technologies, new practices, and procedures and then impose them on others.

We believe that leadership presents the only real hope for resisting and resolving anxiety in the people-systems of the world. In order for people-systems to resist and resolve anxiety, they must have anxiety-resistant leaders. However, such leaders will often increase anxiety before they help reduce and resolve anxiety.

KEY BIBLE PASSAGES

Two Bible passages give us some major insights for becoming anxiety-resistant leaders who might help our people-systems resist and resolve anxiety. We already mentioned 2 Timothy 1:7. We saw that God has given us a spirit of power, love, and self-control. These three ingredients help us become anxiety-resistant leaders.

"Power" reminds us that we have the ability given by God through the Holy Spirit who lives inside us to overcome anxiety. The Holy Spirit has equipped us to resist anxiety. He is the ongoing source of our power as leaders.

"Love" reminds us that only a zealous, self-giving commitment to our people and our people-systems will enable us to help them overcome anxiety. We must resolve to commit fully to our people-system if we are to help it resolve anxiety. Too many leaders flee when things begin to get difficult. We must connect in love.

"Self-control" reminds us that our ability to help our people-system resolve anxiety does not come by trying to control the people-system. Instead, it comes when we exercise self-control. It comes as we learn to resist and resolve anxiety in our own lives while choosing to act and respond to our people-systems in love.

The second Bible passage that helps us as leaders in our people-systems regarding anxiety is Ephesians 6:10–20. The various parts of the armor of God help us deal with anxiety. However, there are two other parts of this passage that have particular importance for us with regard to anxiety.

Paul reminds us that our struggle is not primarily against flesh and blood but against spiritual forces in the heavenly realms. When we are dealing with anxiety it is easy to blame others for the anxiety. We often try to direct our conflict on people. This passage reminds us that anxiety is really a spiritual issue and not just an emotional one. When we direct our struggle with anxiety onto people we simply magnify the anxiety. Anxiety represents one of the devil's schemes to keep our people-systems in bondage.

Paul also reminds us that our primary responsibility as leaders is to take our stand and then stand firm. We often think that we must do a lot of things in order to overcome anxiety. However, we need to remember that overcoming anxiety is primarily an issue of our *being* and not our *doing*. When we learn to stand in the peace of God, we become an anchor point for our people-system so that it might learn how to stand in the peace of God.

FIVE BEHAVIORS IN AND OF ANXIOUS PEOPLE-SYSTEMS

So what are some of the ways a people-system infected with anxiety might behave? Friedman observed five key behaviors in anxious people-systems:

- **Reactivity**
- **Herding**
- **Blame shifting**
- **Quick-fix mentality**
- **Leadership abdication**[3]

We will consider each of these in turn. We will describe what they are and then give some clear strategies for overcoming each one. The effectiveness of each strategy largely depends on how well we are resisting and resolving personal anxiety as leaders. Unless we address our own anxiety first we cannot help our people-systems overcome their anxiety.

REACTIVITY

The first common behavior we can observe in an anxious people-system is what we call "reactivity". Reactivity occurs whenever two or more people (or groups of people) get caught up in a cycle of emotionally intense and reflexive reactions to one another. Reactivity often begins with seemingly small disagreements. If these disagreements remain unresolved, or if people begin to suspect one another's motives or character, then the intensity of the disagreements will escalate. After a while the nature of the disagreements will no longer matter. What will matter is how people get locked into emotionally intense and reflexive reactions to one another. When this happens anxiety will escalate and spread into the entire people-system.

One of the clearest biblical examples of reactivity is the way Saul treated David. For Saul, it did not matter whether David did right or wrong. What mattered was that Saul perceived David as a threat. Saul felt anxious because of David's success. Satan clearly inflamed the situation by provoking Saul into ever more intense emotional reactions to David.

In our struggles at my third church, I allowed myself to get caught up in a number of reactive relationships. One elder and I seemed to go at each other all the time, to the point that our reactivity brought anxiety into our entire leadership. It came to the point that it no longer mattered what we were disagreeing about; what mattered was simply that we disagreed.

Reactive or responsive

As we seek to resolve reactivity, it is important to remember that there is a difference between being "reactive" and being "responsive". When people are acting out of instinct and reflex, then they are being reactive. When we see much emotionality in a relationship then the people are likely being reactive. People who concentrate on winning at all costs are often very reactive.

305

When people are acting out of intention and choice, they are being responsive. Being responsive requires that we exercise self-control. We choose to acknowledge our emotions but then respond in a way that promotes health and understanding. The goal is for everyone to become responsive in a healthy, biblical way.

Characteristics of reactivity

In reactivity, people (or groups of people) effectively get stuck in a negative and sinful way of relating to one another. This leads the relationship to develop along predictable lines. A number of characteristics emerge from this sinful pattern of relating that in turn are sinful.

First, people in reactivity usually experience overly intense emotions. These emotions are generally very negative toward the other person. The intensity of the emotions inhibits the ability of people to hear and understand what others are saying.

Second, a pessimism enters the relationships so that people can only focus on what they perceive to be wrong. This pessimistic focus on our perceptions of what is wrong in the relationships leaves little room for correction or improvement. Instead, it locks the people into a downward cycle that expects further breakdown in the relationships and the emergence of additional problems.

The third characteristic is that people start violating one another's legitimate personal boundaries. They will often interfere with the other person's communication by interrupting them or speaking over them. They refuse to listen to what the other person says. They may even try to disrupt the other person's relationships by doing things such as spreading gossip and rumors or talking behind their back.

The next characteristic is that people will tend to overreact to any perceived hurt, insult or slight. They will take disagreements far too seriously, framing everything in an either/or, "life and death" manner. Even when someone chooses to affirm them or praise them, people caught up in reactivity will put a pessimistic spin on that communication so that what was intended as a compliment becomes yet another insult.

Finally, people will begin to engage in ugly personal attacks rather than dealing with legitimate issues. *Ad hominem* arguments fuel reactivity. People will attack the other person's motives, character, and intentions, always framing these in the worst way possible. They will struggle to identify the real issues in the argument. They may even begin to objectify the other person as something wrong rather than dealing with the person as a fellow human being.

Effects of reactivity on people-systems

Even whole people-systems can get caught up in reactivity. This will happen especially when two or more primary leaders in the system become reactive toward one another. It may also happen when one system starts to be reactive toward another system – for example, most political parties in America and the United Kingdom today.

When a people-system gets caught up into reactivity, several things happen. First, the people-system begins to focus on self-preservation and stability – even if that costs the system everything. For example, if a long-term church member gets into a reactivity cycle with the minister, many churches would rather dismiss the minister than discipline the church member, even when the minister behaves appropriately and the church member behaves badly. What is important is that the people-system returns to stability.

Second, reactive systems will try to defend and even justify their reactive behavior. In the United States, for example, the two main political parties often become reactive toward one another but, instead of finding new ways to work together, they simply justify their behavior as necessary for the preservation of the United States, legitimizing their refusal to work together. This has often led to deadlock and inaction in government.

Reactive people-systems also lose their internal resources for dealing with the problems and issues they face. In order to resolve the problems of the world today, or even the "little" problems of our lives, we need a number of resources. We need to take time and have some distance from the problems in order to see them clearly. We need to be calm, seeking some objectivity. We need to gain clarity about the source of the issues and have the imagination necessary to think creatively. Reactive people-systems lose these resources because of their reactivity and the anxiety it produces.

In the end, if we do not resolve the reactivity of people-systems, they will become demonized and destructive. One can think of churches in the United States that have become so reactive toward problems in society that they would even do something that clearly violated the Bible – such as murdering an abortionist, sending hate mail or picketing a funeral. One might also see reactivity in the responses of some world leaders toward one another. Such reactivity might even lead to war.

Overcoming reactivity

Many people wrongly assume that if we ignore reactivity then it will go away. But ignoring reactivity just increases reactivity and leads to more anxiety. We also cannot hide reactivity. Like anxiety, people will sense reactivity even when they do not know it is present. It will cause anxiety even when we try to disguise it as something else.

But there are ways to disarm reactivity. We begin by exercising self-control, especially as leaders. We must refuse to become reactive ourselves. If we engage in reactivity then we cannot lead our people-system out of it.

If we expose it, identifying it for what it is, we can often overcome it. One of the profound moments in the crisis years at my third church occurred when an elder forcefully interrupted a reactive conversation I was having with another elder. The elder strongly confronted us and challenged us to stop. The elder's action jolted me alert to something happening that I had not perceived – what I now know as reactivity. By taking this action, the elder enabled me to begin a process of change.

If we give grace to one another just as God in Christ has given grace to us (Ephesians 4:32), then we can disarm reactivity. We can choose to be obviously magnanimous, as we discussed in the last chapter. We can show gratitude to the person for the good they have in their character and the good things they have done. If we take a position of mercy and grace toward another and persist in that position, reactivity cannot continue. It normally requires at least two people or groups to remain reactive. If we refuse to participate in reactivity, then reactivity cannot continue.

In order to overcome reactivity, we must carefully identify and evaluate perceptions – our own and others'. Many times we get caught up into reactivity because we have the wrong perception about something. We will often require some outside help to review our perceptions. We need trusted friends to help us face the truth. One thing that helped me through the difficult years was having close friends who knew the situation and were not afraid to tell me when I was seeing things incorrectly.

We need to remember how anxiety distorts everything, including our perceptions. I recall many occasions when I thought I was seeing things clearly only to discover that I had been blinded by my anxiety. On one occasion, I heard about a person that had said something which seemed to betray a confidence that I had shared with the person. Because of my reactivity and anxiety in the relationship, I assumed the worst and immediately became very angry. However, I decided to respond rather than react. I slowed down and took some time to investigate the matter discreetly. In the end, I discovered that my perceptions had been completely wrong and the person had kept my confidence. My reactivity would have harmed or perhaps even destroyed the relationship.

The story above shows how we must learn to respond thoughtfully with gentle firmness. We must choose not to react. This means that we need to step back, take a deep breath and make a good choice. This also means that we must take a firm stand based on our values, not based on our reactive perceptions.

To overcome reactivity, we must focus on what is healthy and healthy processes in the people-system. So often we get stuck in reactivity by focusing on what is wrong and what is unhealthy. We need to look for the good and the good people in our people-system. We need to maintain healthy processes, healthy ways of doing things, that will lead us toward healthy outcomes. Focusing on health creates a sense of hope in our people-system.

Dealing with reactivity requires that we learn how to move in the opposite spirit. Where there is bitterness, we show forgiveness. Where there is anger, we express calm. Where there is criticism, we express appreciation.

I remember dealing with a woman in our church who was fairly critical of her family, most of whom I knew personally. When she would criticize someone, I would not confront her criticism. Instead, I would simply comment on something good about the person she had just criticized. Over time, ministering in the opposite spirit broke the cycle of criticism in her life.

Finally, we must remember the words of Paul to Timothy:

> The Lord's servant must not be quarrelsome but kind
> to everyone, able to teach, patiently enduring evil,
> correcting his opponents with gentleness. God may
> perhaps grant them repentance leading to a knowledge
> of the truth, and they may come to their senses
> and escape from the snare of the devil, after being
> captured by him to do his will. (2 Timothy 2:24–26)

Following Paul's advice will help disarm reactivity. Reactivity can only continue when people become quarrelsome. But as we remain kind, patient, and gentle, God will often intervene by leading people to genuine repentance. With a repentant heart, people will be able to see things as they really are, come to their senses, and escape the devil's snare of reactivity.

HERDING

The second behavior is what Friedman called "herding". Herding occurs when people in a people-system begin to apply or experience a very strong pressure for some kind of fuzzy, idealistic cohesion that does not allow people to take responsibility and act maturely. In herding, the people-system coerces people to sacrifice their own sense of individuality and their own values so that there is no discord or disagreement.

When a people-system engages in herding, the system has little tolerance for individual expression and independent thinking. The people-system does not allow disagreement with the majority opinion and perspectives. When disagreements start, people in the system respond by saying things like, "Can't we all just get along; we need to forget our differences for the common good." People who do not comply or people who disrupt the false sense of peace will be pushed away from or out of the people-system.

Once herding occurs, the people-system begins to adjust itself toward the least mature, most dependent or most dysfunctional members in the system. For example, when an immature person in a herding people-system begins to throw a temper tantrum of some sort, instead of correcting the behavior and expecting the immature person to change the behavior, the people-system will seek to placate or give in to the immature person in order to preserve the false unity and the false peace. When the people-system is herding, the people who are the most messed up tend to be the ones who are in control.

In the Bible, the story about Aaron and the golden calf illustrates the power of herding (see Exodus 32:1-6). Because Moses was delayed coming down the mountain, the people decided that they should make and worship a golden calf. Instead of resisting the anxiety of the people over the lateness of Moses, Aaron capitulated and helped create a false idol that the people worshiped.

Overcoming herding

Leaders can do a number of things in order to overcome herding in their people-system. First, leaders must focus on the mature people in the system. We must seek to promote healthy individuality and integrity among the people. Our goal is to promote maturity throughout the people-system.

Second, leaders need to emphasize the strengths in people and in the people-system itself. The strengths of people and the people-system will enable the system to overcome herding. When a people-system is herding, it will often have an unhealthy preoccupation with anything that is wrong and anything that produces anxiety. By focusing on the strengths, we generate a sense of hope and empowerment for the people-system to develop maturity and to take responsible action to resolve the issues generating anxiety.

As leaders, we must also encourage integrity and maturity in people. We must help people develop a healthy *being*. Mature people will be able to take personal responsibility and resist the power of herding. This means for us as leaders as well that we must be emotionally open and available to people. We cannot close ourselves off. People must be able to see our own maturity if they are to develop maturity themselves.

Finally, in the midst of herding we must resist the powerful force for coercive cohesion and consensus. Instead, we must take clear, principled stands on issues while remaining fully connected to the people around us. We must learn to stand firm with gentleness. We must help others do the same.

BLAME SHIFTING

The third behavior is called "blame shifting". Blame shifting occurs when people focus on forces outside themselves or outside their people-system as the source of their problems. When people focus on forces that they believe have victimized them rather than taking personal responsibility for their own *being* and *doing*, they have succumbed to blame shifting.

In recent years, a number of countries have experienced crises and debates regarding the role of immigrants in those countries. In almost every continent, it has become fashionable for countries to blame any number of societal problems on immigrants. The countries fail to realize that most of the problems attributed to immigrants are more likely the result of internal policies and perspectives within those countries. Even when groups produce research that demonstrates immigrants have made a net contribution to the country, many people continue to assert that immigrants are the problem. This is blame shifting.

Blame shifting is so common that often we fail to recognize it. Businesses blame their declining business on factors such as competition and market forces rather than looking for internal factors that might have led to the decline. Churches blame their declining numbers on various changes in society, refusing to accept the notion that the problem for lack of growth might just lie within the church itself. Some churches even justify their blame shifting by asserting they are the "faithful remnant".

In the Bible, we can see blame shifting occur when the fleeing Hebrews came to the Red Sea (see Exodus 14:10–14). Instead of seeking God for the way to overcome the Red Sea, in their anxiety caused by the pursuing Egyptians, the Hebrews blamed Moses for bringing them to the place they would die. Moses in turn looked to God who brought the deliverance.

Overcoming blame shifting

Several strategies will help leaders overcome blame shifting. First, we need to reframe problems and issues in relation to the people-system, instead of focusing on sources from outside the people-system. For example, instead of blaming our secular society for the decrease in church attendance, churches need to ask themselves what aspect of their church is hindering their growth. Instead of asking why immigrants are taking all the jobs, nations might ask themselves why citizens of the nation are not taking those jobs themselves.

Second, as with herding, we must focus on health and healthy people in our people-systems. For our people-systems to overcome their problems and challenges, it will require healthy people who are working to promote health in the people-system. Having increasingly healthy people provides increasingly varied personal resources we can tap into for meeting our challenges.

Third, we must also re-examine our perceptions and re-evaluate our expectations. We need to ensure that our perceptions of the challenges accurately reflect the truth, not only of our society but especially of our people-system. We need to ensure that we have developed and are maintaining legitimate expectations – first of ourselves and then of others around us. For example, if we are leading a church of 200 people in a village of 1,000 people with ten other churches in it, then we might want to reconsider our goal of building a church of 1,200 people.

Fourth, when we experience challenges to our people-systems, we must describe them and choose our response to them in terms of the healthy aspects of our systems. For example, when we notice an increase in conflict and criticism in our church, instead of using our best sermon against gossip and fault finding, we might choose to describe the situation as an opportunity to show the love and compassion for which our church is known. We can remind people that conflict is a normal part of church life and that we have the ability in Jesus Christ to resolve our conflict in a healthy manner. Instead of lamenting our lack of community impact, churches might ask themselves what strengths and resources they have with which they might better serve their communities and help them reach out with the gospel.

Finally, to overcome blame shifting we must encourage people to take appropriate responsibility for themselves and their own *being.* We do this first by modeling what it means to take appropriate responsibility as a leader. When people see it in us, they will be more likely to do it themselves – those pesky mirror neurons at work again.

QUICK-FIX MENTALITY

The fourth behavior of an anxious people-system comes from that low threshold for pain that causes people to seek a relief from pain rather than healthy change and personal maturity. Friedman called this the "quick-fix mentality". Whenever people seem to think that they can resolve complex issues in a short amount of time, they have fallen into the quick-fix mentality.

The quick-fix mentality increases when people fail to recognize that becoming healthy and mature is a process that takes time. Butterflies must struggle to get out of their cocoons. Without struggle the butterfly will die. Most of the issues in our society, from marital breakdowns to financial crises, developed over an extended period of time. We cannot expect to resolve these issues quickly or even over the course of a few years. Some issues require a generation or two to work themselves out.

Biblically, we see the quick-fix mentality in the life of Saul. In 1 Samuel 13:8–14, Samuel does not arrive in time to make the necessary sacrifice before going into battle. Rather than waiting for Samuel, Saul seeks the quick fix and offers the sacrifice himself. He feels the pressure of the people around him and the pressure of the circumstances to take action quickly, even if it was the wrong action.

Overcoming the quick-fix mentality

We have a number of strategies to overcome the quick-fix mentality. First, we must embrace pain and difficulty. Pain involves anything that we experience to be unpleasant in our spirits, souls or bodies. Emotional pain is just as real to people as physical pain. When we talk about embracing pain, we are not suggesting that we should simply tolerate it. We are suggesting that we must not avoid pain but learn to expect it, endure it, manage it, resolve it (when possible), and use it to help us grow, mature, and overcome things that produce anxiety.

Not only must we embrace pain, but we need also to encourage our people-system to do the same. We do this in part by helping our people-system understand the importance and purpose of pain in our development as human beings. There is truth in the saying "no pain, no gain". We continue to do this as we model what it means to embrace pain. We choose not to react to pain but respond in a way that is healthy and productive.

Second, as leaders we must work very, very hard to encourage, allow, and defend time and space for processes to mature and bear fruit. We must ensure that people do not try to rush the soufflé. When we emerged from our conflict years at my third church, I knew that rebuilding the ministry would require many years of hard work. I knew there was no quick way to experience healing in our people-system. So I continually reminded people about this until they believed me. This gave people a sense of patience and grace with one another and with the processes we set in place.

Third, we must also expose any idealistic distortions – and there are a lot of them! One of the most common distortions that I see is the assumption that people in churches should never have conflict with one another. Whoever came up with this idea never read the Bible. Paul even suggests in 1 Corinthians 11:19 that we need to have disagreements in order to come to a knowledge of the truth.

Another idealistic distortion is that healing and maturity can happen quickly. We know that it takes at least eighteen years for an infant to grow into some sense of adulthood. We understand that certain biological and emotional processes do not reach their fulfillment for even longer than eighteen years. We cannot expect emotional or spiritual maturity to happen quickly. It never does. Nor can we expect healing to happen quickly. Everyone knows that healing requires time, especially when the sickness is severe.[4]

Fourth, in order to help our people-system resist the urge to seek quick fixes, we need to establish some clear, realistic "signposts" showing people that progress is happening. At my third church, when we came out of the conflict we were in very bad shape. At the Annual General Meeting that year I shared what I called the "Way Forward Vision". This document told people that we were in a mess. It told people that it would take a long time to get out of this mess. Then it set forth some things that needed to happen in order for us to become healthy as a church. In the months and years that followed I updated this vision from time to time, sharing it with the church. Gradually, the things I set forth in the vision began to happen.

After a few years, one church member took me aside after worship one Sunday. He said something like this to me: "Rod, when you told us that the church could become healthy, I really did not believe it. However, as I look back now I realize that many of the things you said would happen have happened. This has given me confidence that the other things you said would happen will happen. I can really see our church is getting healthier."

All this means that if we want to overcome the quick-fix mentality then we must heed the popular World War II advice to "keep calm and carry on".

LEADERSHIP ABDICATION

The final behavior for people-systems caught up in anxiety is what I call "leadership abdication". This represents a "failure of nerve" (Friedman's words) that inclines leaders to neglect the responsibilities of leadership and capitulate to all the other behaviors and processes. When in the midst of highly anxious people-systems, leaders will often abdicate their leadership to other people or forces operating within the people-system. Some leaders resign from leadership altogether. Others simply retreat into their own little world of well-defined activities and relationships.

Abdicating our leadership means that we are allowing the forces for anxiety and disease to shape us, rather than taking responsibility to use our leadership to resist these forces. We also abandon the people in our people-system to the whims of these forces that most often use the people and the people-system for their own ends.

Obviously, if we abdicate our responsibilities as leaders then there is really no hope for our people-systems to overcome anxiety. There is really no hope for our systems to achieve their God-given destiny. God reminds us once again as leaders that we are to take our stand for our people-system and then stand firm.

In the Bible, Saul again serves as an example of what leaders should not do. Instead of exercising good leadership and following God's instructions as relayed by Samuel, Saul bows to the pressure of the people as well as his own anxiety and fails to obey God's commands, choosing the desires of the people. He even tries to justify his leadership abdication by appealing to a false attempt to honor God (see 1 Samuel 15:1ff.).

Overcoming leadership abdication

As leaders, the ability to overcome leadership abdication lies within us, at the depths of our *being*. To begin, we must exercise self-control and steadfastness. We must remember that self-control is part of the fruit of the Holy Spirit. Faithfulness is our primary responsibility as stewards of our people-system (see 1 Corinthians 4:2). We must not shrink back; we must hold our ground.

Second, we must seek our own maturity and integrity as leaders. One of the greatest gifts that we can give to our people-system, whether it is a marketplace system or a church, is ourselves as mature leaders. If we are mature as leaders, then we will naturally help other people become mature. We will also attract more mature people to ourselves. The more mature people we have around us the more likely it is that our system will become mature.

Third, we need to walk by the Spirit of God. This means allowing the Holy Spirit to lead us in our decision-making. This also means allowing the Holy Spirit to produce the fruit of the Spirit inside of us. It is so easy for us to get caught up in our own ideas, strategies, and plans. Natural leaders are especially susceptible to this problem. However, we need God's strategies and plans – along with our own obedience – when it comes to leading our people-systems to health.

Fourth, in order to overcome leadership abdication we must fully embrace the responsibilities of leadership. Being a leader often leaves us with responsibilities and challenges that we would never have chosen for ourselves. Along with the responsibilities, we must embrace the costs of leadership. We must recognize that leadership costs us a lot and it is not easy. We must be willing to face loneliness and misunderstanding. We must be willing to accept the consequences of our decisions.

Not only must we embrace our responsibilities, but finally we must also commit to persevere in our leadership. We cannot expect great things to happen in a few weeks. Making significant change and resolving major issues may take many years. We must never give up, never surrender (with a nod to Winston). Genuine love requires perseverance.

This may actually require us to put a symbolic stake in the ground. I know one church leader who decided to express his commitment to his church by purchasing a burial plot in the local cemetery. Although only in his forties at the time, this made a profound statement to the people in this church and the people in his community. Nothing can substitute for perseverance in our leadership.

LEADING SYSTEMS OUT OF ANXIETY

In order to lead our people-system out of anxiety, we must begin with the conviction and the confidence that God wants to use us to lead our people-system. We must know who we are in Christ and that in Christ we have significance, security, and acceptance. We must have the commitment that anxiety does not represent God's good will for his people, but instead represents an emotional state that will inhibit the fulfillment of God's will in our people-system.

Leading people-systems out of anxiety requires leaders who take responsibility for their *being* so they become anxiety-resistant leaders. Our *being* grounded in Christ enables us to lead from a stand of peace. We resist the tyranny of the seemingly urgent in order to focus on the healthy processes that may require time and patience but also lead to lasting results.

If we are leading a people-system bound up with anxiety, we can expect relentless resistance, opposition, and sabotage. We will know that the people who need us the most will often be the same people who seek to undermine us. Therefore, we must practice forgiveness daily. We must refuse to take offence. We must remain committed to our people-system.

In order to overcome the schemes of the devil against us and our people-systems, we need to submit ourselves fully to God. Once submitted to God, we can expose and resist the activities of the demonic in our people-system. Failing to submit to God will only increase anxiety in our people-system as we stumble about trying to implement our own strategies and follow our own wisdom.

Unless we learn to resist and resolve anxiety in ourselves, our people-system bound up in anxiety will shape us and distort our leadership just as anxiety distorts everything else. Once we resist and resolve our own anxiety, we will not be tossed about by the winds of anxiety. Instead we will be able to shape the mindsets of our people with faith, hope, and love.

THE LEADERSHIP DILEMMA

All this leads us to our leadership dilemma. Strong, healthy leaders are the only hope for resolving anxiety in any people-system.

Leaders will become lightning rods for anxiety in any people-system, no matter how big or how small it is. This means that all the pain, discomfort, frustration, disillusionment, disappointment, anger, and other negativity produced in the clouds of anxiety will frequently flash down upon the leader. Serving as a lightning rod is essential for draining away the power of anxiety from the people-system, but it can seem like a harrowing experience.

We cannot avoid serving as a lightning rod as leaders, but it is something we cannot do alone. Serving as a lightning rod demands that we are appropriately "grounded" in Jesus. As we know, lightning would destroy an ungrounded lightning rod. The strength of the lightning rod is not in the rod itself but in the grounding for the rod. In the same way, if we are not grounded in Jesus as a leader, then the anxiety of our people-system will burn us out. Only Jesus has the strength to withstand all the fury of anxiety flowing through the lightning rod leader. Much of the burnout we see among leaders today – in all spheres of society – comes from leaders who are not suitably grounded.

We need this grounding as leaders because anxious people-systems will always try – and often succeed – to eliminate healthy leaders out of the people-system before anxiety is resolved. This is one reason why businesses, governments, and churches all over the world are seeing such rapid turnover in leadership. In a sense, this is good news. If the anxious people-system might fire us no matter what we do, then we might as well choose to lead.

PART V

INCREASING YOUR EFFECTIVENESS AS A LEADER

If you think you are leading and turn around to see no one following, then you are just taking a walk.

Benjamin Hooks

You do not lead by hitting people over the head. That's assault, not leadership.

Dwight D. Eisenhower

Nearly all men can stand adversity, but if you want to test a man's character, give him power.

President Abraham Lincoln

Tax breaks had allowed Tom's financial services company to move into the renovated office building. Although three times larger than what they needed, the tax breaks made it less expensive for the company than a suitably sized space. Tom decided to hire out the remainder of the building as a place where businesspeople could have meetings and set up "hot desks". Tom invited his good friend, Sharon, to locate her small catering business in the building at a reduced rate in exchange for offering occasional catering for the business meetings. Sharon and her husband were close friends with Tom and his wife.

Tom recruited Edna to manage the rooms not used by Tom's company, instructing her to coordinate with Sharon for any catering needed. Edna would take the booking for the rooms and then refer people to Sharon for their catering needs. Sharon in turn would send Edna an email confirming the catering so that Edna could prepare a proper invoice. The business grew rapidly.

Sadly, relationships began to break down just as rapidly. Although Tom, Sharon, and Edna were Christians, Edna did not have her identity grounded in Christ. She had come out of a difficult job situation that had really knocked her confidence. She felt jealous of Tom and Sharon's friendship, and worried they were talking about her behind her back. When Sharon approached her with some genuinely constructive suggestions for how they might work better together, Edna responded harshly, taking every suggestion as a personal attack.

The relationship finally broke down completely when Edna erupted at Sharon because of some email communications. On almost every email, Sharon would write "tcb" after the number of people. Edna could not understand why every catering needed "to be confirmed" later, why Sharon could not simply confirm the number of people when she spoke with the client. Every time Edna would see "tcb" on an email she would become angrier and angrier.

Finally, Edna approached Tom, demanding that he deal with Sharon's poor management skills. Tom called Sharon to his office. Edna exploded at Sharon, expressing her deep frustration at how Sharon would never finalize a catering in her emails. She complained loudly that Sharon always indicated that her bookings were "to be confirmed", making Edna's job very difficult. Sharon completely denied this, explaining how every email gave Edna all the information she needed. Infuriated, Edna called Sharon a liar and pulled up one of Sharon's emails to prove it.

"Look at this email," shouted Edna. "Right here: 'tcb'. 'To be confirmed.' It's on almost every single email you send me!"

"Oh," sighed Sharon. "That is 'tcb', not 'tbc'. It means 'tea, coffee, biscuits', not 'to be confirmed'."

Burl had established a highly successful plumbing business. He employed three men in addition to himself, focusing primarily on residential repairs and home improvement jobs. Burl and his men were good plumbers, but they were not the fastest and they did make some occasional mistakes. Yet, Burl's business had grown much faster than many better plumbers. He also had a higher customer loyalty. Burl had learned some secrets which he used to train every person that worked with him.

Burl's first major job had been an emergency callout. When he arrived at his customer's house, water had almost flooded the kitchen. The woman paced back and forth with worry in her eyes. The children were crying. Burl recognized the woman's anxiety. After shutting off the water, he quickly helped the woman clean up the water in the kitchen. Then he let her settle the children down.

Once everything was calm, Burl sat down with the woman and carefully explained what he was going to do. He investigated the cause of the problem and discovered that a supply line had burst. He returned to the woman and talked her through the repair process. He gave her an estimate of the costs. She asked a number of questions which Burl answered patiently. Once she had agreed to the work, Burl began.

As he worked on the supply line, he noticed two other serious problems with the woman's plumbing. He brought these to the woman's attention. She became suddenly very angry: "You plumbers are all the same – trying to take advantage of people by overcharging them and making up problems!" Burl felt a bit angry and defensive, but stayed calm. He remained quiet and steady, not reacting to the woman's anger and frustration, as he gently and slowly explained the problems, how they had developed and what he could do to repair them. The woman relaxed, paused for a moment, and then told Burl to proceed.

In the end, not only was the woman pleased with Burl's work, but she referred many of her friends to Burl's company. Word of mouth spread quickly and Burl's business grew. The woman herself used Burl's company for every job she had, including installing a new bathroom. She hardly even looked at the detailed quotes Burl provided, and she never questioned his charges.

Burl recognized that how he had approached the situation on this first job had made all the difference. He had diffused the woman's anxiety by his calm *being*. He had instinctively understood the woman's angry outburst as a cry for help and understanding. He had created an atmosphere of trust by his quiet gentleness.

Both stories show two variables that help determine our effectiveness as leaders. The first variable is communication. Communication is the central activity of leadership. However, leaders consistently make some fundamental errors regarding communication, so our next chapter will focus on these errors and how to overcome them.

The second variable is trust. We often do not realize how trust (or lack thereof) influences our leadership effectiveness. However, many in the marketplace have begun to recognize how essential trust is for building a great business and creating a great work environment. We will talk about how to develop and maintain trust as leaders.

We understand that we might discover many ways to increase our leadership effectiveness. In this section, as before, we will not try to consider every aspect of these two variables – communication and trust – but only those which have often hindered our leadership. We will show how our *being* and our *doing* both affect these variables. Implementing the strategies we present will enlarge our leadership effectiveness as we improve our communication and increase trust.

12

IMPROVING COMMUNICATION

Precision of communication is important, more important than ever, in our era of hair trigger balances, when a false or misunderstood word may create as much disaster as a sudden thoughtless act.

James Thurber

If you have nothing to say, say nothing.

Mark Twain

The art of communication is the language of leadership.

James Humes

Great leaders are always great communicators. Communication is the breath of leadership. Without good communication, leadership suffocates and dies. Unfortunately, we often limit our concept of communication to public speaking or oratory. (Just think what came into your mind when you read the first sentence of this paragraph. Most likely it was a person doing some public speaking!) Limiting our concept of communication to public speaking makes us vulnerable to factors that inhibit our communication and undermine our leadership.

We also become vulnerable to factors that inhibit our communication when we think of communication as primarily the conveyance of information and "facts". Particularly in Western contexts, we tend to think of communication as involving clear information exchange without any emotional baggage. However, communication always conveys more than objective, factual information, no matter how we might define information.[1]

THE ESSENCE OF COMMUNICATION

We might define communication in a number of ways, but at its heart communication is the interactive relational process of sharing. Communication always has an interactive component. It is never simply one way. When we communicate, we always receive something back from the communication process.

Communication always involves relationships. Even when communication is seemingly one way – such as with advertising – the communication must engage a relationship in order to communicate. For example, when I see an ad on the television for a new car, if that ad does not establish a relationship with me by connecting with my interests or needs then it will not communicate with me.

Next, communication is always a process. Communication is never simply a one-time event. In order for communication to occur, an interactive process must unfold through the communication. If I refuse to engage with a communication, then I am choosing not to enter the process of communication.

Finally, communication is a process of sharing. However, what we share is not limited to "facts" alone. When we communicate, we share who we are as well as what we do. We share information and emotions. We even share things like our anxiety or our peace. The sharing of communication involves many things beyond simple facts and data.

COMMUNICATION AND LEADERSHIP

Communication is the central relational activity of leadership. Most everything that could be said about leadership could also be said about communication. If we want to communicate well, we need to understand that genuine communication to which others instinctively respond flows from our *being* through our *doing*.

Before people will engage with the content of our communication, they engage with our *being*. We can revise a principle that we introduced earlier and apply it to communication:

> **People will respond to who (they perceive) you are and how (they perceive) you are before they will respond to what (they perceive) you do or say.**

In communication, people respond to our *being* – who we are and how we are – before they respond to our *doing* – what we do or say. However, people's *perceptions* of our *being* make all the difference. If they perceive our *being* as healthy, then they will respond to that health in the communication process. If they perceive our being as riddled with anxiety, then our anxiety will speak louder than the content of our communication.

In communication, our *being* shapes the content of our *doing*. In other words, whether we are authentic and genuine and whether we are calm and self-controlled actually determines the perceived content of what we do and what we say. If people perceive any incongruence between who we are and what we are saying – what we are communicating – then they will refuse to communicate with us. If people perceive that we are healthy and real then they will be more likely to communicate with us, even when the content of communication might be difficult or painful.

As with most employers, I have occasionally had to bring correction to members of staff for mistakes or wrongdoing. I have found that the state of my *being* makes all the difference concerning the success or failure of these meetings. I have learned that I must never be angry or anxious when I speak to employees about their performance. My goal is not to make my job easier or even to protect the company. My goal is to help the staff members serve with excellence and joy, experiencing satisfaction from their employment. I have found that when I am peaceful and focused on the good of the staff person these meetings become much more pleasant and productive. They are more productive because the staff member responds to my *being* (which is oriented toward their well-being) more than the content of my communication.

Having our *being* healthy and grounded in Jesus makes the *doing* of communication much more effective. People can sense instinctively when we are communicating in order to meet our needs for identity, significance, security or acceptance. People may not understand this consciously, but they will perceive when our communication is self-centered and for selfish motives. Conversely, people will also perceive when we are communicating from a healthy *being*. They will perceive that our communication is focused on them and their needs rather than us and our needs.

As leaders, our communication training has most likely focused on *doing* issues – how to shape the content of communication, how to refine our language, how to present information so that people would remember it and the like. These issues are certainly important, but not nearly as important as our *being* issues. In order to communicate more effectively we must focus on having a healthy *being* grounded in Christ. This has become even more important as people today are flooded with various messages begging for their attention.

COMMUNICATION AND EMOTIONAL PROCESSES

Communication engages the emotions of people and people-systems before it engages the minds or wills of people and people-systems.[2] We have mistakenly thought that communication involved intellectual processes primarily, that people would mainly seek to understand our messages with their minds, bypassing any other content. However, we have discovered this is never the case with communication.

Communication engages emotional processes before it engages cognitive processes. We have defined emotional processes as the complex interplay of our impressions, feelings (especially of liking or disliking something), and inclinations in combination with our automatic mental activities of perceiving things around us and remembering experiences from the past which leads us to reflexive thoughts, emotions, and choices. How communication engages emotional processes will either stimulate or stifle deliberation and reasoning. It determines whether people will even bother to engage their minds with regard to our communication.

Communication is fundamentally an emotional process itself rather than a matter of the intellect and reason. Communication interacts with our emotions before it deals with our thinking mind. Messages come through less because of their content than because of the emotional process. People respond reflexively to the emotional process of communication much before they interact with the message.

When I am under a lot of stress, my wife tells me that I tend to have a frown or a scowl upon my face. (Personally, I do not like this so I try to correct it.) If I allow myself to maintain a frown on my face, then I must work doubly hard to communicate positively with my wife. Having a frown on my face means that every message I try to communicate begins with a negative emotional connotation. It is almost impossible for me to transcend this negative emotional connotation by simply using positive language. I must first change the negative emotional package in which the positive message is contained.

The emotional dynamic of communication helps explain why stories and humor help us communicate more effectively. Stories and humor positively engage the emotional processes of people and people-systems. Humor causes people to relax and puts people at ease. Stories that share the emotional content of the message we are trying to communicate prepare people to receive that message. Stories and humor help communicators overcome some of the natural emotional barriers people erect so as not to become overwhelmed with information.

In a people-system, we must remember that the emotional processes of individuals in the people-system as well as the emotional processes of the people-system itself constantly interact with one another. These emotional processes are interconnected within the people-system. Working together, these emotional processes might form an impassable barrier for whatever message we might want to communicate. At the same time, engaging these emotional processes positively will help our communication to become more persuasive and influential.

Mike could sense the tension in the church board before he even sat down. The board had invited him to consult with them about the future of their church. Mike could sense the despair and disagreement that had plagued the board for the past year. He began the meeting by identifying the emotions that he was perceiving in the room and giving the board members a chance to share their feelings. Mike ensured that people could share in a safe environment, asking fellow board members simply to listen without responding.

After about an hour, it seemed that people had shared their dominant emotions. Then Mike decided to share a few stories of other churches in similar situations. The first story was about a church that had failed and had to close. The next three stories were about churches that had made difficult decisions which had led to renewed life and vitality in the churches. He engaged the emotional processes with both a realistic assessment of the church's present situation and genuine hope. After about ninety minutes, the emotional processes of the board had shifted to become more positive, allowing Mike the opportunity to communicate more effectively.

We must shift our understanding of communication as leaders from one that involves primarily intellectual content messages to one that involves primarily emotional content messages. Engaging the emotional content effectively provides the opportunity for us to communicate the intellectual content of our messages. Engaging the emotional content effectively also makes it more likely that people will respond volitionally to our communication. People will become more likely to do something about what we communicate.

SHAPING EMOTIONAL PROCESSES

In order to communicate effectively then, we must learn to shape the emotional processes that influence our communication. We can shape emotional processes in many different ways, but we want to highlight three.

First, we shape emotional processes through our *being* by our presence in the communication process. Three verses from Proverbs 15 indicate how the presence and *being* of a person influence communication:

> A soft answer turns away wrath, but a harsh word stirs up anger. (Proverbs 15:1)

> A gentle tongue is a tree of life, but perverseness in it breaks the spirit. (Proverbs 15:4)

> A hot-tempered man stirs up strife, but he who is slow to anger quiets contention. (Proverbs 15:18)

In each of these verses, descriptions of healthy presence and *being* – soft answer, gentle tongue, slow to anger – shape the communication process for the good, while negative descriptions of presence and *being* influence the communication process for ill.

The presence and *being* of the leader shapes the emotional processes in any communication process in which the leader is involved. This happens both positively and negatively. In order for the presence and *being* of the leader to have a positive influence the leader must have integrity – that is, how the leader engages in the communication process must be consistent with the healthy *being* of the leader. When people perceive that we are healthy in our *being* and that we are communicating in a manner consistent with the fruit of the Holy Spirit, people will allow our communication to shape the emotional processes positively so that they will hear and respond to what we are trying to communicate.

Second, we can shape the emotional processes by shaping the environment of our communication. As leaders, we must become environmentalists. Shaping the environment of our people-systems as well as our communication processes is one of our most important responsibilities as leaders. We must consider everything from the physical environment to the emotional environment.

Many variables in our physical environment affect our communication processes either positively or negatively. The physical temperature in the room, whether it is too hot or too cold, will influence the ability of people to participate in the communication process. The amount of light or darkness in a room will determine how people perceive our communication. The orientation of seating in the room – whether it is in a circle, in a square, facing the front of the room, around tables – shapes the communication process. When we are in a conversation with someone, whether our chair is higher or lower than their chair will influence the communication process. The color of the walls and the size of the room affect the communication process. The ability of people to hear what we are saying – and whether it is too loud, too fast, too soft or too slow – affects the communication process. These are just a few of the physical variables that we need to consider as leaders.

The variables of the physical environment also influence the emotional environment. For example, sitting on opposite sides of a rectangular table when engaging in a difficult conversation might exacerbate the sense of conflict. Additionally, other emotional variables shape the communication process. Whether or not people actually want to communicate with one another shapes the emotional environment. The sense of hope or despair, anxiety or peace, anger or forgiveness, all determine the effectiveness of the communication process. Many other variables such as the gender of people, the cultural background of people, and whether or not people have had what they perceive as a "good" day influence the emotional environment of the communication process.

As leaders we must first become conscious of the environments of our communication processes. So often we fail to consider how these environments influence the effectiveness of our communication. If we fail to become good communication environmentalists, then we will fail to communicate effectively. However, if we become conscious of our environments and choose to shape those environments positively, then we will be amazed at how our communication processes improve.

Third, we can influence emotional processes in communication through spiritual activities. The spiritual realities surrounding our communication processes influence our communication much more than we realize. Demons will always seek to distort our communication. They will try to generate anxiety and negative emotions that hinder effective communication. They may seek to shape a spiritual environment with discouragement and despair. Most leaders have never received training to deal with the spiritual realities surrounding our communication. Yet we have often seen how these spiritual dynamics influence communication.

Spiritual practices and activities will help shape the spiritual realities surrounding our communication processes. Worship can change the spiritual environment in any people-system, even in the marketplace. Prayer and thanksgiving exert powerful influence on spiritual realities around us. Reading Scripture out loud or making declarations taken from the Scriptures might influence spiritual dynamics.

We have seen how spiritual activities influence communication processes on many occasions. I recall one elders meeting where it seemed like we were struggling to accomplish anything. We were not communicating with one another well and we were struggling to make good decisions. Suddenly, we recognized some spiritual dynamic occurring, like a sense of oppression. So we stopped our meeting and spent a few minutes praying. We commanded anything of the darkness to leave us alone. We spent a few minutes thanking God for the church. Afterwards, the meeting progressed in a normal healthy fashion. It was very striking.

I recall another occasion when I was leading a course. As I was speaking, I became aware that people seemed to be very distracted, having difficulty paying attention to what I was saying. In addition, I began to feel poorly, experiencing some nausea and blurred vision. I stopped teaching and called people's attention to what I perceived was happening. We paused as I spent a few minutes praying, asking God to protect us from any evil influences and asking God to help us engage in learning. As I stopped praying, the atmosphere changed completely. My nausea vanished and people suddenly seemed attentive and alert.

As leaders, we must learn intentionally to shape the emotional processes around all our communication. If we fail to shape the emotional processes in a healthy and positive manner then we will fail to communicate well. We must recognize that we have great influence and authority as leaders to influence the emotional processes of our people-system as well as the people we lead.

DIRECTION

In addition to emotional processes, four other variables greatly affect our communication: direction, distance, anxiety, and filters. We need to understand these variables and how to influence them positively if we want to enhance the effectiveness of our communication.

The first variable is direction. Direction refers to the emotional as well as the physical orientation of the receiver to the sender in communication. Effective communication requires positive direction toward one another. People will only hear you if they are moving toward you, both physically and emotionally.

Direction first refers to the physical orientation of the receiver to the sender. If someone is walking away from us then they will be less likely to hear us or understand what we say. If someone has their back turned toward us, then they will be less likely to hear us. If someone has their face turned toward us or is walking in our direction, then there will be a greater chance that the person will understand what we are saying. This is self-evident.

Direction also refers to the emotional orientation of the receiver to the sender. If someone is angry with us then emotionally they are moving away from us. This means that we will have greater difficulty communicating effectively with them. If someone does not respect us, then that person is moving away from us emotionally. They will again struggle to receive our communication.

PURSUIT BEHAVIORS

One leadership conundrum we face regarding the variable of direction is something we call "pursuit behaviors". Pursuit behaviors indicate that the person engaging in the behavior is moving in our direction. They are essentially *pursuing* us. The person engaging in a pursuit behavior wants to get closer to us. They want to have a deeper relationship with us, even if they do not always realize it.

At the same time, pursuit behaviors always turn away the person being pursued. Pursuit behaviors tend to engage our fight or flight responses. When we are being pursued, our natural instinct is to run away. We never tend to experience pursuit behaviors as something good or pleasant. If we cannot run away, then we will tend to turn and fight. However, neither fight nor flight is an appropriate response to a pursuit behavior. In fact, they can tend to intensify the pursuit behavior rather than stop the pursuit behavior.

Rescuing

There are three key pursuit behaviors: rescuing, criticizing, or coercing.[3] Rescuing describes the collection of behaviors where people persistently try to help us in a way that seems pushy and inappropriate. People want to get closer to us so they think the best way to do this is by "saving" us from our stress, difficulties or challenges. They swoop in to offer help, but often in a way that actually makes things much more difficult for us. Their help often seems unsuitable.

One of Sam's responsibilities on the worship team was to help set up and take down equipment each week. Sam was a popular guy and many of the teenagers in the church looked up to him. Each week, whenever Sam would have to set up or take down the sound equipment, a couple of young teenage guys would come and offer to help. He would normally just tell the guys that there was nothing they could do to help and get on with the job.

At first, Sam did not realize what was happening. He thought of these offers to help as more of an annoyance because the guys would not really know what to do. However, eventually Sam recognized that these guys were engaging in the pursuit behavior called rescuing. Once he realized this, Sam approached the situation completely differently. He accepted the guys' offer of help. This gave him an opportunity not only to train them in how to care for the equipment properly but also to talk with them about what was going on in their lives. Since they were coming in Sam's direction, they were open to hearing what he had to say. Sam used the pursuit behavior positively to help them communicate more effectively.

Criticizing

Criticizing describes a collection of behaviors where people persistently try to help us improve, most often in a way that seems pushy and inappropriate. Criticizing indicates that people care about you enough to want to engage with what you are doing. The problem is that people simply do not realize how off-putting criticism actually is. When people are criticizing us, they are coming toward us and they want to engage us in a positive way. They simply do not know how to do it.

Most leaders respond to criticism in completely unhelpful ways. We often try to deflect criticism, which simply makes people try harder. We might turn away from criticism, which simply makes people pursue us – that is, criticize us – more strongly. We might even attack the person criticizing us, by perhaps picking on something in the person for us to criticize. This approach simply wounds the person and leaves them confused as to why we would want to hurt them when all they were trying to do is get close to us.

Like most leaders, I dislike conflict and I dislike receiving criticism. In the past, I have engaged in all the unhelpful behaviors in response to criticism. I have learned from experience that the best way to defuse criticism is simply to stop and allow myself to get "caught" by the one pursuing me. If I maintain an open posture as well as emotional openness to the person while listening carefully to what the person has to say, then I have frequently discovered that once the person feels like they have connected with me they will often leave satisfied and peaceful. I have also discovered that I may often learn something about myself as well.

Coercing

The third common pursuit behavior is coercing, where people try to persuade us to do something they feel strongly ought to be done. When people are coercing us, we often feel manipulated and controlled. People may even use guilt and other emotions to try to coerce us. Our natural tendency is to resist coercion. This only increases the other person's attempt to coerce us.

In the context of a pursuit behavior, coercing does not always mean that the person actually wants to manipulate us or control us. Coercing as a pursuit behavior indicates that the person has identified a problem that they feel we are more competent to address. The person engaging in this behavior normally has a high opinion of us as leaders. So they bring these problems to us with the confidence that we can handle them. They also bring these problems to us with the desire to become closer to us.

As with the other pursuit behaviors, how we respond to the feeling of being coerced determines the outcome. If we respond by simply dismissing the person's concerns, then the person will continue to try to coerce us into doing something about the problem, or they may move on to other leaders to try to coerce them. If we respond by rejecting the person's concerns, then they will feel that we have rejected them personally and no longer want a relationship with them. This will lead to many other bigger problems.

We need to resist the temptation to capitulate to the coercing. Under no circumstances should we just accept the other person's coercion and do what they want us to do. This will both add stress to our lives as well as disappointment to the other person when we fail to do what they want us to do in the way they want us to do it.

I have found a good way of dealing with coercing. We first must show that we understand the problem or concern being raised by the person. This engages the person relationally. Then, we can suggest that whenever God puts such a concern on a person's mind it generally means that God is calling *that* person to do something about it. We can then invite the person to think of what God wants them to do personally and develop a plan of action. We might even offer to coach them along the way as necessary. We invite them to take responsibility for the solution to the problem. This course of action both values the person as well as resists the coercing.

CHANGING DIRECTION

Leaders often mistake pursuit behaviors for personal attacks or rebellion. Most of the time, however, this is not the case. Normally, only people who are really evil or fairly dysfunctional in their behavior really want to harm us. Most pursuit behaviors simply indicate that people want to communicate with us and engage in relationship with us. Pursuit behaviors also indicate that people are coming toward us, that we have positive direction from which to communicate with them.

We have some simple strategies to help us influence direction in a positive way. First, regarding pursuit behaviors, we need to stop and allow ourselves to be caught.[4] When people catch us they have created positive direction which makes our communication with them more effective. People will tend to hear what we say more clearly when they are coming in our direction. Most people engaged in pursuit behaviors do not really expect us to stop and allow ourselves to be caught. Doing so may create real openness for good communication.

Second, we need to practice emotional openness. This requires that our *being* is healthy and grounded in Jesus. Otherwise, we will find emotional openness to be too painful and difficult. We must express our emotional openness both physically as well as personally. We must make sure that our arms are not folded and that our bodies are not turned away from the person. We must make good eye contact when culturally appropriate. We must refuse to react emotionally out of our hurt or our confusion.

Third, we can simply invite a change of direction. When we perceive somebody is moving away from us physically, we can call out to them and ask them to stop for a moment. We might invite them to come closer or allow us to come closer to them. If we feel like they are moving away from us emotionally, we can identify this and ask how we might come together to talk. We have many ways to invite a change of direction.

Finally, we can ask questions. Asking good questions is an effective way to shift direction in a positive way. How we frame the question determines the range of outcomes. So we need to learn to ask open-ended questions, ones in which it is not possible to answer yes or no. Our questions should seek discovery and not be a disguised way to confront or advise the person. Good questions should focus on the present and the future more than the past. We need to keep our questions clear, simple, and short. Once we ask our questions we must then listen actively and carefully.

DISTANCE

Distance is the second variable affecting our communication. Distance refers to the emotional as well as the physical space that separates the sender and receiver in communication. The greater the distance, the greater the effect on communication will be.

We instinctively recognize how physical distance affects communication. If I am standing next to somebody, then it is more likely that they will hear what I say. If a person is standing 100 meters away from me in a crowded room, then that person might really struggle to hear me at all.

Emotional distance also affects communication. If someone is angry or hurt because of something that I have said or done, then their emotional distance will make it difficult for them to hear me apologize. If someone is depressed and I seem to be very happy, then the emotional distance that difference creates will make it difficult for the depressed person to believe that I might understand how they feel.

THE MEANS OF COMMUNICATION

The means we choose to communicate always affects the distance of any communication. People often assume that certain forms of communication are closer than they actually are, such as the use of emails. People can also assume that certain forms of communication contain more distance than they actually do, such as a message on Twitter. The means we choose affects our communication.

The closest means of communication is face-to-face communication. The next closest means of communication is voice communication, such as over the telephone or by some other communication technology such as Skype. Handwritten letters and text messages or instant messaging are closer forms of communication, but obviously not as close as face-to-face communication. Email and public forums such as Facebook give the illusion of close communication but they are not. They are more distant forms of communication.

The greater the distance in any form of communication, the greater the sense of "safety", which is not generally good. We might often say things in an email or on Facebook which we would never say face to face. This would increase the likelihood that we might say something inappropriate or hurtful which we would most likely not say to the person directly. This does not promote healthy communication overall.

The greater the distance, the greater the tendency to abandon self-control and personal responsibility. We have all heard stories about horrendous messages on Twitter. Most people would never dream of saying these things face-to-face, but when they have distance they will say some of the most horrible things.

Social media will often give the illusion of intimacy and good communication while providing distance. This may create a false sense of intimacy. This may also make us more apt to share inappropriate information on what is largely a public forum.

Anonymous communications nearly always tend toward harm and destructiveness. As leaders, we must never tolerate anonymous communication in any form. Personally, I will not even listen to an anonymous complaint. If I receive a letter, the first thing I do is check the signature. If it is not clearly signed and owned, then I will not bother reading it, no matter whether it is positive or negative. Leaders do much damage to their people-systems – in both the church and the marketplace – by allowing anonymous communication.

The greater the distance, the greater the tendency to idealize the other person either positively or negatively. In situations where there is much conflict, the closer people are to one another in terms of distance the better it is. If we allow people to keep their distance, then they will tend to demonize the other person, making them seem far worse than they actually are. In the same way, the greater the distance the greater our tendency to think of someone as better than they actually are. This explains why some followers fail to appreciate their own leaders who are close to them while romanticizing other leaders further away.

DECREASING DISTANCE

Several simple strategies help us to decrease distance in communication. First, we must seek face-to-face communication whenever possible. Technology offers some major advantages by providing a number of ways that we can have face-to-face communication without having to be physically present. When we cannot have face-to-face communication we must prefer voice-to-voice communication.

Second, we must use other means of communication appropriately. Text messages are great ways of sharing little bits of information and making personal arrangements. They are not good for terminations, either of relationships or of employees. Email works well for factual communication, transmitting dates, times of meetings, and other reasonably objective information. Email never serves well as a vehicle for communicating highly emotional content. Social media works well for communicating broader details of one's life, opinions, and perspectives that are not highly emotive, and other non-vital personal information.

Third, we must avoid and reject anonymous communications and comments. As leaders, we must expose everything to the light. Secrets, rumors, and other anonymous communications only harm people and people-systems. We need to create a culture in which people take responsibility for their perspectives, opinions, and communications.

Fourth, we must practice emotional availability. People need to see that we are approachable and that we desire to have close relationships. This does not mean that we create the illusion of being everybody's best friend. Instead, it means that we need to show respect and honor toward all people, whether or not they agree with us.

Finally, we must give grace to others. Paul instructs us to "Be kind to one another, tenderhearted, forgiving one another, as God in Christ forgave you" (Ephesians 4:32). The word translated as "forgive" might also be expressed as "to give grace to". As we are kind and tenderhearted, giving grace to other people as God has given grace to us, people will naturally seek to come closer to us. This will decrease the distance and allow us to communicate more effectively.

ANXIETY

The presence of anxiety in any communication process works like static on the television or radio. The greater the amount of static the more difficult it becomes to receive the signal. The greater the amount of anxiety the more difficult it becomes to communicate well. The presence of anxiety in a person, situation or people-system always affects communication negatively.

To the degree that anxiety is present, people will not receive communication correctly. They simply will not be able to hear accurately what is being said or how it is being said. Anxiety distorts everything, including everything in communication. When anxiety is present, we must assume that nothing we communicate is being received or understood as we intend.

To the degree that anxiety is present, people will put a negative or pessimistic spin on any communication. Rebecca had experienced a major relationship breakdown with Erin. This caused some anxiety in their workplace, not to mention in their relationship. Rebecca really wanted to make things right, so she wrote Erin a kind note to encourage her, leaving it on her desk. When Erin read the note, she was furious. She assumed that Rebecca had written the note because Rebecca was trying to make herself seem better than her. Anxiety had caused Erin to spin the communication in a pessimistic way.

To the degree that anxiety is present in leaders, it will prevent us from accurately expressing and transmitting our communications. We will think that we have said one thing when people actually hear something completely different. We will assume that we have accurately communicated when people really have no idea what we are trying to say. The more anxiety is present, the more we need to build in redundancy to our communication, repeating the same message calmly as often as possible in varying ways.

ANXIETY PRODUCERS

Certain behaviors always produce anxiety in communication. Whenever these things are present anxiety will increase and communication effectiveness will decrease. First, anger and any other form of high emotionality will increase anxiety in communication. Intense emotions always make it difficult to communicate well. We will need to come to peace before we can communicate.

Rumors and secrets increase anxiety. Because of the connectedness in a people-system, rumors and secrets cause anxiety even when people are not privy to these rumors and secrets. Rumors and secrets release a spiritual dynamic that actually creates anxiety. This is one reason that leaders must resist and expose rumors and secrets.

Third, complaining and grumbling increase anxiety. The complaining and grumbling might involve the circumstances of one's own life or the behavior and attitudes of others. Regardless, complaining and grumbling always increase anxiety. They initiate an anxious desire in most people to try to help the person who is complaining.

Fourth, information overload increases anxiety. When people are receiving too much information – someone talking too much, sharing too much, instructing too much – they will experience anxiety. Along with this, when there is too much or too little volume in the communication people will experience anxiety.

Pain and the anticipation of loss create anxiety. Whenever people are experiencing personal or even group pain they will experience anxiety. Whenever people anticipate losing something – whether money or a relationship or an opportunity – they will experience anxiety.

Anxiety might arise from contextual dissonance. For instance, if I am trying to tell my wife that I love her while standing in the middle of a busy highway then we will experience a contextual dissonance that will cause anxiety and interfere with my communication. If we use a public meeting to bring what should be a private correction then we will produce anxiety.

Finally, hurry and busyness produce anxiety in communication. Communication is a process that requires time and concentration. Hurry and busyness undermine both time and concentration, as well as many other aspects of effective communication.

In order to improve our communication effectiveness, we must become aware of these anxiety producers in communication. We must seek to neutralize or minimize these anxiety producers. We also need to engage anxiety reducers in communication.

ANXIETY REDUCERS

We have a number of anxiety reducers that we can use as leaders to increase our communication effectiveness. First, we might practice active listening. We need to listen carefully to what others are saying without trying to formulate a response at the same time. Other people must see that we understand them. This will decrease their anxiety.

We must remain gentle and calm when we are communicating. Gentleness and peacefulness deactivate anxiety, helping people overcome the anxiety they are experiencing in their own lives.

We can practice transparency and openness. If secrets and rumors create anxiety, then transparency and openness disarm anxiety. When people see that we have nothing to hide and no personal agenda to promote they will become more likely to resist anxiety and hear what we have to say.

Thanksgiving and sincere praise help to reduce anxiety. Even in the midst of the most difficult situations, we can often find things for which to be thankful. Expressing thanksgiving and sincere praise for the other person often disarms anxiety. In addition, expressing genuine hope for beneficial outcomes will help resolve anxiety.

Embracing the pain in ourselves and others will help reduce anxiety in communication. We can often experience communication as something very uncomfortable. Learning to embrace our discomfort and then communicate with the other person in the spirit of love and grace will help overcome anxiety. Learning not to react emotionally to the pain others are experiencing but instead to come alongside them with love and grace will help them embrace their pain and overcome anxiety.

Finally, maintaining a moderated tone and speech pattern, while smiling appropriately, helps reduce anxiety in communication. As with many business leaders, we have occasionally had people complain about their experience. We know that almost everyone will experience considerable anxiety when trying to bring a complaint to a leader. So we have found that if we maintain a calm and deliberate pattern of speech while smiling warmly then we can often understand the person's complaint better and develop a more appropriate resolution as we decrease their anxiety.

CLEARING ANXIETY

Like static, we must clear anxiety from our communication. To do this, we offer three strategies. First, we must consciously practice anxiety *reducers* in communication, while recognizing the anxiety *producers* at work. Anyone can learn how to implement anxiety reducers.

Second, we must resist and resolve our own anxiety in order to communicate effectively. We need to put into practice the strategies for overcoming our personal anxiety that we discussed earlier in the book. We also need to understand that whenever we are experiencing anxiety we cannot trust the accuracy of our communication. As we have said before, resolving anxiety requires that our *being* be healthy and grounded in Jesus Christ.

Third, we must remember that using technology generally increases anxiety in communication and very seldom reduces it. This means that the best way to overcome anxiety is through face-to-face communication. This also means that we must never use technology such as email and text messages when we are dealing with highly anxious situations. Email is one of the most effective ways to *increase* anxiety in any difficult communication process.

FILTERS

The final variable affecting our communication is what we call "filters". Filters are the physical and emotional layers through which all communication must pass. Every communication process engages many different filters. These filters operate subconsciously, but we may examine them and change them. The greater the number of filters through which we must communicate the more difficult communication will be.

Processing filters takes great care and patience. Improperly understood and managed, filters become barriers to communication. Properly understood and managed, we may decrease the effect of filters, but we will never remove them entirely. Negotiated wisely, we may actually use filters as aids for communication.

COMMON FILTERS

Every day we experience many common filters, generally fitting into three categories. First, we have cultural filters. These include different languages (such as French and German), different cultures, different religions, and different worldviews. Many resources exist to help us navigate these cultural filters and learn to communicate more effectively.

Second, we have environmental filters. These include the physical environment, such as our physical surroundings, what we see, and what we hear. These also include the emotional environment, such as whether it is peaceful or emotionally charged. In addition, these include the spiritual environment, such as whether we are in a place open or hostile toward God. The effects of environmental filters might help explain why a university student hostile to God in the science classroom might suddenly become open to God during a worship service with friends.

Third, we have personal filters. These include things such as a person's background, gender, values, and focus. These may also include a person's sin issues, whether the person is proud, sexually immoral, prone to lying, and similar sins. Further, personal filters involve a person's preconceptions and biases, as well as their perceptions – no matter whether they are true or false.

Most leaders become easily aware of the cultural and environmental filters operating in any given communication process. However, we often fail to notice the personal filters operating, whether the other person's or our own. Yet often the personal filters have the greatest impact on the effectiveness of our communication. For example, if a person struggles with pride then that pride will often cause the person to overlook essential information in communications. They assume they already know everything being communicated. A person from a wealthy background will often fail to consider how a person from a poor background might respond to her communication. A person who has experienced deep wounding in the past will tend to filter communication through that experience, making communication extremely delicate at times.

COMMUNICATING THROUGH FILTERS

Although filters present a challenge for leaders and communicators, we can learn to communicate more effectively through them. Again, we offer several strategies. First, leaders must identify their own filters, seeking to make them as thin as possible. We need to understand the filters operating in our own lives and how those filters affect our communication either positively or negatively before we can learn to communicate through the filters of other people.

When we first moved to London, many people told us that we "must" do certain things – "You *must* have brussels sprouts for Christmas dinner", "You *must* try this Marmite", "You *must* go to Regent's Park." Telling Americans that they *must* do something is the best way to ensure that they do *not* do something! We felt a bit annoyed at these statements. Suddenly, we recognized how our own filters had determined what we were hearing. So we removed the filters. After that, we realized that the use of "must" was not a command to do something but simply an encouraging and positive suggestion.

Most of the time, simply being aware of our filters will help us communicate through our filters. However, we may also find it helpful to talk about our filters with other people who have different filters. Many years ago I was talking with a group of Croatian friends about American politics. Their observations helped me to realize how much my identity as a Christian had become intertwined with my political identity. It also helped me see how sinful this actually was, leading me to repentance and a change in my filters. This brief encounter helped my ability to communicate more than I can fully relate.

Second, we must identify the filters operating in any given people-system and situation. We need to learn to recognize the various filters that people are using through which to view the world. Our filters may cause us to see the same thing in different ways. Unless we learn how to recognize the filters operating in other people we will not know how to communicate through them. Instead, we will tend to assume that our filters are the same as their filters. This will generally lead to communication failure.

Finally, we need to plan how to communicate through various filters. For most of us leaders, communicating through filters is not something that comes naturally. We set vision as leaders, so we naturally expect other people to see things the way that we see them. This is seldom the case unless we are dealing with a small group of people from the same culture, in the same place, and with generally similar personal backgrounds.

Although some highly gifted leaders communicate through filters naturally and instinctively, most leaders can learn how to communicate well through filters. We can let people know what filters we are using so that they might come to understand us better. We can also make sure that our communication is genuine and authentic to our *being*. We can talk openly with people about what filters they have and how we might communicate better with them. Communicating well takes time and intention, especially when it involves filters – and it *always* involves filters.

THE LEADERSHIP DILEMMA

Once again we have a leadership dilemma. Communication is essential to leadership, yet it is the place where leadership can become the most vulnerable. We often make many incorrect assumptions about communication – that it is primarily an intellectual exercise, that people only need to understand the information content of our communication, that technology actually helps us communicate better, that people criticizing us is bad and not criticizing us is good, and many others.

Our presence and *being* as leaders affects our communication more than most of us realize or understand. We cannot hide who we are as we communicate. Trying to do so will only cause other people not to hear and not to care. When people perceive that we are healthy and grounded in Christ, they will tend to respond to our communication more positively and more openly – provided that the way we are communicating is consistent with who we are.

In the end, we may spend much time shaping the content of our messages before realizing that we *ourselves* are the content of our messages.

13

BUILDING TRUST

*To be persuasive, we must be believable; to be believable,
we must be credible; to be credible, we must be truthful.*

Edward R. Murrow

*Trust is the lubrication that makes it possible for
organizations to work.*

Warren Bennis

To be trusted is a greater compliment than to be loved.

George MacDonald

Franklin had established a good staff team. Individually, none of them was the most naturally gifted or talented in the industry but collectively they achieved consistently good outcomes. Franklin knew each member of his staff team well, including their strengths, weaknesses, and character. He also expected each member of his staff to fulfill their responsibilities with excellence. He accepted how each member of the staff was at the moment but at the same time he expected each member of staff to grow and develop.

Franklin required each member of the staff to give their best. He also expected the staff members to work together as a team, cooperating with one another and helping one another in their assigned responsibilities. Franklin expected people to make mistakes. His only requirement was that people "own" their mistakes and discuss them openly so that the entire staff could learn from the mistakes. In such a positive environment, staff members consistently rated Franklin's company as a good place to work, reporting high levels of job satisfaction.

Franklin's company had not always been such a great place to work. At one time the staff had been riddled with animosity and competition. Staff members had blamed others for mistakes and poor performance. They had withheld and guarded information so they could use it for their own advantage. They had looked for ways to undermine Franklin's leadership and promote their own advantage in the company. They had tried to get their own benefit out of the company, regardless of whether the company succeeded or failed.

Building a good company had presented Franklin with a major challenge. Franklin began by setting new standards for behavior and removing those employees who failed to meet these standards. Next, Franklin removed the hierarchy in the company. Because it was a small company, Franklin required that every employee report to him personally. Then he told the employees that no one would be given a supervisory position but that each employee must learn how to lead by the persuasiveness of their good character and their willingness to cooperate with one another. Franklin reduced the staff team to the bare minimum so that staff members would have to rely on one another and support one another.

Franklin faced many challenges in developing a healthy company. However, over time people saw Franklin's good character, how much he cared for his staff, and that he actually knew what he was doing. They also experienced how the company improved. The whole spirit of the company shifted from negative to positive. Franklin and his staff still encountered many difficulties, but they were able to work together in a healthy and productive manner to overcome these difficulties.

In his experiences with his company, Franklin encountered one of the most important dynamics shaping leadership effectiveness:

trust. Franklin had gone from a company with a low-trust environment to a company with a high-trust environment. In so doing, he had created a company in which people generally enjoyed working and found good job satisfaction. Franklin had achieved this transformation largely because people in his company trusted him personally. He had developed trust in himself as a leader which led to experiencing an environment of trust in his company.

THE NECESSITY OF TRUST

Without trust, we simply cannot lead.[1] If people do not trust us, then they will not follow us – unless somehow we force them to follow us through coercion or the exercise of power, in which case we will further undermine trust. No leader can function without trust. No people-system can function without trust. Everything about leadership breaks down when there is no trust.

Along with the leadership crisis, we are experiencing a trust crisis in our society. One-third of employees in the UK do not trust senior management.[2] We suspect the percentage is similar in the US. About 80 percent of Americans do not trust the government to do what is right.[3] One would suspect that most of the nations of the world would have similar results. Less than half of Americans would rate Christian clergy high on honesty and ethics.[4] These facts show the major trust crisis faced by many societies today.

Low-trust environment

When trust is low in any people-system, the environment may become toxic, leading to dysfunction and dissatisfaction. People-systems with a low-trust environment struggle to exemplify any of the signs of a healthy people-system – mutual submission, unity, and love. Instead, they become susceptible to many kinds of disease and outside interference.

Three dynamics operate in any people-system with low trust: suspicion, anxiety, and friction. These three dynamics influence the very environment of the people-system. By learning to recognize when these dynamics are in operation, we can learn to recognize when a people-system has a low-trust environment.

First, there is the environment of suspicion. People will tend to distort or manipulate facts to their own ends. People will try to spin the truth, revealing only the parts of truth that benefit them or support their positions. On top of this, people will withhold information, treating it like a limited commodity.

In this environment of suspicion, we will find people blaming others for problems, accusing others of mistakes and wrongdoing, and criticizing others – often for insubstantial complaints, issues, and problems. We may also discover that people are sharing many secrets and even holding secret meetings. Secrets and secret meetings are the biggest indicator of a low trust system.

Second, there is the environment of anxiety. High levels of anxiety will often exist throughout the people-system. In the midst of this anxiety, people will not be willing to take risks. They will tend to cover up mistakes or blame them on some other person, circumstance or outside cause. Anxiety will lead people to overpromise and under deliver. When people fail to deliver, they will almost never accept personal responsibility for anything leading to the failure.

Third, there is the environment of friction. We will see a lot of conflict and animosity due to a conflict of wills, temperaments, and opinions. In this environment, people will strive to get personal credit and acknowledgment for their contributions, neglecting the input of others. We will experience open resistance to new ideas and to change. People will set unrealistic expectations, especially for other people, and then feel unduly angry when people fail to live up to these expectations.

Low-trust environments cost money and waste time. Consider the following research. In 2011, one company calculated that mistrust costs companies 14–18 percent annual revenue loss and a 17–24 percent loss of profitability. In the 1960s, if a company released a new product, 90 percent of customers would believe the corporate promise about the product. Today, less than 10 percent believe what the company says about the product. Globally, only half of consumers trust businesses and only 18 percent trust business leaders. Gallup research suggests that 71 percent of American workers are not engaged or are actively disengaged from their workplace, costing around $350 billion every year.[5] These figures do not even begin to consider the costs of low-trust environments for charities and churches.

High-trust environment

Obviously, a high-trust environment has very different dynamics than a low-trust environment. A high-trust environment provides life and joy to everyone associated with it. People who work or serve in a high-trust environment experience greater satisfaction, greater energy, and improved relationships. High-trust environments resist many of the toxins found in low-trust environments.

High-trust environments exemplify three dynamics: openness, honor, and creativity. These dynamics create a positive environment in the people-system. When we experience these dynamics in a people-system, we can know that we are likely in a high-trust environment.

First, there is an environment of openness. People share information openly, freely, and quickly. There is a sense of authenticity and vulnerability among people. People do not fear the possibility of making a mistake. Instead, leaders tolerate and even encourage people to take risks and make mistakes. Leaders understand this is the way many people learn. Of course, in order to make mistakes well high-trust systems encourage a great deal of accountability. People take responsibility for their actions and own their mistakes. Openness leads to improved communication throughout the people-system.

Second, there is an environment of honor. People tend to focus on others first rather than themselves. People will share credit with one another, often giving the biggest share of the credit to others. A high-trust environment encourages honesty among people. People in a high-trust environment will practice loyalty to those who are not present. They will refuse to talk behind another person's back or to engage in gossip and rumors about others.

In this environment of honor, people practice a high degree of collaboration and cooperation. People recognize one another's strengths without feeling threatened by them. People also know one another's weaknesses but choose to minimize them or make up for them with their own activities. Because of this, people can work together to produce beneficial outcomes. Working together produces joy.

Third, there is an environment of creativity. People experience a high degree of energy and vitality. They resist anxiety more effectively. Working together in teams, they generate creative ideas, positive changes, and general improvements. People working in an environment of high trust often find that they feel more innovative and experience better execution of their responsibilities.

Building a high-trust environment presents one of the greatest challenges for leaders. The level of trust will regulate the healthy functioning of the people-system. A high-trust environment alone may determine the overall effectiveness of our leadership. Building a high-trust environment begins with us as leaders. As we become a high-trust person in leadership we influence our people-system to become high trust itself.

TRUST DEFINED

We define trust as placing our confidence in the *being* and *doing* of another. All trust flows from these two dynamics, whether it is trust in ourselves, others, people-systems or God. *Being* involves integrity, motives, and intentions, along with all the factors we discussed earlier. *Doing* involves abilities, skills, and results, along with all the factors we discussed earlier.

The healthy and constructive interplay of *being* and *doing* leads to having confidence in a person or people-system. If people feel that our *being* is healthy and that we are capable of *doing* what we need to do, then they will trust us and follow us. If people believe that either our *being* or our *doing* is not healthy and constructive, then they will not trust us – no matter how good one or the other seems to be.

This understanding of trust shows why only God deserves our ultimate trust. God's being is perfect. He is all-loving, all-holy, and always good. God's doing is perfect as well. He is all-powerful and all-knowing. In addition, God never changes. Because of these things, God alone deserves our full trust.

BUILDING TRUST

Understanding the interplay of *being* and *doing* in trust helps us to see how we can build trust as leaders. In order to have a high-trust people-system, we must become highly trusted people as leaders. Because of our influence as leaders on our people-systems, it is very difficult to have a high-trust people-system if we are not high-trust leaders ourselves.

Two sets of behaviors help us to build trust. When people see these two sets of behaviors operating in us they will naturally begin to trust us as leaders. These two sets of behaviors basically relate to the *being* and *doing* dynamic of leadership that we have discussed throughout the book. These sets of behaviors are especially suitable for helping to build and maintain trust in leadership. We call these two sets of behaviors trust-building behaviors of *being* and trust-building behaviors of *doing* – or behaviors of *being* and behaviors of *doing* for short.[6]

All these behaviors require both a healthy *being* and the capability of *doing* rightly. We cannot separate one from the other. All behavior to some extent flows from our *being* as leaders, so if our *being* is not right then our *doing* will not lead beneficially. Certainly, as long as our *being* is not healthy we will struggle to do any of these behaviors

361

consistently. We have two sets of behaviors because people need to see that we have a good *being* – that we are people of character and integrity – as well as to see that we have the capability of *doing* well as leaders in order for them to trust. Trust depends on the healthy interplay of *being* and *doing*.

We find dealing with the concept of behaviors helpful because we can choose to change our behaviors. We cannot choose whether or not people trust us. We cannot determine how people might feel about us. But we can choose to change our behavior so that we might increase the possibility that people will choose to trust us. We have found that certain behaviors naturally lend themselves to building trust among people. When we model these behaviors as leaders, we increase the likelihood that the people in our people-system might choose these behaviors as well. Thus, we increase trust throughout our people-system by engaging in trust-building behaviors.

Trust-building behaviors of being

In light of our earlier discussions about *being*, to talk about "behaviors" of *being* might seem rather strange. After all, the word "behavior" suggests the concept of *doing*, not the concept of *being*. However, our outward behaviors represent the only way that people might have a sense of whether our *being* is healthy and grounded in Christ. As Jesus said, we will know people by their fruits (see Luke 6:43–44, for example).

Several behaviors reveal what is going on in our *being*. We call these behaviors of *being* because they are difficult to do consistently and authentically unless our *being* is reasonably healthy. People simply will not express these behaviors faithfully unless their *being* has a good degree of health and vitality.

Once again, Christians have a major advantage. As Christians in leadership, we have our identity grounded in Christ along with a sense of significance, security, and acceptance. People who fail to do behaviors of *being* consistently often fail because they have identity issues wrapped up in the failed behavior. For example, when someone fails to speak the truth in love, it is often because they fear that if they do speak the truth then people might not accept them. When someone fails to model transparency, it is often because they have a sense of insecurity. Knowing who we are in Christ gives us the confidence to do these behaviors of *being.*

Having the Holy Spirit dwell inside of us also gives us an advantage as Christians in leadership. The Holy Spirit establishes us in the truth of who we are in Christ. The Holy Spirit reminds us of the things we need to do to show that we have good character. The Holy Spirit convicts us of wrongdoing and leads us to repentance.

We have identified nine trust-building behaviors that reveal a healthy *being.* Engaging in these behaviors shows others that we are people worthy of trust. First, we need to *speak the truth in love* (see Ephesians 4:15). Truth in this context is not the same thing as our opinion. It is not simply an expression of our perspective. Truth involves an accurate representation of reality, especially in light of the Bible as God's Word.

We need to speak this accurate representation of reality out of genuine love. Love involves the self-giving commitment to others for their benefit. Love seeks the good of other people. Love does not include demanding our own way or simply doing that which benefits us. When we speak the truth in love, we are speaking truth to other people for their benefit.

Second, we *show respect and honor* (see Romans 12:10). Respect focuses on the abilities and the qualities of another person. Honor focuses on the inherent value and worth of the other person, that which is good in the person. Showing respect and honor means that we look for what is good in other people and emphasize what is good. People who are always criticizing, grumbling, and complaining about other people do not show respect or honor.

Third, we need to *model transparency* (see James 5:12 and Matthew 5:14–16). We need to be ourselves, without masks and deceptions. We mean what we say and say what we mean. We refuse to present ourselves as something we are not. When we fail and make mistakes, we refuse to hide these things or blame others. We are honest about our strengths as well as our shortcomings.

Fourth, we need to *right wrongs* (see Matthew 5:23–25). When we make a mistake, we choose to correct the mistake as soon as possible. When we fail to do something, we seek to admit our failures openly and then make the necessary changes. Righting wrongs also includes seeking reconciliation when we hurt other people. We do not wait for people to come to us but instead we choose to take the initiative ourselves in order to rebuild relationships.

Fifth, we choose to *show loyalty* (see Proverbs 20:6). Loyalty is "a noble, unswerving allegiance, born of faith and love, that binds hearts together in a common purpose".[7] Loyalty is not blind or naïve toward another person. Loyalty does not acquiesce to sin in the life of another person. Instead, loyalty looks for God's favor in the life of another person and seeks to unite us with that person at the point of God's favor to achieve a common purpose. One test of loyalty is how we talk about another person or think about another person when that person is not present.

Sixth, we need to *pay attention to others* (see Philippians 2:4). Paying attention to someone involves taking an interest in that person. When we pay attention to someone, we focus on that person while seeking to ignore other distractions. Paying attention includes allowing ourselves to become engaged with the life of another person so that we show a genuine concern for the person.

Seventh, we must *exercise self-control* (see Proverbs 25:28). Self-control means that we practice care and intention with regard to our mind, will, and emotions. Self-control involves not allowing our emotions to dominate our thinking and our choosing. Instead, self-control leads us to pause, consider our circumstances thoughtfully in light of the truth, and then make the best decision possible. When we exercise self-control, we do not allow our emotions to control us or to get the better of us.

Eighth, we *express gratitude* (see Ephesians 5:4). We must learn to show thankfulness toward other people for their contributions. We must show appreciation for the strengths and wisdom of other people. Expressing gratitude helps us to realize that we do nothing on our own but always depend on the team of people around us for our success. Expressing gratitude looks for the best in other people and acknowledges that openly.

Finally, we must *give grace* (see Ephesians 4:32). Grace is undeserved kindness and favor. Giving grace includes showing kindness to others, especially when they do not deserve it. When we give grace, we give other people the benefit of the doubt. We assume the best about their motives and intentions, even when their actions do not measure up. Giving grace includes giving people the freedom to fail without judging them harshly. The measure of giving grace is how God in Christ has given grace to us.

When we practice these behaviors of *being* we show people that in the core of our personality we have health and vitality. We demonstrate that there is something positive inside of us that governs our motives and intentions. Behaviors of *being* suggest to others that we are people worthy of trust because of our good character. Consistent behaviors of *being* lead people to have confidence in who we are as a leader.

Trust-building behaviors of doing

Trust-building behaviors of *being* serve as the first step for establishing trust. However, behaviors of *being* alone will not help you build trust in other people. After all, we can be very good people but terrible leaders! We need to have trust-building behaviors of *doing* to accompany our behaviors of *being* in order to develop a healthy sense of trust in our followers for us as leaders.

Behaviors of *doing* help show that we are capable of achieving what we set out to achieve. These behaviors demonstrate that we are competent as leaders to achieve beneficial outcomes. Without these behaviors of *doing*, people may like us as individuals but they will not have the conviction that we are able to do what we say we will do. Behaviors of *doing* alongside behaviors of *being* help people see that we have credibility as leaders.

Once again, we have identified nine trust-building behaviors of *doing*. First, we must *deliver results* (see Colossians 1:10 and 1 Peter 2:12). People need to see that we are getting things done. When we tell people that we will do something we need to do it and do it well. Instead of overpromising and under delivering, we need to under promise and over deliver. We must resist the temptation to make excuses when things do not work out as we had hoped.

Second, we need to *get better* (see Proverbs 9:9 and Philippians 4:17). One of my favorite words is the Japanese word *kaizen*. This word suggests making continuous, incremental improvements. People normally do not expect us to make many improvements suddenly. However, when they see us making consistent, gradual improvements, they begin to feel they can trust our ability to accomplish things.

Third, we must learn to *confront reality* (see 1 Samuel 15:13–16 and Nehemiah 2:13–17). As leaders, we need to see things as they really are, not as we would hope them to be. We must look at our situations openly and honestly, acknowledging the problems and issues truthfully. We must refuse to put a veneer on reality so that what we try to convey does not really reflect truth.

Fourth, we need to *clarify expectations* (see 2 Corinthians 9:5–7 and Nehemiah 5:6–13). We need to tell people what to expect in a realistic and forthright manner. We also need to clarify what we expect from ourselves and what we expect from others. We need to make sure that all our expectations are legitimate – that is, that they are realistic and agreed by everyone involved. So much anger and frustration comes from unmet expectations. So many expectations are unmet because they were unrealistic to begin with. Clarifying expectations gives people a sense of assurance that things are getting done.

Fifth, we need to *practice accountability* (see Matthew 5:21–25 and Romans 14:12). Masters require stewards to give an account of their stewardship. We all serve as stewards over the resources God has given us. Not only do we give an account to God, but we also give an account to one another for how we exercise our stewardship. In God's economy everyone has multiple points of accountability. As leaders we not only give an account of ourselves to God but we also give an account of ourselves to our followers and our people-systems.

Sixth, we must *listen actively* (see James 1:19). Many leaders fail to listen actively to their people. In so doing, they unwittingly undermine the people's confidence in their ability to lead. Listening to people, especially when they are bringing us concerns and difficulties, creates a sense of assurance that we as leaders might be able to do something about their concerns. When we listen and show understanding, we build a sense of trust for our abilities in other areas.

When listening to people, I try to focus completely on the person with whom I am talking, not allowing other things to distract me. I have a rule for my staff: we cannot answer the telephone or respond to a text message when we are meeting with someone. The only time we permit this is when we have told people at the beginning of the meeting that we might be receiving an important call or text message that we must answer. Otherwise, I expect people to mute their phone so they can concentrate on listening to the other people in the room.

Seventh, we must *keep our commitments* (see Psalm 15:4b). When we tell people that we are going to do something, we need to ensure that we do what we tell them. We need to keep our commitments even when what we have committed does not work out in the way that we had thought. The psalmist says that the people who dwell with God are, in part, those who make a commitment and keep it even when it hurts them. Keeping our commitments builds a track record of trustworthiness in the hearts and minds of those who follow us.

Eighth, we need to *extend trust* to others (see 1 Chronicles 12:16–19). Trust is a risky thing. When people choose to trust us, they are choosing to take a risk that we are trustworthy people. One of the best ways to build a sense of trust in us as leaders is to extend trust to other people. Leaders who micromanage or seek to control others break down the sense of trust in any people-system. In order for trust to flourish, we must choose to give trust more than we want people to trust us in return.

Finally, we must *meet the needs* of followers (see Nehemiah 9:14–19 and Acts 6:1–6). All followers have certain needs for which they look to their leaders and their people-systems to meet. In this context, we are not talking about the fundamental needs that everyone has which may only be met ultimately in a relationship with Jesus Christ. We are also not talking about general needs, perceived or real, for things such as food, clothing, and shelter. We are talking about a different set of more relationally based needs that leaders might address. We might call these needs "longings" in a sense.

Our followers long for a sense of confidence that their contribution to our shared purpose has value and importance. They long to experience compassion from us as leaders, a genuine sense that we care for them. Our followers long for a sense of stability in us as leaders as well as in our people-systems. They need to know that we have steadiness, balance, and strength. Our followers also long for a sense of hope, a sense that something good will happen in our people-system. When we meet these needs – these longings – as leaders, people will trust our ability to accomplish what we set out to do.

When we engage in these behaviors of *doing* alongside our behaviors of *being*, we will build high trust in the people who follow us. Building trust in us as leaders is often the first part of creating a high-trust people-system.

PRINCIPLES FOR BUILDING TRUST

As leaders, we often find it much easier to lose trust than we do to build trust. We can work for months and months on end to create trust in our people and people-systems only to lose it in a moment of anger or frustration. Sometimes, we might even find the whole issue of winning and losing trust rather mysterious. However, two principles will help us understand how we can avoid losing trust as well as how we can help to build trust:

> **The quickest way to decrease trust is to violate a trust-building behavior of being.**
>
> **The quickest way to increase trust is to demonstrate a trust-building behavior of doing.**[8]

Whenever we violate or fail to maintain any of the behaviors of *being* we will decrease trust in our followers and in our people-system. If people do not feel that they can trust our good character, then they will never really trust what we do no matter how good it seems. If people begin to doubt our motives and intentions, then they will not trust that what we do might lead to mutually beneficial outcomes. They will often become suspicious of what we are doing and whether it is actually for our own benefit.

For example, if we fail to speak the truth or to speak the truth in a loving way, then people will wonder whether anything we say is true. If we fail to show loyalty, talking behind someone's back, then people will wonder what we say behind their backs. If we do not demonstrate self-control but allow ourselves to burst into fits of rage, people will not believe that we have the self-discipline to accomplish what we promise.

When we find ourselves violating any behavior of *being*, the first priority is to stop violating it! If we continue to violate behaviors of *being*, then we will completely undermine anyone's trust in us as leaders. Violating behaviors of *being* destroys trust and undermines our leadership effectiveness.

When trust has been broken, or when we need to build trust from scratch, demonstrating behaviors of *doing* provides the quickest way to increase trust. The reason why behaviors of *doing* are so important at this point is because it takes time for people to see our healthy *being* or our good character. Everyone knows that people may fake behaviors of *being* for little while. However, no one will consistently do behaviors of *being* if those behaviors are not consistent with who they really are. Unfortunately, it takes time to see this in a leader.

Consistently performing the behaviors of *doing* suggests to people that we have the capability of being good leaders. Behaviors of *doing* indicate to people that we have a competence for leadership. When they see our capabilities, people begin to think that perhaps they can trust our *being* – our motives and character. When we do things like deliver results, make improvements, confront reality, and listen actively, people begin to assume the best of us and extend trust to us. We confirm the perception that we are trustworthy by adding behaviors of *being* to our behaviors of *doing*.

We experienced the importance of this dynamic for rebuilding trust when we emerged from the crisis time in the life of the church. People in the church wanted to trust me, but others had attacked my *being* so forcefully that even some of my strongest supporters wondered whether I was trustworthy. People had accused me of lying, of building my own kingdom, of selfishness and greed, along with many other things. A minority of people felt that they could trust me fully, but many people took a "wait and see" attitude.

I had no way to convince people immediately that my *being* was healthy and grounded in Christ. So I worked carefully not to violate any behaviors of *being*. I sought to speak the truth about our situation and the problems that we had encountered as a church in love. I tried to model transparency by admitting my weaknesses, as well as my faults and my failures. I strived to exercise self-control at all times. Above all, I sought to give grace to people, even people who had wounded me deeply. It certainly helped that people recognized I was not violating behaviors of *being*, but that is not what really rebuilt trust.

What really began to rebuild trust in people after our time of crisis were my behaviors of *doing*. I confronted the reality of our situation and how most churches do not recover from the kind of conflict that we had experienced. I set out a course of action in order to establish and clarify good expectations. I tried carefully not to make promises that I could not keep. I practiced accountability not only with our board of elders but also with our church meeting, letting them know when we had failed to achieve our objectives as well as celebrating the times when we did achieve our objectives.

After a number of months, I began to notice a change in the attitudes and actions of a number of people. Many people seemed to warm to me and begin to relax around me. I began to hear a number of comments like these:

> "You told us that we would achieve certain things. We have now achieved those things. I remember how people before used to make promises but then did not keep them."

> "I used to hear people talk about you behind your back all the time. But I never heard you talk behind anyone else's back. When I talked to some other people, they never seemed to listen to me. But you do listen to me."

> "You have really demonstrated your commitment to us and this church. You have really persevered. I sense that our church has a new degree of stability. I also feel like you really care for people."

Because people had witnessed good behaviors of *doing*, they began to trust my *being* and give me the benefit of the doubt. When they further saw that I was not violating behaviors of *being*, they began to see that what some people had said about me was not true. They began to trust me more and more. Once they trusted me, it enabled me to begin building a high-trust church, something which is an ongoing process.

If we maintain the trust-building behaviors of *being,* then we will receive more grace when we violate behaviors of *doing*. Violating behaviors of *doing* will not decrease trust in the same way as violating behaviors of *being*. For example, suppose someone comes up to speak with me, but I am distracted and fail to practice active listening. If I had shown them respect in the past, if they had seen me consistently pay attention to others, if I now exercise self-control so that I am not rude or dismissive to them, and if I now transparently apologize for not being as attentive as I would like – all trust-building behaviors of *being* – then they would more likely forgive my failure in that moment and continue to trust me. If I had not practiced these behaviors in the past then they would begin to lose their trust in me. What happens in our *being* determines whether we increase or decrease trust in any interaction we have with people.

Trust-building behaviors of *being* and trust-building behaviors of *doing* do not represent the latest management techniques. We can learn to develop and improve these behaviors. We might intentionally seek to grow in them. However, for these behaviors to build trust, they must flow authentically from our *being*. People will sense instinctively if we try to feign these behaviors. Only when flowing from a healthy *being* will these behaviors build and maintain trust.

TRUST AND ANXIETY

As with everything else, anxiety has a corrosive effect on trust. Unmanaged or unresolved anxiety in a leader or a people-system will degrade trust. Anxiety leads to a corrosive pessimism toward leaders and people-systems with respect to trust. If the leader is bound up with anxiety, then the people in the system will instinctively not trust that leader. If the leader is actually generating anxiety then the people-system will become bound up with mistrust and conflicts of will. Ultimately, the system will spin into dysfunction and disunity.

Leaders who resist and resolve anxiety will help enable the people-system to resist and resolve anxiety. In these situations, the level of trust in the people-system will actually increase due to the healthy functioning of the leader. In order for this to happen, leaders have to serve as a lightning rod in people-systems to drain away anxiety and enable people to trust. However, we need to remember that when we are a lightning rod the people will focus their anxiety onto us as leaders. This means that we must remain healthy and grounded in Christ in our *being* so that we do not become overwhelmed or burned out by the people-system's anxiety.

David and his church faced some fundamental changes due to the changing demographics of their community. The church had experienced decline as many people moved away and others did not take their place. The expectations for styles of worship had changed among people looking for churches, which meant that the more traditional style of worship would no longer reach those moving into the community. As David led the church through the changes, he encountered a lot of confusion and anger among his people. However, David remained calm with his *being* grounded in Jesus. As he listened to the anger and the confusion caused by the anxiety people were feeling, the anxiety would drain away from people. Over time, many of his congregation actually became excited about the new opportunities they had in their community. The church remained healthy.

FAILURE AND TRUST

Most people try to avoid failure at all costs. However, failure can be normal and healthy. After all, we learn and grow through failure, individually and together. As we talk about failure in this context we are not talking about "moral failure" – sin. Obviously, sin or "moral failure" is never good. We are talking about times when people try something new, experiment, take risks and stretch themselves, yet fail.

Failure is essential to healthy leaders, healthy followers, and healthy people-systems. Failure might even increase trust in a people-system. Failure helps to increase our resilience and develop our maturity. It stretches our perceived limits and provides opportunities for growth. Failure will often prompt innovation as we look for new ways to succeed. It motivates us to improve.

The level of trust determines whether people are willing to take risks and possibly fail. High levels of trust give people the ability to benefit from failure. Modeling healthy responses to failure increases trust. In order to build trust in the midst of failure we must evaluate failures openly, encouraging responsibility and learning.

While in a casual conversation with a regular client, John offhandedly suggested that the client might use a certain room for a special function over the weekend. John had forgotten about the normal client who had already booked the room. The client forgot to confirm the room with the booking manager, and just assumed that they could use the room as suggested by John. When the weekend came, the staff on duty had to scramble to undo the mess created, apologizing to both clients and feeling rather embarrassed.

Sarah decided to review the failure at the weekly staff meeting. Because she had already created an environment of trust where people were free to fail, John openly admitted his mistake, enabling everyone to examine what had happened and why it had happened. The whole failure became a way for Sarah to review the procedures for booking rooms, how to practice good customer care in similar conversations with clients in the future, and what to do if the staff discovered a similar mistake in the future and had a situation to resolve. Failure became an opportunity for growth. How Sarah handled the failure increased trust.

Certain responses to failure will damage trust. If we explode at the person who fails then we will undermine trust. If we try to blame others for failures or if we try to cover up failures, then we will diminish trust. If we back away from people who have failed instead of supporting them, then they will not trust us. In order to build trust through failure, we refuse to quit with people but continue to support and encourage them.

In dealing with failure, we find it helpful to remember that God expects more failure from us than we expect from ourselves. Our failure never surprises God. God knows what we are going to do and how we are going to do it and yet gives us the freedom to fail. One of the most significant things we can do as a leader is ensure that we understand and receive the grace of God in our lives. Then we extend that grace to others as God has extended grace to us.

THE LEADERSHIP DILEMMA

Building and keeping trust will increase our leadership effectiveness. It will also greatly increase our joy in leading. Few things bring more joy than leading a high-trust people-system. People serving in high-trust people-systems will also experience greater joy, along with greater creativity and greater overall satisfaction. Working with people who trust us improves our leadership effectiveness even when we do not make any other changes in our leadership.

Building and keeping trust is a process that takes time. People learn to trust over weeks, months, and years, not over a few days. As leaders we need the confidence to know that we can build trust, even in the most difficult situations. At the same time, we can lose trust very quickly, in an instant. Even when this happens, providing we persevere, we can rebuild trust while also building up a high-trust people-system.

The people-systems of our society need trust in order to function properly. The people-systems of our society must trust their leaders in order to accomplish beneficial outcomes and experience real joy in working together. Yet, people in all the people-systems of our society are actively seeking to destroy trust in leaders. This is our leadership dilemma. We see this all around us, from how people treat those in government to those in business to those in the clergy. So we must persevere in our leadership with grace, remembering that we can build trust with patience and perseverance. All this begins with a healthy *being* grounded in Christ.

PART VI

OVERCOMING LEADERSHIP PITFALLS

Good things do not come easy. The road is lined with pitfalls.

Desi Arnaz

Success is to be measured not so much by the position that one has reached in life as by the obstacles which he has overcome.

Booker T. Washington

The rationalist imagines an imbecile-free society; the empiricist an imbecile-proof one, or even better, a rationalist-proof one.

Nassim Nicholas Taleb

Security is mostly a superstition. It does not exist in nature, nor do the children of men as a whole experience it. Avoiding danger is no safer in the long run than outright exposure. Life is either a daring adventure or nothing.

Helen Keller

When I came to my first church as a pastor, I had many hopeful expectations. The near unanimous vote to call me gave me a sense of assurance and excitement that we would all work well together and achieve many things for God. The people seemed genuinely excited to have a new minister. In the process of calling me, we had agreed a number of important goals for the ministry of the church, including expanding the youth ministry, growing Sunday attendance, and possibly a new educational wing for the church.

Before entering professional Christian ministry, I had many good experiences working in the marketplace. I had worked in cinema management for several years. I really enjoyed managing people and dealing with the challenges of workplace leadership. One company I had worked for even offered me a job with their company on the West Coast of the United States. Although I was tempted for a short time, I knew that God had called me into full-time Christian ministry so I declined the job offer. But I had expected my positive experiences to continue into church ministry.

From the beginning, we saw God change many lives with the good news about Jesus Christ. I enjoyed many of my responsibilities as the pastor of a church. We had many excellent people in the life of the church. I really expected things to go smoothly, people to work together cooperatively, and generally for the church to become healthier and healthier as it grew. So, one can imagine my surprise when I began to face an increasing number of difficulties. Real world Christian ministry turned out to be more difficult and more demanding than I had ever anticipated.

I quickly discovered that leaders always encounter a large number of pitfalls. These hidden or unsuspected dangers and difficulties confront and surprise leaders at every turn. One reason I can write about these pitfalls is that I personally have encountered almost every single one of them. Some of these pitfalls I avoided, many of these pitfalls I stumbled into unwittingly, and a few of these pitfalls I leaped into with gusto – much to my dismay. Looking back, I cannot believe how many pitfalls we face as leaders. I am astounded that any of us actually survive them.

Seminary had left me totally unprepared for what I would face as a leader. For that matter, so had university. Although some colleges and universities do better today, most leaders are left to discover these pitfalls on their own and hopefully to avoid them. Looking back, I realize that I may have done a much better job had someone told me the pitfalls I would face and how to avoid falling into them.

One of my biggest problems – and perhaps the biggest problem that I have seen with other leaders – was that the pitfalls I encountered took me completely off-guard, which meant that most of the time my reaction to these pitfalls was completely inappropriate. I had believed that the pitfalls I encountered were unusual, abnormal, and a sign that I was failing as a leader or that people were opposing my leadership. What I discovered was that these pitfalls were normal and a sign that I was actually succeeding as a leader.

In a sense, it is a strange irony: although I was succeeding as a leader I was also failing to deal with pitfalls in a healthy and appropriate way. So my reactions to the pitfalls undermined my own leadership success. Sadly, I have seen this happen time and again with many leaders on many different continents and in many different leadership contexts.

In this section, we will examine three kinds of leadership pitfalls: personal pitfalls, systemic pitfalls, and leadership delusions. These pitfalls alert us to some things to expect as leaders, especially when we are leading well. When we expect to find a pit, it is much easier to avoid falling into the pit. When we expect to find a leadership pitfall, it is much easier to overcome the pitfall and not allow it to undermine our leadership effectiveness.

Perhaps the most important message that we want to give leaders in this section is that we should not see the presence of a leadership pitfall as a sign that we are failures as leaders. If we were failing, the world, the flesh or the devil would not even bother to place a pitfall in our way.

Perhaps the second most important message is that we can overcome all these leadership pitfalls. We do not have to be victims of the pitfalls. Instead, God has designed and equipped us as victors who overcome leadership pitfalls.

14

OVERCOMING PERSONAL PITFALLS

The difficulty, my friends, is not in avoiding death, but in avoiding unrighteousness; for that runs faster than death.

Socrates

We are certainly in a common class with the beasts; every action of animal life is concerned with seeking bodily pleasure and avoiding pain.

Augustine

If men as individuals surrender to the call of their elementary instincts, avoiding pain and seeking satisfaction only for their own selves, the result for them all taken together must be a state of insecurity, of fear, and of promiscuous misery.

Albert Einstein

That no one seemed to help during hectic times frustrated Phil no end. He often felt angry at people because they would not take responsibility to help out, but he stuffed the feelings inside (most of the time) because he felt that perhaps this was just his "cross" to bear. Secretly, he thought that without him the whole place would fall apart. Day after day he shouldered the full weight of the things that needed to get done, frequently reminding people of all the work he had to do. Of course, if he needed some office supplies at home he would help himself to supplies from the work office; after all, he had earned it in a way because of all his extra work. When people suggested that perhaps Phil should become more of a team player and work better with others, he would irritably suggest that people just needed to learn how to work better with him since he was the leader. When Phil suddenly died of a heart attack, his colleagues did not even notice his absence for two days.

Phil represents an amalgamation of many leaders I have met over the years. However, I feel reasonably confident that as people read his story they will have recognized leaders that they know personally in Phil. So often leaders undermine their own leadership fruitfulness by stumbling – or rushing headlong – into a number of predictable personal pitfalls. In this chapter we will examine a number of these pitfalls and present some strategies for overcoming the pitfalls.

PERSONAL LEADERSHIP PITFALLS

All leaders face a number of personal dangers and difficulties that simply go along with the role of leadership. We call these dangers and difficulties "pitfalls" because quite often we fail to expect them or we fail to see them before suddenly we get caught up in them. (The Bible often uses the word "snare" to refer to what we are calling a "pitfall".) Sometimes, we might even deny that these are problems in the first place and instead try to justify the fact that we are caught up in them as good leadership.

Leaders stumble into these pitfalls so frequently that some people begin to think that the issues represented by the pitfalls are normal character flaws for leaders. They give up hope that leaders might not fall into these pits and begin to assume that all leaders naturally have these problems. Oftentimes, leaders begin to justify these behaviors, trying to excuse themselves or blaming others for their failures. While it is true that all leaders face these pitfalls, it is not true that leaders must inevitably fall into them. We can overcome them.

The hope of overcoming personal pitfalls lies within us as leaders. The reason so many leaders fall into personal pitfalls is that they become weary of trying to *do* things to overcome the pitfalls. They make overcoming pitfalls a matter of *doing*. However, overcoming personal pitfalls involves our *being* more than our *doing*.

When our *being* is healthy we experience greater strength and creativity for leaping over personal pitfalls. When our *being* is healthy and grounded in Jesus, we experience the strength and vitality of Jesus himself by the power of the Holy Spirit, which energizes our *being* and provides our best opportunity for overcoming personal pitfalls. Leaders most often fall into personal pitfalls when they allow their *being* to become weak and weary. Leaders who have nurtured a healthy *being* have the ability to resist personal pitfalls.

We have identified at least four kinds of personal leadership pitfalls. Leaders face temptation pitfalls, egocentric pitfalls, emotional pitfalls, and exhaustion pitfalls. We face many other pitfalls as well, but these will be some of the most common pitfalls. We will look at each kind of pitfall in turn and then provide some strategies for overcoming these pitfalls.

TEMPTATION PITFALLS

Leaders face many strong temptations to sin. These temptations tend to revolve around three areas: money, sex, and power.[1] These three things are not inherently sinful; in fact, they are part of God's good creation. However, these three areas have great influence in our lives and may awaken very strong temptations for wrongdoing. Sadly, almost every day we read stories about leaders, even Christian leaders, who succumb to temptations in all three areas and shipwreck their leadership.

Money

The first area of temptation is money. When we talk about money in this context we are talking about all material resources and not just "cold, hard cash". One aspect of this area is greed, but greed might manifest in many different ways. We can become greedy for more money, a higher salary or more personal benefits. We can become greedy for more things, more technology to use in our business, a bigger house or better car. The constant desire for more shows greed, no matter how that constant desire for more shows itself. Whenever we allow ourselves to become greedy in any way we have fallen into this pit.

Another aspect of this area includes how we manage the money and resources of our people-system. Again, this area is not just about cash money. We would include in this area all of the physical resources of our people-system, from buildings to office supplies to technology such as computers.

We can ask ourselves many questions to help us discern whether we have fallen into the pit of a money temptation: are we following best practice in how we manage our organization's finances? Are we setting and following budgets? Are we caring for the physical resources of our organization, such as our building? Are we taking proper care of our computer systems, protecting them against loss and damage? Are we using the resources of our organization properly, to advance the purposes of our organization and not for our own personal benefit? These questions represent some of the questions we need to ask ourselves to ensure we do not fall into this pit.

A third aspect of this area involves how we manage our personal money and resources. Many leaders allow their personal finances to become quite messy. They allow themselves to get into large debts, especially consumer debts. They fail to pay their bills on time. They do not exercise good stewardship over the physical resources God has given them. For example, I have seen many leaders who failed to take care of their cars.

If we cannot manage our personal money and resources appropriately, then no one can expect us to be able to manage the money and resources of our organizations properly. Jesus reminds us of this:

> One who is faithful in a very little is also faithful in much, and one who is dishonest in a very little is also dishonest in much. If then you have not been faithful in the unrighteous wealth, who will entrust to you the true riches? And if you have not been faithful in that which is another's, who will give you that which is your own? (Luke 16:10–12)

Poor personal money management has a great impact on our leadership. It undermines our integrity as leaders. Poor personal money management exposes leaders to many temptations and struggles, undermining their leadership effectiveness.

One reason money becomes such a powerful temptation is that we often try to meet our needs for security through money. When we have a lot of money or a lot of resources we tend to feel secure as people. When we have little money and little resources we tend to feel insecure. So trying to gain more money and resources might actually indicate that we are seeking to meet our need for security through the acquisition of money. However, as we have seen, only Jesus truly and fully meets our need for security. Whenever we are trying to meet this need for security outside Jesus, and especially in our leadership roles, we distort our leadership and undermine our effectiveness.

Sex

The second area of temptation is sex. Sex is God's good gift to us as humans, providing that we experience this gift within the parameters set by God in the Bible. Too often Christians seem like prudes when it comes to our sexuality. However, we believe that sex is good within

385

the covenant of marriage between a man and a woman. Still, sex has great power in our lives as human beings, which means we face many temptations with regard to sex – especially as leaders.

The most obvious aspect of this area is sexual immorality – that is, sex outside the covenant of marriage. We sadly read stories almost every week about Christian leaders who have fallen into adultery or other kinds of sexual immorality. Sexual immorality has become so common in the marketplace that hardly anyone pays attention to it anymore. However, sexual immorality destroys leadership as we have described it in this book.

Another common aspect of this area is pornography. Pornography has become a great problem throughout society, including the church. Here are just a few statistics: at the time of writing, there had been over 873 million searches for internet porn in the first half of 2015. A quarter of smartphone users admit to having pornography on their phone. Sixty-four percent of Christian men and 18 percent of Christian women admit to watching porn at least once a month. Nine out of ten boys and six out of ten girls are exposed to pornography before they are eighteen years old.[2] Pornography drains vitality away from leadership and makes leaders more likely to commit sexual immorality.

Leaders often overlook a third aspect to this area: fantasy and daydreaming. Many leaders will avoid sexual immorality and pornography only to allow themselves to wander into daydreaming about a colleague. They might engage in fantasizing what it might feel like to be involved with a co-worker. In our experience, female leaders face this temptation especially, although men are not excluded from this. Often, reading certain kinds of books or watching certain films will expose people to these temptations.

One reason sex becomes such a powerful temptation is that we often try to meet our needs for acceptance through sex. God created sex in part to allow a husband and a wife to experience complete acceptance of one another, as a foreshadowing of how God accepts us in Christ Jesus. Sexual immorality, pornography, and fantasy all give us an allusion of acceptance. They give us a sense that our needs for acceptance are being met. However, only Jesus truly and fully meets our need for acceptance. Whenever we are trying to meet this need for acceptance outside Jesus, and especially in our leadership roles, we distort our leadership and undermine our effectiveness.

Power

The third area of temptation involves power. We often struggle to persuade or influence people to follow our leadership. People often resist our suggestions, believing their own ideas to be better or simply wanting to do things their own way. Such responses can weary leaders at times, making our jobs much more difficult. In these moments, we can easily fall into the desire to dominate and manipulate our followers. We try to coerce them into following us or wear them down until they comply. When this happens we have fallen into a pit.

Leaders may sometimes crave a certain leadership position or place of authority. We might then engage in all sorts of political maneuvering in order to gain that position. We might think that once we gain a position then people will naturally follow us – or, if they do not naturally follow us then we can force them to follow us because of our position. Whenever we begin to think that either gaining or using a position will make us better leaders, we are beginning to lean into this pit – and we may quickly fall into it.

Sometimes we simply want people to show us respect as leaders. We long for people to acknowledge our contribution and honor us as we perhaps feel we should be honored. We have expectations that people should respect and honor leaders no matter what. When we begin to try to gain that respect or demand that respect then we have begun to fall into this pit. Some degree of respect will always be given to leaders but having someone's respect does not make us better leaders. Craving respect will actually undermine our leadership as we seek to use others to meet our desires.

As with money and sex, the quest for power becomes a quest to meet another of our fundamental needs – the need for significance. God has created power structures and given us the ability to influence others in order to promote the up-building and well-being of people and society. God uses his power always in the context of his grace and his love. When we crave power and seek power we are actually trying to gain significance. However, whenever we are trying to meet our need for significance outside Jesus, and especially in our leadership roles, we distort our leadership and undermine our effectiveness.

AVOIDING TEMPTATION PITFALLS

To overcome temptation pitfalls we must first understand that temptation itself is not sin. To experience temptation is not the pitfall; committing the sin associated with the temptation is the pitfall. As long as we live on the earth, we will never be entirely free from temptation. However, we never need to succumb to temptation.

We deal with temptation pitfalls best by avoiding temptation and situations where we might experience temptation. Once we fall into a temptation pitfall the damage will have been done. We will need to repent – confessing our sin and turning away from it – and we will also need to seek reconciliation with those we have wronged. But it may take months and years to rebuild our leadership after falling into a temptation pitfall. So the best strategy is to avoid these pitfalls.

We can avoid temptation pitfalls as we lead from our *being* fully grounded in Jesus Christ. When our identity flows from our relationship with God through Jesus Christ and when our fundamental needs for significance, security, and acceptance are being met in our relationship with God through Jesus Christ, we will avoid temptation pitfalls more naturally and instinctively because the Spirit of God will alert us when these pitfalls arise. We cannot stress enough the importance of having a healthy *being*.

Understanding the nature of temptation will help us resist it. Temptation is the enticement to have our core needs for significance, security or acceptance met outside God in Jesus Christ. Anything to which we look to meet these needs, other than God himself, becomes an idol in our lives. This understanding of temptation helps explain why having our *being* grounded in Christ helps us to resist and overcome temptation.

A second strategy is to guard our hearts. David said, "I will walk with integrity of heart within my house; I will not set before my eyes anything that is worthless" (Psalm 101:2–3). We need to take care that we are living appropriately, even in the private places of our lives, our "house". We must choose carefully what we look at and what we listen to. We can practice what we call "threshold thinking", in which we do not allow anything over the "threshold" of our minds that dishonors God or the Bible.

David also gives us another way to guard our hearts: "For your steadfast love is before my eyes, and I walk in your faithfulness" (Psalms 26:3). He said that he would keep God's love before his eyes so that he would not engage in anything that dishonored God. Paul gives us a similar idea when he says, "Set your minds on things that are above, not on things that are on earth" (Colossians 3:2). We can guard our hearts by focusing on the superior delights of God and his ways.

Third, we must learn to rest. Failing to rest makes us vulnerable to every single temptation we discussed in the section. Most leaders would never even consider doing some of these things when they feel rested and alert. It is only when we allow ourselves to become weary and worn out that we face these temptations most strongly. In our tiredness we might resort to becoming dominating and manipulative toward our followers simply because it takes too much energy to persuade them. In our weariness we might feel that we are entitled to buy a few more things to make us feel good, even if it takes us into debt. In our exhaustion we might fail to take care of what we are watching on the television. Rest becomes a strong weapon to use against all the temptation pitfalls.

EGOCENTRIC PITFALLS

We call our second group of pitfalls "egocentric" pitfalls. We label them "egocentric" because they arise from a self-centered perspective regarding our leadership. These egocentric pitfalls entice us to think that our people-system depends on our leadership or that what we do in our leadership has the greatest importance for our people-system.

Messiah complex

We describe the first egocentric pitfall as the "messiah complex". We might also call it the "God complex". The messiah complex arises when we begin to think that we are the savior of our people-system. We start to believe that we alone are the people who have the ability to lead our people-system successfully. We might start to think that we are always right. We might begin to believe that our contribution makes all the difference in the success or failure of our people-system, that without us everything would fail or fall apart.

Leaders with a messiah complex often exhibit arrogance and pride. They will have a lot of selfish ambition where they are in competition with other leaders both inside and outside the people-system. They will often engage in manipulation or intimidation but feign innocence when they are challenged about it.

Having a messiah complex always undermines leadership fruitfulness. People instinctively resist those who think they are "God" or who think they are God's gift to our people-system. God himself will also oppose leaders who have a messiah complex because God always resists the proud and gives grace to the humble (see James 4:6).

The messiah complex arises from our need for significance. People who try to find their sense of significance in their leadership role become susceptible to the messiah complex. We delude ourselves into thinking that we must be significant because our people-system depends on us so much. Trying to meet this need in someone other than Jesus always undermines our leadership.

Martyr complex

Having a martyr complex is another egocentric pitfall. The martyr complex arises when we begin to think that our people-system requires our suffering or our sacrifice in order to function well or achieve good outcomes. Sometimes we might attribute our difficulties or suffering to the fact that we are simply great leaders, at least in our own minds. Other times, we might assume that we need to embrace (often needless) suffering in the name of love or duty.

For example, over the years I have encountered a number of pastors who were willing to respond to every cry for help from people immediately, even if it meant loss of sleep, loss of family time or loss of other important activities, such as prayer. These leaders embraced the pain of neglecting their families or neglecting their health for the sake of others. These behaviors might have seemed sacrificial but they were most often evidence of the martyr complex. Most of the time, the people demanding their time and attention could have easily waited until the pastor had a better opportunity to minister to them. Occasionally, these people really did not have a genuine need at all, but simply wanted the attention of the pastor.

Occasionally, having a martyr complex might indicate that people are trying to avoid taking personal responsibility for something. For example, we might choose to pray for four hours for the outreach team rather than going out for an hour with the outreach team to share our faith with people on the streets. The "sacrifice" of four hours in prayer disguises the fear of taking responsibility to share our faith. People can develop many different ways of avoiding responsibility through the martyr complex.

Leaders with a martyr complex often use their apparent self-sacrifice to manipulate others. They might try to motivate people by using guilt or shame, particularly in light of their "shining" example. They might seek the admiration and affirmation of other people for the suffering they are enduring. They may even make themselves seem like victims, being bullied and harassed by others in the people-system.

The martyr complex proceeds from our need for acceptance. Leaders want people to accept them so they offer themselves as a "sacrifice", assuming that people would never reject such an expression of "love". The problem comes because this "love" is not genuine biblical love but a false love and a self-love. Trying to meet our need for acceptance in someone other than Jesus always distorts our leadership.

Hermit complex

The hermit complex is our third egocentric pitfall. The hermit complex often emerges when we begin to feel overwhelmed by stress, conflicts, problems or the flood of leadership responsibilities. When we have too many things to do or too many responsibilities we become susceptible to the hermit complex. The hermit complex causes us to retreat into ourselves and away from the people in our system. In the hermit complex we focus on a narrow range of activities – some important and some not – that we feel able to do successfully and peacefully. We will often ignore other people or the legitimate needs of our people-system. Sometimes, we may even feel that we need to do this in order to survive.

When we fall into the hermit complex, we are experiencing a cowardice or a failure of nerve, often stemming from weariness that leads to passivity and an ungodly compliance to others. We retreat from our responsibilities of leadership and we retreat from our relationships with other people because we feel unable to cope and unable to lead. In the hermit complex we shrink our world so that it becomes manageable and safe.

Leaders who fall into the hermit complex often ignore other people. They might ignore or deny reality, deceiving themselves into thinking things are better than they truly are. They surrender their leadership responsibilities and allow their people-system to come under the influence of many different forces that may seek to use the people-system for their own ends. These leaders lose all ability to lead, negating their influence in the people-system.

The hermit complex emerges from our need for security. We try to create a safe environment to fulfill those leadership responsibilities that seem easiest for us. We resist anything that challenges us, stretches us or threatens us. In so doing we miss all the genuine opportunities for leadership. Trying to meet our need for security in someone other than Jesus always distorts our leadership.

AVOIDING EGOCENTRIC PITFALLS

We have four strategies for avoiding egocentric pitfalls. We have already discussed the first two under avoiding temptation pitfalls. First, we must lead from our identity grounded in Jesus Christ. Second, we must also pursue healthy rest. Lack of rest makes us susceptible to many unhealthy influences.

Our third strategy is to pursue humility. Paul urges us not to think of ourselves more highly than we ought, but instead to think of ourselves with sober judgment, having a clear sense of our strengths and abilities through faith by the grace of God (see Romans 12:3). Having a healthy concept of ourselves in light of the Bible and placing our confidence in God who makes us sufficient for our leadership responsibilities (see 2 Corinthians 3:4–6) enables us to avoid the egocentric pitfalls.

When we have humility, we will realize that there is only one God and Savior for our people-system and we are not that God. Humility protects us from the martyr complex where we are tempted to think that our sacrifice makes all the difference. Humility reminds us that we cannot deal with all our responsibilities and challenges alone, but we can do all things through Christ who gives us strength (see Philippians 4:13).

Fourth, we need to clarify our expectations and responsibilities. We need to know what we are responsible for and what God is responsible for. We cannot do God's responsibilities and God will not do our responsibilities. So often our struggle as leaders comes because we have failed to understand our responsibilities. For example, we might try to convince someone about their sin or wrongdoing when that is the responsibility of the Holy Spirit.

We will also struggle when we try to fulfill the responsibilities of other people. Some leaders think that they themselves must pick up all the slack in their people-system. When we try to do this we will doom ourselves to failure. We cannot take on the responsibilities of others. We cannot forgive for other people, do the work of prayer others need to do, or take on other people's jobs.

Along with our responsibilities, we need to clarify expectations. We need to clarify what we are expecting from ourselves and whether those expectations are realistic. We also need to work with the people in our people-system to clarify the expectations they have for us. In any people-system, the people will have a great diversity of expectations for those who are in leadership. Many of these expectations are completely unrealistic. Unmet expectations will cause anger and frustration. Therefore we must clarify and agree all the expectations that the people-system has for us as leaders. Expectations that have not been agreed are not legitimate expectations.

EMOTIONAL PITFALLS

We leaders often experience very strong emotions. These emotions naturally spring up from the variety of encounters we have as leaders. Many of the emotions we experience have a positive and pleasurable impact, such as when we take delight in the successes of the people we are leading. Negative emotions we experience bring challenges for our leadership. If we allow ourselves to follow these stronger, negative emotions we may find ourselves stuck in major difficulties. So we call our third set of personal leadership pitfalls "emotional" pitfalls.

We need to understand that our emotions are inherently neither good nor bad. Emotions occur naturally as part of life. We cannot control our emotions; they just happen. However, we can choose how we will think and act in light of our emotions. We can choose how we will respond to our emotions. We can accept that we will experience some emotions as pleasurable and other emotions as painful. We need both kinds of emotions.

Emotions alert us that we need to address something in our lives. Pleasurable emotions remind us to pause, pay attention, and enjoy whatever is giving rise to those emotions. Negative or painful emotions remind us to evaluate what is happening and respond carefully. Both types of emotions alert us that we need to pay attention.

Emotional pitfalls tend to occur in three varieties: anger, bitterness, and defensiveness. We are not only referring to these three emotions specifically but also to a whole cluster of emotions that surround these three. Each of these three emotions has many other kinds of emotions associated with them. But rather than try to focus on a dozen or more emotions we find it helpful to focus on these three clusters.

Anger

Anger normally signals that we have unmet expectations or blocked goals. Whenever people fail to live up to our expectations, whether agreed or not, we will experience anger. Whenever we have what we feel is a legitimate goal that someone or something else seems to hinder, we will experience anger. Leaders often feel tempted to justify their anger as something warranted and appropriate. Nonetheless, as James reminds us, "the anger of man does not produce the righteousness of God" (James 1:20).

We might experience a whole range of emotions associated with anger. We might feel resentment toward other people. We might struggle with feelings of frustration when people or things let us down. We might become cross with people, losing our patience with them. We might feel irritation when things do not go away. Occasionally, leaders might even feel rage as their anger becomes really intense.

We need to remember that feeling these things is neither right nor wrong. These are simply normal emotions. What matters is what we choose to do with these feelings, how we choose to respond to them. Trying to stuff our anger deep inside of us may lead to many kinds of serious problems, from physical problems to problems such as depression. Losing all self-control and expressing these emotions indiscriminately will also lead to serious problems. Either of these responses are pitfalls that will cripple or undermine our leadership.

The healthy response to the cluster of emotions we call anger involves acknowledging these emotions and choosing to express them carefully and appropriately. We must maintain self-control at all times. We must remember that it is never healthy to engage with people in our people-system when we are feeling anger or any of these other emotions strongly. Anger and similar emotions should lead us to evaluate what is happening around us carefully and to look out for unmet expectations or blocked goals.

Bitterness

The second variety of emotional pitfall is the emotions that cluster around the idea of bitterness. Bitterness arises when we fail to forgive others. Whenever we allow any degree of unforgiveness to remain in our lives, we are planting the seed for bitterness. Bitterness works like a poison that affects everything in our lives. The only antidote for this poison is biblical forgiveness.

Many people misunderstand forgiveness. Some people think that forgiveness means saying that whatever the other person has done does not really matter. Other people think that forgiveness means forgetting. Still others think that forgiveness means going to the person who has wounded you and telling them that you forgive them. A few people might even think that forgiveness means tolerating sin and wrongdoing. However, none of these ideas reflects the biblical concept of forgiveness.

Biblically, forgiveness means releasing to God what the other person has said or done that has wounded us. The core meaning of the biblical word "forgive" is to "release". Forgiveness is between us and God; it is an act of prayer. When we forgive, we are telling God that we release what has been done to us, and the pain it has caused, to him so that he might bring justice to the situation and healing to our lives.[3]

People often misunderstand forgiveness as applying only to matters of sin and wrongdoing. We then assume that in order to forgive we must judge something that someone else has said or done as sinful. Sometimes, we might even think that we cannot forgive unless the other person acknowledges that what they have said or done is wrong. This traps people in a cycle of unforgiveness, because often the other person will not admit that what they have said or done is wrong or the other person may not even know that they have done something to hurt us.

The real issue of forgiveness is not whether the other person has done something sinful but whether the other person has caused us pain. Sometimes people cause us pain because they do something wrong. Other times people cause us pain when they have not done something wrong, such as if someone accidentally steps on our toe. Occasionally, people may cause us pain by doing something right, such as when a parent might bring correction to a child. Whenever someone causes us pain, we need to forgive them. We do not need to judge whether the person is right or wrong. We only need to know that they have caused us pain.

We need to remember that God commanded us to forgive and that we can choose to forgive at any time. Forgiveness is a choice, an act of the will. God has already empowered us to forgive as his people. We forgive by choosing to release the pain we experienced to God, choosing not to seek revenge on the other person, and releasing what has been said or done to God for his justice.

Refusing or failing to forgive destroys our leadership, allowing bitterness to flood our lives. Bitter leaders cannot lead effectively. Bitterness may cause many physical problems, such as ulcers or even cancer. Bitterness also disrupts and destroys relationships. It poisons everything in our lives and our leadership, rendering us ineffective. Left unchecked, bitterness will lead to malice and hatred.

Defensiveness

Defensiveness involves emotions in which we seek to protect and justify ourselves. Defensive leaders are often oversensitive and thin-skinned. They may exhibit prickly and difficult emotions to keep people away from them. Sometimes they might seem uptight and hardened. Defensiveness is ultimately designed to keep people out of our lives.

Leaders may often feel defensive when people challenge them or seek to correct them. In these times we need to remember that if we have done something wrong then we have no defense. Our best response is to admit our mistake, repent, and seek to make things right. If we have not done something wrong then we need no defense. God will become our defender. (But we need to remember that God does not always act as quickly as we would like him to!)

Leaders may also feel defensive when they feel offended. Feeling offense leads us to erect strong defense. We may find it helpful to remember that the only way we can be offended is if we choose to *take* offense. Offense is a matter of the person *receiving* it, not the person *giving* it. Many people might try to *give* us offense but we cannot be offended unless we choose to *take* offense. As leaders, we can become unoffendable. When we become unoffendable, we will strengthen our leadership immeasurably.

Defensiveness undermines leadership because it causes us to erect emotional barriers for people. Defensiveness keeps people out, which means that we cannot lead those people. Defensiveness sends a message to people that they cannot trust us and they cannot approach us with the really difficult issues of their lives. Defensiveness also suggests to people that we are selfish and self-centered in our leadership.

AVOIDING EMOTIONAL PITFALLS

We have a number of strategies to avoid emotional pitfalls. The first two are common to all the pitfalls: lead from your *being* grounded in Christ and rest. In addition to these, we need to practice openness and emotional availability. People need to see who we really are, even our faults and failures. They need to know that we are real people with real emotions. At the same time, they need to know that we are approachable, that we will exercise self-control even in the midst of difficult situations and difficult emotions. When people approach us with difficult emotions such as anger, we need to keep our guard down and listen to what the person has to say carefully.

Next, we need to repent and forgive ruthlessly. As soon as we notice that we have done something wrong, we need to confess what we have done and renounce it. If we realize that we have hurt someone, we need to go to that person and seek reconciliation. We also need to forgive immediately whenever we feel pain, no matter how small. Sometimes we can remember to forgive the seemingly big things but forget to forgive the seemingly small things. However, when we fail to forgive even something small we open the door to the root of bitterness, along with these other emotional pitfalls. So we must forgive immediately whenever we experience pain.

Along with the above, we must evaluate our perceptions carefully. In Freedom in Christ Ministries, we often say that it is not what happens to us that matters; it is how we *perceive* what happens to us. If what we perceive is not the truth then what we feel will not reflect reality. In these situations, we cannot trust our feelings. So when we experience these emotions, before we fall into the pit of wrong responses to the emotions we must evaluate our perceptions and ensure that our perceptions accurately reflect what is really happening.

Sam had gone through a very difficult time in his workplace. One colleague in particular had chosen not to like Sam. This person would often write mean-spirited letters and put them on Sam's desk unsigned. Eventually, Sam's boss fired this person because he had failed to do his job in other areas. A few months later, Sam came into work to find another blank envelope sitting on his desk. Immediately, all the terrible feelings that Sam had experienced before flooded his mind. He wanted to run away. Nervously, he picked up the envelope and opened it. Inside he discovered a letter from a co-worker thanking Sam for helping her during a difficult project. Immediately his emotions changed from negative to positive. It was not the letter that had caused the negative emotions; it was Sam's perception of the letter before he opened it.

Finally, we need to bless others. We can speak words of blessing over their lives. The Bible suggests that our words have power and influence in the lives of others (see, for example, Proverbs 12:18). Speaking words of blessing will calm troubled emotions and change the focus from ourselves to others. Often, we are tempted to express the strong emotions of the emotional pitfalls through hurtful words, so choosing to speak blessing instead helps us guard our tongues and refrain from saying things we might later regret.

EXHAUSTION PITFALLS

We call the final variety of pitfalls "exhaustion" pitfalls. Exhaustion pitfalls occur when we fail to rest and recharge our spiritual, emotional, and rational batteries as leaders. When we fall into exhaustion pitfalls, we break down as leaders and cease to function in any fruitful capacity. In some cases, exhaustion pitfalls may either lead us to give up leadership entirely or cause us to lose our leadership completely. We have three exhaustion pitfalls to consider: burnout, blowout, and bankruptcy.

Burnout

Most leaders think of burnout as the only exhaustion pitfall. Burnout certainly seems like the exhaustion pitfall that most psychologists and leadership experts have considered most often. Burnout is a long-term physical, emotional, mental, and spiritual exhaustion causing people to feel increasingly overwhelmed, helpless, hopeless, cynical, and resentful. When people experience genuine burnout they often take a year or more to recover. Many burned-out people never fully recover and instead change their careers and their lives completely. Burnout most often happens suddenly, with little warning.

Blowout

Blowout does not mean that we go out and have a big party. A blowout refers to what happens to a car tire when it suddenly fails or falls apart because the owner has allowed the tire to wear too thinly. For a car, blowouts most frequently occur when we are driving at speed, perhaps on the highway. Blowouts indicate that the owner of the car has neglected proper maintenance. Blowouts cause many accidents, which is why in most Western nations it is illegal to drive with improperly maintained tires. When a tire blows out we have no choice but to pull to the side of the road and change the tire or wait for a tow truck.

On some occasions, blowouts occur because we run into some debris in the road. The debris might have been left intentionally or as the byproduct of another accident or problem. We often hit the debris because we are driving too fast or not paying careful attention to the road. How well our tires have been maintained often determines whether we will experience a blowout.

As an exhaustion pitfall, a blowout refers first to what happens when a leader suddenly falls into sin, particularly a sin that forces the leader to stop leading and move to the side. The leaders normally fall into sin because they have worn themselves too thinly and failed to maintain their emotional, mental, and physical health. Sometimes they fall into sin because they are not paying careful attention to their lives and their surroundings in their leadership.

Some of the sins of blowout may seem quite major, such as sexual immorality. Other sins of blowout might seem comparatively minor at the time – such as stealing a few office supplies – but they can lead to a loss of leadership. At the least, they will lead to a loss of integrity that undermines our leadership.

Sudden sickness is a second way blowout might manifest as an exhaustion pitfall. When we fail to get good rest, eat right, and get some exercise, we can suddenly become sick, especially if we are feeling under a lot of stress and pressure. These things weaken our body's immune system, making us susceptible to various illnesses. Most frequently, we have only minor illnesses, such as colds. However, we may also have very serious illnesses, such as heart attacks and strokes. How long we allow ourselves to live unhealthily often determines the severity of the blowout and its damage, much as how long we try to drive with a damaged tire might determine the damage done to the car.

Bankruptcy

When we experience actual bankruptcy, we run out of the money necessary to pay our bills and live our lives. We accumulate so much debt that we cannot repay it. As an exhaustion pitfall, bankruptcy indicates the point at which we run out of spiritual, mental, and emotional reserves and insights. Bankruptcy results from the failure to replenish these reserves regularly.

All leaders will live through seasons in their lives where they seem to draw down their personal reserves until their spiritual, emotional, and mental "bank" is overdrawn. Most of us can survive and even thrive in the midst of these seasons for a while. However, we must all come back into a time in which we actively and intentionally replenish these personal reserves. Replenishing reserves requires time and patience.

When we fail to replenish our personal reserves regularly, we will eventually come to a point when we run out of these reserves entirely. We will have nothing more to give. We will lose all sense of creativity and vitality. One of the saddest things to see, for example, are ministers who have so run out of personal reserves that their preaching simply recycles the same sermons year after year without ever providing a fresh word from God. Sometimes we never rebuild the reserves at all.

AVOIDING EXHAUSTION PITFALLS

To avoid exhaustion pitfalls we must strongly emphasize the strategy of rest. Of course, we must continue to lead from our identity grounded in Christ, but rest is absolutely essential. We need to have regular sabbath days, regular days off, and regular holidays. We also need regular retreats at which we seek God and restore our relationship with him. We cannot emphasize rest enough.

Second, we need to practice lifelong learning. We need to read books, listen to lectures, attend conferences, and do any other thing that will help us continue learning throughout our lives. Learning is not just for the young, but leaders of all ages must actively practice learning. We need to seek out learning opportunities on a regular basis. As we learn, we need to look for learning in disciplines other than just our primary occupation. Learning in this context might include developing new skills and picking up new hobbies.

Third, we need to prioritize prayer and Bible reading. In prayer, we would include activities such as worship. Prayer engages us with God and leads to daily refreshing and renewal in the presence of God's Spirit. Bible reading renews our spirits with God's holy Word, challenging us to grow and improve and enabling us to think more deeply about how God sees the world around us. We would urge leaders to make prayer a significant priority every day, thinking in terms of hours rather than minutes.

Finally, seeking to live a well-balanced life of moderation will help us avoid exhaustion pitfalls. We need to ensure that we have a healthy balance of work and play in our lives. Cherishing relationships and investing time in them will help bring balance to our lives. Instead of living in the extremes, we can seek moderation in all things. Everything God has created is good (see 1 Timothy 4:4) and God has given us all things to enjoy (1 Timothy 6:17). We have many good things in our lives that we might celebrate with moderation.

THE LEADERSHIP DILEMMA

We have personal leadership pitfalls all around us just waiting to trap our leadership. These pitfalls will hinder or even destroy our leadership if we allow ourselves to fall into them. Simply being alert to the presence of these pitfalls will help us avoid them. After all, people who see a pit seldom fall into the pit. Being alert to the presence of these pitfalls requires that we pay attention to ourselves and maintain a healthy *being* grounded in Christ. We have everything we need to avoid these pitfalls, but even so we often fall into them. This is our leadership dilemma.

15

OVERCOMING SYSTEMIC PITFALLS

*I've always found that anything worth achieving will always
have obstacles in the way and you've got to have that drive
and determination to overcome those obstacles en route to
whatever it is that you want to accomplish.*

Chuck Norris

*Kindness and intelligence don't always deliver us from the
pitfalls and traps: there are always failures of love, of will,
of imagination. There is no way to take the danger out of
human relationships.*

Barbara Grizzuti Harrison

*Avoiding occasions of expense by cultivating peace, we
should remember also that timely disbursements to
prepare for danger frequently prevent much greater
disbursements to repel it.*

George Washington

Difficulties are just things to overcome, after all.

Ernest Shackleton

 enrietta's New York consultancy had almost collapsed. She had built a strong business by bringing together five top-quality consultants and an excellent support staff. They had won several contracts with key government

agencies and private-sector companies which had provided significant capital for the business. They developed such a good reputation that others wanted to learn from them, so they set up several training courses to pass on their skills. They had a very generous stance when it came to helping others.

The combination of global financial problems and intense competition for contracts suddenly shifted the fortunes of the business. A poor support team hire and the resulting internal conflicts weakened the business further. However, Henrietta was not a quitter. She made several staff changes. She convinced her partners to double their efforts and sacrifice some of their salaries to rebuild the business. The strategy worked. Although it took three years, they rose from staff dysfunction and financial difficulty to become stable again, even beginning to grow a little.

What happened next caught Henrietta completely off guard. One of her key consultants told Henrietta that she would now work from home and demanded a 30 percent increase in her consultancy fees. Another consultant asked to reduce his days to three days a week, but wanted the same salary. A third consultant, Sam, had talked with the office manager behind Henrietta's back and they decided together that they could lead the practical side of the business better than Henrietta. They asked her to surrender the day-to-day leadership of the business to them. They suggested that Henrietta could stay on as the "face" of the business.

These things completely confused Henrietta. They had just come through such a difficult three years, bringing the business back from the brink of closing entirely, only to have all these things happen. She even began to doubt her own leadership competence. The behaviors of her colleagues confused and frustrated her.

Henrietta had encountered a number of normal, and highly predictable, people-system pitfalls.

SYSTEMIC PITFALLS

Leaders not only face many personal pitfalls but we face other pitfalls as well. Our effective leadership will *always* trigger a number of predictable reactions among the people we lead in our people-system. We call these "systemic pitfalls" or "group pitfalls".

Systemic pitfalls indicate that our leadership is being effective, not that we are poor leaders. Most leaders become discouraged when they encounter systemic pitfalls because they assume these pitfalls signify that they have either failed in their leadership or that they have weak leadership skills. Sometimes leaders who face these pitfalls even quit because of them. Realizing that these pitfalls suggest our leadership is actually succeeding rather than failing might encourage us to continue leading.

Systemic pitfalls occur when people seek to neutralize our leadership and return our people-system to its previous condition, even if that condition was unhealthy or dysfunctional. Occasionally systemic pitfalls occur because our leadership is succeeding but some person has a different opinion on what our people-system should look like. People simply do not like change and they are instinctively afraid of what they might lose. This means they naturally resist good leadership – even when they suspect the leadership may lead to good outcomes – because good leadership always brings about change.

The key thing to remember is this: it is not these situations by themselves that are the pitfalls, but our *wrong reactions or responses to these situations as leaders.* We need to remember that a certain degree of conflict and uncertainty will always occur in any people-system. The point is that we do not have to allow conflict and uncertainty to lead us into wrong or inappropriate behavior as leaders – the pitfalls. So when we talk about "pitfalls" here we are not only talking about the things themselves but how we react or respond to these things as leaders.

If we react or respond to these pitfalls inappropriately, we will create anxiety and instability in our people-system, undermining our leadership. Our unsuitable reactions to these pitfalls will actually make them worse. So we need to learn to avoid or deal with these pitfalls effectively.

DILEMMAS AND PROBLEMS

Leaders should understand systemic pitfalls as dilemmas instead of as problems. We have to understand the difference between the two. Neglecting to recognize the difference creates more problems than most leaders realize.

Problems are issues that can be solved and resolved. Problems have solutions. Normally, we can think through problems in order to achieve a satisfactory resolution. Problems may often respond to the application of technology, such as various computer programs.

For example, "2+2 = 4" is a common mathematical problem. It has a solution. If someone gets into debt, then there are numerous solutions to get them out of debt. They can change their spending habits. They can live within their means according to a budget. If someone drives into our car and dents the fender, we can take the car to the body shop and have it repaired. If we want to drive from London to New York City, we can look on a map and discover that we will have a problem with the Atlantic Ocean. Although the solution might be challenging, we can find a solution to this problem. That is the nature of problems – they have solutions.

Dilemmas are issues that by their nature resist solutions. We have no easy way to resolve them. Normally, we can only manage them while we work our way through them. Dilemmas often require a lot of time as well as a thoughtful response from leaders to work themselves out. Occasionally, the best we can do is learn to live with the dilemma and not allow it to undermine our people-system or our leadership.

For example, climate change is a dilemma. It has no quick fixes. It will require the cooperation of many people and nations who normally would not cooperate with one another to begin to resolve climate change. Even scientists themselves debate how to resolve this complex issue, with some scientists questioning whether there is an issue called "climate change".

A husband and wife who are having struggles relating to one another well are facing a dilemma. We might try to identify certain behaviors of the husband or the wife as problems, but when we understand the complex nature of human relationships we quickly realize that these so-called "problems" have no easy solutions. As soon as the husband changes his behavior in one area the wife will often change her behavior in another area, thereby continuing the relational struggles. Bringing health to this relationship does not have straightforward answers.

A church struggling with changing demographics has a dilemma. The church cannot simply decide to adopt a new style of worship or some new technology in order to reach the newcomers in the community. Churches in these situations face a number of complex issues, including how the church is organized, the kinds of ministries the church offers, the interrelationships of the people within the church, the average tenure of people within the church, and the socioeconomic backgrounds of people in the church. We simply cannot tell these churches to do one or two things that will lead to a clear resolution of these issues.

The key is this: when we have a dilemma, by definition there are no easy answers. If we try to find a quick fix for a dilemma, it will cause problems. If we mistake a dilemma for a problem as a leader, then we will create crises and conflicts of will in our people-system.

The challenge is that dilemmas and problems look very similar to one another, but they are radically different.

Annie enjoyed challenging things and pushing boundaries. Because of this, she had attended many different churches in the last ten years. In each church she had experienced the same cycle.

The churches warmly welcomed her at first. Then they became annoyed at her behavior. They tried to "solve" her behavior with various techniques and tools. Finally, they would ask her to leave the church. Annie began to expect these cycles, which encouraged her to behave in ever more challenging ways.

Few people understood Annie's background. When she was a young girl, her father had rejected her and her mother had neglected her. She learned that the only way she could get her mother's attention was to act out and misbehave. She also learned that poor behavior would get her more attention at school. Although she knew that such behavior damaged her relationships, she continued to behave in these ways because they saved her from the pain of rejection that she had come to expect from all her relationships.

Annie finally came to Frank's church. Frank's church embraced the principles of Freedom in Christ Ministries, seeking to create a relational culture based on our identity in Christ, forgiveness, repentance, and grace. Annie joined a course during the weekly fellowship night. From the very first evening, she challenged the course leader. The course leader remained calm, addressed some of the issues Annie raised, and then calmly continued with the course. When Annie challenged her a second time, the course leader simply asked her to hold her comments until the end so that others could have an opportunity to participate.

When Annie later complained to Frank about the course leader, Frank listened to Annie's concerns but calmly supported the course leader. Although Annie raised one or two legitimate points, Frank still supported the course leader as he spoke with Annie. He did raise the issues later in private with the course leader, who received Frank's encouragement and made the necessary corrections.

Although she tried her best to force Frank's church to reject her, they continued to show Annie grace and forgiveness. They did not try to "fix" or "solve" Annie, but neither would they allow Annie to distract them from their healthy functioning. Annie felt attracted to the health she encountered in the church. She also began to change her behavior so that it became healthier as well. Annie remained involved in Frank's church for almost two years.

Annie's behavior created a dilemma. Her behavior had no easy solutions. Annie was not a problem that needed to be fixed, but a person who needed to experience love and grace. Churches who had tried to "fix" Annie and force her to conform had only driven Annie away. They had also created more turmoil and strife within the church as they sought to "fix" Annie.

Most of the situations leaders face are dilemmas, not problems. We cannot solve them; we can only look after them as they work themselves out. The challenge is that most leaders feel more confident solving problems than resolving dilemmas. We like to develop clear-cut solutions to the issues we face. We do not like the messiness of dilemmas with no clear or easy resolution. Generally, problems are easier than dilemmas, requiring less time and energy to deal with.

Leaders must remember that people are not problems to be solved. Even their so-called "problem" behaviors often have no easy solutions. Of course, in one sense, "problem" behaviors do have an easy solution – repent and stop doing them! – but the complex personalities that give rise to these behaviors cannot be "solved" in the same way. People normally create dilemmas. Systemic pitfalls are also dilemmas.

VARIETIES OF SYSTEMIC PITFALLS

We have identified at least four common pitfalls when it comes to people-systems: selfishness, sabotage, strife, and suffering. These systemic pitfalls may emerge at any time within a people-system. We cannot predict exactly when they will occur, although we have noticed some discernible patterns. Systemic pitfalls most often occur in the presence of healthy, effective leadership. Systemic pitfalls will also frequently occur when our people-system is becoming healthier.

SELFISHNESS

Ironically, selfishness most often appears when a people-system has begun to change for the better. When a people-system becomes stronger or healthier the people who have sacrificed or suffered for the sake of the system often want to get the benefits they feel they deserve. The feeling is similar to the desire to take dividends from a company in which we have held stock during difficult periods in the company's history. Investors want to get something in return for their efforts. This may lead them to become selfish.

Selfishness is an inappropriate focus on oneself – being self-centered, self-seeking, or self-referential. At its heart, it is the refusal to take appropriate personal responsibility for our character or our perceived needs. When we are feeling selfish, we want other people to meet our needs. We want other people to make the effort to care for us. We want to get what we feel we have earned or deserved. Selfishness does not depend on a truth-filled assessment of a situation, but on our self-centered feelings.

Selfishness is a form of immaturity. Immaturity is the unwillingness or inability to take responsibility for our own mind, will, and emotions. Immature people will always demand that other people adjust toward their immaturity, problem or difficulty. Immature people expect others to cater for their perceived needs and to make adjustments for their demands and requirements.

Immaturity and rebellion

One dilemma for leaders is the tendency to mistake immaturity for rebellion. Initially, immaturity and rebellion may look very similar. Both involve selfishness. Immaturity often reacts to leadership out of emotionality and willfulness, but generally not with much intention and deliberation. This is similar to how small children might react reflexively to a parent when told to put away their toys. Or, immaturity might react to leadership with overly compliant and acquiescent behavior.

Rebellion, on the other hand, actively resists and repels leadership. A rebellious person might also react to leadership out of emotionality and willfulness, but this will lead to intentional choices not to cooperate with leadership. Rebellion always involves defiance, disobedience, and insubordination. People choose to rebel, either in an instinctive way or in a deliberate way.

Leaders often treat immaturity as they treat rebellion. This always creates problems. People are generally unaware of their level of immaturity. Because of this, when we deal with immature people as if they are rebellious, they will perceive our treatment of them as harsh and hurtful. The resulting confusion will ironically often push people into a rebellious stance toward leadership. However, when we deal with immature people with patience, exposing them to healthy maturity along the way, they will grow and develop as any healthy person will.

John was always questioning leadership. When asked to do something by his boss, he was continually asking why and trying to suggest a better way. He often had an edge to the way he asked things, possibly giving the appearance that he thought he knew more than his boss. At first, John greatly frustrated his boss. Several times he felt tempted to yell at John and say, "Just do it because I said so!" However, John's boss recognized that this was just John's youthful enthusiasm. John genuinely cared about his job and really liked his boss. So John's boss patiently worked with him to help him "mature" in the job. John became one of the company's best assets.

Leaders occasionally treat rebellion as if it is immaturity. When we treat rebellious people as if they are simply immature, we will actually reinforce their rebellion. They will continue their dysfunctional behavior.

John's co-worker, Lou, was very different from John. He was genuinely rebellious. Lou also questioned everything. Lou also had an edge to how he said things. But Lou did not respond to his boss's patient leadership. He would listen to what his boss had to say, but then he would go ahead and do things his own way. Sometimes the way Lou did things was actually better, which always worsened his behavior. Eventually, his boss recognized his behavior as rebellion, so he did the only thing he could do – fire Lou.

Immaturity is a dilemma that people must work through in order to become mature. Rebellion is a sin problem that requires repentance. Both require some degree of discipline. The discipline for rebellion involves setting clear boundaries and providing explicit expectations. The discipline for immaturity involves setting clear boundaries and providing patient coaching and encouragement.

Discerning the difference between immaturity and rebellion takes time and patience. Initially, they look almost exactly the same. However, time will always expose the difference. Rebellious people will persist in their rebellion, even when given good training and coaching. They will also become more demanding and selfish as time goes on. They may become subtly manipulative and controlling. Immaturity will usually respond to good coaching and encouragement. Immature people want to become mature, and will usually respond well to health and grace.

Overcoming the pitfall of selfishness

To help our people overcome the pitfall of selfishness, we must model healthy self-giving as leaders. Healthy self-giving means that we love our people and our people-system, giving out of our strengths and skills to help them become strong and healthy themselves. One of the greatest dangers we face as leaders is becoming selfish ourselves. So we must watch out for the personal pitfalls that often indicate our own selfishness.

We can also help our people avoid the pitfall of selfishness by promoting maturity throughout our people-system. We first promote maturity by becoming mature ourselves, taking responsibility for our mind, our will, and our emotions. We then must insist that people in our people-system take and fulfill their own responsibilities. We must resist the temptation to rescue or save people by taking over their responsibilities.

As difficult as it might be, we need to focus on healthy and mature people in our people-system, without capitulating to the demands of selfishness. This final tactic means that we cannot allow selfish people to draw away our focus from our essential mission and vision. We cannot capitulate to selfishness, even when people threaten to storm off or throw their "toys out of the pram" and stop serving. The focus on health will draw mature people, as well as immature people who want to become mature, to the healthy core of the people-system. The focus on health will lead others to decide to become healthier or decide to leave the people-system. Accept either response.

SABOTAGE[1]

David and his board had worked together for three months to redevelop the church's prayer ministry team. That it had taken so long had surprised David, but now that they were ready to adopt the new ministry he grew more and more excited. David started to ask for the vote when one of the board members suddenly asked, "How are we going to screen the people who do prayer ministry?" David felt confused, since the board had discussed how potential ministry team members would have to go through the new training process as the way to be admitted to the ministry team. He expressed this. The board member replied, "Oh no, that wouldn't be sufficient. We need to have a proper process for screening ministry team members." The board member had just sabotaged the whole process, requiring another two months of deliberations.

The second common pitfall for people-systems is sabotage. Sabotage includes seeking to destroy, damage, obstruct or hinder leaders or change, sometimes for personal or political advantage. Sometimes people will sabotage the leader because secretly (or not so secretly) they want to be in charge of the people-system. People often engage in sabotage when they want to have their own way or seek their own ends.

Sometimes people will sabotage leaders because there are shifting relationships in the people-system. For example, the best friend of the former pastor is often the person who will sabotage the relationships of the new pastor. In these situations, people are expressing a longing for relationship, even though their sabotage will often damage relationships.

People may also sabotage leaders because of their own flesh, that sinful aspect of our humanity. We all have certain sin issues in our lives that influence our behavior. One person might feel insecure and so engage in sabotage in order to make themselves feel important. Our pride might make us think we are right and others are wrong, so we sabotage their efforts in order to prove ourselves right. Our anxiety about possibly losing some perceived personal benefit in our people-system might lead us to sabotage change in our system.

Occasionally, demons may inspire sabotage. An employee may have thoughts that her supervisor is going to destroy the company so she needs to take action in order to expose her supervisor as a fraud. Church members may hear a voice tell them that it is their pastor's responsibility to grow the church (when, in fact, it is God's responsibility – see 1 Corinthians 3:7). When the pastor does not produce growth quickly they then look to get rid of the pastor and find one who can grow the church. Satan can whisper thoughts into people's minds that, left unchecked, may lead them to sabotage something. As Paul says in 2 Corinthians 2:11, we do not want to be ignorant of Satan's schemes.

Sabotage involves complex issues, not easily discerned and understood. The nature and extent of sabotage is not linked to specific issues, structures, and goals. A person might sabotage a new program at work because she harbors a secret desire to be promoted. Another person might not like a new co-worker, so he undermines a person on the new co-worker's team to make the co-worker look bad. Because of sabotage's complexity, we may struggle to resolve it sometimes.

There are a number of common ways that sabotage manifests itself. First, people might spread discontent about other people or about the people-system. Next, people might magnify the potential loss from some course of action. A church member might suggest that people would get mugged all the time if the church started the new outreach to homeless persons.

Third, people might misrepresent a leader or a decision that has been made. When a manager institutes a new procedure for purchasing supplies, an employee might assert that this means the manager is a control freak who does not trust people any longer when it is simply the manager trying to cut costs.

Fourth, passive aggressive behavior is a form of sabotage. When someone seems to acquiesce about a decision when they are in fact actively undermining the decision, they have engaged in passive aggressive behavior. Passive aggressive behavior allows the person to seem innocent and supportive even while they engage in sabotage.

People changing their minds after the group has made a decision indicates a fifth way that people practice sabotage. Alongside this is the practice of putting in extra conditions on an agreement late in negotiations or even after negotiations have been completed.

Next, people might agree on something publicly while undermining it privately. They save their best arguments regarding a decision or a situation to express privately in order to erode support. Along with this comes spreading gossip and rumors. Gossip and rumors sabotage a people-system by undermining confidence in both the people and the leader of the system.

Finally, people might sabotage things by using bullying and intimidation, especially with those people whom they perceive to be weak. Another way of practicing intimidation involves using charm and flattery. Some people seek to control others by charming them and flattering them. The flattery persuades people that the flatterer really must know what they are doing because they are so charming or so intuitive about the person receiving the flattery.

Overcoming the pitfall of sabotage

Perhaps the best way to overcome the pitfall of sabotage is to expect sabotage in the first place. Most leaders feel very surprised when they are sabotaged, as if it is something unusual and strange. However, when we realize that sabotage is normal and to be expected, we will respond differently to it. When we expect sabotage we are less likely to feel angry and frustrated. We will thus avoid falling into one of the personal pitfalls. In addition, when we realize that sabotage is a normal reaction to healthy leadership and healthy change, we will take sabotage as an indicator that we are doing something right rather than as a suggestion that we are failing in our leadership.

We must also ensure that our *being* is healthy and fully grounded in Jesus Christ so that we can respond calmly and intentionally to sabotage. Most of the time sabotage succeeds when we allow it to create anxiety in us and in our people-system. When we respond calmly and purposefully to sabotage, choosing a course of action that reflects truth and embodies healthy values, we can often overcome sabotage rather quickly.

As with selfishness, to work through the dilemma of sabotage we must focus on building healthy people and healthy processes in our people-system. Healthy people persevere in spite of sabotage. Healthy processes help to protect our people-system from sabotage. For example, if we have healthy decision-making processes in our people-system, then we can expose the sabotage of gossip and rumors as the unhealthy and inappropriate behaviors they are, suggesting that *healthy* people would only use the healthy processes in our system. When someone tries to change their mind after a decision has been made, we can point them to how we have followed the agreed process and resist their attempt to sabotage us.

STRIFE

The third common systemic pitfall is strife. Strife is just another word for friction and conflict. It can include reactivity, arguments, conflicts of will, criticism, and even personal attacks. Basically, strife describes problems within interpersonal relationships. When people seek to work through differences and differences of opinion, they will experience some degree of strife as a natural byproduct.

We need to remember that strife will often increase as people are learning to become mature. When children become teenagers, becoming disagreeable and argumentative to some extent is a normal process for the self-differentiation necessary for maturity. When people are becoming mature, they are learning to take responsibility for their own mind, will, and emotions in a way that naturally leads them into conflict with the mind, will, and emotions of other people who are also learning to become mature.

We cannot avoid strife. Conflict might actually indicate health and vitality in a people-system. Disagreement suggests that people have a sense of individuality along with a desire to work together. Thus, disagreement becomes an essential part of any healthy people-system. Paul even suggests that we need disagreement in order to discern what is true (see 1 Corinthians 11:19). The key is learning how to work through strife and conflict in a healthy manner.

As leaders, we tend to do a number of things instinctively that are completely ineffective when it comes to strife. Sometimes we might respond to strife by trying to explain or justify our position. We mistakenly believe that if only people understood why we do what we do then they would naturally agree with us. Explaining and justifying ourselves only intensifies strife; it seldom diminishes it. People often want us to understand *them* rather than wanting to understand us.

Trying to defend ourselves also intensifies strife. Defending our position only makes people want to attack it that much harder. Defensiveness may even make us look weak as leaders. People will often perceive our defensiveness as an unwillingness to have an open relationship with them.

Many times we assume that the best thing to do is simply withdraw from the conflict and refuse to engage in it. We can pretend that we are above the conflict. We can ignore that the strife is occurring at all. This response to strife only redirects strife to other parts of our people-system, as those who have issues will take those issues to anyone who will listen to them.

We might try to blame someone else or something else for the issues causing strife. We act like it is not our problem as leaders. Blame shifting only intensifies strife and anxiety within any people-system. It never works to resolve the strife.

Finally, we can make one of several person-centered attempts to resolve strife. We might try to placate the other person by making promises or agreements, some of which we will not be able to keep. We can try to appease the other person by giving in to some of their demands. Or we might try bargaining with the person, appealing to a sense of fairness or fair play, seeking a compromise.

These person-centered responses to strife may lead the other person to believe that we agree with them when we do not. They also may encourage the other person to continue in the conflict, seeking ever more concessions and capitulations. If the person is rebellious, these responses to strife will intensify their rebellion. They will never disarm rebellion. In strife, we are not seeking compromise; we are seeking resolution through agreement and cooperation.

All these common responses generally increase strife. They seldom reduce or resolve strife. These responses may also represent an attempt to avoid strife. Trying to avoid strife always empowers it and encourages it to become stronger.

Overcoming strife

In order to overcome strife, we need to ensure that our *being* is grounded in Christ and that we are resolving our personal anxiety well so that we do not try to avoid strife. One of the best ways to overcome strife is to face it head on as something natural and even beneficial for our people-systems. If we allow strife to create anxiety in us as leaders, then strife will create anxiety in our people-systems.

Second, we need to shift people's understanding of strife. People need to know that strife can be healthy and beneficial for everyone, allowing us to learn and grow stronger while becoming more mature as people and as Christians. We need to help people gain new, healthier perspectives on strife. For example, we might help people understand that strife is one way that God forms our character.

Third, we need to lead by example as we encourage people to work through strife with love, mercy, and grace. People need us to model appropriate responses to strife. They need to see how we work through strife ourselves. They especially need to experience our sense of peace and patience in the midst of strife.

SUFFERING

The final people-system pitfall, suffering, is essentially the collective effect of all the other pitfalls. Suffering is experiencing something that we perceive to be negative or unpleasant. We will generally experience strife, sabotage, and selfishness as unpleasant. We might experience what we have to go through in order to resolve strife, sabotage, and selfishness as something unpleasant as well. Few genuinely healthy people enjoy these things.

Both leadership and life itself involve many forms of suffering. However, all suffering is not inherently bad. Some suffering promotes many good outcomes. For example, students learn because they have to endure the suffering of exams. We can grow in our discipleship through suffering, which Jesus' command to take up our cross and follow him suggests.

Pain itself is a natural part of our growth and development. If we could not feel pain, then we would not be healthy. Pain alerts us that something might be wrong, just as pleasure alerts us that something might be good. Sometimes good leaders even need to cause a certain amount of pain in order to be effective. For instance, a surgeon will cause us pain in order to cut cancer out of our system, but in causing us this pain he might also save our lives. A leader might challenge someone to do something that stretches them, such as teaching a course or serving the homeless. The discomfort we might experience will help us grow in our discipleship.

Good leaders might often lead their people into a time of suffering in order to achieve beneficial outcomes. A business leader might require her employees to adopt a new computer system, causing a lot of grief and consternation in the process, but helping the business to become stronger. A church leader might lead his people into a season of fasting and prayer, using the discomfort of fasting to encourage people to draw closer to God. Suffering can promote good results and healthier people-systems.

Overcoming suffering

In order to endure and overcome suffering we need first to understand that various difficulties will always accompany a people-system that has effective leadership. In other words, suffering is normal and to be expected. The Bible tells us not to be surprised when we experience suffering, as if something strange were happening to us (see 1 Peter 4:12).

Second, we need to model how to deal with suffering as leaders. Our willingness and ability as a leader to embrace suffering will determine the willingness and ability of our people and our people-system to embrace suffering. Our example will help people endure suffering well.

Third, we must refuse to "medicate" people or try to relieve suffering too quickly. We need to help discern the possible good outcomes for suffering. When we love people we do not want to see them suffer. At the same time, we know that some degree of struggle and suffering promotes health and growth in other people.

This means that if we try to take someone out of suffering too quickly we might short-circuit the good that suffering might bring in their lives.

Fourth, in order for people to experience the benefit of suffering they need to distinguish suffering that is caused by sin and other unrighteousness from suffering that is a natural part of our lives. People can avoid the suffering caused by sin, most often through repentance and forgiveness. Akin to the suffering caused by sin is suffering caused by our failure to take responsibility for ourselves and become mature. People might avoid much of the suffering they experience if they obey God and live by the Holy Spirit.

AVOIDING THE SYSTEMIC PITFALLS

As leaders, we can help our people-systems avoid these systemic pitfalls. To do so, we must lead from our identity fully grounded in Christ while maintaining a peaceful and strong leadership presence in our people-system. Having our *being* healthy and grounded in Jesus Christ and keeping well connected to our people-system provides the best way for our people-system to avoid or resolve systemic pitfalls.

Second, we can seek fresh and different perspectives on what is happening in our people-system. One of the things that enabled me to endure the difficulties we experienced at my third church was having many friends with whom I could share in order to gain their perspective. When we are in the midst of challenges in our people-system, or perhaps when we have even fallen into a systemic pitfall, we might struggle to see our way out or to see how we might resolve our situation. We often have blind spots and weaknesses that prevent us from seeing things the way they truly are. We need other perspectives to help us discern the truth.

As leaders we can, thirdly, welcome conflict as normal and even as an opportunity for growth. Just as the human immune system becomes healthier as it fights off various diseases, so a people-system will become healthier as it goes through various conflicts. This means that we need to embrace conflict as part of our calling in leadership. We simply need to ensure that we engage in conflict in healthy ways with a healthy attitude, always maintaining a sense of love and grace for other people.

Fourth, in order to avoid falling into these pits, we must identify and resist idealistic distortions and expectations. To think that churches should not have conflict is an idealistic distortion that has no biblical foundation. To assume that sabotage is not a normal part of leadership is an idealistic expectation that has no foundation in the real world. To wonder how we might resolve these systemic pitfall issues quickly and easily shows an idealistic distortion, denying the biblical call for faithfulness and steadfastness in our leadership. In order to identify an idealistic distortion or expectation we must compare it with the Bible as God's Word, seeking a truth-filled view of the world in which we live.

There is an ancient story about a philosopher who was walking together with an elderly woman. They were walking along on a beautiful clear night. The philosopher could not help but gaze at the stars and dream about the future. Suddenly, the philosopher fell into a deep pit. Laughing as she looked down at him in the pit, the elderly woman said: "Perhaps you should spend less time gazing at the stars and more time with your feet planted firmly on the ground." Sometimes we set such lofty, idealistic expectations for what life in the church or the workplace should be like that we miss the importance of what is happening around us.

THE LEADERSHIP DILEMMA

Overcoming systemic pitfalls requires a lot of courage and endurance. It requires that we exercise self-control, ensuring that we maintain a healthy connection with the people we are leading. It requires that the love of God for people and our people-system consumes us, so that our self-giving reflects the self-giving of God in his Son Jesus Christ. It requires that the Spirit of God fills us with his power, so that we can serve as Jesus served.

When we are most successful in our leadership is when we often face the most difficult challenges and pitfalls. This is our leadership dilemma, and it is unavoidable. So as leaders, we must remember the words of Paul to his spiritual son, Timothy: "For this reason I remind you to fan into flame the gift of God, which is in you through the laying on of my hands, for God gave us a spirit not of cowardice but of power and love and self-control" (2 Timothy 1:6–7).

16

OVERCOMING LEADERSHIP DELUSIONS

The human brain is a complex organ with the wonderful power of enabling man to find reasons for continuing to believe whatever it is that he wants to believe.

Voltaire

You can avoid reality, but you cannot avoid the consequences of avoiding reality.

Ayn Rand

Nothing is so difficult as not deceiving oneself.

Ludwig Wittgenstein

Every society produces its own cultural conceits, a set of lies and delusions about itself that thrive in the face of all contrary evidence.

Jack Weatherford

C harlie was a self-professed Christian conference junkie. As a pastor, he loved to go to as many conferences as possible so that he could learn new things and discover new programs and techniques to bring back to his church. Excitedly he would seek to implement his new learning in the life of the church, believing that each new idea might bring growth, health, and even revival to his church. Although his church stayed reasonably healthy, it never experienced the growth that he desired. Charlie never really allowed any new program to take hold before he was seeking the next new thing to bring to his church.

Christine had some major struggles with one of her employees, Hank. Hank behaved in some very aggressive and obnoxious ways, intruding into conversations and wasting people's time with various concerns and complaints, none of which had any real substance. Christine had a deep concern for all her employees. She was very compassionate and grace-filled, willing to listen to any concerns brought by her employees. So Christine followed her natural inclination and assumed that if she only would spend time with Hank, listening to Hank's concerns and agreeing appropriate boundaries and expectations for Hank, then Hank would finally come round and behave responsibly. Every meeting she had with Hank seemed to go very well, and she left the meeting with the sense both that finally Hank felt that he had been heard and that Hank would now follow the agreed boundaries and expectations. However, Hank's behavior only became worse and worse.

Both Charlie and Christine had fallen victim to very common patterns of behavior in leaders that we call "leadership delusions".

LEADERSHIP DELUSIONS

Any leader might experience some common leadership delusions. Even people in our people-systems might experience these delusions as well. A delusion is a false belief or impression we maintain even when it is contradicted by reality. When we do the same thing over and over and expect different results we have fallen prey to a delusion. When we think that our activities might achieve substantially different outcomes than other people doing the exact same activities then we have become subject to a delusion. Conversely, when we assume that we can achieve the same results as another leader by doing the same thing in a completely different environment or context, we have fallen into a delusion.

427

The four leadership delusions are: the delusion of expertise, the delusion of empathy, the delusion of togetherness, and the delusion of position.[1]

None of these four things is bad or wrong. All leaders want expertise in their field. We all believe that empathy is a good quality for leaders to have. We know instinctively that we may often achieve things with a sense of togetherness that we might otherwise not achieve. We recognize that sometimes having the right position in an organization helps us to lead more effectively.

The delusion of these things is that they necessarily make us *better leaders*. As we have seen, great leadership flows from our *being*, not our *doing*. Many people mistake these good things as the heart of leadership, what makes leadership effective. Some of these things may help us improve as people, but they may not help us improve as leaders. In fact, if we actually pursue these things as a primary activity of our leadership, then these things will undermine our leadership effectiveness.

Leadership delusions trap us in an endless cycle of activity that fails to lead other people well. Not every great leader was an expert; take the apostle Peter, for example. Not every great leader has a lot of empathy; take the apostle Paul, for example. Not every great leader always sought to promote togetherness; take David, for example. Not every great leader had a recognized position; take Gideon, for example.

We do not need expertise, empathy, togetherness or a position in order to lead people well. We only need a healthy *being* grounded in Christ and the willingness to do what is necessary in our leadership role. We need the willingness to persevere faithfully until we achieve the beneficial outcomes for our people-system.

So let us examine each delusion in turn.

THE DELUSION OF EXPERTISE

The delusion of expertise is the misapprehension that if we only have the right knowledge or use the right techniques then we will be effective leaders. In this delusion, we believe that success involves overcoming a series of problems for which there are clear-cut solutions provided by the right knowledge or the right technique. We lose the distinction between dilemmas and problems, seeking problem-oriented solutions rather than health-fully processing dilemmas.

Often, the solutions we seek are perceived to be technological solutions, such as having the right computer brand! We can assume that having the right program or the right product will enable us to lead more effectively. But as my wife reminded me years ago, if I cannot hit the ball with my current golf club then buying a new club is not likely to help me very much!

The delusion of expertise also includes the misconception that if something succeeds in one people-system then it will succeed in another similar people-system. People all over the world try to import the successes of other leaders into their present people-system, failing to recognize that every leadership success has a unique context and environment which contributes to the success as much or more than the activities of the leaders themselves. We cannot assume that what works in London will also work in Shanghai.

There are many examples of this delusion in operation. We might assume that starting a popular evangelism course will make our church effective at outreach. Or we might assume that if we have a great website then people will flock to our church and become members. Yet there are many great churches with terrible websites and there are many great websites with terrible churches. As a business leader we might think that a new computer software system would help us serve our customers better even when we have failed to train our employees in customer service.

When we fall into the delusion of expertise, we become overwhelmed or seduced by knowledge, techniques or technology. We can spend days and days looking at the web, searching for a great book, or trying to connect with some great leader doing the stuff, only to discover at the end of it all that we have failed to lead. We can wrongly assume that if we only have the latest gadget then we could lead more effectively. Having good information or technology is not necessarily wrong, but these things alone will not make us effective leaders.

THE DELUSION OF EMPATHY

The second delusion that we can fall prey to is the delusion of empathy. This is the deception that if we only let people know that we understand them and are sensitive to how they feel then we will lead them. Of course, empathy itself is a good thing. People like leaders who can show that they empathize with their situations and feelings. But having and showing empathy does not mean that people will follow us. Often, people may even take advantage of our sensitivity.

The delusion of empathy also includes the error that we can overcome inappropriate, unhealthy or destructive behavior in others by appealing to reason, fairness, and sensitivity. As Friedman observed, "There are forces on this planet that, because of their inability or unwillingness to self-regulate, are by nature all take and no give."[2] Appealing to reason, fairness or sensitivity will have no effect on these forces. In fact, it may give these forces more strength and energy with which to undermine our leadership.

Leaders do not need a lot of empathy in order to lead effectively. Leaders do not need to "feel" or even understand another person's pain in order to lead that person. Some people do not even want or expect their leaders to have a lot of empathy. If I need a heart surgeon, then it does not matter to me whether or not the heart surgeon has experienced heart problems. It does not matter to me whether she can stand next to my bed and tell me, "I know exactly how you feel." If I need a heart surgeon, then I want the best surgeon possible, the person who has the most success in conducting heart surgery.

As suggested above, not only is empathy ineffective as a leadership strategy, it may also be detrimental. Leaders who use empathy as a leadership method often reinforce people in their unhealthy state. Empathy may not encourage them to become responsible, mature, and healthy. When people who are immature and unhealthy get our attention (our empathy), they often lose their drive to become healthy and mature. They will often take our empathy as affirmation of their present situation. They might even use their "pain" or their immaturity to control us or our people-system.

Sometimes as leaders we will have to do things that cause some pain and make people feel uncomfortable. The delusion of empathy may deceive us into thinking that we must avoid causing pain or discomfort at all costs. When we face these situations, although it may be good to be able to say "this will be unpleasant for you", we still will need to lead the people through the painful situation.

THE DELUSION OF TOGETHERNESS

The next delusion is the delusion of togetherness. We might also call this the delusion of "consensus". This is the deception that we can lead people more effectively by promoting strong "togetherness" (that is, consensus) in our people-system. Togetherness in this sense discourages individuality and self-expression for a sense of consensus or general agreement.

In the delusion of togetherness, we simply want people to agree harmoniously and sacrifice their principles or perspectives for the greater good so that we might achieve some fuzzy consensus about what we should do. Once this is achieved we assume that people will play well together and follow our leadership. But it does not happen this way.

Leaders may easily mistake togetherness for unity. Obviously, unity is one of the signs of a healthy people-system. However, unity and togetherness are not the same thing. Unity is a Spirit-filled force that promotes diversity, maturity, and community among people. Within unity, people can disagree with one another even as they submit to one another out of reverence for Christ, cooperating with one another so that together they achieve good outcomes.

Having togetherness or consensus does not mean that a people-system has unity. Togetherness means that people forsake – or at least set aside for a time – their sense of self or individuality, subsuming their values, perceptions, and thoughts to the greater consensus. Togetherness often gives a false sense of unity.

The quest for "togetherness" may become a coercive force that compels homogeneity and concurrence among people. People feel forced into an agreement that betrays their values and integrity. We cannot underestimate the power of social approval to bring about severe change to a person's behaviors and personality.

At its worst, togetherness may actually promote immaturity among people. It compels people to surrender their responsibility for their mind, will, and emotions to the larger group. In some situations, disruptive or dysfunctional people may hold a togetherness-seeking leader or people-system hostage by demanding that the leader or system adjust to their demands before they will cooperate in seeking "togetherness".

Let us illustrate this delusion with a comparison of two churches. Metro Chapel believed it had a great vision from God. When the leaders received the vision and presented it to the people, there was much excitement and a lot of anxiety. It seemed like a great vision, but a few people had some doubts and many people had questions. At first, the leaders answered the questions patiently. But after a while, the leaders began to respond with more and more antagonism. They began to say things like: "God will only give us this vision if we have 100 percent agreement"; or, "if you question this vision, then you are really questioning God because we are sure this vision is from God";

or, "we need to stick together regarding this vision because Satan would like nothing more than to see this vision fail". Some people left the church. But most people who stayed simply decided to shut up and let the leaders have their way. In the end, the leaders were not fully accurate regarding the vision, and the church almost died.

Grace Chapel also believed it had a vision from God. When the leaders received the vision and presented it to the people, there was much excitement and a lot of anxiety. People had doubts and people had questions. However, because unity was important to the leaders, they encouraged people to express their doubts and ask their questions. They encouraged people to discuss and debate whether the vision was from God. They dealt patiently and lovingly with dissent. They encouraged people to engage in conflict lovingly and gracefully. In the end, the leaders discovered that although the vision was from God they did not understand everything. Although it took a few years to work through everything, God used the process of discussion to reveal even more about the vision. The church grew and people became even more united.

In order to resist the delusion of togetherness, we must have a well-defined sense of our *being* – our principles, values, and calling – while remaining fully connected to our people-system. We must also help other people achieve a well-defined sense of *being.* We need to encourage people to be mature, assuming responsibility for their own minds, wills, and emotions. If we do not promote maturity, even in the midst of "togetherness" we may find that we have factions and the loss of community.

THE DELUSION OF POSITION

The final delusion is the delusion of position. This is the lie that if we only have the right position or title, or if we only have enough power, then we might be good leaders. Although we would like to think that this delusion is self-evident, many Christian leaders fall prey to it. We strive after power, positions, titles or degrees in order to convince people that we are the ones who should be the leaders. We assume that having these things would convince people that we are qualified to be leaders. We forget that many of the great leaders of history had no position whatsoever or refused to use their position as a way to control others.

One variation of this delusion suggests that if we only had the right public position then we would be able to influence people for the gospel. So if I could only become a professional athlete making millions of dollars, then I could lead people to Jesus. Or if I only became a superstar actor, then I could promote the kingdom of God. We might assume that if we got into a senior government position then we could make good policies in line with our Christian faith. We ignore the reality, which is the nature of a delusion, that many if not most Christians who achieve these things often sacrifice their Christian integrity in order to achieve them or to maintain them.

If we try to lead from a position of power, assuming that our position gives us the authority to instruct or command people, we will always create conflicts of will that will disrupt our people-system. We will bring ourselves into conflicts with people who believe that they have better ideas or that they are the ones who should be in the position of power. These conflicts will be highly contentious. People will often attempt to disguise them with charm, niceness or appeals to "fairness". They may also respond to our attempts to lead from power with passive aggression and sabotage.

As a leader, Jesus embraced the place of weakness and servanthood. He emptied himself and took on the form of a servant. We must follow his example if we are to escape the delusion of position. It is so important to remember what Jesus said in Mark, that if we want to become great then we must become the servant of all (see Mark 9:35). Humility provides the greatest antidote to the delusion of position.

DISPELLING DELUSIONS

As leaders, we begin to dispel these delusions by exposing them for the deceptions they are. Part of this involves identifying where we have believed a delusion and then repenting. As we renew our minds with truth we can eliminate these delusions from our lives.

Second, we need to help reset our expectations and the expectations of our people-system. We can refuse to allow people to adopt the concept that the real leaders are the people with the right title or position. We can help people to resist the idea that if we only have a good sense of togetherness then we can assume that we are in God's will. We can embrace the idea that understanding one another is a good thing while resisting the notion that if we only understand each other well enough then we can get things done. We can flee the fantasy that if we only have the right knowledge or technology, or apply the right strategy or technique, then we will succeed.

Finally, the greatest way to dispel leadership delusions is choosing to lead from our identity in Christ as the person God has made us to be. So often we succumb to these delusions because we think we have to become like someone else in order to lead well. This is perhaps the greatest delusion of all. We are leaders by God's calling and by God's design, but our worth as a person does not depend on or come from our leadership.

THE LEADERSHIP DILEMMA

The leadership dilemma is contained within the nature of the delusions themselves. We can spend a lot of time engaged in these delusions, thinking we are leading, only to discover that we have completely failed to lead anyone. We can easily invest all our leadership energy in things that fail to lead.

We are leaders, and God has made us sufficient for the task. God does not intend for us to lead like anyone else (except possibly his

Son, Jesus), but as the persons he has created us to be. As a leader, we must hold everything loosely – our job, our title, our sense of skill and expertise. What really matters is who we are in Jesus Christ and who Jesus Christ is in us as leaders. So we must hold everything loosely – except Jesus.

CONCLUSION – TRANSFORMING LEADERSHIP

In literature and in life we ultimately pursue, not conclusions, but beginnings.

Sam Tanenhaus

I have come to the conclusion that the most important element in human life is faith.

Rose Kennedy

No one should ever say that it was my ignorance if I did or showed forth anything however small according to God's good pleasure; but let this be your conclusion and let it so be thought, that – as is the perfect truth – it was the gift of God.

Saint Patrick

It's more fun to arrive a conclusion than to justify it.

Malcolm Forbes

As a young man, I spent many years trying to learn how to do leadership. I read books, listened to recorded teachings, and attended many seminars and conferences. None of these things really prepared me for leadership. Reflecting back, I also realize that my university studies, seminary studies or doctoral studies did not prepare me for leadership either. I value these experiences greatly and they have influenced me in many beneficial ways, but they did not make me a leader.

One of the reasons that I wanted to learn how to *do* leadership better is that I had noticed people were following me. From my very first job in the marketplace to my very first church I saw how people followed me as their leader. This was both exciting and intimidating, so I wanted to do leadership in the best way possible.

Looking back, an encounter in my first church initiated the change in my perception of leadership. A woman had come to me for counsel. I applied all the counseling techniques that I had learned in seminary – active listening, asking questions, and the like. At our second meeting together, I could tell that the woman had become a bit agitated with me. Finally, she turned to me and said something like, "I'm not coming to you just to talk so you can listen to me. I'm coming to you because I trust you and I want to know what *you* think."

The woman did not come to me for counseling; she had come to me for leadership. She had not come to me because she thought I was a great listener; she had come to me because she felt I was a leader. She did not want me to take responsibility for her decisions. She knew these were her responsibility, not mine. She wanted to connect with me as her leader – as well as her pastor and friend – so that she could gain new perspectives and make good decisions. She had responded to who she perceived me to be in her life more than anything I had done as a leader.

Around this time, Neil Anderson had published *Victory over the Darkness.* This book showed me the Bible from a new perspective and shifted my understanding of my identity in Jesus Christ. I suddenly understood that I was a saint, a holy one, because of what Jesus Christ had done for me in the cross and the empty tomb. I chose to believe what the Bible said about me is true, which began the renewing of my mind.

These two encounters – one with a follower and the other with a book – began the process of shifting my understanding of leadership from one of *doing* leadership to one of *being* a healthy leader that people would follow. My journey has required a lot of discipline from God as he purified my mind, will, and emotions. I had a lot to learn, and I still have a lot to learn – it is a lifelong process after all. But we have seen many people and people-systems transformed by the grace of God in and through leadership.

CHRIST IN YOU, THE HOPE OF GLORY

Genuinely transforming leadership begins with the reality of Jesus Christ in us as leaders. As new creations in Christ, our self (*being*) has been redeemed and renewed. The mystery for us as Christians is that Christ is in us, which gives us the hope of glory. The goal is that we will become mature in Christ, improving and increasing our leadership.

Christ in us is the greatest reason we do not have to become like someone else in order to lead. Christ in us means that we are the leaders God desires just as the people God has made us to be. God does not want us to be someone else. Christ is in us so that we might become authentically ourselves as leaders because we are new creations in Christ.

Christ in us gives us real hope that our leadership will bring glory to God. Christ in us also gives us real hope that our leadership will manifest the glory of God that will change lives and people-systems. It is Christ in us that might make our leadership truly transformative. We not only become great leaders but our leadership might represent Jesus Christ to the world.

Leadership begins with who we are, our *being*, which has been redeemed and renewed through a living relationship with Jesus Christ. Because of this, as our *being* grows healthier in Christ we can become stronger leaders. Growing to maturity as "sons" of God becomes the key for growing in effectiveness as leaders.

Because Jesus Christ is in us, we can develop several personal abilities that will facilitate our growth and effectiveness as leaders. These abilities represent things that we can do to nurture the reality of Christ in us, develop our *being* in a healthy way, and share our healthy *being* with others through our leadership. Any Christian can do all these things because the Holy Spirit has already given us all we need for life and godliness (see 2 Peter 1:3). Any Christian leader practicing these things will grow in leadership impact because Christ is in us.

CHRIST IN YOU AS A LEADER

Actively developing and engaging in these activities helps our *being* grow stronger with the reality of Christ in us. They help us become more alive to the reality of Christ in us as well as communicating that Christ is in us. These activities help leadership flow more fruitfully from our *being.*

First, we must *humble ourselves.* Humility is about placing our confidence in Jesus Christ and not in ourselves. When we humble ourselves, we remind ourselves that God is sovereign over our leadership. We also remind ourselves that every person we lead has great value as a human being loved by God. Every person deserves our respect. Humility allows people to experience our leadership more authentically and with less anxiety.

Second, we must *know ourselves.* We need to know the person that God has created us to be and rejoice in that person. We see many leaders who are not conscious of who they really are – their strengths and weaknesses, their foibles and fortes, how they affect the people around them. Many leaders, especially Christian leaders, believe that true leaders must diminish themselves or lose all sense of self in their leadership. However, effective leadership requires knowing who you are and maintaining a high degree of integrity.

Knowing ourselves means that we give up trying to be someone or something other than who we really are. Many leaders get lost because they try to emulate other leaders. They seem to think that if only they could be someone else then they would be better leaders. But God has made each of us unique and given us uniquely important leadership roles. We need to accept that God has designed us to be the leaders we are. Therefore, we need to know ourselves rather than trying to be someone else.

Third, we must *control ourselves.* Self-control is the only biblical form of control. Many leaders lose their leadership in just an instant by losing their self-control in the heat of the moment. We must exercise self-control at all times under the leadership of the Holy

Spirit. Exercising self-control by pausing for a minute or two often makes all the difference between success and failure in any given situation.

Next, we can learn to *connect ourselves*. We need to connect ourselves both with individuals and also with the people-systems that we lead. This connection must be authentic and genuine in order to influence our leadership. Many people think that connections happen only spontaneously, with the right chemistry. But we can choose to connect ourselves with others. Choosing to connect with others demonstrates love and concern. We cannot influence others unless we connect ourselves with them in some way.

Fifth, we need to *communicate ourselves*. People long to know who we are – our passions, our dreams, our visions. As we have seen, leadership involves communication, but communication involves much more than facts and information. Communication engages people emotionally. When we choose to communicate ourselves, we engage with the emotional core of people, giving them a sense that they know us and helping them decide to follow us.

Next, we have to *distinguish ourselves from processes and outcomes*. We often invest ourselves so much in particular processes or particular outcomes that we begin to identify ourselves with those processes and outcomes. If they fail, then we assume that we are failures. If they succeed, then we assume that we must be effective leaders. However, we are not the sum of processes and outcomes. Whether we succeed or fail, we are still a unique and valuable person that God designed. Whether we achieve the outcomes we desire does not define who we are. We will seldom know the ultimate outcome of our leadership and how we have influenced the lives of people.

Seventh, we must *make ourselves vulnerable*. Being a leader means that sometimes we will get hurt. Yet we must open ourselves up to other people. They need to be able to get close to us. They need to see the person we really are. Vulnerability indicates strength, for only a strong person will have the courage and ability to become vulnerable. The incarnation of Jesus Christ demonstrates this reality

441

most clearly. We may become vulnerable because Jesus Christ has made us strong in our *being*.

Eighth, we must choose to *align ourselves*. Many leaders try to remain aloof from their people and their people-system. They might see themselves as some sort of "expert" parachuted into a situation in order to save the day. Unfortunately, many seminaries reinforce this idea of remaining aloof by suggesting that somehow church leaders must not get too involved with the people they lead. However, real leadership will only occur when we align ourselves fully with our people and our people-system. We must align ourselves with God's purposes and plans for our life. We must align ourselves with God's purposes and plans for the people-system that we lead. We must align ourselves with the hopes and dreams of the people we lead.

Finally, we must learn to *deny ourselves, take up our cross, and follow Jesus*. Denying ourselves is not the opposite of knowing ourselves. Denying ourselves suggests that we do not focus on meeting our own wants and desires through our leadership. It suggests that we do not make self-centered demands in our leadership. Our leadership is not about us; it is about bringing glory and honor to our Lord and Savior Jesus Christ. It is about seeing his kingdom come and his will done on earth as it is in heaven. It is about achieving the best outcomes for our people and people-system. Ultimately, denying ourselves suggests that leadership is primarily a matter of discipleship.

LEADERSHIP BEYOND LIMITS

Embracing the mystery of Jesus Christ in us brings us into a realm where we can lead beyond limits, where our leadership becomes transforming – not only for the people we lead but also for us. Embracing Jesus Christ in us as leaders turbocharges our leadership. Too often we limit our leadership to the realm of perceived possibilities rather than understanding that the presence of Jesus Christ in us enables our leadership to achieve more than we might ask or imagine (see Ephesians 3:20).

Embracing Jesus Christ in us allows us to be ourselves as leaders, serving others genuinely and authentically. It frees us from the constant quest to become someone else, reminding us that we are the people God has intended to lead. This allows us to relax and enjoy leadership, which often increases the enjoyment of those we lead.

Based on the reality of Jesus Christ in us, several qualities will transform our leadership and make it transformative as well. These qualities do not replace other aspects of *being* and *doing* in leadership, but they enhance and intensify them. These qualities enable leaders to leave a legacy in the lives of people.

LOVE

The first quality is love. Love is a zealous, self-giving commitment to others for their benefit. This love is not romance, sentimentality, emotionalism, tolerance, indulgence, and similar things. This love is a costly, passionate focus on God's best for others. We often cheapen love in the world today, reducing it merely to a set of feelings that might easily change. The Bible presents a greater vision for love, grounded in the self-giving love of God in Jesus Christ.

Christian love is gritty and grounded in the cross. Love is the basis for our spiritual authority as leaders. Years ago at a conference I heard Francis Frangipane say that "spiritual authority is the muscle of your love". In other words, the more love we have for people the more spiritual authority they will give us in their lives. Spiritual authority expresses the amount of genuine influence we have with other people.

Without authentic love for our people we do not have spiritual authority in their lives. Without authentic love for our people-systems, we do not have spiritual authority in those systems. Our spiritual authority, flowing from our love, deepens and intensifies the influence and effect we may have on the lives of others.

Having love recognizes that all people and people-systems have their faults and failures but chooses not to focus on these faults and failures. I have heard many leaders secretly (or not so secretly) disparage their city, people-system or people. Without realizing it, by doing this they undermine their spiritual authority because they are undermining their love. Love does not focus on that which is ugly but chooses to focus on that which is beautiful.

Having love involves choosing to commit ourselves to others even when it is difficult or not what we would prefer. I have heard many leaders daydreaming about what their next leadership challenge might be or longing for another person's leadership context. Without realizing it, by doing this they undermine their spiritual authority because they are undermining their love. Love chooses to give itself in a full commitment to the other.

FAITH

The second quality is faith. Leadership requires faith in God that releases a spirit of adventure which optimizes God's providence. Faith in God enables us to have new perceptions beyond the control of our normal thinking processes. This faith operates at the intersection of risk and reality. The search for safety and certainty are enemies of faith.

Unfortunately, many Christians do not understand what Christian faith really is. Christian faith is choosing to trust and act, often beyond our natural abilities, based on true knowledge of God and God's ways founded in relationship with God through Jesus Christ in the power of the Holy Spirit.[1] All people live and operate by faith. Even atheists have faith; it is just not faith in God.

Faith can only come when we have a true knowledge of the object of our faith. As I write this, I have faith that the chair in which I am sitting will not collapse on me. My faith in this chair is very strong because I have a true knowledge of the chair. I know its materials and how it was constructed. I base my faith on the true knowledge I have and because of my faith I choose to sit on the chair.

We can only have genuine faith as Christians when we have a true knowledge of God and his ways. Our knowledge of God and his ways will only come in relationship with God through Jesus Christ in the power the Holy Spirit. Our relationship with God through Jesus Christ enables us to embrace the Bible as God's revelation of himself, providing us with a reliable source for a true knowledge of God and his ways. Faith is grounded in the reality of who God is as God has revealed himself to us. Faith comes only as we know God in all his glory and majesty.

Having a true knowledge of God and his ways based on the Bible as God's self-revelation enables us to trust him and then act accordingly. When we do this, God takes us beyond our natural abilities and empowers our leadership with an aspect of himself that allows our leadership to become more effective and more transformative in the lives of people.

We need to rescue faith from the common distortions and misrepresentations of faith present in the world around us, even among Christians. Faith is not positive thinking, sincere opinions strongly held, emotionalism, blind commitment, tradition, willpower, closed mindedness, dogmatism or irrational belief in the face of contrary evidence. We must reject these misconceptions of faith. These misconceptions of faith undermine the power of faith in our lives.

Faith adds a dynamic character to our leadership. This faith cherishes uncertainty and keeps us from the deception that we are omniscient. This faith opens us up to the surprises of God's providence that will liberate us from preconceived notions of reality and possibility. This faith gives rise to sanctified imaginations of possibilities within God's kingdom. Such faith acts as a binder of anxiety, especially in the leader.

EMBRACING THE CROSS

The third quality is embracing the cross. Power is a major issue in leadership – who has it, who can get it, who benefits from it. The fundamental error that many people make is to think they must get and keep power in order to lead well. People want to feel strong and power-filled. People think they need to exert power, even spiritual power, over other people. Jesus showed us another way.

For Christians, the issue of power becomes especially evident when we talk about spiritual warfare. People assume that we must fight demonic spiritual power with Christian spiritual power. Yet we often forget that Jesus disarmed the principalities and powers through the cross, a symbol of weakness and brokenness (see Colossians 2:15). If power had ever been the solution, Jesus never would have embraced the cross.

Jesus' leadership leads straight to the cross. We must be willing to embrace the cross in order to have Christlike leadership. Embracing the cross means, at least in part:

- **offering up our reputation and good name;**
- **allowing people to revile us and say all manner of evil against us falsely;**
- **being excluded and rejected;**
- **laying down our "weapons" and refusing to defend ourselves;**
- **accepting the pain of leadership.**

When we embrace the cross, we align ourselves with Jesus' plans and purposes for our lives. We remind ourselves that real leadership does not begin with the exercise of power and force but with a life surrendered to God in Jesus Christ.

Leadership involves helping other people learn to embrace the cross and follow Jesus. Even in the marketplace, we can see that genuine Christlike character traits – even when we do not present them as such – enable people to work more fruitfully. As leaders, we must willingly embrace the cross before our followers will embrace the cross. When people see that we are willing to embrace the cross in our own lives, it will help them to have the courage to embrace the cross in their lives.

PERSEVERANCE AND ENDURANCE

The fourth quality is perseverance and endurance. These two words are related but slightly different. Perseverance is steadfastness in doing something despite the difficulty or delay in achieving the beneficial outcome. Endurance is bearing up under something that is difficult or unpleasant without giving way. Leaders need both perseverance and endurance in order for their leadership to have its full effect.

One of my favorite quotes comes from Roger Bannister, the great runner, who said that "the man who can drive himself further once the effort gets painful is the man who will win". I also saw another quote on a poster one day: "The race does not always go to the swift, but to the ones who keep running." Perseverance and endurance call us never to quit, no matter how difficult it seems.

Modern life gives us an illusion of the quick fix – ATMs, fast-food, supermarkets – which undermines perseverance and endurance. But people develop their personalities, issues, and strongholds over months and years. People-systems may even develop their personalities and issues over the course of generations. Significant and lasting change or transformation requires perseverance and endurance.

Perseverance and endurance require that we embrace the pain and struggle of leadership. I do not think it is any accident that Paul told us that after having done everything we could we just needed to stand firm (see Ephesians 6:13–14). Sometimes it will not seem like our leadership makes any difference whatsoever. Sometimes we might feel that everything is actually becoming worse rather than better. Especially in these times we need to choose to persevere and endure. So often leaders give up just before the battle is won.

PERSPECTIVE

The final quality is perspective. Perspective determines our leadership. Our point of view makes all the difference in whether we see something as beautiful or ugly, as easy or difficult. When I was in my first church, I perceived the conflict we experienced as something really terrible. However, looking back from the perspective of three churches now, I realize that what I experienced was not as awful as I thought. In many respects, it was little more than "family squabbling". I now use my perspective to help other leaders who are struggling.

Perspective is a function of our reference point. We can choose to change our reference point and therefore choose to change our perspective. Leaders must choose their reference points – and those used by their people-systems – carefully. We might even ask God to give us a new reference point.

I remember a vision God gave me about City Temple. I do not get many visions, but this one was very profound for me. In this vision, I was being held in the air over City Temple. I was looking down on the top of our building and it seemed very large. After a few moments God began to lift me further and further away from the building. In a bit, the building began to look fairly small, but the City of London looked very big. Then I could barely see City Temple because London looked so large. Soon, London began to look small as I began to see the entirety of the United Kingdom. Then, the United Kingdom began to look small on the face of the earth. As I went further and further away into space, the Earth itself began to look smaller and smaller until I could no longer see it in the vastness of the universe. In that brief vision, God shifted my perspective and I began to see things completely differently. I began to recognize how everything I had seen as large was so small in the eyes of God.

As leaders, we must actively seek God's perspective. God's perspective is revealed to us in the Bible. It comes to us in prayer. It may also be revealed through the prophetic. But God's perspective is vital to us as leaders. When we see the universe as God sees it, we learn two things among others. We learn what a privilege it is that God has chosen us to lead and become agents of transformation in the world that he created. We also learn that our leadership does not depend on our strength and wisdom but on the God who filled us with his Holy Spirit. God himself makes our leadership transformative.

From our perspective, the most significant contribution leaders make is not achieving any given beneficial outcomes. The most significant contribution we make is to the long-term development of people and people-systems so they can adapt, change, prosper, and grow. We cannot determine our success, effectiveness or fruitfulness as leaders by simply looking at short-term outcomes and objectives. Leadership success involves transformed people and people-systems, not particular accomplishments. Many leaders have achieved what they thought of as leadership success only to discover later that ultimately they had failed in their leadership because their leadership had achieved numerous accomplishments but left a wake of destroyed lives and destroyed people-systems.

God is a generational God, calling for a long-term perspective. As leaders, we live in the flow of God's holy history. We are an important part of God's history, but that history began before us and will continue long after we cease to lead. We entrust our leadership to this generational God knowing that he will determine the long-term transformative impact of our leadership.

The challenge for us is to lead from the perspective of the legacy we would like to leave, knowing that our God is one who declares the end from the beginning (Isaiah 46:10). The legacy that we leave in the lives of people and people-systems is what will endure long after we are gone.

APPENDIX:
THE STEPS TO FREEDOM FOR LEADERS

Introduction

The Steps To Freedom In Christ by Neil T. Anderson is a resource used around the world to help Christians resolve personal and spiritual issues. Based on his books *Victory Over The Darkness* and *The Bondage Breaker*, and founded on the teaching in the Freedom In Christ Discipleship Course, the "Steps" have become an essential discipleship tool for many churches around the world. Churches use the Steps in a variety of ways: in corporate settings, where people pray through the Steps personally as part of a large-group process; in personal settings, where people pray through the Steps with an encourager and a prayer partner; and in individual settings, where people pray through the Steps or use portions of the Steps as part of their personal discipleship. For many churches the Steps are a fundamental part of their ministry, serving as a doorway into church membership or ministry.

The Steps To Freedom For Leaders is a resource focused on the personal and spiritual issues common to people in leadership, be it leadership in the marketplace, leadership in the church, or leadership in the home and community. This resource will enable you to identify and resolve personal and spiritual issues that can weaken, undermine, or even destroy your leadership. In some cases, these issues have become so entwined with our understanding of leadership that we do not even realize that what we are doing is actually preventing us from being the leaders God desires.

How to use the leadership steps

You may use *The Steps To Freedom For Leaders* in the same ways as you can use the original Steps To Freedom: group settings; personal settings; and individual settings. As with the original Steps, we most strongly recommend using the Leadership Steps in a personal setting with an encourager and a prayer partner. Alternatively, two leaders praying through *The Steps To Freedom For Leaders* together would prove very effective.

However you choose to work through the Leadership Steps, it is essential to give yourself time for reflection as you go through the prayer process. Make notes about the various things you sense that God is showing you about yourself and your leadership. Ideas and strategies may come to your mind regarding your present leadership context. Write these ideas down immediately so that they do not distract you from listening to God for how He is calling you to change and grow as a leader.

In order to receive the maximum benefit from using *The Steps To Freedom For Leaders*, we recommend the following:

- Participating in the Freedom In Christ Discipleship Course, reading the four accompanying *Discipleship Series* books by Steve Goss or reading *Victory Over The Darkness* and *The Bondage Breaker* by Neil T. Anderson
- Engaging in *The Steps To Freedom In Christ* in a personal setting
- Familiarity with the "Truth About My Father God" exercise in Step Two of *The Steps To Freedom In Christ*
- Familiarity with the "Stronghold-Busting" exercise taught in the Freedom In Christ Discipleship Course
- Integrating the discipleship truths from the above fully into your life in an ongoing way
- Participating in the *Freed To Lead* course or reading the *Freed To Lead* book by Rod Woods.

In addition to the above, we would also recommend *The Grace Course* from Freedom In Christ Ministries, a course designed to help people overcome common issues regarding grace and legalism. Such legalism is one of the most destructive forces in the life of a leader – just consider the Pharisees in Jesus' day.

Discipleship for leaders

As with the general Steps, *The Steps To Freedom For Leaders* provide a number of discipleship resources that may be used outside the overall

Leadership Steps process to keep your leadership free in Christ and healthy. For example, we would encourage the use of Step 2 (Forgiveness) on a regular basis to ensure that you are forgiving those who wound you in your leadership context. By so doing, you will overcome the unforgiveness and bitterness issues that have destroyed or seriously damaged many leaders. You could use Step 3 (Anxiety and Reactivity) to help your team work together more smoothly and overcome the anxiety in the face of change that often undermines a team's creativity.

As with *The Steps to Freedom In Christ*, we encourage you to use *The Steps To Freedom for Leaders* annually as scheduled maintenance for your leadership.

However you may use *The Steps To Freedom For Leaders*, we pray that God will richly bless your leadership wherever He has called you. We pray that your exercise of leadership will result in praise and glory to our Lord and Savior, Jesus Christ.

Opening prayer and declaration

Before you begin with the opening prayer and declaration, spend a few minutes reflecting on the following questions (or discussing them with your encourager if you are doing this in a personal setting):

- Who is the most influential leader in your life?
- What qualities do you admire most in a leader?
- What qualities most annoy you in a leader?
- What do you remember most about the leadership qualities of your parents?
- Do you see yourself as a leader? Why or why not?
- Do you see yourself as a good leader? Why or why not?
- What talents, skills, knowledge, and spiritual gifts do you have that you use regularly in your leadership?
- What qualities of Jesus' leadership would you like to see grow in your own leadership?
- How would you like to be remembered as a leader ten years from now?
- What is the greatest legacy that you would like to leave as a leader?

If you have a journal, you may want to make notes about your responses to these questions for review each time you work through *The Steps to Freedom For Leaders*.

Opening prayer

Dear Heavenly Father, I acknowledge You as the one true living God, existing as the Father, Son and Holy Spirit, and the only Lord of my life. I choose to surrender myself fully to You, so that I may become the leader You have created me to be. I give thanks to You that you have reconciled me to Yourself by grace through faith in Your Son, Jesus Christ. I pray that You, the God of our Lord Jesus Christ, the Father of glory, may give me the Spirit of wisdom and of revelation in the knowledge of Jesus. I pray that I may have the eyes of my heart enlightened, so that I may know what is the hope to which You have called me and what are the riches of Your glorious inheritance in the saints. I pray that I may know the immeasurable greatness of Your power toward us who believe, according to the working of Your great might that You worked in Christ when You raised Him from the dead and seated Him at Your right hand in the heavenly places (Ephesians 1:16–20). I want to know and choose to do Your will in the leadership to which You have called me. To that end, I welcome Your Holy Spirit and Your people to lead me in this process. I choose to cooperate with You fully to the glory of my Lord and Savior, Jesus Christ. Amen.

Declaration

In the name of Jesus Christ, as one sealed by the Spirit of God, I declare that I submit fully to God and resist the devil (James 4:7). I command Satan and all evil spirits to release me and have no influence over me so that I can know and do God's will. I exalt the living Lord Jesus Christ as the One who died on the cross and rose bodily from the dead, who is now seated far above all rule and authority and power and dominion, and above every name that is named, not only in this age but also in the one to come. This Jesus has all things under His feet and is the head over all things for the benefit of the Church, which is His body, the fullness of Him who fills all in all, and of which I am part (Ephesians 1:21–23). I declare that I, _____(name), belong to Christ and the evil one cannot touch me (1 John 5:18). I declare that I surrender myself fully – my hopes, dreams and leadership – to God the Father, through Jesus Christ the Son, and in the power of the Holy Spirit. Amen.

Step One: Embracing our identity in Christ, not leadership

The purpose of this Step is to help discern ways in which you have sought identity, significance, security, or acceptance in leadership roles, positions and titles rather than in Jesus Christ.

To the degree that we try to find our sense of significance, security, acceptance, or identity in our leadership, our leadership is likely to be distorted or dysfunctional. To the degree that we find all these things in Jesus, we will discover true freedom to lead as the people God has created us to be.

You are not free to lead if you are finding your identity in your role as a leader, or if you are basing your acceptance on the approval of others, hoping for job security, or finding your significance in what you do as a leader.

If you could no longer function as a leader or serve in your current leadership capacity, would you still be the same person, having the same sense of acceptance, security, and significance?

Use Part 1 below to help you determine the degree to which you have found your significance, security, acceptance, or identity in leadership.

Part 1 –Discerning wrongful identity in leadership

Dear Heavenly Father,
I thank You that by Your grace through faith in Your Son Jesus Christ I have become your chosen child, holy and precious to You. I thank you that in Christ I know that I am significant, secure, and accepted. However, I confess that I have not always chosen to believe that my identity was fully in Christ. I have sought significance, security, and acceptance through my leadership. I ask that Your Holy Spirit reveal to my mind all the ways that I have sinned against You in this regard, so that I might repent. In Jesus' name, I pray. Amen.

Consider the following four lists. Rate each statement in them on a scale of 1 to 5, with 1 being something that is not at all true for you and 5 being something that is very true for you.

Write the total at the base of each section.

Discerning whether we have sought our identity in leadership:

Identity is more than a label. It speaks to the essence of who we are and why we are here. When we begin our journey on earth, the world seems to revolve around us. Inevitably flesh patterns develop over time until we discover who we are in Christ and learn to centre our life around Christ. Such flesh patterns will hinder our ability to lead.

- ❏ I have trouble imagining my life without my leadership responsibilities.
- ❏ I often feel that my "world" revolves around my leadership role.
- ❏ I often take my electronic gadgets on holiday with me so that I can keep up with my leadership responsibilities.
- ❏ I often struggle to stop thinking about my work/leadership role, even when I have a day off or a holiday.
- ❏ All my hobbies and leisure activities tend to relate to my leadership role.
- ❏ I feel that my leadership role is the most significant and meaningful part of my life.
- ❏ My spouse, children, or friends often complain that I spend too much time in my leadership role (or at work).
- ❏ I feel proud to have attained the leadership position I have
- ❏ I deeply relish all the benefits of the leadership position I have attained and would find it very difficult to lose them.
- ❏ When I am talking with people, the first thing I tend to talk about is something to do with my leadership role or responsibilities.
- ❏ **Total**

Discerning whether we have sought our significance in leadership:

What is forgotten in time is of little significance. What is remembered for eternity has the greatest significance. Believing we are insignificant or that our ministries are insignificant will cripple our leadership as will try to find our significance in leadership roles.

- ❏ I feel that if I did not do the work myself then everything would fall apart.
- ❏ My leadership role or position gives me a sense that I have a place in this world.
- ❏ I am a very important part of my organization, perhaps the key to its success.

- ❑ I focus a lot on the number of people who attend my event, or the publicity it receives.
- ❑ How much money I make shows the value of my leadership. (Or: How much money I could be making if I were in another field shows the value of my leadership.)
- ❑ I enjoy telling people the number of emails that I receive each day, the number of people I supervise, or how important my responsibilities are.
- ❑ I feel hurt or upset when I do not get the credit that I deserve.
- ❑ I pay much attention to – or draw others' attention to – the number of titles and degrees I have.
- ❑ I find it difficult to rest because people really need my help or input.
- ❑ My leadership role helps me feel good about myself.
- ❑ **Total**

Discerning whether we have sought our security in leadership:

Security relates to eternal rather than temporal matters, which we have no right or ability to control. Insecure leaders will try to manipulate people and events that they believe will offer them some sense of security.

- ❑ I'm not sure what I would do in my life if I could not continue in my current leadership role or position.
- ❑ I often feel that I must remain in control of the situation.
- ❑ When people criticize me, I often find myself getting very defensive.
- ❑ . All my friends and social circles seem to revolve around my leadership role.
- ❑ If someone were to wrong me at work or in my leadership capacity, I would quickly seek redress through appropriate channels.
- ❑ As a leader, it is important for me to remain in charge of situations.
- ❑ I often find myself reminding people how busy I am.
- ❑ I feel competitive or jealous when others seem to do well at the same things I do.
- ❑ I feel threatened when I am with others who seem to be more successful than I am.

- ❏ I spend a lot of time thinking about how much I am paid for my leadership role.
- ❏ **Total**

Discerning whether we have sought our acceptance in leadership:

Acceptance by God is more than being tolerated. It means that we are fully forgiven, adopted as a child of God, made a new creation in Christ, and welcomed as a valuable member into the family of God. Knowing this is essential for leaders, who are likely to receive more criticism and rejection than followers.

- ❏ I struggle to say "no" to new responsibilities.
- ❏ I find it difficult to share my personal struggles with others in my leadership sphere or with the people I lead.
- ❏ As a leader, I feel it is very important for me to be liked by those around me.
- ❏ I conceal my thoughts and feelings because if others see the "real me" they would not want me or allow me to be a leader.
- ❏ I really want people to address me by my title or position.
- ❏ I have a difficult time admitting when I make a mistake, especially regarding my leadership.
- ❏ I will often do something others want me to even when I know that it might not be for the best.
- ❏ I find myself spending much of my time as a leader simply reacting to the needs and crises of others.
- ❏ I often neglect to take a day off because people urgently need me.
- ❏ I find it very difficult when people criticize or reject me.
- ❏ **Total**

Look at your totals in each of the four areas above and take some time to assess before God how significant an issue each area is for you.

We would suggest that a total of 40–50 in an area indicates that this area is definitely an issue for you; 30–40 indicates it is probably an issue for you; 20–30 indicates it may be an issue for you; and less than 20 suggests it is probably not an issue for you.

The "Nudge" Test

Pause and listen to the Holy Spirit. Do you feel a "nudge" that perhaps you have sought identity, significance, security, or acceptance in your leadership?

Pray the following prayer in light of what God has shown you above:

Dear Heavenly Father,
I confess that I have sinned against You in how I have sought my identity, significance, security, and acceptance in leadership roles, positions, and titles rather than in my relationship with You. In particular, I confess that I have sought my identity, significance, security, or acceptance outside of You in the following ways:

_____ (list what the Holy Spirit has shown you or brings to your mind now). I acknowledge that this is sin. Thank you that in Christ I am forgiven. I renounce seeking my identity, significance, security, and acceptance in these ways. I choose to base my life in You alone, through faith in Your Son Jesus Christ. Please fill me with Your Spirit and help me trust in You alone. Through Jesus Christ, my Lord. Amen.

Part 2 – Affirming who we are in Christ as leaders

God loves us and wants us to be firmly rooted in Christ, and that must happen before we can freely lead others. Trying to discover who we are in leadership roles, and hoping such roles will make us more significant, secure, and accepted can only lead to disaster. On the other hand, leading others can be very fulfilling if we are deeply rooted in Christ. Read the following affirmations aloud and let the Word of God dwell richly within you:

My identity in Christ affirmed

I renounce the lie that I depend on any leadership role for my significance, because in Christ I am deeply significant. God says that:

I am the salt of the earth and the light of the world (see Matthew 5:13, 14)

I am a branch of the true vine, Jesus, a channel of His life (see John 15:1, 5)

I have been chosen and appointed by God to bear fruit (see John 15:16)

I am a personal, Spirit empowered witness for Christ (see Acts 1:8)

I am a temple of God (see 1 Corinthians 3:16)

I am a minister of reconciliation for God (see 2 Corinthians 5:17–21)

I am Christ's ambassador to the world (see 2 Corinthians 5:20)

I am God's fellow worker (see 2 Corinthians 6:1)

I am seated with Christ in the heavenly realm (see Ephesians 2:6)

I am God's workmanship, created for good works (see Ephesians 2:10)

I may approach God with freedom and confidence (see Ephesians 3:12)

I can do all things through Christ who strengthens me! (see Philippians 4:13)

I renounce the lie that I depend on any leadership role for my security, because in Christ I am totally secure. God says that:

I am free forever from condemnation (see Romans 8:1, 2)

I am assured that all things work together for good (see Romans 8:28)

I am free from any condemning charges against me (see Romans 8:31–34)

I cannot be separated from the love of God (see Romans 8:35–39)

I have been established, anointed, and sealed by God (see 2 Corinthians 1:21, 22)

I am confident that the good work God has begun in me will be perfected (see Philippians 1:6)

I am a citizen of heaven (see Philippians 3:20)

I am hidden with Christ in God (see Colossians 3:3)

I have not been given a spirit of cowardice, but of power, love, and a sound mind (see 2 Timothy 1:7)

I can find grace and mercy to help in time of need (see Hebrews 4:16)

I am born of God and the evil one cannot touch me. (see 1 John 5:18)

I renounce the lie that I depend on any leadership role for my acceptance, because in Christ I am completely accepted. God says that:

I am God's child (see John 1:12)

I am Christ's friend (see John 15:5)

I have been justified (see Romans 5:1)

I am united with the Lord and I am one spirit with Him (see 1 Corinthians 6:17)

I have been bought with a price: I belong to God (see 1 Corinthians 6:19, 20)

I am a member of Christ's body (see 1 Corinthians 12:27)

I am a saint, a holy one (see Ephesians 1:1)

I have been adopted as God's child (see Ephesians 1:5)

I have direct access to God through the Holy Spirit (see Ephesians 2:18)

I have been redeemed and forgiven of all my sins (see Colossians 1:14)

I am complete in Christ. (see Colossians 2:10)

My identity in Christ declared

Now get together with one other person. Sit or stand directly opposite each other. Each person should read the following aloud to the other person. One person in turn should read the entire list to the other person. (If you are working through the Leadership Steps on your own, try looking at yourself in a mirror as you read these statements.)

I declare to you, _____ (name), that you do not depend on any leadership role for your significance, because in Christ you are deeply significant. God says that:

You are the salt of the earth and the light of the world (see Matthew 5:13, 14)

You are a branch of the true vine, Jesus, a channel of His life (see John 15:1, 5)

You have been chosen and appointed by God to bear fruit (see John 15:16)

You are a personal, Spirit empowered witness for Christ (see Acts 1:8)

You are a temple of God (see 1 Corinthians 3:16)

You are a minister of reconciliation for God (see 2 Corinthians 5:17–21)

You are Christ's ambassador to the world (see 2 Corinthians 5:20)

You are God's fellow worker (see 2 Corinthians 6:1)

You are seated with Christ in the heavenly realm (see Ephesians 2:6)

You are God's workmanship, created for good works (see Ephesians 2:10)

You may approach God with freedom and confidence (see Ephesians 3:12)

You can do all things through Christ who strengthens you! (see Philippians 4:13)

I declare to you, _____ (name), that you do not depend on any leadership role for your security, because in Christ you are totally secure. God says that:

You are free forever from condemnation (see Romans 8:1,2)

You are assured that all things work together for good (see Romans 8:28)

You are free from any condemning charges against you (Romans 8:31–34)

You cannot be separated from the love of God (see Romans 8:35–39)

You have been established, anointed, and sealed by God (see 2 Corinthians 1:21, 22)

You are confident that the good work God has begun in you will be perfected (Philippians 1:6)

You are a citizen of heaven (see Philippians 3:20)

You are hidden with Christ in God (see Colossians 3:3)

You have not been given a spirit of cowardice, but of power, love, and a sound mind (see 2 Timothy 1:7)

You can find grace and mercy to help in time of need (see Hebrews 4:16)

You are born of God and the evil one cannot touch you. (see 1 John 5:18)

I declare to you, _____ (name), that you do not depend on any leadership role for your acceptance, because in Christ you are completely accepted. God says that:

You are God's child (see John 1:12)

You are Christ's friend (see John 15:5)

You have been justified (see Romans 5:1)

You are united with the Lord and you are one spirit with Him (see 1 Corinthians 6:17)

You have been bought with a price: You belong to God (see 1 Corinthians 6:19, 20)

You are a member of Christ's body (see 1 Corinthians 12:27)

You are a saint, a holy one (see Ephesians 1:1)

You have been adopted as God's child (see Ephesians 1:5)

You have direct access to God through the Holy Spirit (see Ephesians 2:18)

You have been redeemed and forgiven of all your sins (see Colossians 1:14)

You are complete in Christ. (see Colossians 2:10)

If you did the above with a partner, finish this step by praying for each other.

Step Two: Forgiveness in leadership

Conflicts in leadership are inevitable. We will experience criticism, sabotage, ingratitude, and any number of pains and offences. Leaders who do not forgive will become bitter and angry and may ultimately experience burnout or other negative spiritual, mental, and physical outcomes.

Leaders must forgive others in order to relate to others in healthy ways and to maintain a healthy connection with both people and people-systems. However, we must forgive mainly for the sake of our own relationship with God (see Matthew 18:23–35). This Step will enable you to do that.

We are to forgive others as Christ has forgiven us. He did that by taking all the sins of the world upon Himself. Essentially, forgiving others is agreeing to live with the consequences of their sins. That may seem unfair, but we will have to anyway. The only real choice is to live in the bondage of bitterness, or forgive from our hearts others who have hurt us. It is for our own sake that we make that choice.

We forgive someone who has hurt us because the pain will not go away until we forgive. We don't heal damaged emotions in order to forgive. We forgive and our restored fellowship with God is what brings the healing.

Forgiveness does not mean tolerating sin. We have every right to set up scriptural boundaries to stop further abuse. Leaders who forgive their followers must still carry out discipline when appropriate. The difference is that they don't do it in the bitterness that would make it less effective.

Forgiveness does not necessarily mean that the other has done something wrong, but is merely an acknowledgement that the other has caused us pain. Of course, we do need to forgive when someone sins against us, but we also need to forgive when someone does something that is not sinful but causes us pain — such as when they give us godly correction.

As we forgive, we release the pain of what was said or done to us to God through Jesus Christ. Whenever the memory of what was said or done returns and causes pain again, we need to forgive again. As we continue to forgive, God will come and begin to heal the pain we have experienced. Forgiveness is not the same as reconciliation, although both are biblical concepts. If you have been wounded or sinned against, you have a responsibility to forgive (see Matthew 18:23–35 or Matthew 6:12–15). If you know you have wounded or sinned against someone else, you have a responsibility to seek reconciliation (see Matthew 5:23–26) – although either party may initiate reconciliation. As you go through this Step, the Lord might bring to your mind people with whom you need to initiate reconciliation. Make a list of them.

Begin with this prayer:

Dear Heavenly Father,
As a leader, I know that I have sinned many times. I have wounded others, knowingly and unknowingly. I thank You for the riches of Your kindness, forbearance, and patience toward me, knowing that Your kindness has led me to repentance. I confess that I have not shown that same kindness and patience toward those leaders or followers who have hurt or offended me. Instead, I have held on to my anger, bitterness, and resentment toward them. Please bring to my mind all the people I need to forgive who have wounded me either as a leader or a follower, in order that I may now choose to forgive. In Jesus' name. Amen.

(See Romans 2:4.)

List everyone the Lord brings to your mind – other leaders, followers, or anyone else who has wounded you:

Remember, it matters not whether these people have actually sinned against you. If you *feel* they have, the need to forgive them still exists. That is why many need to forgive God. Even though we know that God has not sinned, we may feel that He has let us down.

In order to forgive others from our hearts, we have to allow God to reach our emotional core and we need to acknowledge all hurtful and hateful feelings, especially the ones we have tried to suppress. God wants to surface such feelings so we can let them go. That happens when we forgive others for the specific things they have done that God brings to mind, and acknowledge how those things made us feel.

Forgiving yourself is actually acknowledging that God has forgiven you, but it is extremely helpful for some to say, "Lord I forgive myself for (tell

God the mistakes you made and other things you are beating yourself up for)."

Forgiving others is a crisis of the will. Don't say, "Lord, I want to forgive" or "Lord, help me forgive". God will always help us. We *choose* to forgive people for specific things we believe they have done.

Pray the following prayer for each person on your list, and stay with that person until every painful memory has been acknowledged:

Lord, I choose to forgive _____(name) for _____(what they did or failed to do) which made me feel _____(describe the pain).

After you have prayed through your list, pray the following:

Lord, I choose not to hold on to my resentment. I renounce all bitterness. I give up my right to seek revenge or to punish those who have wounded me. I thank You for setting me free from my bondage to bitterness and I ask You to heal my damaged emotions. I choose to bless those who have hurt me. In particular, I choose to bless _____(name the people). In Jesus' name. Amen.

Reconciliation

List the names of all the people with whom you may need to seek reconciliation.

If we have sinned against another person, we need to go to that person and specifically ask them to forgive us for what we have done, or not done, and make restitution if it is called for (Matthew 5:23, 24). It is always better to do that personally rather than by letter, phone, or email. Begin the process of reconciliation now by praying as follows:

Almighty God, I confess that I sinned against _____(name of person) by _____(state what you did or said). By Your Holy Spirit, please show me how to seek reconciliation with this person. In Jesus' name I pray. Amen.

If you have said or done something that may have wounded the person but which was not necessarily sinful (such as speaking an appropriate word of correction), then use this prayer:

Dear Heavenly Father, I ask You to heal the wounds that I may have caused to _____(name of person) when I _____(state what you did or said). Please reveal to my mind any way that _____(state what you did or said) was sinful, so that I might repent. By Your Holy Spirit, please show me how to seek reconciliation with this person. In Jesus' name. Amen.

Be sure to follow through in any way the Lord shows you. Be patient in the process and note that reconciliation can never be guaranteed as it depends on the response of the other person (Romans 12:18). However, if you have forgiven them and sought their forgiveness, you will have peace with God. For much deeper discussion about reconciliation read Neil Anderson's book *Restoring Broken Relationships* (Bethany House Publishing, formerly *The Path to Reconciliation*, Regal Books).

Step Three: Overcoming anxiety and reactivity in leadership

Anxiety disables leadership by immersing us in the problems and tensions around us in such a way that it prevents us from seeing God's truth and gaining perspective from God on how to move forward in obedience. Anxiety blinds leaders so that they lose any sense of vision and direction from God. Anxiety distorts our perspectives and our communication.

When leaders are anxious, they are more prone to reactive relationships: relationships where people instantly oppose one another and cease giving one another grace and forgiveness. In these relationships, we react out of our flesh instead of our spirits. Leaders can choose to respond thoughtfully and gracefully toward others who are reactive, especially those who oppose or criticize them personally. In order to do so, they must first recognize these relationships and choose to break the reactivity by responding in grace and love.

Part 1 – Overcoming anxiety

Anxiety often operates in the background of our minds. The particular source(s) of anxiety may be any number of issues: too much to do; too much information to process; financial struggles; relationship struggles; problems at work; problems at home; etc. Often, several sources of anxiety may be operating at the same time. In order to overcome anxiety, we must ask the Holy Spirit to reveal the source(s) of anxiety. Then we need to repent of this anxiety, choosing to present the matter to God in prayer and thanksgiving. If the anxiety is deep-seated or chronic, we may need to do a "stronghold-busting" exercise to eliminate it (see the *Freedom In Christ Discipleship Course* for more information). To begin discerning anxiety in your life, pray the following:

Dear Heavenly Father,
You are the omniscient God. You know the thoughts and intentions of my heart. You know the situations I am in from the beginning to the end. I place my trust in You to supply all my needs according to Your riches in glory and to guide me into all truth. Please reveal to my mind all the emotions and symptoms that I have been experiencing which are evidence of anxiety in my life. In Jesus' name. Amen.

Tick the emotions and symptoms of anxiety below that are true for you. Add others that the Spirit brings to mind.

- ❑ General uneasiness or nervousness
- ❑ Impulsiveness
- ❑ Unforgiveness
- ❑ Defensiveness
- ❑ Lack of concentration
- ❑ Restlessness
- ❑ Hyperactivity
- ❑ Loss of creativity
- ❑ Not thinking clearly
- ❑ Highly emotional
- ❑ Loss of objectivity
- ❑ Procrastination
- ❑ Stubbornness
- ❑ Sense of helplessness or self-doubt
- ❑ Difficulty in making choices
- ❑ Vivid nightmares
- ❑ Blaming
- ❑ Criticism and judgmentalism
- ❑ Willfulness
- ❑ Demanding your own way
- ❑ Gossip or rumours
- ❑ Feeling victimized
- ❑ Exaggeration
- ❑ Moodiness
- ❑ Miscommunication
- ❑ Too much TV or media
- ❑ Too much drink or food
- ❑ Money concerns
- ❑ Working too hard
- ❑ Others:

Selecting more than three indicates that anxiety may be a problem. More than seven suggests that you may be chronically anxious.

Pray the following prayer:

Loving Father,
Your Word tells us not to be anxious, but I realize that I have not
obeyed Your Word. I have allowed myself to be anxious about many
things, as the emotions and symptoms above have shown me. I confess
that my anxiety shows a lack of trust in You. I now ask You to search
me, O God, and know my heart; try me and know my anxious thoughts;
and see if there be any hurtful way in me, and lead me in the
everlasting way. Please reveal to my mind all sources of anxiety that I
might commit each of them to You in trust and obedience. In Jesus'
precious name. Amen.

(Matthew 6:31–34; Philippians 4:6; Psalm 139:23, 24)

1. List the sources of anxiety (evidenced by the emotions and symptoms above) that the Holy Spirit reveals to your mind, being as specific as possible:
(Example: I have so much to do that I'm afraid I will miss something important.)

2. For each source of anxiety, describe what you are believing or assuming (these are generally "lies") that is causing you apprehension or emotional pain.
(Example: I need to do everything I'm doing.)

Respond with this prayer:

Dear Heavenly Father,
I choose to trust in You alone. I do not trust in myself or my own
abilities to resolve the situations in my life. I do not trust in my
relatives and friends to resolve the situations in my life. I do not trust
in my work to resolve the situations in my life. I do not trust my church
to resolve the situations in my life. I choose to trust in You alone. I now
commit the following sources of anxiety to You in prayer:

1. List the anxiety or source of anxiety.
2. Describe the emotions or symptoms that accompany it.
3. Pray for the appropriate resolution or outcome.

In the name of Jesus Christ, I now renounce the lies that I have believed about these sources of anxiety. In particular, I renounce the lie that: _____(list each lie you have believed or assumed).

Thank You that You are sovereign over my life. Thank You that You are in control of the situations of my life. Thank You that You always work for my good in every situation. Thank You that through Jesus Christ I am not a victim of anxiety, but I am an overcomer of anxiety. I choose to walk in obedience to You, resisting anxiety by keeping my focus on You. Through Jesus Christ. Amen.

Part 2 – Breaking cycles of reactivity

Reactivity cycles occur whenever we become stuck in a relationship where we are opposing, resisting, and criticizing the other. We become reactive when we begin to engage with other people out of our flesh, that sinful aspect of our humanity that resists God's will. When we are reactive, others often become reactive to us as well, entrapping us in a reactivity cycle.

We may become reactive not only toward individuals, but also toward groups and organizations. For example, people can become reactive toward a political party, so that no matter what the leader of a certain political party might say these people will find something to oppose. This may lead to intractable disagreements among people regarding politics, which prevent people from working together for the good of their country.

At any time, we can break reactivity cycles by persistently choosing to respond to the other out of grace, love, and forgiveness. Respond to God as you pray this prayer:

Dear Heavenly Father,
Your Word says that You are merciful and gracious, slow to anger, and
abounding in steadfast love (Exodus 34:6). Although I have received
Your mercy, I confess that I have not always extended this mercy to
others. Instead, I have allowed myself to react out of my flesh. Please
reveal to my mind anyone with whom I have been reactive, so that I
might repent and find freedom. In Jesus' name. Amen.

1. List each person that the Spirit brings to your mind.

2. For each person, describe how you have been reactive toward that person.

3. For each person, pray the following prayer:

Lord,
I confess that I have been reactive toward _____ (name the person
or group) by _____ (describe the ways in which you have been
reactive). Thank You that in Christ I am forgiven. I now choose to
respond to _____ (name the person or group) in grace, love, and
mercy. I choose to give _____ (name the person or group) grace as
You have given grace to me through Your Son Jesus Christ. I ask that
You would make me an agent of reconciliation with (name the person
or group). I choose to bless (name the person or group) in the name of
Jesus Christ, my Lord. Amen.

(Ephesians 4:32)

As appropriate, you may need to seek reconciliation with those on your list
(see Step 2). Allow the Holy Spirit to lead you in this. Often, as we choose
to break the cycle of reactivity, reconciliation with that person naturally
begins to occur by the Holy Spirit.

Step Four: Embracing our leadership responsibility

The purpose of this Step is to help us understand and embrace who God has created us to be as leaders, whether we are a natural leader, a leader in our people-system, or a leader in a particular situation. Natural leaders are people who lead as a matter of course, no matter what context they seem to be in. Their normal disposition is leadership. Other leaders may be called to lead in a particular people-system (group of people). They may be leaders at home or at work, but they do not generally lead outside their people-system. Almost everyone will need to lead from time to time as the situation requires. Because almost everyone will lead from time to time, there is not an activity for discernment in this aspect of leadership.

After helping identify how you are called to leadership, this Step then helps you resolve the times when you have failed to exercise leadership or when you have exercised leadership in the wrong way. If we fail to lead as God requires or if we exercise our leadership in the wrong way, then we have sinned. So we must resolve these areas of sin if we are to lead appropriately.

Part 1 – Identifying the scope of your leadership

Dear Heavenly Father,
I rejoice that You have saved me by grace through faith, and that I am
Your workmanship created in Christ Jesus for good works that You
have prepared for me (Ephesians 2:8–10). I know that You have created
each person differently, and You have given each person different
spiritual gifts, callings, and ministries by Your Holy Spirit (1
Corinthians 12:4–7). I pray that You would reveal to my mind how you
have created me and called me to lead. In Jesus' name. Amen.

Natural leadership

Please rate the following statements on a scale of 1 to 10, with 10 being the highest:

- ___ No matter whether I am at work, church, home, or other organizations, I find that people consistently ask me to lead.
- ___ Whenever I am leading, I feel confident.
- ___ Whenever I am leading, I feel positive.
- ___ Whenever I am leading, I feel energized.

- _ I usually serve more effectively by leading a team than I do as a general team member.
- _ I generally do not feel threatened or jealous when I am around other leaders.
- _ People seem to enjoy following my leadership.
- _ The best way I can serve people is by leading them.
- _ I find it relatively easy to get a clear vision from God for my work, church, home, or other organization of which I am part.
- _ I can point to a record of good fruit stemming from contexts in which I was leading.
- _ **Total**

If your score is 70 or above, it is likely that God has called you as a natural leader. (It is often best to verify your responses with your spouse or a close friend, who can assist you in your discernment.)

Once you have completed this exercise, pray the following:

Dear Heavenly Father,

Thank you for creating me to be the leader that I am, whether or not I am a natural leader. I surrender to Your purpose in my life regarding leadership. I affirm that Your Son Jesus was the greatest leader of all, the perfect example of genuine leadership. By Your Spirit, I choose to follow His example of leadership, using leadership to serve others in humility. May my leadership always reflect and be filled with the life of Jesus. Amen.

People-system leadership

Review the list of people-systems below. Put a tick next to those in which you already serve as a leader or you believe God is calling you to serve as a leader. Write a note next to any people-system that requires additional specification (e.g. "budget team at work" or "Girl Guides troop").

- ❏ Your immediate family
- ❏ Your extended family
- ❏ Your work
- ❏ Teams or other groups at work
- ❏ Your profession or professional associations
- ❏ Your church

- ❏ Church cell group/home group
- ❏ Community and social organizations
- ❏ Others:

Pray the following in light of your answers above:

Dear Heavenly Father,
I thank You for the person You have created me to be. I now freely and
wholeheartedly choose to walk in the ways You have prepared for me,
accepting the leadership responsibilities You have given me. In
particular, I affirm that You have called me to lead in _____ (list all
specific contexts). By Your Holy Spirit, empower me to serve others
through my leadership in whatever people-systems or situations You
place me, so that I might bring glory and honor to my Lord Jesus
Christ. Amen.

Part 2 – Identifying situations and people-systems in which you failed to lead

Every leader makes mistakes; every leader fails. This part of the Step focuses on times when we have neglected our leadership responsibilities or times in which we sought to fulfill our leadership responsibilities in a sinful way. Begin by praying the following prayer:

Dear Heavenly Father,
I thank you for Your mercy and kindness, knowing that Your kindness
leads me to repentance (Romans 2:4). I confess that I have not always
led when I have needed to lead, neglecting my responsibility before
You. I also confess that I have not always led in the way I should lead,
but have led out of selfish motives and in sinful ways. Please reveal to
my mind any and all ways that I have not led as You have wanted, so
that I might repent. In Jesus' name. Amen.

1. List the people-systems above in which you have failed to lead as God wanted:

2. List the situations in which you have neglected your leadership responsibilities or have failed to lead as needed:

3. List the situations in which you have led wrongly:

4. Put a mark next to any of the following that are true for you:
   - ❑ I have used guilt or shame to get others to do what I want or think best.
   - ❑ I have demanded that others do what I want or follow my rules.
   - ❑ I have controlled others by my strong personality, heavy-handed persuasion, or the use of fear or intimidation.
   - ❑ I have expected to be in charge because I am the leader.
   - ❑ I have tried to get others to do what I want using rules, regulations, and standards.
   - ❑ I have striven to get or maintain a position or role in order to accomplish my agenda.
   - ❑ I have assumed responsibility for the lives and well-being of other adults under my leadership.
   - ❑ I have driven others and myself harder and harder in order to achieve the vision.
   - ❑ I have been stubborn and rigid in my leadership.
   - ❑ I have required people under my leadership to do what I say, when I say it and how I say it.
   - ❑ I have expected others to work as hard as I do if they want my approval.
   - ❑ I have never been really satisfied with the performance of others I lead.
   - ❑ Other things the Lord may show you:

Pray the following prayer, including the items you have listed above:

Lord, I confess that I have not led when I should have. Specifically, I confess my sins in these areas: _____(list the ones indicated in 1 and 2 above). I also confess that I have led wrongly. Specifically, I confess these wrong ways of leading: _____(list the ones indicated in 3 or 4 above). Thank You that in Jesus Christ I am forgiven. I now commit myself to leading in whatever situation You ask and in a manner worthy of Jesus Christ, the greatest leader of all. Amen.

Conclude this Step with the following prayer:

Gracious and loving God,
Thank You for allowing me to serve people through leadership as the person I am in Christ. I pray that I might fulfill all my leadership responsibilities humbly, joyfully, and lovingly, in the manner of Your Son, Jesus. Empower me by Your Holy Spirit to live in obedience to You and serve in love. Through Jesus Christ. Amen.

Step Five: Money, sex, and power in leadership

When a leader fails, most often it is because of one (or more) of the following: money, sex, and power. When any of these three things are out of balance in our lives, it will undermine our leadership ability. This will be true even if the issue does not seem to be directly related to our leadership context. This Step asks the Holy Spirit to reveal to our minds all ways that we have sinned or are sinning in each of these areas.

Part 1 – Money

When we use the term "money", we are referring to all the financial and material resources (car, home, computer, etc.) God has provided for us. In this Step, we are asking God to reveal not only our behaviors but also our attitudes concerning our financial and material resources. Greed is the desire to have more and more or to have more than you actually need. Covetousness is the longing to possess things that other people have. Envy is a feeling of discontent or resentful longing arising from someone else's situation.

Begin with this prayer:

Dear Heavenly Father,
I thank You that You richly supply me with all the resources I need
through Your Son Jesus Christ. You have said that the love of money is
the root of all kinds of evil (1 Timothy 6:10). Because of this, You have
told us to keep our lives free from the love of money and choose to be
content with what we have (Hebrews 13:5). You have promised that if
we seek first Your kingdom, then You would add to us all the things we
need (Matthew 6:33). I confess that I have not always done this.
Instead, I have sinned through greed, envy, and covetousness. I have
also sinned by failing to be a good steward of the financial and material
resources that You have supplied to me. I now ask You to reveal to my
mind any and all ways that I have sinned regarding money, that I might
fully repent. In Jesus' name. Amen.

Ways that we may sin as leaders regarding money:

- ❑ Failing to live within my means or according to a budget
- ❑ Not paying off my credit cards each month or carrying a large balance on my credit cards with no ability to pay them off
- ❑ Having large amounts of consumer debt
- ❑ Taking small items from my workplace for my personal use
- ❑ Failing to file or pay my taxes on time and in full
- ❑ Trying to disguise money problems that I may be having
- ❑ Failing to exercise good stewardship of the resources God has given me (e.g. failing to maintain my car or my home, failing to care for my computer and phone, etc.)
- ❑ Using or administering the financial resources of my workplace without transparency and appropriate financial controls
- ❑ Failing to insist that others use appropriate financial controls and stewardship of our common resources (at home, in the workplace, or in church)
- ❑ Ignoring financial practices that I know to be wrong (for myself, at home, in the workplace, or in church)
- ❑ Feeling rebellious or defensive when I'm asked to give appropriate account for my financial activities and expenditures
- ❑ Failing to ensure that my current account and savings account balance each month
- ❑ Finding myself practicing "retail therapy" or conspicuous consumption
- ❑ Envying or coveting the resources of other friends, co-workers or leaders in similar situations to myself
- ❑ Finding it difficult to share my financial needs with others who may be able to help me
- ❑ Failing to give financially as God has instructed me
- ❑ Spending a lot of time thinking and worrying about money matters
- ❑ Being overly concerned about getting the financial remuneration that I feel I deserve
- ❑ Feeling that I am entitled to a certain level of financial remuneration
- ❑ Other ways that God is showing me:

Respond to what God has shown you by praying this prayer:

Dear Heavenly Father,
I thank You for the riches of Your kindness toward me, leading me to
turn away from my sin. I confess that I have sinned regarding money in
the following ways: _____(list them). Thank You that in Jesus
Christ I am forgiven. I choose to turn away from my sin and exercise
good stewardship over the financial and material resources that You
have entrusted to me as a person and as a leader. Help me to be
faithful in little, so that I may receive much to use for Your kingdom
(Luke 16:10–12). Through Jesus, my Lord. Amen.

Part 2 – Sex

In this section, we are not looking to deal with all the ways that we have sinned regarding sex, but we are focusing primarily on our leadership context. However, it is important that we repent of all immoral sexual activity according to the Bible and ensure that we resolve all outstanding personal and spiritual issues regarding our sexuality. (See *The Steps To Freedom In Christ*, Step 6, for guidance on how to resolve issues regarding immoral sexual activity more fully.) In this Step, we are asking God to reveal not only our behaviours but also our attitudes regarding sexual issues.

Pray the following:

Dear Heavenly Father,
I thank You that sex is Your good gift to be exercised according to Your
Word in the covenant of marriage between one man and one woman. I
acknowledge that immoral sexual activity includes a range of sins that
undermine our relationship with You and with others. I confess that it
ruins our ability to lead as Christians. I now ask You to bring to my
mind any sexual sin in thought, word, or action that I might repent of
these sexual sins and break their bondages. In Jesus' name. Amen.

Ways that we may sin as leaders regarding sex:
- ❑ Thinking about co-workers or those I lead in a lustful way
- ❑ Looking at co-workers or those I lead in a lustful way
- ❑ Looking at pornography
- ❑ "Channel surfing" or internet surfing when I am tired or stressed

- ❏ Watching films and TV programs that contain strong sexual images
- ❏ Daydreaming about immoral sexual activity
- ❏ Finding myself longing to spend time with people of the opposite gender (who I am not either dating or married to), especially in one-to-one circumstances
- ❏ Not taking time to develop healthy friendships with people of the same gender
- ❏ Thinking too much about past relationships, especially if they involved immoral sexual contact
- ❏ Dwelling on temptations toward homosexuality or paedophilia
- ❏ Not giving sufficient attention and effort to nurturing my sexual relationship with my spouse
- ❏ Using sex with my spouse as a means of fulfilling my sinful lust
- ❏ Other ways that God is showing me:

Once you have considered this list, choose to repent by praying this prayer:

Dear Heavenly Father,
I admit that I have not always exercised self-control and obedience to You and Your Word regarding my sexuality. I confess that I have sinned against You by _____ (list them). I renounce all these sexual sins, and I admit to any willful participation. I choose now to present my eyes, mouth, mind, heart, hands, feet, and sexual organs to You as instruments of righteousness. I present my whole body to You as a living sacrifice, holy and acceptable. I choose to reserve the sexual use of my body for marriage only (see Hebrews 13:4). I now loose myself from any sinful bonds I have made with any co-worker or follower in my heart or in my behavior. In the name of the Lord Jesus Christ, I cancel any effects my sin has on my leadership and take back any ground I have given to the devil. Thank You that You have totally cleansed and forgiven me and that You love and accept me just the way I am. Therefore, I choose now to present myself and my body to You as clean in Your eyes. In Jesus' name. Amen.

Part 3 – Power

Power is a complex concept in leadership. Leaders have authority and responsibility for people in order that people may experience God's best for them. However, as leaders we can often use our authority and responsibility as a means to control and manipulate others. Most leaders unintentionally fall into this from time to time. A few leaders consciously choose to control others. Some leaders will try to control others because they enjoy having positions of power and influence. Other leaders try to control people out of fear and self-protection. Some people will seek positions of leadership in order to use these positions of leadership to achieve their own desires or their own agenda.

In this section, we are asking God to reveal to us all the ways that we have sought to control or manipulate people using our leadership. Begin with this prayer:

Almighty God, You are the Sovereign Lord of all creation. We know that nothing is outside the control of Your Son Jesus Christ, even though it does not always seem that everything is under His control. Lord Jesus, You uphold the universe by Your power. As Your people, the power we have comes by Your Holy Spirit and through godliness. Your power is at work within us, but it enables us to live fully for You. You have not given us power over others. It is the love of Christ that controls us, and You do not allow us to control others. Instead, You call us to self-control. I confess that I have used my leadership as a means to gain or exercise power over others. I repent of this sin and ask You to reveal to my mind all the ways that I have used my leadership as a means to control others. Please reveal all the ways that I have become intoxicated with my power and position over others. In Jesus' name. Amen.

(See Hebrews 2:8; Hebrews 1:3; 2 Timothy 3:5; 2 Timothy 1:7; Ephesians 3:20; 2 Corinthians 5:14.)

Ways that we may sin as leaders regarding power and control:
- ❑   Expecting (or trying to force) people to follow me because of my position, title, degrees, or achievements
- ❑   Using guilt or shame to persuade others to do what I think is right
- ❑   Using biblical verses such as "Touch not my anointed ones" (Psalm 105:15) to defend myself or persuade others

- ❏ Not sharing requested or needed information in an open and timely manner
- ❏ Withholding pertinent information needed by my co-workers or followers
- ❏ Acting or speaking in deceptive ways in order to control others or protect myself
- ❏ Spending time and energy trying to control people and situations instead of exercising self-control
- ❏ Using harsh or judgmental language with others, especially when I want them to do something
- ❏ Threatening others with bad consequences in order to get my way
- ❏ Threatening others with my own resignation or withdrawal in order to get my way
- ❏ Having the tendency to think that my way is the right way
- ❏ Giving people responsibility but expecting them to fulfill it in the way I determine
- ❏ Not allowing, actively or passively, other people to take leadership responsibility as appropriate
- ❏ Not giving people open access to the resources needed in order to fulfill their responsibilities fully and in a timely way
- ❏ Giving different people different information about the same activity, responsibility or situation
- ❏ Using rules, regulations, or the Bible in a way that stifles discussion and tries to force people to listen to me or obey me
- ❏ Using phrases such as "because I said so" or "the Lord told me" when people raise questions about my decisions or opinions
- ❏ Using technical, obscure or complicated language in order to persuade people that I am right
- ❏ Being harsh, critical, or abusive with others, especially if they do not agree with me
- ❏ Taking responsibility for someone else's obedience and discipleship
- ❏ Other ways that God may be showing you:

Pray the following:

Almighty God,
I confess that I have used my leadership as a means to control people and situations. In particular, I confess _____ (list them). I renounce all ways and means of using leadership to control others, especially the ones that I have listed. Thank You that in Jesus I am forgiven. I cancel all ground gained in my life through my sin in this

area. I choose to lead in the way of Jesus, who for our sakes emptied Himself and made Himself nothing, becoming the servant of all (Philippians 2:5ff.). Fill me with Your Holy Spirit, that I might live for You. In Jesus' name. Amen.

Step Six: Renouncing pride, defensiveness, and selfish ambition in leadership

This Step addresses three key areas that deeply affect leadership: pride, defensiveness, and selfish ambition. These three factors are at the root of the lack of healthy unity, not only in the Church but also in the workplace. These factors cause a lot of dysfunction and disease among leaders as well as followers. They prevent people and people-systems from working together effectively for the benefit of society.

Part 1 – Pride

Pride is one of the great leadership sins. Pride involves having a high opinion of oneself or one's importance, which can show itself in many ways. Pride often puts leaders in situations where people will oppose, resist, or resent them. Pride always puts leaders in opposition to God. Left unchecked, pride functions like a cancer in leadership, eating away at our leadership until it dies. Even many secular books and authorities on leadership recognize the destructive influence of pride in a leader.

Begin with the following prayer:

Dear Heavenly Father,
You have said that pride goes before destruction and an arrogant spirit before a fall. As a leader, I confess that I have often considered myself more highly than I ought. I have wanted to be first and not last. I have chosen to serve myself, seeking my own desires and disguising it as serving others. As a result, I have given ground to the devil in my life and I have compromised my leadership. I have sinned by believing I could know and choose what is best for others on my own. In so doing, I have placed my will before Yours, and I have centered my life around myself instead of You.

I repent of my pride and selfishness in leadership and pray that all ground gained in me by the enemies of the Lord Jesus Christ would be canceled. I choose to rely on the Holy Spirit's power and guidance so I will do nothing from selfishness or empty conceit. With humility of mind, I will seek to lead by Your Holy Spirit with the love and grace of Jesus.

Please show me now all the specific ways in which I have led in pride. Enable me through love to serve others and in honor to prefer others. I ask all of this in the gentle and humble name of Jesus, my Lord. Amen.

(See Proverbs 16:18; Matthew 6:33; 16:24; Romans 12:10; Philippians 2:3.)

Allow the Holy Spirit to show you any specific ways in which pride has infected your leadership. As the Lord brings to your mind areas of pride, use the prayer below to guide you in your confession.

Ways that pride might become evident in leadership:

- ❑ Having or showing a stubborn and determined intention to do what I think is best
- ❑ Leading from my own understanding and experience rather than patiently seeking God's guidance through prayer and His Word
- ❑ Leading from my own energy and effort instead of depending on the power of the Holy Spirit
- ❑ Leading in ways that control or manipulate others instead of using self-control
- ❑ Having impatience when it comes to seeing the change or getting the outcomes I want in my leadership contexts
- ❑ Being too busy doing important things as a leader to take time to do little things for others
- ❑ Having a tendency to think that I do not need anyone's help to lead
- ❑ Finding it hard to admit when I am wrong
- ❑ Being more concerned about pleasing people than pleasing God with my leadership
- ❑ Being concerned about getting the credit I feel I deserve as a leader
- ❑ Thinking that as a leader I am more humble, spiritual, religious, or devoted than others
- ❑ Being driven to obtain recognition for my leadership abilities, especially because of the size or scope of my leadership responsibilities
- ❑ Feeling that my needs are not as important as others' needs so that I must sacrifice myself
- ❑ Feeling that others do not have the same level of commitment or ability in leadership as me
- ❑ Often feeling that if I do not do something as a leader then no one else will
- ❑ Thinking that I must keep things going as a leader otherwise they may fall apart

- ❏ Considering myself better than others because of my accomplishments or position as a leader
- ❏ Other ways I have thought more highly of myself than I should:

For each of the above areas that has been true in your life, pray:

Lord, I agree I have been proud by _____(list the ways). Thank You for forgiving me for my pride. I choose to renounce pride and humble myself before You and others. I choose to place all my confidence in You and none in my flesh. In Jesus' name. Amen.

Part 2 – Defending ourselves wrongly

Self-defense can be another sign of pride in a leader, or it may reflect that the leader is seeking his or her significance, security or acceptance in leadership. Self-defense is always problematic: if we have done something wrong, we have no defense; if we have not done anything wrong, we need no defense because God will defend us. Defensiveness will always undermine leadership, especially by undermining other people's trust in the leader. Pray the following:

Dear Heavenly Father,
You have promised to be my shelter and my fortress. By Your grace, You surround me and defend me. I admit that I have not always trusted in You as my defender. Instead, because of pride or insecurity, I have often struggled as a leader to admit that I was wrong or that I made a mistake. I have resisted attempts by others to show me my faults in accordance with Your Word. I have chosen to defend myself wrongly. In so doing I have wounded others and myself and I have offended You. Please reveal to my mind any ways that I have failed to trust You by trying to defend myself wrongly. In the name of Jesus. Amen.

Ways we defend ourselves wrongly:

- ❏ Pretending or thinking that I have not done anything wrong
- ❏ Pretending or thinking that my behavior is better than it really is
- ❏ Focusing on my own best motives and another's worst behaviours
- ❏ Denying or distorting reality, evidence, or the truth
- ❏ Retreating into entertainment, drugs, alcohol, or food

- ❑ Trying to portray myself in a better light than others
- ❑ Withdrawing from people or keeping people at a distance
- ❑ Regressing to less threatening times or to immature attitudes and behaviors
- ❑ Showing displaced anger or irritability
- ❑ Projecting my problems on to others; blaming others for my problems; shifting the focus on to others
- ❑ Rationalizing my behavior or my circumstances
- ❑ Lying, disguising the truth, or giving partial truths
- ❑ Presenting a false image of myself or my motives
- ❑ Framing motives, behaviors, attitudes, and situations in ways that are deceptive or that present myself as better than I am
- ❑ Adopting a martyr complex
- ❑ Adopting a messiah complex
- ❑ Adopting a hermit complex
- ❑ Showing a lack of openness and transparency
- ❑ Refusing to trust and release others
- ❑ Other ways that the Holy Spirit may show you:

In light of the above, pray the following:

Gracious Lord,
I confess that I have defended myself wrongly by _____ (list them).
Thank You for Your forgiveness. I choose to trust You to defend and protect me. In Jesus' name. Amen.

Part 3 – Selfish ambition, envy, and jealousy

Envy, jealousy and selfish ambition are three related sins. They lead to unholy comparisons with others and unrighteous competition. These sins are related to the sin of pride (see Philippians 2:3). In a sense, jealousy is an intensification of envy, and selfish ambition is an intensification of jealousy. This part of the Step seeks to reveal these sins in our lives so that we might repent.

There are four primary sources of envy, jealousy, and selfish ambition. First, people may feel or fear that they are being displaced in terms of their relationships with others or in terms of their status (position or influence) in their leadership context. Second, feeling insecure (or having our sense of security in someone other than Jesus) may lead to these sins. Third, people may develop an entitlement mentality, believing that they deserve something (especially something someone else has) because of their own efforts. Finally, these sins may result from an unwillingness to pay the price for – or trying to find a shortcut to get – what one wants. All these flow from pride and conceit. They may all be corrected by finding our significance, security, and acceptance in Jesus rather than our leadership.

Envy

Envy is a feeling of discontent or resentful longing aroused by someone else's possessions, qualities, or circumstances – including God's blessings. Envy is related to covetousness. Envy refers to wanting what someone else has. Ultimately, it will seek to destroy the one who is envied. Envy leads to rivalry, divisions, and quarrels (see Mark 15:10; Galatians 5:18–21; Philippians 1:15). Pray the following:

Dear Heavenly Father,
You have promised to supply all our needs according to Your riches in glory in Christ Jesus. You have commanded us not to desire what others have, whether it is relationships or property, talents or resources. Such envy is a work of the flesh, not the Spirit. I confess that as a leader I have often envied what other leaders have. I ask You to reveal to my mind all the ways that I have envied others, so that I might repent. In Jesus' name. Amen.

(See Philippians 4:19; Exodus 20:17; Galatians 5:21.)

Some ways that we envy as leaders:
- ❑ Longing for the financial resources of another
- ❑ Longing for the material resources of another
- ❑ Feeling that if I only had what someone else had, then I would be successful or happy
- ❑ Longing for the relationships of another
- ❑ Longing to be like another in terms of talents, abilities, spiritual gifts, skills
- ❑ Longing for the leadership position of another
- ❑ Feeling resentful toward others because of what they have
- ❑ Not feeling content with what God has provided me

- ❑ Feeling that I need to work harder or smarter in order to get what others have
- ❑ Other ways the Holy Spirit may show you:

Once you have considered the items above, pray the following:

Gracious God,
I confess that I have sinned by envying others. Specifically, I have envied others by: _____(list them, being as specific as possible). I repent of my envy. Thank You that in Jesus I am forgiven. I ask You to wash me clean from the stain of envy. I choose to trust You and rejoice in Your provision for me. I choose to be content with what I have, knowing that You will use what I have to bring glory to Your Son Jesus. In His name I pray. Amen.

Jealousy

Jealousy is feeling or showing resentment toward someone because of that person's achievements, successes, perceived advantages, or relationships. Whereas envy focuses on what another has, jealousy focuses on the other person. Like envy, jealousy usually leads to quarrels and strife. Left unchecked, jealousy becomes an unholy zeal directed against another.

(There is a holy jealousy based on covenant faithfulness. This jealousy is aroused when someone gives to another the loyalty and affection belonging to one in covenant relationship. For example, when God's people worship idols or when a wife has affections for a man not her husband. See Exodus 20:5.)

Begin with this prayer:

Holy God,
Your Word says that You are a jealous God, calling us to a faithful love for You. At the same time, Your Word says that jealousy in us is a work of the flesh leading to arguments and dissensions. I confess that I have often resented other leaders because of their positions and accomplishments. I have sometimes even harbored ill will against them. This is sin. I ask You to reveal to my mind all the ways that I have been jealous and all the people of whom I have been jealous, so that I might repent. Through Jesus Christ, my Lord. Amen.

Ways that we can be jealous as leaders:

- ❑ Feeling that if I only had the same advantages as other leaders then I would have their accomplishments
- ❑ Feeling resentment toward others because of the relationships they have or enjoy
- ❑ Having hard feelings toward others because they have unfair advantages over me
- ❑ Feeling discontented because of the successes of others
- ❑ Secretly hoping that another leader would fail
- ❑ Feeling disgruntled with God because of the relationships others seem to enjoy with Him
- ❑ Other ways the Holy Spirit may show you:

People of whom I have been jealous:
Write the names of people and organizations the Lord shows you.

Reflecting on your answers above, pray this prayer:

Almighty God,

I confess that I have committed the sin of jealousy. I confess that I have been jealous by _____ (list them). Thank You that in Jesus Christ I am forgiven. Cleanse me completely from the sin of jealousy.

I now ask You to bless abundantly all those I have been jealous of: _____ (list the people). I ask You to heal any relationships broken because of jealousy, especially my relationship with _____ (list them).

Thank You for saving me by Your grace. Thank You for who I am in Your Son, Jesus Christ. Thank You that I am Your child and that You love me fully and completely. I rejoice in Your love for me. I choose now to walk in the good works that You have prepared for me to do. Help me love You faithfully. Through Jesus. Amen.

Selfish ambition

Zeal or ambition can be a good trait in a leader. Leaders with a healthy sense of ambition will seek to achieve great things for God, for people and for their organizations. Such zeal is a healthy, godly quality that inspires

491

leaders for excellence. Leaders with a healthy sense of ambition will not care who gets the credit as long as the godly outcomes are achieved. Leaders with a healthy zeal will put others first and promote their well-being.

Selfish ambition is not the same as healthy ambition. Selfish ambition is a desire to put oneself forward as deserving of something someone else has. It flows from envy and jealousy. It is self-seeking instead of serving others. Selfish ambition is a partisan and factious spirit that will do almost anything to get its way and to get ahead. As such, selfish ambition always leads to a sense of rivalry and unholy competition with others. Selfish ambition is always destructive, leading to many evil practices (see James 3:14–16). When leaders become selfishly ambitious, they ultimately destroy themselves, other people, and sometimes the very organizations they lead.

Pray this prayer for discernment of selfish ambition in your life:

Loving Father,
You have told us to do nothing out of selfish ambition or vain conceit, but in humility of mind to count others as more significant (Philippians 2:3). I know that in Christ I am significant. However, I have repeatedly tried to find my sense of significance in other things. I confess that I have often sought my sense of significance in comparison and in competition with other leaders. I have allowed envy or jealousy to lead to a spirit of rivalry. This is sin. Please reveal to me all the ways that I have been selfishly ambitious, that I may repent. Also reveal to my mind all those with whom I have had an unhealthy rivalry and sense of competition. Through Jesus, my Lord. Amen.

Ways selfish ambition can manifest in our lives:
- ❏ Having a strong sense of competition regarding something that is not normally competitive (such as a game or a sport)
- ❏ Striving against another person
- ❏ Acting in ways that seem to set people against each other or seem to create disunity
- ❏ Comparing oneself with others in terms of numbers and quantities (e.g. size of budget, number of church members, scope of responsibilities)

- ❑ Thinking myself significant because I have a larger _____ (ministry, budget, workload, membership, etc.) than another leader
- ❑ Speaking or acting in ways that criticize, undermine, disparage, tear down, or in other ways harm another leader or his/her organization, ministry, achievements, etc.
- ❑ Speaking or acting in ways that harm another leader's relationships
- ❑ Other ways the Holy Spirit may show you:

List all the leaders and organizations with which you have developed an unhealthy rivalry or sense of competition:

Using your answers above, pray this prayer:

Gracious God,
Although I have been created and called by You for leadership, I have not led as You desire. I realize that I have not led by the wisdom that is pure, peaceable, gentle, open to reason, full of mercy and good fruits, impartial, and sincere (James 3:14–17). Instead, I have harbored selfish ambition in my heart by: _____(list them). In all these ways I have sought to put myself forward and advance my own agenda. I have not served others, but I have harmed others with my competition and rivalry. Thank You that in Christ I am forgiven. I ask You to cleanse me completely from every trace of selfish ambition. I ask You to bless and give success to all the other leaders around me, in particular _____(list them). I pray that You would heal any damage I have done through my selfish ambition. By the grace of Jesus. Amen.

The Holy Spirit may ask you to go to leaders in connection with whom you have had selfish ambition in order to seek reconciliation and in order to bless that leader.

Close this Step with this declaration:

I here and now, in the name and authority of the Lord Jesus Christ, renounce all envy, jealousy, and selfish ambition. I choose to rejoice in God's provision for me, in the person God has made me to be as His

child, and in where God has called and placed me as a leader (Luke 10:20). In Jesus' name, I cancel all ground gained by Satan in my life, my leadership, my ministry, my work, and the organizations of which I am part because of my envy, jealousy, and selfish ambition. In Jesus' name, I now break every unholy bond I have created with people _____(list any that come to mind) through envy, jealousy, and selfish ambition.

In humility, I now choose to consider others more significant than myself. I choose to honor God and honor other leaders. I choose to rest in God's sovereignty over my life and my leadership, rejoicing that my name is written in heaven. Amen.

Step Seven: Choosing faith for leading

Unbelief is another sin that acts like a cancer for leadership. Unbelief is not the same as doubt. Doubt, a sense of uncertainty, is common to all people. The Bible tells us to be merciful to those who doubt (Jude 22). Unbelief is the opposite of faith, resistant and hostile toward belief. Unbelief undermines our confidence in God and leads us away from the truth. Unbelief blinds our minds and hardens our hearts. As leaders we must repent of our unbelief and be transformed by the renewing of our minds.

Faith is a state and act of believing on the basis of the reliability of the one trusted. Faith depends on relationship with the object of faith. (In the New Testament, "faith", "belief", and "trust" generally flow from the same word, which can be either a noun or a verb.) Faith is never blind, but depends fully on the dependability, capability, and nature of the object of faith. Faith has no power in itself; its effect flows from the power and nature of the object of faith.

Healthy leadership confidence flows from a faith in God that opens our hearts and minds to the full range of possibilities for how God might act in our leadership context. Having faith in God for leading – no matter whether the context is the Church or the marketplace – awakens us to the surprises of God's providence in our lives and the potential for God to work in any situation to bring about beneficial outcomes. Faith enlivens our leadership with joy and hope.

Begin to identify unbelief in your life with this prayer:

Dear Heavenly Father,
You have warned us to take care that we do not develop an evil, unbelieving heart that would cause us to fall away from You (Hebrews 3:12ff.). You have told us to be exhorted every day by one another and Your Word, so that we will not become hardened by the deceitfulness of sin. You have challenged us to keep our eyes fixed on Jesus so that we might hold our confidence throughout our lives (Hebrews 12:1ff.). Although I have been saved by grace through faith in Jesus Christ, faith that You have given me, I have not always applied that faith to my daily life. Although I am a believer, I have often lived practically as an unbeliever. Although I am a Christian leader, I have often led without

495

reference to You. Please reveal to my mind all the ways that unbelief has infected my life, so that I might repent. In Jesus' name. Amen.

Some common manifestations of unbelief:

Prayerlessness

- ❑ I do not take time every day to read the Bible and pray.
- ❑ I do not pray as much every day as God would like me to pray.
- ❑ When I encounter someone who is unwell, praying for them is not the first thing that comes to my mind or my first response.
- ❑ I do not intercede for others daily.
- ❑ I often forget to pray for someone when I said I would pray for them.
- ❑ I do not regularly pray for people to become Christians.
- ❑ When I say "grace" for a meal, I often find myself praying longer than I should.
- ❑ I do not regularly pray for those I am leading.
- ❑ I do not always pray before making key leadership decisions.
- ❑ I do not regularly pray for God to fulfill His vision for my life, ministry, work, or leadership.
- ❑ I do not ask others to pray for me as a leader.
- ❑ I do not have a sense of God's vision for my life, ministry, work, or leadership.
- ❑ Other ways that God may reveal prayerlessness to you:

Four or more ticked areas above suggests that prayerlessness is an issue.

Busyness and hurry

- ❑ I often feel stressed because I have too many things to do.
- ❑ I often find myself walking or driving faster than I should.
- ❑ People often feel stressed and hurried when they are around me.
- ❑ People often feel that I am too busy for them.
- ❑ I get a sense of personal satisfaction from how busy I am.
- ❑ If I were not so busy, I am not sure what I would do with myself.
- ❑ I often discover that I have scheduled too many appointments in a day.
- ❑ I struggle to say "no" to new commitments and responsibilities, especially if they look really good to me.
- ❑ I do not have time to do little things for the people closest to me.

❑ I repeatedly fail to keep my promises and commitments to myself and others.

❑ I often find myself trying to make things happen.

❑ I often feel frustrated and irritable, especially when I think of all I need to do.

❑ I rarely come away from my busy life to pray and seek God.

❑ Other ways that God may reveal busyness and hurry to you:

Four or more ticked items above suggests that busyness and hurry are issues.

Failure to rest

❑ I have difficulty slowing down.

❑ I often do not have or take a day off every week.

❑ I do not practice some kind of "Sabbath".

❑ I do not always take all my holidays, or I tend to take them only a few days at a time.

❑ I tend to stay up too late.

❑ I generally do not get as much sleep as I should.

❑ I do not have much that I enjoy doing outside of my work or ministry.

❑ I do not have enough time for the people who are closest to me.

❑ Other ways that God may reveal your failure to rest to you:

Three or more ticked items above suggests that failure to rest is an issue.

Putting one's ministry or work before relationship with God (idolatry)

❑ Although I hate to admit it, I often find myself spending so much time on ministry or work that I do not have enough time to pray, worship, and read the Bible.

❑ People sometimes tell me that they feel I put my ministry or work before them.

❑ I spend so much time doing ministry that I find it difficult to receive ministry.

❑ If someone examined my life, especially how I spend my time, they might struggle to see that my priorities were God first and family second.

- ❑ I often feel irritated by those who want to spend time with me, especially those close to me.
- ❑ I often feel condemned or guilty because I have not spent time with God.
- ❑ Other ways that God may reveal about how you put things before Him:

Three or more ticked items above suggests that you may be putting your ministry or work before relationship with God.

Other manifestations of unbelief:

- ❑ I have trouble accepting that what God says in the Bible is true, especially for me.
- ❑ If I ordered my life according to the Bible, I would struggle to survive in this world.
- ❑ It is easier for me to apply the Bible to my personal life than my professional life.
- ❑ I often feel that the Bible may work for others but it doesn't work for me.
- ❑ I often think that God will not use me because I don't pray enough, don't know the Bible well enough, am not holy enough, or (list the reason).
- ❑ Other people's spiritual gifts, skills, or talents are more important for advancing God's kingdom than mine are.
- ❑ I do not generally sense that my leadership, ministry, or work really make any difference for God and others.
- ❑ Because of my past sins and mistakes, God will not use me like He uses other people.
- ❑ Other ways that God may reveal unbelief to you:

If you ticked any of the items above, it may suggest that unbelief is an issue. Turn away from unbelief using this prayer:

Dear Heavenly Father,
Because of unbelief, Your Son Jesus could do no mighty works in Nazareth. Because of my unbelief, I have not often seen Your Son Jesus do mighty works in my life, work, ministry, and leadership. I have not always chosen the way of faith, but I have often hardened my heart and

closed my mind to the truth of Your Word. I confess that my unbelief is sin. I confess the specific ways that unbelief has manifested in my life: _____(list them).

Thank You that in Jesus Christ I am forgiven. I renounce all the ways unbelief has shown itself in my life as sin. Wash me clean of unbelief. I choose to renew my mind in the truth of who You are and in the truth of Your Word.

By faith I believe that You have cleansed my heart. I receive my place among those sanctified by faith. I choose to live by faith. I thank You that I am justified by faith and redeemed by faith. I choose to walk by faith and not by sight. I choose to exercise my leadership, do my work, and serve in ministry all by faith. By faith, I choose to receive and exercise the stewardship that You have given me. By faith I choose to obey You. By faith I choose to live my life as You decide.

I thank You for the faith You have given me, knowing that even if I have faith as small as a mustard seed, I will see the mountains move and the glory of the Lord revealed in my life. Thank You, most of all, that I have been saved by Your grace through faith, faith which You have given me through Your Son Jesus Christ in the power of Your Holy Spirit. Amen.

(Acts 15:9; Acts 26:18; Romans 1:17; Romans 3:23ff.; 2 Corinthians 5:7; Galatians 2:20; 1 Timothy 1:4; Hebrews 11; Ephesians 2:8)

Declaration of faith

Conclude these Steps with this declaration of faith:

I here and now, in the name of the one Lord Jesus Christ, declare my faith in the living God. I declare that there is only one God who exists as the Father, Son, and Holy Spirit. He is the creator and sustainer of all things.

I declare that Jesus Christ is the Messiah, the Word who became flesh and dwelt among us. I declare that Jesus died on the cross for the forgiveness of sins and rose bodily from the dead on the third day. I declare that He came to destroy the works of the devil, and that He has disarmed the rulers and authorities and made a public display of them, having triumphed over them by the cross.

I declare that the Holy Spirit, who lives in me, is fully God, who by His indwelling presence causes people to be born again into the Kingdom of God. The Holy Spirit seals God's people until the day of redemption. By His empowering presence, the Holy Spirit enables people to live for God and extend God's loving rulership into the whole world.

I declare that I have been saved by grace through faith in Jesus Christ, and not as a result of any works on my part. I declare that God has delivered me from the dominion of darkness and transferred me to His Kingdom. I declare that I am now seated with Christ in the heavenly places as a fully adopted child of God.

I declare that apart from Christ I can do nothing, but I can do all things through Christ who strengthens me. So I declare my complete dependence on Jesus Christ. I declare to the spiritual realms that Jesus is my only Lord and Savior.

I declare that the Bible is trustworthy and true, the only reliable standard for faith and life. I declare that the promises God makes in the Bible are dependable and the revelation of God in the Bible is faithful.

I declare that I belong to Christ for I was bought with a price. I declare my entire being to be a living sacrifice, holy and acceptable to God through Jesus. I declare that my life and my leadership, my work and my ministry, all belong to the Lord Jesus Christ and I submit them freely to Him. I declare that Christ is in me, the hope of glory.

I declare by faith that I receive the Holy Spirit as the Father has promised. I declare by faith that I will do the works that Jesus did to the glory of the Father. I declare that I will live by faith and not by sight, seeking to please and honor God in all I say and do, to the glory of Jesus Christ.

I fully commit myself to the leadership to which God has called me: _____(name or describe that leadership). I fully commit myself to loving and serving the people to whom God has called me. I fully commit myself to humble leadership within the sphere God has given me. I fully commit myself to bringing glory and honor to Jesus Christ through my leadership.

I declare that the Lord Jesus has all authority in heaven and on earth. I declare that Jesus Christ is coming soon. Jesus is the Alpha and the Omega, the beginning and the end. I declare that by His blood Jesus ransomed people for God from every tribe and language and people and nation, and He has made them a kingdom and priests to our God, and we shall reign on the earth.

I declare that holy, holy, holy is the Lord God Almighty, who was and is and is to come. I declare that worthy is the Lamb who was slain to receive power and wealth and wisdom and might and honor and glory and blessing. Amen!

(See Exodus 20:2, 3; Colossians 1:16, 17; John 1:1, 14; Colossians 2:15; 1 John 3:8; John 3:1ff.; Ephesians 1:13; Acts 1:8; Colossians 1:13, 14; Galatians 4:5–7; John 15:5–8; Philippians 4:13; 2 Timothy 3:15–17; 1 Corinthians 6:20; Romans 12:1; Luke 11:13; John 14:12; 2 Corinthians 5:7; Matthew 28:18; Revelation 22:12–13; Revelation 5:9–12.)

Next Steps – changing faulty beliefs

We are transformed through the renewing of our minds. Before you finish the process, ask God to highlight for you where you need to change your belief system. What faulty beliefs has He helped you identify as you have gone through *The Steps To Freedom For Leaders*? Where do you need to do some work to renew your mind?

Pray the following prayer:

Heavenly Father,
I commit myself to living according to the truth. Thank you for revealing to me ways in which I have not been doing that. I ask you now through the Spirit of Truth to show me the key strongholds in my mind, the areas where my belief system has been faulty. I commit myself to renewing my mind so that I will be transformed and will become the person and the leader you want me to be.

In Jesus' name. Amen.

Sit in silence and write down areas where you realize your thinking has been faulty (i.e. does not line up with what God says in His Word). There is space for this on pages 190–191. Bear in mind that the faulty thinking will still *feel* true to you. It might help to look back through the Steps and the notes you have made in *Freed To Lead*.

Then pick no more than three key areas that you will commit to focus on to renew your mind and write them on pages 188–189. On the left-hand side write down the faulty belief and on the right side write what God says in His Word. Write as many verses as you can find that say what is really true.

For the first area, write a stronghold-buster along the following lines:

I renounce the lie that....
I announce the truth that.... [list the truth from the verses you found]

Declare it every day for the next 40 days or until you know that your belief system has changed. Then come back and do the same for the second one and then the third one. Imagine how much more effective you could be as a leader if you could deal completely with these issues. And you can!

NOTES

Part II

1. Brittney Helmrich, "30 Ways to Define Leadership", http://www.businessnewsdaily.com/3647-leadership-definition.html. Accessed 4 January 2015.

2. "Leadership definitions", University of Warwick, www2.warwick.ac.uk/fac/sci/wmg/ftmsc/modules/modulelist/le/content_store_2012/leadership_definitions.doc. Accessed 4 January 2015.

Chapter 4

1. Of course, we do believe that society must defend the rights of individuals, including Christians. We must certainly stand up for and support one another. However, we have not always done a good job of encouraging Christians to take responsibility for the well-being of society.

Chapter 5

1. See, for example, Daniel Kahneman's *Thinking Fast, Thinking Slow* (London: Allen Lane, 2011) for a thorough review of the science of human decision-making.

2. See www.capuk.org for more information.

3. "Weakness" here is not referring to sin. We must repent of sin and wrongdoing. Weakness in this context refers to areas in which we have no aptitude or ability.

4. See, for example, *Freedom in Christ Leader's Guide: A 13-week Course for Every Christian* (Oxford: Monarch Books, 2009). Session 10 presents the "Stronghold Busting" exercise.

Part III

1. From the Royal Museums Greenwich website, http://www.rmg.co.uk/explore/sea-and-ships/facts/explorers-and-leaders/sir-john-franklin-(1786-1847). Accessed 14 April 2015.

Chapter 6

1. Systems theory began to emerge as a discipline of its own in the early twentieth century. After WWII, Dr. Murray Bowen began to apply the theory to the human family and society in general, eventually developing his Bowen

theory. Since the 1960s, many researchers have advanced the research and application of systems theory in general, and the Bowen theory in particular, to the family and other human systems.

The insights of Edwin Friedman in his book *A Failure of Nerve* (New York: Church Publishing, 2007), which deals with some of the issues of leadership and human systems, have guided my own thinking in this chapter and in part four regarding anxiety. Friedman inspired me and challenged me in *A Failure of Nerve*, serving as a catalyst for my thinking on people-systems. I had been familiar with systems theory prior to reading Friedman but I had not fully recognized its importance for leadership.

Regarding the application of family systems theory to the church, Peter Stienke has written a trilogy of books: *How Your Church Family Works: Understanding Congregations as Emotional Systems* (Herndon: The Alban Institute, 2006), *Healthy Congregations: A Systems Approach* (Herndon: The Alban Institute, 2006), and *Congregational Leadership in Anxious Times: Being Calm and Courageous No Matter What* (Herndon: The Alban Institute, 2006). Stienke was a student of Friedman, and Friedman encouraged the application of his work to the life of churches. We highly recommend these books for pastors and other church leaders. The Postscript of *Congregational Leadership*, "People of the Charm", is an important observation on an unfortunately repeated dynamic in churches that is worth the price of the book.

2. If someone ever says, "I don't think we need leaders; we should just have a flat structure" (or something similar), that person usually wants to be the leader!

3. See Edwin Friedman, *A Failure of Nerve*, pp. 16–17. It was Friedman that first alerted me to developments in brain science that had implications for leadership. The more we learn about the brain the more we see applications for leadership. The research also seems to confirm our understanding of the importance of *being*.

4. Many people talk about "emotional processes" but it is difficult to find anyone with a clear definition. I developed our definition of "emotional process" using some of the insights of Daniel Kahneman in *Thinking, Fast and Slow* (London: Allen Lane, 2011). Kahneman identifies "System 1" thinking as something that happens quickly and involuntarily, including impressions and feelings (pages 20–21). This describes how emotions operate. We have taken this concept and applied it to what happens in the people-system as a person.

5. George Barna, *The Power of Vision* (Ventura: Gospel Light, 2009), pages 26–27.

6. The argument to support this understanding of submission would require too much space to explicate fully. In short, the biblical word for "submission"

is the idea of self-subordination to another, surrendering one's own rights and preferences in order to benefit another. In the church, we are to subordinate ourselves to one another in honor of Jesus. The word does not include the idea of "obey", nor does it include the idea that one can force the submission of another. Unfortunately, many misunderstand the biblical concept of "submission". Many leaders – including church leaders – have used it to try to subjugate or control others. Consequently, we have chosen the word "cooperation" since it both has a more positive connotation and represents the general sense of what the Bible is teaching.

7. Having different political parties is not inherently factional. History has shown that different political parties may disagree strongly while working together for the common good. Factionalism develops when political parties begin to "demonize" the others, blaming the other parties for all that is wrong and refusing to acknowledge when the other parties get something right.

Chapter 7

1. I am indebted to Philip Zimbardo's book *The Lucifer Effect* (London: Rider, 2007) for many of the insights in this chapter. The situational forces at work have been written about throughout the literature of psychology and are commonly known. Zimbardo's strength is showing how these situational forces might lead us to do evil. I found his insights especially helpful for how religious groups might influence people in evil ways. He provides many strategies in his book for recognizing and overcoming evil in our daily lives by resisting situational forces. It is a very long book, but significant sections deal with two case studies, and these sections might be skimmed or avoided altogether without losing the heart of the book.

2. Even the title of *The Lucifer Effect* would lead us to believe situational forces are inherently evil. Certainly the book itself focuses on two examples of how situational forces have led to evil. However, it is our blindness to situational forces, and the tendency of many people to use them to dominate and manipulate others, that leads people toward the idea that situational forces are evil.

3. Zimbardo, page 8.

4. We would include "laws" under the rubric of "rules".

Part IV

1. It is difficult to overestimate the influence Friedman has had on my thinking regarding anxiety. His influences are found throughout this book and especially in this section of the book. Although I have taken Friedman's work and moved it to an explicitly Christian context, his work is foundational to all my own thinking regarding anxiety.

Unfortunately, Friedman died while writing his book, so although it is great in terms of diagnosis, he never did complete what he would have written about how to address the issue of anxiety. However, without Friedman I may never have detected the issue of anxiety and then learned how to resolve it. So I owe a greater debt to Friedman than a few footnotes might repay.

Chapter 9

1. Emily Caldwell, *Phobia's effect on perception of feared object allows fear to persist* (http://researchnews.osu.edu/archive/sizebias.htm, 2-22-2012. Accessed 5 May 2015).

2. Edwin Friedman, *A Failure of Nerve*, page 3.

Chapter 10

1. Christian meditation is not the emptying of our minds as in Eastern religions but filling our minds with truth and with God.

2. As we talk about embracing pain, we are aware that some people suffer from chronically painful physical and emotional conditions. Such conditions are beyond the scope of what we are trying to address in this discipline, normally requiring professional help of some kind.

3. Adapted from the *Freedom in Christ Leader's Guide: A 13-week Course for Every Christian* (Oxford: Monarch Books, 2009). Session 12 deals with godly goals and godly desires.

4. This is why I prefer the more accurate translation of "debts" in the Lord's Prayer to the more popular translations of "trespasses" or "sins".

Chapter 11

1. Edwin Friedman, *A Failure of Nerve*, page 57.

2. Friedman, page 57.

3. Friedman, pages 53–54. These five behaviors of anxious people-systems form the entirety of chapter two in *A Failure of Nerve*, pages 51–94. The only one I have changed somewhat is the last behavior, the abdication of leadership. Friedman approaches these behaviors from the perspective of family systems theory. This chapter in Friedman presents a tremendous overview of these issues with insight and depth too great to cover in this book. In the chapter, Friedman hints at some of the ways to address these behaviors, but he does not present a systematic way to approach them as we have sought to do.

4. Of course, we believe that God might intervene supernaturally in these situations, bringing maturity or healing more quickly. However, God most often chooses the slower route to maturity in his people.

Chapter 12

1. Information theory has begun to raise a number of issues regarding communication. However, it is beyond the scope of this chapter to consider these issues.

2. A short passage from Friedman's *A Failure of Nerve* initiated my thinking in this chapter: "[C]ommunication itself is an emotional phenomenon, rather than a matter of the intellect that is influenced by feelings or the emotions, and [it] depends on three interrelational rather than 'mental' variables: direction, distance, and anxiety... Messages... come through less because of the quality of their content than because of the emotional envelope in which they are delivered", page 128.

3. Friedman, page 128.

4. Of course, it is important to note that some people *are* out to get you!

Chapter 13

1. Stephen M. R. Covey's book, *The Speed of Trust: The One Thing that Changes Everything* (London: Simon & Schuster, 2006), in particular "The Second Wave – Relationship Trust" (pages 125–232), forms the basis for this chapter. I highly recommend *The Speed of Trust*, which is one of the best books available on the subject and deals with the issue of trust more broadly than here. I am also grateful to Steve Goss who helped me refine and reframe our discussion of trust in the overall context of the *being* and *doing* dynamic of our understanding of leadership.

2. Michelle Stevens, "Third of employees don't trust senior management", http://www.cipd.co.uk/pm/peoplemanagement/b/weblog/archive/2013/10/24/third-of-employees-don-t-trust-senior-management.aspx. Accessed 2 October 2015.

3. http://www.gallup.com/poll/5392/trust-government.aspx. Accessed 19 May 2015.

4. "The Six People Americans Now Trust More Than Their Pastor (2013)". http://www.christianitytoday.com/gleanings/2013/december/seven-people-americans-trust-more-pastor-gallup-honesty.html. Accessed 19 May 2015.

5. Barbara Kimmel, "The Hard Costs of Low Trust: Take the Test", http://www.trustacrossamerica.com/blog/?p=859. Accessed 20 May 2015.

6. Covey, page 133. Covey talks about behaviors of character and behaviors of competence. Covey only identifies thirteen behaviors. We have added another five in light of our Christian discipleship.

7. Bob Sorge, *Loyalty: The Reach of the Noble Heart* (Lee's Summit: Oasis House, 2004), page 15. This book provides the best study of the biblical idea of loyalty.

8. Covey, page 133.

Chapter 14

1. Richard Foster identified these three areas in his seminal book, *Money, Sex and Power* (Hodder & Stoughton, 2009), first issued in 1985.

2. "Pornography Statistics: Annual Report 2015", http://www.covenanteyes.com/pornstats/. Accessed 23 May 2015.

3. Many biblical passages deal with forgiveness. See, for example, Matthew 6:9–15 and Matthew 18:21–35. The *Freedom in Christ Discipleship Course* has an entire session on forgiveness.

Chapter 15

1. Friedman points out the issue of sabotage throughout *A Failure of Nerve.* (See the Index at page 259 for references.) He first alerted me to the way sabotage was a normal response to healthy leadership. Prior to this, I had frequently experienced it but I had always perceived it as unusual and unhealthy. This shift in my own thinking was fundamental, resetting my own perceptions and expectations.

Chapter 16

1. Friedman discusses similar issues using the word "fallacy". He deals with what he calls the "fallacy of expertise" in chapter three of *A Failure of Nerve* (pages 95ff.). He considers the "fallacy of empathy" in chapter four (pages 132ff.). In chapter five, he introduces the "fallacies of self" along with the concept of "togetherness" as an enemy of self (pages 158ff.). I developed the concept of these leadership delusions from the central ideas Friedman explored in these chapters.

2. Friedman, page 135.

Conclusion

1. I have adapted this definition from one I learned from Dallas Willard. Unfortunately, I have lost the original source. Of course, this definition is for "faith" that is explicitly Christian.

SELECTED BIBLIOGRAPHY

Neil T. Anderson. *The Bondage Breaker.* Oxford: Monarch Books, 2002.

_____. *Steps to Freedom in Christ.* Oxford: Monarch Books, 2009.

_____. *Victory over the Darkness.* Oxford: Monarch Books, 2002.

Neil T. Anderson and Steve Goss. *Freedom in Christ Leader's Guide: A 13 Week Discipleship Course for Every Christian.* Oxford: Monarch Books, 2009.

George Barna. *The Power of Vision.* Ventura: Gospel Light, 2009.

Stephen M. R. Covey. *The Speed of Trust: The One Thing that Changes Everything.* London: Simon & Schuster, 2006.

Edwin H. Friedman. *A Failure of Nerve: Leadership in the Age of the Quick Fix.* New York: Church Publishing, 2007.

Steve Goss. *Break Free, Stay Free: Don't Let the Past Hold You Back.* Oxford: Monarch Books, 2008.

_____. *Free to Be Yourself: Enjoy Your True Nature in Christ.* Oxford: Monarch Books, 2008.

_____. *Win the Daily Battle: Resist and Stand Firm in God's Strength.* Oxford: Monarch Books, 2008.

_____. *The You God Planned: Don't Let Anything or Anyone Hold You Back.* Oxford: Monarch Books, 2008.

Daniel Kahneman. *Thinking, fast and slow.* London: Penguin Books, 2011.

Bob Sorge. *Loyalty: The Reach of the Noble Heart.* Lee's Summit: Oasis House, 2004.

Peter L. Steinke. *Congregational Leadership in Anxious Times: Being Calm and Courageous No Matter What.* Herndon: The Alban Institute, 2006.

_____. *Healthy Congregations: A Systems Approach.* Herndon: The Alban Institute, 2006.

_____. *How Your Church Family Works: Understanding Congregations as Emotional Systems.* Herndon: The Alban Institute, 2006.

Philip Zimbardo. *The Lucifer Effect: How Good People Turn to Evil.* London: Ryder, 2007.

Freedom In
Christ Ministries

Freedom In Christ Ministries is a resource ministry that exists to serve the Church. Our role is to equip church leaders around the world with tools and resources to help them make **disciples** (not just converts) and set their people, marriages and ministries free in Christ. We are trusting God to raise up people to take our discipleship approach to every country where He wants it established. For the latest details of where we operate and for contact details, see our international website at **www.ficminternational.org**

As well as the Freed to Lead course, Freedom in Christ produce a range of other resources, including *The Freedom in Christ Discipleship Course* and *The Grace Course*.

The Freedom In Christ Discipleship Course is a straightforward and effective way for any church to implement discipleship that really works. With clear, concise teaching – each of the 13 sessions focuses on just a few key points – it is excellent for new Christians and mature Christians alike.

The Grace Course is a tool for churches to help Christians recover their first love for God so that they go on to love others and make a great impact on the world. Its objective is to enable Christians to experience God's grace in such a deep and real way that love for Him becomes the main motivator in their lives.